second edition

High-Tech
CYCLING

Edmund R. Burke, PhD

University of Colorado at Colorado Springs

editor

Human Kinetics

Library of Congress Cataloging-in-Publication Data

High-tech cycling / Edmund R. Burke. -- 2nd ed.
    p.   cm.
Previous ed. cataloged under the m.e. Burke.
Includes bibliographical references and index.
    ISBN 0-7360-4507-4
    1. Cycling. I. Burke, Ed, 1949-2002
RC1220.C8 B873   2003
612'.044--dc21   2002152619

ISBN-10: 0-7360-4507-4
ISBN-13: 978-0-7360-4507-0

Copyright © 1996, 2003 by Edmund R. Burke

Acquisitions Editor: Ed McNeely; **Developmental Editor:** Cynthia McEntire; **Assistant Editor:** John Wentworth; **Copyeditor:** Patsy Fortney; **Proofreader:** Joanna Hatzopoulos Portman; **Indexer:** Betty Frizzéll; **Permission Manager:** Toni Harte; **Graphic Designer:** Robert Reuther; **Graphic Artist:** Francine Hamerski; **Art and Photo Manager:** Dan Wendt; **Cover Designer:** Keith Blomberg; **Photographer (cover):** © Jim Whitmer; **Photographer (interior):** Dan Wendt (unless otherwise noted); **Illustrator:** Mic Greenberg; **Printer:** Versa Press

Human Kinetics books are available at special discounts for bulk purchase. Special editions or book excerpts can also be created to specification. For details, contact the Special Sales Manager at Human Kinetics.

Printed in the United States of America   10 9 8 7 6 5 4 3

Human Kinetics
Web site: www.HumanKinetics.com

United States: Human Kinetics
P.O. Box 5076
Champaign, IL 61825-5076
800-747-4457
e-mail: humank@hkusa.com

Canada: Human Kinetics
475 Devonshire Road, Unit 100
Windsor, ON N8Y 2L5
800-465-7301 (in Canada only)
e-mail: info@hkcanada.com

Europe: Human Kinetics
107 Bradford Road
Stanningley
Leeds LS28 6AT, United Kingdom
+44 (0)113 255 5665
e-mail: hk@hkeurope.com

Australia: Human Kinetics
57A Price Avenue
Lower Mitcham, South Australia 5062
08 8372 0999
e-mail: info@hkaustralia.com

New Zealand: Human Kinetics
Division of Sports Distributors NZ Ltd.
P.O. Box 300 226 Albany
North Shore City, Auckland
0064 9 448 1207
e-mail: info@humankinetics.co.nz

High-Tech Cycling is a special book, as it presents the latest scientific knowledge for training and racing applications to the sport. It also is special because it was the final book published by editor Ed Burke.

Shortly after completing his work on the manuscript, Ed died doing what he loved—riding his bike with a group of friends. His death rocked the cycling and academic communities, from those who were fortunate to receive his training advice directly, to students and faculty at the college where he taught, to those who valued what they had gained from reading his work.

Ed authored and edited many books and articles in his 53 years. He spawned useful research in the fields of performance, diet, and recovery. He taught eager students at the university and at hundreds of private seminars around the world. He played an active role in every Olympic Cycling Team since 1984 and was a regular at the Olympic Training Center. In his later years, Ed became an athlete himself, completing some of the hardest bike events on earth, including the Leadville 100 and IdidaBike. And he did it all with his ever-present smile.

While we all sorely miss him, we also can thank him for leaving such a lasting contribution to the sport. On Ed's behalf I hope you enjoy and benefit from this book, for that would certainly have pleased him—and, no doubt, made him smile.

Andrew Pruitt, EdD
Boulder Center for Sports Medicine

Contents

Preface

During the last decade, a remarkable expansion of the application of scientific principles has occurred in the sport of cycling, both road cycling and mountain biking. More and more cyclists, from elite competitors to fitness enthusiasts, are applying these principles to their own programs.

The need for this book became clear after the completion of the first edition of *High-Tech Cycling* (1996), when I continued to see scientific information being produced that needed to be disseminated to all of us to help us perform at our best. This book picks up where the first edition left off. In it you'll find the most recent research in the many facets of cycling science, training, equipment, and physiology.

This edition of *High-Tech Cycling* has been possible only because the contributors made time to write their chapters while balancing research and teaching responsibilities. My request of them was to provide scientifically accurate, comprehensive, and readable reviews of the information available on their topics. I also asked them to suggest how to use this information in training and competition and how it might be used to stimulate further research. The authors have met these objectives, and as a result, this book is a valuable resource for those who compete, coach, perform research, or engage in the clinical practice of sports medicine. Serious recreational riders with an appetite for accurate and up-to-date information about their sport will also want this book in their collections.

This edition begins with criteria for equipment selection in road cycling. Chester Kyle presents information he has collected from his research during the last few years and explains the impact of the new UCI rules on bicycle equipment.

Next, in chapter 2, John Olsen instructs us on the basics of mountain bike suspensions for comfortable and efficient off-road cycling and on the selection of other equipment such as tubeless tires and shifting mechanisms.

In chapter 3, Andrew Pruitt and I focus on the importance of proper positioning on both road and mountain bikes for increased efficiency and injury prevention. Cycling is a marriage between the somewhat adaptable human body and a somewhat adjustable machine.

The next three chapters investigate the important topics of optimization of pedaling and the biomechanics of cycling. We often think of pedaling cadence for the serious cyclist as needing to be above 90 rpm, but what about individual preferences? What is the most efficient cadence for climbing on a mountain bike or time trialing on a road bike? In chapter 4, Alejandro Lucía discusses these important questions for the road cyclist. In chapters 5 and 6, Jeff Broker gives us a comprehensive review of the biomechanics of road and mountain bike cycling and current and future research, and shares data he collected on some of the world's elite cyclists while working at the U.S. Olympic Training Center. Dr. Broker shows how the use of SRM and other field power-measuring devices have opened a new way of measuring performance both on the road and on single tracks.

In chapter 7, Chester Kyle and David Bassett discuss the evolution of the hour record in cycling and considerations for training and site selection for the most coveted record in competitive cycling.

In chapter 8, Randy Wilber discusses the concept of living high and training low to improve aerobic capacity and the use of high altitude training sleeping chambers to supplement training.

Chapter 9 discusses the nutritional practices and demands of competitive cyclists both in training and from data collected from some of the leading races around the world. Asker Jeukendrup presents information on nutritional intake during training and competition and on the caloric needs of cyclists in competition.

Finally, we discuss the physiological demands of both road and mountain biking. Alejandro Lucía, in chapter 10, presents data he has collected on the physiological and performance characteristics and demands of competitive road cycling while working with some of the top professional teams in Europe. Information on heart rate, energy demands, and intensity during road racing are discussed. The book closes with Holden MacRae's discussion of the physiological characteristics and demands of off-road cycling. Much of this information has never before been presented to the cycling public.

Successful competition in cycling is only as effective as the preparation time invested. Preparation and the selection of equipment for competition and training should be approached systematically and scientifically with attention given to both the obvious and discreet concerns related to the event. These and many other unique characteristics of both road and off-road cycling are carefully investigated in this second edition of *High-Tech Cycling*.

1

Selecting Cycling Equipment

Chester R. Kyle

Appropriate cycling equipment can save time and energy and increase convenience, comfort, maneuverability, and safety. Every year at bike shows, major corporations, smaller companies, and private individuals promote hundreds of new items, all with the hope of finding a winning ticket into the market.

The majority of new products disappear quickly due to insufficient capital for marketing and production, a market crowded with similar products that are better and cheaper, or their own lack of benefit to cycling performance. The information in this chapter should help cyclists avoid products in this last category.

All-terrain bicycles are discussed elsewhere, this chapter will concentrate on bicycles that are normally ridden on paved surfaces, including conventional recreational or commuting road bicycles as well as competition road and track bikes and hybrid bikes that can be ridden either on or off the pavement. However, before we talk about cycling equipment, let's briefly discuss the principal ingredient that makes a bicycle go fast—human power.

Human Power

More than the equipment and technique you use, the speed at which you can propel a bicycle depends on how much power you apply to the pedals. Almost any healthy adult can produce about 75 to 100 W (0.1 hp) continuously—even someone older than 70. This will move you along at about 16 to 24 kph (10 to 15 mph), depending on what kind of bicycle and what riding position you use (Kyle 1973; Kyle and Edelman 1975).

In setting the world cycling hour record, elite athletes have produced in excess of 450 W (0.6 hp) for one hour (Padilla et al. 2000). In 1975, professional cyclist Eddy Merckx produced over 455 W (0.6 hp) for one hour on a cycling ergometer (Kyle and Caiozzo 1986b). In 1972, Merckx set a world record of 49.431 km (30.7 mi) in one hour at Mexico City using a classical track bike without aerodynamic components (Okajima 1990; Peronnet et al. 1991). During the 1980s and 1990s, Merckx's record was broken several times by cyclists on modern aero bikes. In an hour ride, modern equipment can make a significant difference in speed (about 6 kph or 3 to 4 mph); however, speed principally depends on athletic ability.

The capability of most cyclists lies somewhere between the performance of an average healthy adult and that of a champion professional athlete. The power a cyclist can produce is a direct function of muscle mass. This depends on weight and percent body fat; well-conditioned male cyclists normally have 7 to 18% body fat (women have slightly more). Figure 1.1

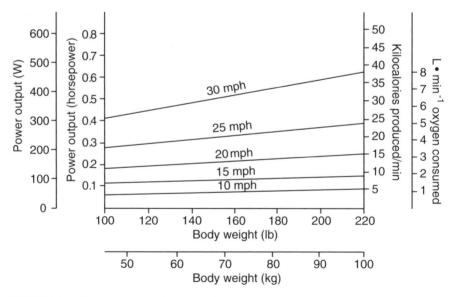

FIGURE 1.1   Power, speed, calories, and oxygen consumption versus body weight.
Data from Swain et al. 1987 and Sjogaard et al. 1982.

shows the amount of power cyclists can produce versus body weight and the speed they can maintain on the level with no wind. The curves were drawn for cyclists of average build using lightweight racing bicycles and riding in a low racing position with hands on the drops (Sjogaard et al. 1982; Swain et al. 1987). For example, a cyclist who maintains 32.18 kph (20 mph) and weighs 77 kg (170 lb) will produce about 160 W (0.21 hp). In riding positions other than a low racing position, cyclists would have to produce more power to go the same speed.

Cyclists who are taller than average for their weight will have a higher wind resistance and will therefore have to produce more power. Those who are more compact and muscular need less power. Since the body surface area and frontal area, and thus wind resistance, all increase as the height does, squared, thin, tall bicycle racers are rare.

Potential for endurance or speed depends more on muscle type and cardiovascular conditioning than on body type. Fast-twitch muscle fibers, which make up the bulk of a sprinter's muscle mass, are great for short bursts of speed but do not process oxygen as efficiently as slow-twitch muscle fibers, which make up the bulk of an endurance athlete's muscle mass. This is why a superbly muscled athlete who can power a bicycle 65 kph (40 mph) or more in a 200-m sprint can easily be beaten over longer distances by a cyclist with much less physical strength.

Lighter cyclists have an advantage when climbing hills. You can observe this in a pack when gaps expand and contract as the slope changes. Heavier riders have the downhill advantage and sometimes can catch up if they haven't lost too much distance on the uphill. The optimum weight for an elite male endurance racing cyclist seems to be 64 to 73 kg (140 to 160 lb). Good sprinters, on the other hand, are massive, often weighing over 91 kg (200 lb).

For intervals of a few seconds, the body can produce perhaps five times the power it can produce continuously over intervals of several minutes (Whitt and Wilson 1982). Short-term anaerobic exercise rapidly uses energy stored in the muscles and does not involve the slower metabolism of oxygen. Once steady state is reached, the amount of long-term aerobic power you can produce depends on the amount of oxygen you can absorb in the blood and convert to energy. You can improve your capacity to absorb oxygen approximately 20 to 30% by training (Sjogaard et al. 1982). Figure 1.2 shows the variation of power with the duration of exercise for typical cyclists.

For those who wish to use cycling as a tool for weight reduction, figure 1.1 shows the number of calories burned per minute versus speed and body weight and the oxygen absorption capacity of the cyclist. At 32 kph (20 mph), a person weighing 68 kg (150 lb) will use about 790 calories per hour and absorb about 2.8 L of oxygen per minute into the blood. Figure 1.3 shows the number of calories burned per mile on a level course. The energy consumed per mile is fairly constant until about 19 kph (12 mph), when wind resistance causes it to increase rapidly.

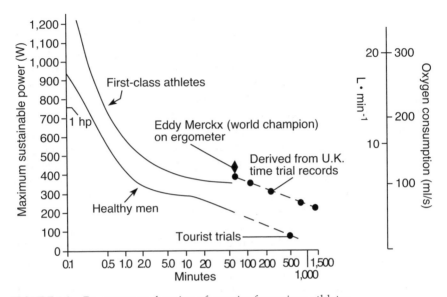

FIGURE 1.2   Power versus duration of exercise for various athletes.

Reprinted, by permission, from F.R. Whitt and D.G. Wilson, 1982, *Bicycling Science* (2nd ed.) (Cambridge, MA: MIT Press), 51.

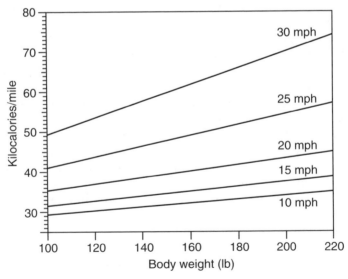

FIGURE 1.3   Calories per mile versus speed and body weight.

For a fixed distance, you burn more energy by traveling fast. If you prefer to ride more slowly, you can compensate by traveling longer distances. Cycling takes about one-third the energy per kilometer of walking or running, so you must travel longer distances on the bike to burn the same number of calories (Margaria et al. 1963; Pugh 1971). Because you travel faster, however, the time consumed per calorie burned is about the same.

Effects of Bicycle Equipment on Speed

When a bicycle moves in a straight line, the resistance forces retarding motion are balanced by the thrust component developed by the rear wheel. Efficient bicycle equipment can decrease all of these forces. Resistance forces are of five types:

1. Aerodynamic forces caused by wind and the bicycle's motion through the air
2. Gravity forces when the road is not level
3. Inertial forces experienced when the bicycle is accelerating or decelerating
4. Tire rolling resistance forces
5. Bearing friction

On a level road with no wind at speeds below 13 kph (8 mph), tire and bearing rolling resistance are the dominant retarding forces. However, wind resistance increases as the square of bicycle speed, while rolling resistance increases only slightly with speed. Above 13 kph, air resistance overshadows rolling resistance. In fact, at speeds above 40 kph (25 mph), wind resistance is responsible for over 90% of the retarding force on a traditional road racing bike (Kyle 1988a).

A simple equation will serve for analysis of the relative importance of the resistance forces and the benefits of equipment modification:

1.1 $$m(dv/dt) = T - [WSin(ArctanG) + WCrr_1Cos(ArctanG) + NCrr_2V + 1/2C_dA_\rho(V + V_w)^2]$$

where m is the equivalent mass of the bicycle and rider, dv/dt is acceleration rate, T is propulsive thrust at the tire contact patch, W is weight, Crr_1 is rolling resistance coefficient, G is fractional slope (the rise divided by the horizontal distance), N is the number of wheels (the equation also covers tricycles), Crr_2 is a factor defining the variation of rolling resistance with velocity, V is cycle velocity, C_d is aerodynamic drag coefficient, A is frontal area, ρ is air density (a value of 1.2 kg/m^3 = 0.00233 slugs/ft^3 was used in all calculations), and V_w is the velocity of a headwind or tailwind with the sign being positive for a headwind.

The first term in equation 1.1 gives the inertial force due to acceleration. The second term gives the rider-generated net thrust after losses through the chain, gears, and rear wheel. The third term gives the force component of gravity in ascending or descending. The sign of G is positive uphill and negative downhill. The fourth term gives the static rolling resistance of the tires and bearings. The sixth term gives the aerodynamic drag of the bicycle and rider.

The fifth term in equation 1.1 combines the velocity-dependent drag due to wheel bearing and windage losses (rotational air drag) and also the velocity-dependent losses in the tires. Wheel bearing friction is a function of velocity and of total weight on the bearing. The friction of roller bearings is extremely small compared to other losses. The drag of tires increases with velocity because of dynamic friction in the tread and sidewalls. However, with high-pressure tires of 100 psi or more, dynamic friction is very small at moderate speeds (16 to 70 kph, 10 to 40 mph). The rotational air drag of the wheel is also a function of velocity. A spinning wheel encounters air friction even on a stationary bicycle trainer.

For simplicity, it will be assumed that the coefficient Crr_2 includes the windage losses of the wheels and that it is just a function of the number of wheels (N) and of the speed (V). In a test using the General Motors tire test drum in 1987, a value of $0.0502\ N \cdot s/m$ ($0.00344\ lb \cdot s/ft$) for Crr_2 was measured for a Moulton 17-in. bicycle tire with the spokes covered by smooth plastic wheel disks (Moore 1987). Since this factor has not been measured for other wheel sizes, a conservative value of $0.0502\ N \cdot s/m$ for Crr_2 will be used for all of the calculations.

Multiplying the equation by the speed gives us

1.2 $$mV(dv/dt) = P - WV[Sin(ArctanG) + Crr_1Cos(ArctanG] + NCrr_2V^2 + 1/2C_dA_pV(V + V_w)^2$$

where P is the net mechanical power produced by the rider. If there is no acceleration, then the power shown is the mechanical power necessary to overcome drag forces. Depending on the problem, these equations can either be solved directly or integrated numerically (Kyle and Burke 1984). Now let's take a closer look at the factors that slow one down while cycling.

Aerodynamic Drag

You can decrease aerodynamic forces by choosing shapes that move through the air efficiently. This is streamlining, an energy-conserving process used by all creatures that must move rapidly through air or water. The drag coefficient C_d gives a relative measure of the aerodynamic drag: The higher C_d, the higher the drag. See figure 1.4 for the drag coefficients of typical shapes.

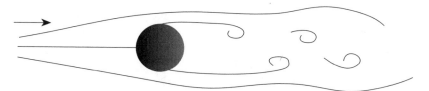

Air separates from a circular cylinder and leaves a turbulent wake with a low-pressure region in the rear of the cylinder. The pressure difference between the front and back creates a high drag. $C_d = 1.2$.

Shapes with sharp edges are much worse than cylinders. All edges should be rounded to avoid unnecessary drag. By putting a radius about 0.2 times the height on the corners of this box-shaped cylinder, the drag can be lowered from $C_d = 2.0$ to $C_d = 1.3$.

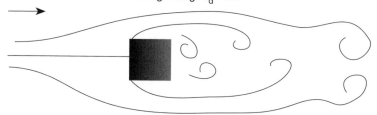

Air flows smoothly around a streamlined airfoil without turbulence. A wing shape takes less than 1/10 the energy to move through the air than a cylinder and less than 1/20 that of a box shape. The longer the airfoil is with respect to the thickness (chord-to-thickness ratio), the lower the drag. $C_d = 0.1$ or less.

When the rear of an airfoil is cut off, the drag increases because of the higher base drag due to turbulence at the rear. $C_d = 0.3$.

A two-to-one ellipse (width-to-height ratio) has a drag lower than that of a cylinder, but not as low as that of a cut-off airfoil section. $C_d = 0.6$.

FIGURE 1.4   Aerodynamic drag of various shapes.

From Hoerner 1965.

A standard road bike with a rider in racing position has a drag coefficient of 0.8 to 0.9; total frontal area is usually 0.32 to 0.37 m² (3.4 to 4 ft²). Unfortunately, a traditional bike is made up of round tubes and cables and other unstreamlined shapes that have a relatively high degree of aerodynamic drag. Streamlining the components on a bicycle can significantly reduce air resistance. A round tube perpendicular to the wind, with a drag coefficient C_d of 1.2, takes more than 10 times the energy to move through the air than an airfoil, which can have a C_d of less than 0.1.

Objects with sharp edges, like many cranks, pedals, and sprockets, are even worse than cylinders. A sharp-edged box with a C_d of 2.0 takes more than 20 times the energy than an airfoil to move through the air. Drilling holes in components may help save weight, but it is bad for aerodynamic drag. Speed loss due to air turbulence far outweighs the benefits from weight savings. Rounding sharp edges can decrease drag 15 to 50% (Hoerner 1965). Unfortunately, since rounding the sharp edges on a bicycle can escalate production costs, this detail is often neglected.

Apart from streamlining by changing the profile, there are other ways to lower aerodynamic drag. One way is to decrease frontal area. Bicycles with small-diameter tubes have lower drag than bicycles with wide tubes. A bicycle pump parallel to the wind (like an arrow) has lower drag than the same pump placed perpendicular to the wind (like a flagpole). A bicycle rider who assumes a racing crouch both streamlines the body and lowers frontal area. Components placed in the wind shadow of others create a lower profile and a lower drag. A water bottle behind the saddle would have a lower drag than the same bottle on the down tube.

Smooth bicycle frame tubes have lower drag than rough ones (Brownlie et al. 1991). There are two kinds of aerodynamic drag: surface friction drag and pressure drag. Friction drag is caused by a viscous shear in the thin layer of air moving parallel to a surface. A rough surface traps more air mass and increases friction. Wind tunnel studies show that smooth, polished surfaces are almost always better within the speed range of a bicycle (Brownlie et al. 1991).

Pressure drag is caused by the difference in surface pressure between the leading and trailing sections of a moving object. When airflow separates from the trailing edges (see figure 1.4), a low-pressure cavity develops. On the leading edge, pressure is higher than average. Differential pressure acting over the entire surface results in a drag force. At bicycle speeds, pressure drag is much higher than friction drag. Streamlining is the most effective way to lower pressure drag.

Figures 1.5 and 1.6 show the effect of lower aerodynamic drag on a 40-km (25-mi) time trial (Kyle 1991d). For example, if the measured drag on a bicycle in a wind tunnel is lowered by 50 g (0.11 lb) at 48 kph (30 mph), a cyclist who normally travels 32 kph (20 mph) can save 26 s in a 40-km time trial.

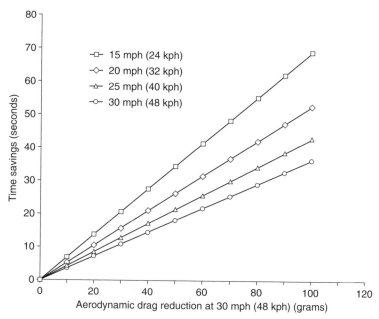

FIGURE 1.5   Time savings in 40-km (25-mi) time trial versus aerodynamic drag reduction, small scale.

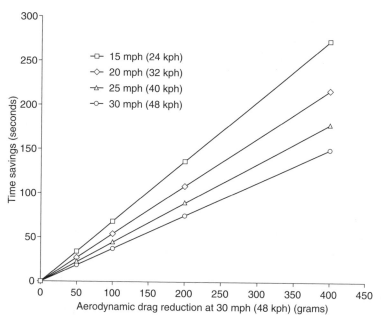

FIGURE 1.6   Time savings in 40-km (25-mi) time trial versus aerodynamic drag reduction, expanded scale.

Gravity Forces and Weight

Gravity forces have two important effects on bicycle speed. First, when a cyclist is climbing a hill, gravity slows the rate of ascent; during descent, gravity speeds up the bike. Unfortunately, since high downhill speeds never compensate for the slower climbing rate, a cyclist's average speed on hills will be less than on flat terrain. Lowering the bicycle's weight increases climbing rate, and the net time to cover a hilly course improves. See figure 1.7 for the effect of weight on bicycle speed on hills.

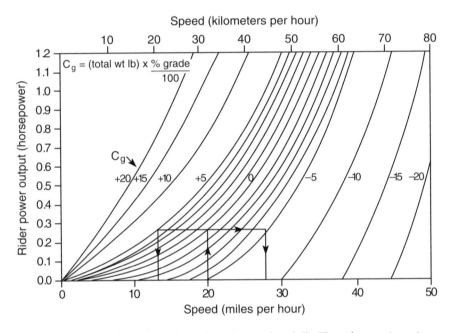

FIGURE 1.7   The effect of weight on bicycle speed on hills. The rider was in racing position on a Le Jeune bicycle. For a 200-lb cyclist riding on a 2.5% grade, $C_g = 200 \times (2.5/100) = 5$. Level speed = 20 mph; downhill speed = 27.8 mph; uphill speed = 13.2 mph.

The second effect of gravity is more subtle. Higher weight deforms the tires and raises the bearing loads, resulting in a higher rolling resistance. Even on level ground at constant speed, a heavier bike is slower. However, the effect of weight on bicycle speed is small compared to that of aerodynamics. Figure 1.8 gives the time lost over a 40-km distance by the addition of weight to a bicycle, assuming a level course. Lowering the aerodynamic drag only 10 g equals the effect of removing one whole kg (2.2 lb) from a bicycle. Air resistance of 10 g is equal to a 12-cm (4.5-in.) pencil held perpendicular to a 48-kph (30-mph) wind. Exposed cables can easily cause more than 10 g of drag. Cables should be run inside the handlebars and frame.

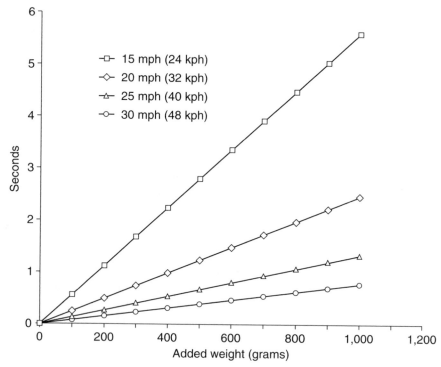

FIGURE 1.8   Time lost in 40 km versus added weight.

Historically, cycle designers have put enormous effort and money into building lighter bicycles. No doubt that effort has paid off. Today's elegant road bicycles can weigh less than 9 kg (20 lb). During the past 20 years, the relatively brief effort spent improving bicycle aerodynamics has produced more record results than has any other equipment development.

Inertial Forces

When a rider applies a force higher than equilibrium to the pedals, the bicycle accelerates until the retarding force balances the new thrust force. Newton's second law of motion states that net thrust force (F) equals mass times acceleration, so the only way to boost the acceleration rate is to increase the applied force or decrease the mass.

Lighter bikes are quicker than heavier ones. In racing, weight's effect on acceleration is relatively small but very important. Acceleration is roughly proportional to the square root of the ratio of the masses. Imagine that a racing cyclist and bicycle weigh 80 kg and can accelerate from a stop to cover 100 m in 10 s. If the bicycle is 1 kg heavier, the cyclist will lose about 0.06 s in 100 m, a gap of about 0.8 m against an equal opponent on the lighter bike.

Most roads are up and down, and there are always stops, so acceleration and deceleration is a constant process. Lighter equipment will get you there faster. As cynical observers often say, it costs a lot less to drop 1 lb in body weight than to lower the weight of a bicycle by 1 lb. The effect is the same.

Rolling Resistance

Although tire friction is small compared to wind drag, better tire designs have led to significant improvement in racing performance (Kyle 1988b; Kyle and Burke 1984). A good racing tire can weigh as little as 130 g (4.5 oz) and hold pressure as high as 15 atm (220 psi). The tires with the lowest rolling resistance have extremely thin walls; thin, smooth tread; and thin tubes.

As a tire rolls, it flattens where it touches the ground, deforming the tread and the casing and scrubbing against the pavement. Internal and external friction and inelastic deformation of the tread cause energy losses that are exhibited as resistance to rolling. Rolling resistance usually is expressed in terms of a coefficient *Crr*, which is friction force (*F*) divided by wheel load (*W*). Rolling drag decreases as a function of pavement roughness, casing and tread construction, tube construction, tire pressure, wheel load, tire cross-sectional diameter, wheel diameter, speed, tire temperature, drive torque, and steering angle. Of these, pavement roughness, tire materials and construction, tire pressure, and wheel load are the major contributors to rolling resistance.

Tires deform to fit small irregularities in the surface. Smoother pavement causes less tire distortion. Rolling resistance can easily double on rough pavement. See table 1.1 for the effect of pavement type on rolling resistance and the rolling resistance of typical bike tires (Kyle 1988a).

In general, thinner and more flexible, resilient casings and tread have lower rolling resistance. Natural rubber (latex) is better than manufactured butyl. Pinching tires between your fingers and feeling the ease with which they deform and rebound gives a good indication of their rolling resistance. The best wall materials are made from thin threads of silk, nylon, or Kevlar, since they have a high strength-to-weight ratio and are extremely flexible, thus minimizing both weight and hysteresis (internal friction) losses.

Tread pattern also influences rolling resistance. Tire tread concentrates the pressure at the contact patch where the tread squirms and deforms as it moves through the contact patch. Tread is meant to improve traction, not lower rolling resistance. Fine tread patterns are better than coarse ones, but slick tires are best for low rolling resistance. Hybrid tread that has a broad, smooth band in the center with tread lugs on both sides is a good compromise to give superior traction in corners or on soft surfaces and low rolling resistance on smooth pavement.

Thin, lightweight natural rubber (latex) tubes have the lowest rolling resistance. The tube flexes with every wheel revolution, which influences rolling resistance one-half to one-tenth as much as the tire does. Unfortunately,

TABLE 1.1   Rolling Resistance of Bicycle Tires

Tubular tires

Type	Pressure (atm)	SURFACE*		
		Linoleum	Concrete	Smooth asphalt
Continental Olympic 27 in. × 19 mm	6.8	0.19	0.17	0.22
Continental Olympic 24 in. × 19 mm	6.8	0.26	0.23	0.27
Clement Colle Main 27 in. × 19 mm	6.8	0.16		
Clement Colle Main 24 in. × 19 mm	6.8	0.21		
Clement Colle Main 20 in. × 19 mm	6.8	0.29		

Wired-on "clincher" tires

Type	Pressure (atm)	SURFACE*		
		Linoleum	Concrete	Smooth asphalt
Specialized Turbo S 700 × 19 C	6.8	0.26		0.29
Specialized Turbo S, Kevlar, with latex tube 700 × 19 C	6.8	0.23	0.27	
Same tire, butyl tube	6.8	0.28		
Same tire, butylized latex tube	6.8	0.25		
Same tire, thin polyurethane tube	6.8	0.29		
Same tire, polyurethane liner, latex tube	6.8	0.54		
Same tire, thick latex liner, latex tube	6.8	0.32		

(continued)

TABLE 1.1 (continued)

Type	Pressure (atm)	SURFACE*		
		Linoleum	Smooth Concrete	asphalt
Touring tire 700 × 25 C	6.8	0.31		0.35
Same tire	8.2	0.28		
Knobby tread tire 27 in. × 2 1/4 in.	3.1	1.30		
Knobby tread tire 20 in. × 2 1/4 in.	3.1	1.70		
Avocet fastgrip 20 in. × 1 3/4 in.	5.4	0.40		
Same tire	6.8	0.37		
Same tire	8.2	0.32		
Same tire, worn tread	6.8	0.30		
Avocet fastgrip 26 in. × 1 3/4 in.**	6.8			0.35
Same tire	6.8			
Moulton 17 in. × 1 3/4 in.	5.4	0.34		
Same tire	6.8	0.30		0.39
Same tire	8.2	0.27		

* Rolling resistance coefficient in percent. To get the resistance in motion, multiply the weight of the tire by the coefficient divided by 100.

** Glass = 0.30; smooth asphalt = 0.35; rough macadam = 0.54

Tests performed from 1984 to 1988 at California State University, Long Beach, for the U.S. Cycling Team, Specialized, General Motors, and Tom Petrie of Velimpex Marketing, El Cerrito, California.

latex tubes lose air rapidly. A mixture of latex and butyl gives both good rolling resistance and good air retention. Butylized latex tubes are commercially available.

Thick polyurethane tire liners, intended for flat protection, can nearly double rolling resistance. Puncture sealants, latex liners, or puncture-resistant belts on tires cause less drag than thick polyurethane liners. Probably the best solution for most riding conditions is to use tires with slightly more tread thickness. This will prevent most flats and will provide relatively low rolling resistance (see the 700 × 25 C touring tire in table 1.1).

With equal loads, higher tire pressures decrease tire deformation. High tire pressure also helps prevent pinch flats, but the vibration dampening of the tire deteriorates. See figure 1.9 and table 1.1 for the effect of tire pressure on rolling resistance. In racing, competitors will carry as high a pressure as is practical to decrease rolling resistance. Typical pressures are 120 to 150 psi (8 to 10 atm) in road races and 150 to 220 psi (10 to 15 atm) in track races. Clincher tires will not carry such high pressures and are usually restricted to 90 to 120 psi (6 to 8 atm) by the manufacturer.

Rolling resistance is directly proportional to wheel load. Lighter loads lessen tire deformation. Depending on tire design and road surface, the retarding force caused by tire friction can vary from 0.22 to 0.5% of the weight on the tires (Kyle and Burke 1984). The tire's weight has three effects. Lighter tires have thinner casings and tread and less internal friction. A lighter tire also decreases wheel load, although this is a comparatively minor effect.

One effect that is not negligible is the added drag force in cornering. On a bicycle track, racers sometimes undergo two times gravity because of the centrifugal acceleration. This doubles tire rolling resistance. Also, if the bicycle wheel has a steering angle (slip angle), this also adds to rolling

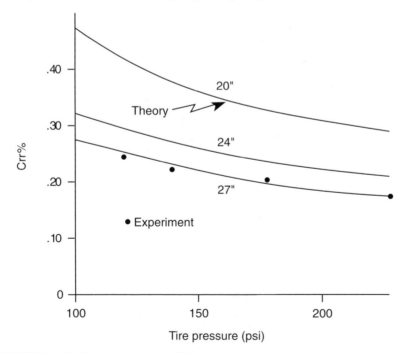

FIGURE 1.9   Rolling resistance coefficient versus tire pressure and wheel size.
From Kyle 1988c.

resistance. Cyclists always note the rapid deceleration when they corner sharply. This is caused by increased download and tire scrubbing from the corner.

Another effect of added weight is wheel inertia. Because tire weight is concentrated at the rim, extra tire weight magnifies inertial effects during acceleration. Energy is required to spin the wheel and accelerate it forward. The sum of the two effects causes the apparent mass of an accelerating wheel to be higher than that of a constant-speed wheel. The equivalent inertial mass of a tire is double the inertial mass of a nonrotating weight, so light tires are doubly effective for quick starts. See table 1.2 for the typical inertial mass of wheel types. If the mass were entirely concentrated at the rim, the inertial mass would be twice the mass of the wheel. For a pure disk, the inertial mass would be 1.5 times the static wheel mass. If the wheel mass were entirely at the hub, the equivalent mass would be the same as the wheel mass. The inertial masses of the wheels in table 1.2 are between 1.4 and 1.8.

Larger tire cross sections deform less under equal loads, given the same tire construction and tire diameter. However, narrow tire profiles are still extremely efficient, and they have lower air resistance than wider tires.

Larger wheels have less tire deformation for equal loads. They also roll over surface irregularities with less applied torque. As the wheel size decreases, the tire must deform progressively more to support an equal weight. Tires with smaller wheels have an unavoidable higher rolling resistance even on perfectly smooth pavement (see figure 1.9). On rough pavement they are at a double disadvantage. Overcoming irregularities in the pavement requires a greater propulsive force for a small wheel than for a large wheel, and the friction losses are correspondingly greater (consider a roller skate trying to go over a rock half the size of the wheel). See table 1.1 for the effect of wheel size and pavement roughness on rolling resistance.

Lower speeds decrease bearing friction, wind resistance, and dynamic tire distortion. All of these usually are included in some way in rolling resistance measurements. With high-pressure bicycle tires, dynamic distortion is very small, but bearing friction and wind resistance are always present.

Rubber viscosity decreases with higher temperatures, cutting internal friction. Air expands with heat, causing higher tire pressure. Hot tires roll more easily than cold tires.

Tire deformation decreases with lower drive torque. The rear bicycle tire wears much faster than the front because about 60% of the weight is on the rear tire and the thrust force causes increased scrubbing on the pavement. For these reasons, rear tires last about half as long as front tires.

When the bike turns, tire friction goes up because the tire scrubs the pavement and centrifugal force increases the weight on the wheel. Steering a straight line will get you there faster (Kyle 1991b). In an experiment on a 250-m bicycle track, the steering angle of the bicycle during steady pedaling at about 48 kph (30 mph) was measured (see figure 1.10). The rider used standard aero bars. With every pedal stroke, the steering angle

TABLE 1.2 Apparent Mass of Accelerating Aero Wheels

24-inch wheels, radius = 0.2561 m[a]

	Static mass (g)	Moment of inertia (Nms² = Kgm²)	Apparent mass (g)	Ratio of apparent mass to static mass[b]
Mavic 3-spoke composite	654	0.0221	970	1.49
Mavic cosmic 12-spoke	840	0.0407	1,430	1.70
HED CX 12-spoke	663	0.0296	1,094	1.66
Mavic G2 disk	885	0.0307	1,350	1.53
HED disk	926	0.0386	1,480	1.59
Aerosports kevlar disk	622	0.0201	910	1.47

26-inch wheels, radius = 0.2868 m[a]

	Static mass (g)	Moment of inertia (Nms² = Kgm²)	Apparent mass (g)	Ratio of apparent mass to static mass[b]
Mavic 5-spoke composite	740	0.0280	1,070	1.45
Mavic cosmic 12-spoke	795	0.0727	1,420	1.78
Mavic 3G 3-spoke composite	872	0.0335	1,270	1.46
HED disk	1,090	0.0478	1,660	1.52
HED deep rim CX 16-spoke	867	0.0589	1,580	1.82

700 C wheels, radius = 0.3141 m[a]

	Static mass (g)	Moment of inertia (Nms² = Kgm²)	Apparent mass (g)	Ratio of apparent mass to static mass[b]
Mavic G2 disk rear	1,180	0.0555	1,745	1.63
HED disk	1,250	0.0722	1,986	1.59
Rolf Detrich 14-spoke	722	0.0540	1,291	1.79
HED 3-spoke[c]	850	0.0420	1,301	1.53
Spinergy 8-spoke[c]	833	0.0543	1,408	1.69
Specialized 32-spoke[c]	900	0.0539	1,467	1.63
Aerolite 16-spoke[c]	510	0.0346	859	1.68

[a] Radius measured at the center of the inside of the bare rim.
[b] Total mass concentrated at the rim would be 2.0; 1.5 would be a plane disk; and 1.0 would be total mass concentrated at the hub.
[c] Clincher wheels. All others are sew-ups.

swung back and forth about 2.5°. Since the track was cambered (sloped) even on the straights, about a 1° steering angle was necessary to hold the bike on the straight. On the curve, the average steering angle increased to 4°. The steering angle variation with each pedal stroke and the average steering angle along the straights and into the curves are clearly shown in figure 1.10. Figure 1.11 shows the variation of tire rolling resistance with steering angle (Moore 1987). A 2.5° steering angle would increase the rolling resistance coefficient by 15%. So it pays to steer a straight line.

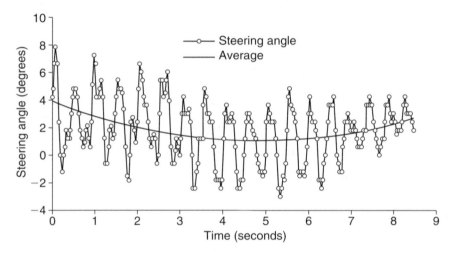

FIGURE 1.10   Steering angle versus time, 250-m track, transition from a curve to a straightaway.

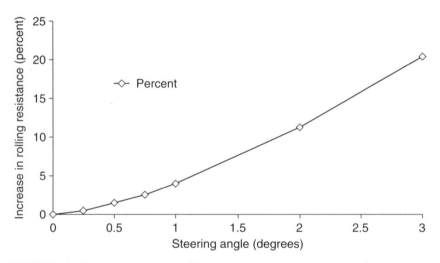

FIGURE 1.11   Percent increase in rolling resistance versus steering angle.

Bearing Friction

Bicycle wheel bearings are of two basic types—cup and cone ball bearings and cartridge bearings. Bicycle manufacturers lubricate bearings with grease. Ball bearings have low friction and cause about 1/20th to 1/50th as much drag as high-pressure racing tires. Friction in bearings is so low that it can be measured only with very accurate laboratory tools. Cartridge ball bearings usually contain seals that add to the bearing friction.

Danh and colleagues (1991) measured the friction of bicycle wheel bearings of several types. They found enormous differences between lubricants and bearing types (see figure 1.12). They concluded the following:

▶ Properly adjusted cup and cone bearings lubricated with 20w oil have the lowest friction. The friction of a cartridge bearing with no seal and lubricated with 20w oil is about seven times higher than that of cup and cone bearings. For racing, standard cup and cone bearings are superior.

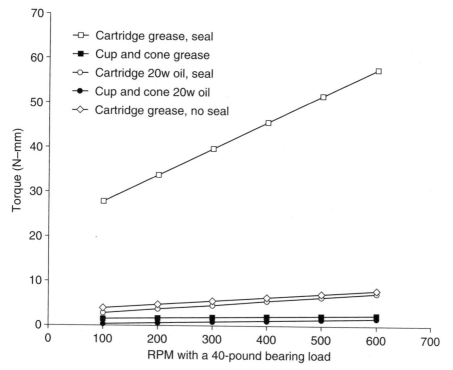

FIGURE 1.12   Effects of lubricant and seals on cartridge and cup and cone bearing friction.

▶ Bearings with grease have a friction about six to seven times higher than the same bearing with light 20w oil. For racing, bearings should be cleaned and lubricated with light oil. The loss resulting from the use of grease is the equivalent of climbing a 15-m hill during a 40-km time trial, enough to lose a close race.

▶ Cartridge bearing seals can cause up to 10 times the friction of a free-running bearing without a seal. For racing, cartridge bearings should be of the shielded type, not sealed (the shield doesn't rub). For racing, the inner shield should be removed and the bearing lubricated with light oil.

▶ The friction of bicycle wheel bearings does not seem to be affected much by load. However, friction increases linearly with speed. Friction approximately doubled from 50 to 600 rpm.

These conclusions are generally correct with one qualification. Danh and colleagues used new cartridge bearings, which give very high friction measurements. Worn bearings and seals have much lower friction than new bearings. In any case, a well-worn bearing has lower friction than a new bearing has. Racing bearings should be well worn in before use.

Using a different test procedure, Kyle (1988a) reached basically the same conclusions. According to Danh's data, cone bearings could produce a 7-m lead in a 40-km time trial against an equal opponent using cartridge bearings with the seals removed and lubricated with light oil (Danh et al. 1991).

To estimate the combined energy losses in the chain, sprockets, and bearings, a bicycle ergometer driven by an accurate dynamometer can be used (Kyle and Caiozzo 1986b). Drive train losses are 2 to 4% of energy input. This extremely high efficiency is typical for a well-oiled sprocket and roller chain transmission. To minimize transmission energy losses, the bicycle chain and gears should be clean and well lubricated.

A factor not often considered by inventors seeking to improve bicycle transmissions is the extremely high energy efficiency of a chain-sprocket drive—above 96%. Hydraulic transmissions often are proposed as a solution to bicycle gearing, but they are less than 75% efficient, meaning that more than 25% of a rider's energy is wasted. This is clearly impractical. Beware of new, infinitely variable transmissions or other drive schemes until the inventor measures the energy losses in the transmission. Anything with higher losses than a chain-sprocket transmission will not sell because the rider must overcome the added losses with muscle power.

The design and shape of various bicycle components also have a significant effect on aerodynamics. We will begin with wheels.

Wheels

Numerous types of bicycle wheels are currently manufactured: round-spoked wheels with flat rims, bladed-spoked wheels with aero rims, composite disk wheels, Kevlar membrane aero wheels, composite three-spoked aero wheels, and an endless variety of combinations of spoke types and patterns, shapes, sizes, and weights. Several factors influence the performance of a bicycle wheel, including stiffness, weight, aerodynamic drag, strength and durability, and the efficiency of the braking surface.

The fact is that almost any type of wheel can be built to meet all of the important performance criteria except two—aerodynamic drag and weight. In other words, almost any type of wheel can have adequate strength, durability, stiffness (which influences ride quality and stability), and a good braking surface; however, all wheel types can't have low aerodynamic drag and low weight.

Table 1.3 shows the time advantage for elite cyclists when small aerodynamic drag reductions are achieved by the use of better equipment. Table 1.4 shows the air drag and weight of racing bicycle wheels tested at the University of California at Irvine low-speed wind tunnel and at the University of Washington, Kirsten wind tunnel. The measurements listed in table 1.4 are for front wheels only. The rear wheel would provide about 60% of the advantage listed because the rear wheel is drafting in the slipstream of other components.

From the wind tunnel wheel tests, the following conclusions about the aerodynamics of wheels can be drawn (Kyle 1991d).

TABLE 1.3   Racing Advantage of Aerodynamics

Drag increase (g)	Ft/mi advantage	Time decrease, s/mi	1,000-m time trial (s)	4,000-m pursuit (s)
10	5	0.11	0.07	0.28
20	10	0.22	0.12	0.62
40	20	0.45	0.23	1.12
80	41	0.93	0.47	2.22
120	61	1.39	0.70	3.39
160	91	2.06	0.94	4.53
200	111	2.51	1.17	5.62

Adapted, by permission, from C.R. Kyle, 1990, "Wind tunnel tests of bicycle wheels and helmets," *Cycling Science* 2(1):27-30.

TABLE 1.4 Bicycle Wheel Tests

	DRAG IN GRAMS AT 30 MPH		
	Wheel weight (g)	Static tests (average)*	Rotating (average)*
24-inch wheels			
Flat carbon disk 18-mm tire	950	74	97
Kevlar lens disk 18-mm tire	480	76	100
12-spoke deep aero rim 18-mm tire	790	86	109
18 bladed spokes, aero rim 18-mm tire	490		136
28 round spokes, flat rim 22-mm tire	610		182
26-inch wheels			
Kevlar lens disk 18-mm tire	590	78	95
Flat carbon disk 18-mm tire	900	73	101
HED CX 18 aero spokes 18-mm tire	850	109	139
18 bladed spokes, aero rim 18-mm tire	530		145
32 round spokes, flat rim 22-mm tire	700		208
27-inch wheels			
27-in. composite spoked wheels (3 and 4 spokes)			
Aerosports 3-spoke prototype 18-mm tire	720	90	106
Trispoke (3 spoke) 18-mm tire	720	87	112
Specialized (3 spoke) 18-mm tire	1,330	89	114
Zipp (forward) (3 spoke) 18-mm tire	850	102	129
Corima (4 spoke) 18-mm tire	1,590	100	131
Zipp (backward) (3 spoke) 18-mm tire	850	108	146

TABLE 1.4 (continued)

	DRAG IN GRAMS AT 30 MPH		
	Wheel weight (g)	Static tests (average)*	Rotating (average)*
27-in. disk wheels			
Gipiemme lens disk 18-mm tire	1,110	72	101
Flat carbon disk 18-mm tire	1,040	76	105
Zipp 950 carbon disk 18-mm tire	1,040	76	105
HED flat carbon disk 18-mm tire	1,050	77	114
Kevlar lens disk 18-mm tire	710	99	118
27-in. steel spoked wheels			
18 aero spokes, aero rim 18-mm tire	680	122	149
24 aero spokes, aero rim 18-mm tire	770		147
28 aero spokes, aero rim 18-mm tire	820		173
28 oval spokes, aero rim 18-mm tire	780		175
18 round spokes, aero rim 18-mm tire	700		206
36 round spokes, standard rim 18-mm tire	960		258

* The basic accuracy of the wind tunnel balance is ± 5 g, so many of the listed differences are not significant.

Tests performed for the U.S. Cycling Federation, Specialized, and Aerosports at the University of California, Irvine wind tunnel and University of Washington, Kirsten Wind Tunnel, 1987, 1989, and 1991.

Wheel Size

Aerodynamically, there doesn't seem to be too much difference among the best wheels in terms of diameter: 24, 26, and 27 in. Even though the 24- and 26-in. wheels have a smaller frontal area, they must spin faster to achieve the same rim speed, so the corresponding drag is about the same. However, smaller wheels have many other advantages. They are lighter and stronger, and the bicycle frame can also be made lighter and stiffer with a consequent advantage in acceleration, cornering, and hill climbing. The center of aerodynamic lift of a disk wheel is ahead of the axle by about one fourth of the wheel radius, so steering torque is generated by crosswinds. Since small front disk wheels have more stability in unsteady crosswinds, you can ride them in more severe wind conditions.

In a pace line, small-wheeled bikes can draft closer and therefore achieve a lower average wind resistance (see figure 1.13). Using 24-in. wheels, each drafting rider can have 5% lower wind resistance compared to riders in the same pace line with 27-in. wheels, so the pace line can travel faster. A reasonable estimate is 2 s faster in a 4000-m team pursuit.

As noted earlier, the only obvious disadvantage to small wheels is a higher rolling resistance. Considering the combined aerodynamic drag and rolling resistance, racing bikes can be built with a mix of wheel sizes and be competitive. Table 1.5 compares several wheel combinations at 30 mph on a level course with a pair of standard 27-in. wheels as the baseline (Kyle 1991d). Wheels of 24 in. (550 C), 26 in. (650 C), and 27 in. (700 C) have been used in competition and are still UCI (Union Cycliste Internationale) legal as long as both wheels are the same size.

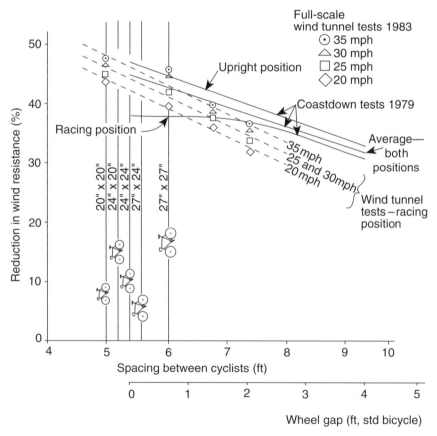

FIGURE 1.13 Wind resistance of drafting riders in a pace line.

TABLE 1.5 Net Drag of Various Wheel Combinations

Wheel combination	Difference in drag (g)
27 × 27	0
27 × 26	−1
27 × 24	9
26 × 26	3
26 × 24	13
24 × 24	29

Adapted from Kyle 1991d.

The difference in aerodynamic drag among the various wheel size combinations used by time trial bikes is not very large, only about 29 g at 30 mph. This translates into a time difference of about 10 to 15 s in 40 km. Considering that small-wheeled bikes can be made much lighter, I suspect that all of the bikes listed would be about equal on a level course with no wind. On a rolling course where climbing is necessary, the lighter bikes with smaller wheels should be superior. And in a road race where there is constant acceleration and deceleration, the small-wheeled 24 × 24 should be best. Time trial bikes of 27 × 27 (700 C), 26 × 26 (650 C), and 24 × 24 (550 C) have won international races.

Wheel Type

A comparison of the wheels in table 1.4 shows that composite aerodynamic wheels have a uniformly lower drag than the best bladed, oval-, or round-spoked wheels by 35 to 50 g per wheel.

When we compare composite three- or four-spoked wheels to lens-shaped or flat disk wheels, the three types are about the same. There is another major difference, however, between disk wheels and three- or four-spoked aero wheels. In a buffeting crosswind, a front disk wheel often causes steering instability that makes it impossible to ride a straight line. Rear disk wheels cause few problems—they can be ridden in nearly any wind condition.

Three- or four-spoked composite front wheels have much more stability in crosswinds, making them ideal for racing under almost any conditions. In fact, the aero drag of both three-spoked composites and disk wheels decreases in a mild crosswind because the wheel actually develops lift (the sail effect). In contrast, the drag of conventionally spoked wheels increases in a crosswind (Kyle 1990). Thus, the advantage of aero wheels over steel spoked wheels improves with side winds.

Tire Width

The width of tires should be about equal to the width of the rim for minimum aerodynamic drag. Air should flow smoothly around the tire and rim. If the tire is wider than the rim, it causes flow separation and turbulence, raising the drag. The wider the tire, the higher the aerodynamic drag. Since tire width makes little difference in rolling resistance, there is no advantage to using wide tires in time trialing or road racing, except on rough pavement. On rough pavement or in gravel or dirt, wide tires handle much better than narrow tires.

Bicycle Frames

Because of UCI regulations passed in 2000, bike frames must have a traditional double diamond frame. However, the tubes can still be streamlined with a maximum length of 8 cm and width of 2.5 cm for main frame members and 8 cm by 1 cm for forks, seat, and chain stays.

Modern bicycle frames come in a bewildering variety of shapes and materials. Frames of different styles have sloping top tubes, composite frame members, various wheel sizes, different seat tube and head angles, and so on. Because of this variety, it has become difficult to classify frame size by traditional methods. In fact, the frame size (58 cm, 60 cm, etc.) has little meaning for many custom bicycles. What is important is that the bars, the

© Jim and Mary Whitmer

Equipment choices should be based on the comfort of the cyclist, the regulations of the governing agency of the race, and the demands of the course.

saddle, and the relative position of the cranks be adjustable enough to fit the preferred riding position of the cyclist.

For rider comfort, the triangle composed of the body contact points—crank, saddle, and handlebars—should remain unchanged no matter what frame style the rider is using. From a side view, the riding position should be identical from one bicycle to the next. A variety of bicycle sizes and geometries can feel comfortable and provide stable riding. Jeukendrup and Martin (2001) provide an excellent summary of the effect of bicycle equipment on aerodynamics and bicycle performance.

Bicycle Stability

Stability is an obvious necessity for any bicycle. A rider must be able to ride a straight line and corner cleanly with near effortless control. Unfortunately, there is really no useful way to define bicycle stability except subjectively through rider feel.

Bicycle geometry has few absolutes. Dimensions and angles can vary greatly and still be suitable. For most bicycles the steering head angle is between 65 and 75° as measured from the horizontal. The trail is the most critical geometric parameter. This is the distance between a projection of the steering axis where it hits the pavement and the center of the tire contact patch. The trail normally runs 3.8 to 6.4 cm (1.5 to 2.5 in.). Within these ranges, bicycles feel stable and are very ridable. A head angle of 73° and a trail of 4.4 cm (1.75 in.) is typical of a racing bicycle, and 65° and 6.4 cm (2.5 in.) is typical of mountain bikes.

Steeper head angles and less trail make a bicycle quicker to steer but less stable at racing speeds. More trail and lower head angles make the bicycle sluggish to steer but very stable and easy to handle over bumps and rough pavement. Preferred bicycle geometry (frame size, rake, trail, etc.) is a matter of personal preference. Cyclists can ride anything from a child's sidewalk bike to a unicycle.

Riding Position

Unlike bicycle size, rider position and aerodynamics is not a matter of personal preference but is subject to the laws of physics. With aero bars that place the rider in a low crouch and the torso close to horizontal, the position of the steering axis is important. If the rider is too far forward over the steering axis, the added forward mass can make the bicycle difficult to steer.

Lengthening the top tube, and thus the wheelbase, makes steering more sluggish but easier to manage. At 48 kph (30 mph), the combined air resistance of a bicycle and a rider 182 cm (6 ft) tall and 75 kg (165 lb) varies from about 2.5 kg (5.5 lb) to over 4.5 g (10 lb), depending on the riding position and the bicycle. The aerodynamic drag of the bicycle is only 25 to 35% of the total, with the cyclist's body being the remainder. Consequently, body position is the biggest single factor in achieving low aerodynamic drag.

Figure 1.14 shows the effect of riding position on the power required to pedal a standard racing bicycle (Kyle 1991c). The hill descent position (hands together, elbows in, low crouch) is the most efficient aerodynamically. This is only slightly better than the position achieved with the use of elbow-rest aero handlebars. With aero bars, wind tunnel studies show that the drag of a rider is usually lowest if the back is flat, not arched. However, an arched back can still have very low wind resistance. Tour de France winner Lance Armstrong rides with a radically arched back and can time trial at over 53 kph (33 mph). The elbows should be held in so that the front arm profile is narrower than the body. The angle of the forearms can be from 0 to 30° as measured from the horizontal (Kyle 1989); however, 0° is best.

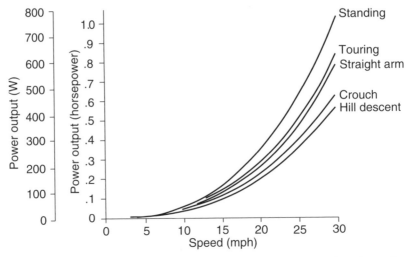

FIGURE 1.14   Power versus speed for various riding positions. The bicycle used was a Raleigh track bike; the rider was 187 cm (6 ft 2 in.) tall and weighed 82 kg (180 lb). Results of coastdown tests conducted by Chester Kyle at California State University at Long Beach, 1983-1984.

The invention of modern aero bars is due to California engineer Pete Pensayres. In 1986, he set a record in the Race Across America using bars that were built according to his own specifications. Soon after, commercial bars were introduced by Scott and Profile. By 1988, they were being used by triathletes in Ironman races. Later, aero bars were adopted by traditional bicycle racers.

Elbow-rest aero bars allow a rider to maintain an efficient aerodynamic posture for long periods without fatigue. In 1993, Scottish amateur time trialist Graeme Obree invented a new aero position with which he broke the world hour record. By placing his hands on horizontal handlebars about chest width apart, doubling up his arms, and resting his chest on the bars,

Obree succeeded in improving on the aerodynamics of standard aero bars. This position was promptly banned by the UCI, so Obree invented an even better aero position with his arms in diving position ahead of the front wheel. In 1994, he again broke the hour record with the so-called super-man position. In 2000, the UCI banned the superman position. However, they did not ban standard elbow-rest aero bars; they are still legal for time trials.

In mass-start races, traditional drop bars are still required by the UCI. In the traditional crouched racing position, with hands on the drops and the elbows bent at 90°, the air drag is still higher than it is with aero bars. The only way to achieve the low drag of aero bars is to assume the descent position, grabbing the bar in the center, on either side of the stem, tucking in the elbows, and staying in a low crouch with the crank horizontal and the knees touching the top tube.

Body Type and Air Drag

A cyclist's body type makes an enormous difference in aerodynamic drag. For the same weight and height, riders can have a wide variety of limb lengths, chest and neck sizes, and so on, and consequently a widely vary-ing aerodynamic drag. Table 1.6 shows the physical characteristics of six cyclists, and table 1.7 shows the aerodynamic drag of these same subjects on a triathlon bike in identical riding positions.

One of the shortest and lightest subjects had a stocky build and surpris-ingly the highest aerodynamic drag. A slender torso is an advantage in cycling as far as aerodynamic drag is concerned (Kyle 1991e). Many cy-clists have a slender torso and arms but well-developed leg muscles—a body type ideal for cycling.

TABLE 1.6   Physical Characteristics of Subjects (See Table 1.7)

Initials	Gender	Age (years)	Height in m (ft/in.)	Weight in kg (lb)	Body type
M.R.	Female	34	1.619 (5'4")	47.7 (105)	Slender
K.K.	Female	19	1.625 (5'4")	54.5 (120)	Stocky
K.S.	Male	25	1.753 (5'9")	59.9 (132)	Slender
R.R.	Male	23	1.797 (5'11")	69.0 (152)	Medium
C.C.	Male	22	1.829 (6'0")	65.8 (145)	Slender
D.M.	Male	26	1.854 (6'1")	79.2 (160)	Slender

Reprinted, by permission, from C.R. Kyle, 1991b, "The effect of crosswinds upon time trials," *Cycling Science* 3(3-4):51-56.

TABLE 1.7 Wind Tunnel Tests on Bicycles With Varying Yaw Angles

Bike	YAW ANGLE DEGREES							
	0°		10°		20°		30°	
	Drag force (lb)	Side force (lb)	Drag force (lb)	Side force (lb)	Drag force (lb)	Side force (lb)	Drag force (lb)	Side force (lb)
M.R., triathlon bike	5.171	0.07	5.360	5.967	5.537	13.392	5.715	21.509
K.K., triathlon bike	5.925	0.29	6.021	4.678	6.062	11.82	6.696	20.66
K.S., triathlon bike	5.219	0.14	5.460	5.522	5.446	12.968	5.779	22.486
R.R., triathlon bike	5.619	0.66	5.764	5.612	5.656	13.386	5.674	23.258
Average, triathlon bike	5.484	0.29	5.651	5.437	5.675	12.892	5.966	21.978
C.C., track bike	8.006	0.21	8.398	4.062	9.098	7.990		
C.C., aero bike	7.597	0.30	7.484	4.752	8.216	8.346		
D.M., road bike*	10.575	1.913	11.437	1.643	12.026	5.580	13.709	13.118

* The road bike test was actually performed at 20 mph. To get comparative drag figures at 30 mph, the measured drag was multiplied by $2.25 = (30/20)^2$.

Wind speed 30 mph. All speeds and forces are given with respect to the bike axis.

Triathlon bike: Vitus aluminum frame, special flat 100k bars, 27 in. × 19 mm front wheel with aero rim and 18 bladed spokes, 27 in. × 19 mm Hed lens rear disk, single disk front sprocket. Riders wore Giro Aero helmets with a Lycra cover and Lycra skin suits. All riders were in aero position with back flat, elbows pulled in resting on bars with hands together in front. Wind tunnel tests performed January 1990 at Texas A & M by Chester Kyle, Mike Melton, and Gary Hooker at the Hed Triathlon camp.

Track and aero bikes: The track bike was a conventional Raleigh with drop bars and two 27 in. × 22 mm standard rim 36 round spoke wheels. The aero bike was a prototype with helicopter aero strut tubing, bull horn bars with aero tubing, two 20-in. 18 round spoke wheels with aero rims, 60-mm narrow front hubs, 110-mm rear hubs, a single disk front sprocket with aero cranks. Riders sat upright, head up, with elbows straight. On the aero bike, riders' hands were on the bull horns. Riders were bare headed and wore loose Lycra USA suits and high wool socks. Track and aero bike wind tunnel tests performed June 1983 by Chester Kyle and Jack Lambie at Texas A & M for USOC.

Road bike: Conventional round tube frame with drop bars, conventional 27-in., 36-spoke wheels and a carrier rack in the rear. Rider crouched with hands on drops. Rider wore a loose cotton T-shirt, wool ski cap, and loose cotton touring shorts. Wind tunnel tests performed at Calspan in New York October 1980 by D.M. for Alex Moulton Bicycles.

Air Drag of Bicycles

The data in table 1.7 also include the drag of bicycles at wind yaw angles up to 30°. The yaw angle is the apparent angle of the wind with the bicycle direction. Yaw angles are produced by any wind not directly along the line of travel, a crosswind. The yaw angle data demonstrate that bicycles with disk wheels or aero tubing perform far better in crosswinds than round-tube bicycles with conventional wheels.

Actually, the condition of no wind and zero yaw angle is very rare. There is almost always some wind outdoors. On an indoor track, a different situation causes relative wind. When a bicycle turns on a track, the relative wind shifts, causing a wind yaw angle whenever the track curves. Jeff Broker and Chester Kyle have measured this effect on track bikes traveling at 30 mph on a 250-m track. Figure 1.15 clearly shows the relative wind angle as a bicycle tours a 150-m track. In the curves, the yaw angle averages about 10°; in the transition zone and straights, the yaw angle is about 3°. So aero equipment can be of added benefit wherever turns are frequent, even when there is no wind.

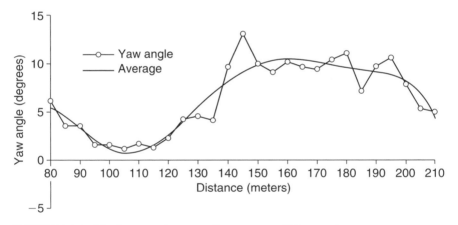

FIGURE 1.15   Wind yaw angle versus distance on a 150-m track.

Another factor that affects the air resistance of a bicycle and rider is the change in body configuration as the legs move around the crank cycle. Figure 1.16 shows the effect of yaw angle and crank angle on air drag as determined in the General Motors wind tunnel (Kyle 1997). The bicycle that was tested in the wind tunnel had aero tubes with aero bars, a rear disk wheel, and an aero three-spoke front wheel. A crank angle of 0° means that the right leg is straight up. Turning the crank forward, when the crank reaches horizontal, the angle is 90°, and so on. Starting with the wind straight on, positive yaw angles occur when the bicycle turns away from the wind to the right, and negative yaw angles occur when the bicycle turns to the left.

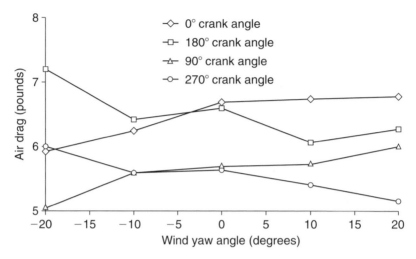

FIGURE 1.16   Drag versus yaw angle and crank angle.

In general, the minimum drag comes when the crank is either at 90 or 270°, which confirms the standard practice of cyclists in coasting down steep hills.

Figure 1.17 shows the same data plotted a different way. As the yaw angle changes, the drag depends on the position of the windward leg with respect to the wind. If it shields the other leg, then the drag is low. If the downwind leg is open to the wind, then the drag is high. For example, the curve for 0° crank angle continually increases from a yaw angle of –20° to +20° as the legs change position relative to the wind.

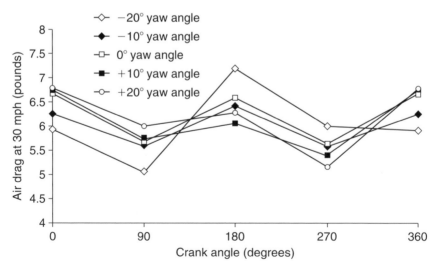

FIGURE 1.17   Drag versus crank angle and wind yaw angle.

Table 1.8 shows the air drag of various bicycle types in wind tunnel tests (Kyle 1989, 1991b, 1991e). At 30 mph, aero funny bikes have almost 1 lb less drag than standard road bicycles, giving them an enormous advantage in time trials. The two Dupont bicycles had prototype monocoque frames similar to that of the Lotus/Mike Burrows funny bike used by Chris Boardman in winning the 1992 Olympic 4,000-m individual pursuit. The Dupont bikes were built by Don Guichard and Chester Kyle for the 1988 U.S. Olympic cycling team but were declared illegal by the UCI before the Olympics. The UCI reversed the ruling in 1991, making composite monocoque bicycles legal. In 2000, the UCI again declared such bikes illegal. However, composite bicycles with near optimum aerodynamic shapes are still commercially available, if expensive, and they are UCI legal. Such bikes are extremely popular with triathletes and road time trialists. Two manufacturers with excellent aero composite time trial or triathlon bikes are Trek of Waterloo, Wisconsin, and Cervelo of Toronto, Canada. Both have had success in international racing.

Shifting Systems

Index shifters with fingertip controls have several advantages over conventional systems in which the shifters are on the down tube. Fingertip shifters allow faster and more frequent shifts, giving the proper gear when it is required, not later. If the shifter is on the down tube, the rider must release the handlebar and reach down. This sometimes causes steering problems and often interrupts the pedaling effort. Index shifters also permit changing gears under load, which permits a steadier pace.

At least two manufacturers (Shimano and Campagnolo) sell unique combined brake and shift levers for use on road bikes. The brake levers operate as usual, but fingertip shift levers, overlapped by the brake levers and parallel to the brake lever, pivot at right angles to the brake levers. They permit either braking or shifting while keeping the hands either on the brake hoods or on the drop handle grips.

Electronic rather than manual shifting is still in the development stage, but it could be an improvement that would save time and weight and make shifting more accurate. Shimano and Browning offer something in the lower price range (not meant for racing), and Mavic has a solenoid-operated derailleur. The definitive electronic bicycle transmission is yet to be invented.

Optimum Gearing and Mechanical Efficiency

The mechanical efficiency of a bicycle gear train is the power output at the wheel divided by the power input at the crank. Higher gear efficiency means lower energy losses and higher speed with identical power input. Derailleur transmissions are very efficient, usually from 95 to over 98%, under power inputs from 100 to 400 W (0.13 to 0.54 hp).

TABLE 1.8   Aerodynamic Drag of Bicycles at 30 MPH

		DRAG (LB)		
Bike	**Wheels**	**Bike, bare**	**Bike with rider**	**Drag (g)**
Road				
Gleb Derujinski, aero-composite[a]	27-in. × 28 aero spokes front, 32 spoke rear	1.90	6.89	3,128
Trimble prototype, aero-composite[a]	27-in. × 36 round spokes, front and rear	2.46	7.07	3,210
Kestrel prototype, aero-composite[a]	27-in. × 36 round spokes, front and rear	2.52	7.27	3,301
GIOS (standard round steel tubes)	27-in. × 36 round spokes, front and rear	2.64	7.37	3,346
Trek (aluminum round tubes)	27-in. × 36 round spokes, front and rear	2.71	7.36	3,341
Cannondale (aluminum round tubes)	27-in. × 36 round spokes, front and rear	2.72	7.25	3,292
Road time trial				
Kestrel prototype, (steel aero tubes)	27-in. rear flat disk, 24-in. front lens disk	1.45	6.48	2,942
Hooker Elite[b]	27-in. flat disk rear, 24-in. × 18 aero spoke front	1.38	6.66	3,024
1986 Huffy aero-composite[a]	27-in. rear lens disk, 24-in. front lens disk	1.89	6.71	3,046
Kyle prototype[b]	27-in. flat disk rear, 24-in. flat disk front	1.33	6.72	3,051
Huffy Triton[b]	27-in. flat disk rear, 24-in. × 18 aero spoke front	2.23	6.80	3,087
KHS[b]	27-in. flat disk rear, 24-in. × 18 aero spoke front	2.29	6.94	3,151
Time Machine[b]	27-in. flat disk rear, 24-in. × 18 aero spoke front	2.93	7.03	3,192
Rigideol Aero (steel aero tubes)[b]	27-in. lens disks, front and rear	2.02	7.06	3,205

TABLE 1.8 (continued)

Bike	Wheels	DRAG (LB)		
		Bike, bare	Bike with rider	Drag (g)
Team pursuit				
Huffy aero-composite	24-in. lens disks, front and rear	1.54	6.33	2,874
Individual pursuit				
Gleb Derujinski, aero-composite[a]	27-in. rear lens disk, 24-in. front lens disk	1.44	6.30	2,860
Dupont aero-composite #1, frame[a]	27-in. rear lens disk, 24-in. front lens disk	1.20	6.41	2,910
1986 Huffy aero-composite[a]	27-in. rear lens disk, 24-in. front lens disk	1.57	6.42	2,915
Dupont aero-composite #2, V frame[a]	27-in. rear lens disk, 24-in. front lens disk	1.21	6.56	2,978
Brent Trimble composite monocoque[a]	27-in. rear lens disk, 24-in. front lens disk	1.44	6.56	2,978
Tesch Aero (aluminum aero tubes)	27-in. rear lens disk, 24-in. front lens disk	1.56	6.84	3,105
Schwinn Track (steel round tubes)	27-in. × 32 bladed spoke wheels with aero rims, front and rear	2.41	6.98	3,169

Tests performed at California Institute of Technology, November 4–10, 1986, except where indicated. The same rider was used in all tests and was in the same crouched racing position. Rider was 6'2" and 170 lb. Rider wore Lycra tights with a long-sleeved wool jersey and a U.S. team aero helmet. Road bikes used standard drop bars except the Gleb, which used composite bars with an aero cross-section and standard drop hand grips. Road and time trial bikes included water bottles.

[a]These composite aero bikes were illegal for UCI-sanctioned races prior to 1991, when the rules were changed to permit monocoque bikes with no restrictions on tubing dimensions. They are again illegal as of 2000.

[b]Tests performed at Texas A & M, January 9–10, 1990. The same rider was used in all tests with elbow rest bars and with the torso horizontal. Rider was 6'1" and 170 lb and wore a Lycra skin suit with a Giro aero helmet. The Kyle prototype is the same bike listed above except with special aero elbow-rest handlebars designed by David Spangler of Hooker Industries. The bars are nearly identical to those on the Hooker Elite.

What gear combination is best to achieve a particular gear ratio has always been in question. For example, a 52/15 tooth gear combination has almost the same ratio as 42/12. Which one has the highest efficiency? In 2001, Frank Berto and Chester Kyle used a stationary crank dynamometer along with a special wheel ergometer to measure the efficiency of several bicycle transmissions. After comparing different gear combinations at varying levels of power input (Kyle and Berto 2001), we came to several conclusions:

1. Efficiency generally increases with load. For example, in tests of a 27-speed Shimano derailleur transmission, efficiency went from 94 to 98% with loads increasing from 50 to 350 W (see figure 1.18). Apparently, the residual bearing and chain friction increase at a slower rate than the increasing load, so the ratio of friction losses to power input declines as the load goes up. In other words, the faster you go, the more efficient your gear train is.

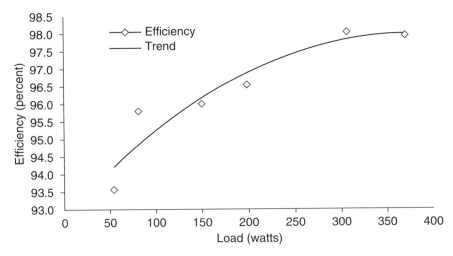

FIGURE 1.18   Mechanical efficiency versus load watts, Shimano 27-speed, gear 25, 44/16.

2. Efficiency is fairly constant with gear ratio. See the trend line in figure 1.19. The test is on a Browning 12-speed transmission at 200 W crank input. There are efficiencies above and below the trend line. The efficiency of a derailleur transmission depends on things such as the load, chain tension, chain bend, crank rpm, gear size, gear combination, chain type, chain position, and lubrication. The main factors seems to be load and gear size.

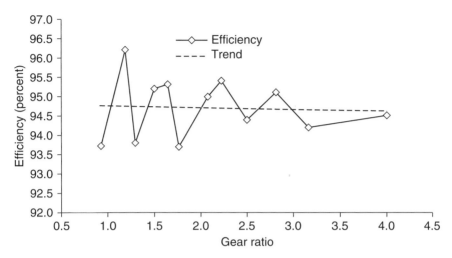

FIGURE 1.19   Gear efficiency versus ratio, Browning 12-speed, 200 W load.

3. In a derailleur transmission, there is often a difference of 1 to 3% in efficiency between adjacent gears (see figure 1.19). A 1% improvement in efficiency will mean 12 s or more in a 25-mi time trial. Choosing the right gear is important in time trials. For high efficiency, the trick seems to be to avoid combinations using sprockets smaller than 14 teeth. In figure 1.19, from left to right, the efficiencies below the trend line (lower than average efficiency) were chain ring/sprocket combinations of 30/32, 30/23, 30/17, 30/12, 38/12, and 48/12. The combinations above the trend line (higher than average efficiency) were 38/32, 48/32, 38/23, 48/23, 38/17, and 48/17. Tests on the Shimano 27-speed transmission gave similar low efficiencies for the 12-tooth sprocket (see figure 1.20). If possible for a particular gear ratio, a larger chain ring combined with a larger sprocket will yield a higher efficiency. So the answer to the question is: A 52/15 gear combination will have a higher efficiency than a 42/12.

4. If the derailleur chain is in maximum misalignment, crossing from the outer chain ring to the inner sprocket or from the inner chain ring to the outer sprocket doesn't seem to greatly affect efficiency. Modern chains bend so freely that with index shifting, which assures proper derailleur alignment, cross chains don't seem to cause appreciable added friction.

5. Modern derailleur transmissions are from 2 to 3% more efficient than hub gear transmissions. Older European commuter bicycles that use hub gears pay an energy penalty in many ways—the riding position as well as the bicycle and wheels have higher air drag. The wheels and tires have higher resistance, and the gear system is less efficient. On the plus side,

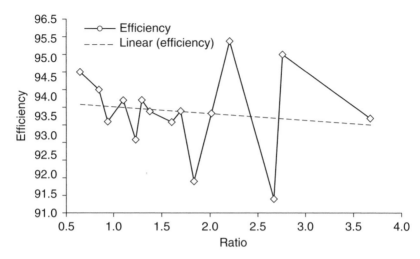

FIGURE 1.20   Gear efficiency versus ratio, Shimano 27 speed.

riders get about 40% more exercise per mile at the same speed than riders on racing bicycles.

Drinking Systems

In rides of one to two hours, liquid supplements are not necessary for maximum performance (Coggan 1990; Coyle 1989; Noakes 1990). But Coyle has shown that the onset of exhaustion in exercise over two to three hours can be extended from 30 to 60 min by the intake of a carbohydrate supplement during exercise. To do this, a cyclist must drink frequently and ingest about 50 g (1.8 oz) of carbohydrate per hour (Coyle 1989).

Drinking from bottles carried on the down tube or seat tube works well, but there are problems. When riding in a pack, riders often find it hard to take one hand off the bars to drink. When they do, they must relax their pedaling intensity, reach down for the bottle, tilt the head back, squeeze the bottle, drink, and put the bottle back in the cage, all of which slow them down. When riders relax their pedaling efforts to drink, their heads and arms move out of position, causing increased aerodynamic drag.

Several systems allow cyclists to drink without changing position or slowing down. Probably the simplest is to place a pressurized bottle with a plastic straw on the handlebars or behind the seat. The rider drinks by biting on a squeeze valve in the mouthpiece. Though this solves the problem of ready access to liquid, unnecessary aerodynamic drag can result from either the exposed straw or the bottle.

Another device places water on the back in a flat soft bag worn either outside or under the jersey (the CamelBak). The cyclist drinks though a tube attached to the helmet strap. This works well, doesn't raise aero drag significantly, and permits the cyclist to concentrate on riding. However, many cyclists don't like the extra weight on the back or the feel of the bag if it is worn inside the jersey. Despite some minor problems, the new drinking systems are probably superior for most racing or recreational applications.

Clothing, Helmets, and Shoes

Bicycle clothing has many functions. It provides safety, protection, and comfort; keeps the wearer cool or warm; lowers aerodynamic drag; and adds color, decoration, or commercial advertising to the rider. Except for the last three items, all of these can help improve performance.

Clothing

During wind tunnel tests, we conducted some experiments with clothing (see table 1.9) (Kyle 1991e). At the time the tests were run, efficient aerodynamic clothing was not as common as it is today; however, the results still contain valuable information.

Briefly, the use of slick, tight-fitting, smooth clothing without wrinkles can reduce air drag dramatically. A polyurethane-coated Lycra suit was the best, but plain Lycra spandex was nearly as effective. Rougher materials such as wool or polypropylene used in jerseys or tights could slow a rider down over 1 min in 40 km.

If a separate jersey must be worn, it should be as tight fitting as possible with no wrinkles when the rider is in position. Loose, fluttering fabric has

TABLE 1.9   Air Drag of Bicycle Clothing at 30 MPH

Clothing	Drag (lb)	Drag (g)
1986 USA rubberized Lycra skin suit, long sleeves	5.78	2,624
Full Lycra skin suit, long sleeves, tights	5.80	2,633
1986 USA Lycra skin suit, long sleeves	5.83	2,647
Wool jersey, long sleeves	6.31	2,865
Polypropylene warm-up suit	6.46	2,933

All tests are at 0° yaw angle. Rider was on the Kyle aero road bike in crouched racing position wearing a USA team aero helmet. Rider was 6'2" and 170 lb. Tests performed at Texas A & M, January 9–10, 1990.

super high air drag. The tests merely verified that a well-fitting skin suit is a requirement for any racing cyclist. As a matter of interest, skin hair raises the air drag of the human body, so for minimum air resistance serious racers should shave the limbs exposed to the air and cover the head with a helmet (Kyle 1986).

There is another way to lower the drag of cycle clothing. In 1990, Len Brownlie of the University of British Columbia tested various fabrics on a cycling mannequin in a full-scale wind tunnel (Brownlie et al. 1991). He found that a material called cosmopion with a slight surface roughness had a significantly lower drag than Lycra. I noticed a similar phenomenon in wind tunnel clothing tests in 1986 (Kyle 1986; Kyle and Caiozzo 1986a).

At bicycle racing speeds, cylindrical or oval shapes such as the legs, arms, or body undergo a transition in which the flow in the wake changes from laminar to turbulent. When this happens, the size of the wake decreases and the pressure on the trailing surface rises, lowering drag abruptly to one half to one third of what it was. If the flow transition can be prematurely induced at a lower speed by a slightly rough surface, then a significant drag reduction can occur (Brownlie et al. 1991; Hoerner 1965; Kyle 1986; Kyle and Caiozzo 1986a).

In field tests, Brownlie found that his wind tunnel data were correct; the cosmopion suit was the fastest of the several suits he tested. Unfortunately, this material (made in Japan) is no longer produced, but other similar materials are definitely worth developing.

Applying this concept, Nike developed what they called the Swift Suit for running track sprinters in the 2000 Olympics. Aerodynamics consultants Chester Kyle and Len Brownlie extensively tested experimental versions of the single-piece suit in the University of Washington wind tunnel. Nike placed different fabrics on various regions of the limbs and torso. The fabric had carefully graded textures that caused transition air flow on these zones at running speeds. In 2002, Nike again applied the zoned fabric idea to provide speedskating skins to the Dutch and American teams in the Winter Olympics. Skaters, wearing the suits, won all of the gold medals in men's long track speedskating. Nike developed cycling time trial suits for the United Postal Service team for the 2002 Tour de France. So far, Nike's zoned fabric Swift Suits for high-speed sports have been highly successful. Whether the clothing will be commercially marketed for cycling is not certain.

Larry Berglund (1987) has shown that in direct sunlight, light-reflective clothing can lower sweat loss and improve cooling in exercising cyclists. At high noon, the uncovered human body can absorb about 100 W of radiative energy from the sun, and this energy must be dissipated by convective cooling, radiation, or evaporative cooling.

Berglund found that aluminized fabric was best for cycle clothing, followed by white and light-colored fabric. The aluminum-impregnated fabric was superior to bare skin in the ability to dissipate heat. The right fabric, in other words, can cut down on water losses in endurance events (Berglund 1987).

Helmets

As with clothing, helmets can lower aerodynamic drag while providing head protection and adequate cooling. Aero helmets that have no ventilation holes and a teardrop shape produce the lowest drag. Examples include the aero helmets that were used by the U.S. Olympic cycling team from 1984 to 1996, the helmet used by Greg LeMond to win the Tour de France in 1988, and the helmets used in almost all world record time trial attempts. Lance Armstrong wore a Giro aero helmet in the 2001 Tour de France time trials. Helmet tests on a mannequin in the wind tunnel have uncovered some interesting facts (Kyle 1990; Kyle and Burke 1984):

▶ Aero helmets have a lower drag than no helmet at all. The drag of even short human hair is higher. An aero helmet smoothes the flow over the head and lowers the drag by about 100 g at 30 mph.

▶ Unstreamlined, blunt, blocky helmets, commonly used in racing today, may weigh little and have good cooling, but their air resistance is from 110 to 180 g higher than that of a good aero model. Standard helmets will lose more than 1 s per mile to an aero helmet. Therefore, aero helmets should be used in all important time trials up to one hour, where cooling is not usually a problem. Helmets with smooth, rounded edges and a polished surface are superior to those with a rough finish and sharp edges or ridges.

▶ Each helmet has an optimum head position at which the drag is minimal. If the head is tipped higher or lower than this, drag will increase. Usually the best position for aero helmets is such that the bottom of the helmet is parallel to the upper back and a gap occurs between the back and the helmet. Some recent aero helmets, such as the one used by Graeme Obree and Lance Armstrong, have a streamlined tail specially contoured to fit the rider's back; the helmet curves over the ears and under the chin. These potentially have a lower drag than older aero models.

Shoes and Pedals

Today's bicycle shoes are made for service and comfort, not speed. An ideal aerodynamic shoe would have a very low weight and a smooth contour to streamline airflow around the foot. In contrast, almost all cycling shoes have straps that disturb airflow; a rough cloth and leather exterior surface with seams, ridges, and holes; plus a thick sole for rigidity that adds to the weight. Although aerospace materials and design concepts are used elsewhere on the bicycle, they have seldom been applied to commercial cycling shoes.

In 1984, Peter Cavanagh built a pair of prototype streamlined cycling shoes with an integral pedal (the pedal was part of the shoe and only the axle protruded from the side of the shoe). Cavanagh's shoe/pedal lowered air drag of the feet over 200 g at 30 mph (Kyle 1986). The streamlined shoes would have provided over a 1-min advantage in a 40-km time trial. Fully streamlined cycling shoes are not commercially available, but smooth fabric shoe covers work very well as a substitute.

In purchasing shoes and pedals for racing, there are several points to consider. Shoes should have as smooth an upper surface as possible. Pedals should have a small frontal area and be as smoothly contoured as practical. The pedal should allow lateral motion of the foot and also be smoothly contoured. The shoe cleat and pedal should be as small and light as possible. The Shimano SPD pedal system is as suitable as any for road use.

Recumbent Bicycles

So far we have talked only about conventional road bicycles. What about recumbent bikes? With their laid-back, easy chair riding posture, recumbent bikes have several major advantages over conventional bicycles. They are more comfortable to ride. The head and eyes face straight forward so visibility is better. In crashes, the feet and legs, not the head, are forward, and the rider is closer to the ground so falls are usually not serious. Since the body is supported in a sitting position, there is no pressure on the hands. Because of the comfortable seat, there are no saddle sores and no injuries to the nether regions.

Several years ago, Ed Pavelka, a former editor of *Bicycling Magazine*, wrote an article about his seat numbness and impotence because of riding long distances on a conventional hard saddle. He bought a recumbent, and after a month or so recovered completely. Pavelka's article started a revolution. Sales of recumbents shot up, and saddles with open channels in the center, which removed pressure from the pelvic region, became runaway best-sellers. The trend continues. Both recumbents and pressure relief saddles are selling briskly.

There are also disadvantages to recumbents. They are not off-road machines since the rider is forced to remain seated to pedal. A cyclist cannot shift body position for balance and power. Some riders reportedly have problems climbing, although with modern gearing this doesn't seem to be a serious drawback. Some feel that recumbents are more dangerous since they are lower and not as visible to automobile traffic. Because of the lower body position, a recumbent rider can't peer through an automobile's rear windows to monitor the road ahead.

Recumbents are also more unstable at the start because the center of gravity is lower and balance is harder at low speed. However, once they get moving, they are rock solid and easy to ride. They do take a bit of getting used to, but so does a conventional bicycle.

Despite the drawbacks, there is no doubt that recumbents are fast and can be ridden comfortably for long distances. Greg Miller of Seal Beach, California, has finished first in the Davis, California, double century riding an Easy Racer recumbent against some formidable cyclists on conventional bicycles.

Directions for Future Research

Future cycling research should demand a more cycling-specific approach with a greater focus on cycling-specific experimental design, equipment, subject selection, and protocols to answer questions particular to the competitive and recreational aspects of cycling. The following areas need to be studied.

Alternative Drive Mechanisms

Oval sprockets, linear lever drives, infinitely variable transmissions, variable-length cranks, and cam drives—for the past hundred years, inventors have sought a better way to propel a bicycle. They are still seeking an alternative drive system to replace the traditional sprocket and chain transmission. This is a daunting challenge. To be competitive, an alternative drive mechanism must be at least as good as the traditional system. This means that it must meet certain criteria, including the following (Kyle 1991a):

▶ Weight—the drive system must be relatively light.

▶ Cost—cost should compare to that of a chain drive.

▶ Gear changes—there should be a wide range of gear ratios.

▶ Noise—the transmission should be relatively silent.

▶ Maintenance—the drive should require little maintenance or adjustment. Repair costs should be low; maintenance or adjustments should be simple enough that the owner can easily perform them. With any successful drive, it should be easy to remove the rear wheel and change a tire.

▶ Reliability—the transmission should be rugged and almost failure free.

▶ Mechanical efficiency—the internal mechanical efficiency of the drive system should be greater than 95%. In other words, only 2 to 5% of the energy input should be wasted in internal friction. This automatically eliminates small hydraulic transmissions that are only about 60 to 75% efficient.

▶ Biomechanical efficiency—the caloric efficiency of human power production should not be impaired by the pedaling motion. Even today, inventors often claim that their new drive mechanism will allow a rider to immediately increase power production from 15 to 25%. Given the high mechanical efficiency of a chain-sprocket drive and the high metabolic efficiency of the circular crank motion, this is an absurdly false claim. If it were true, the new mechanism would instantly be adopted by all bicycle racers, and this has not happened yet.

▶ Operation—the drive system should shift easily and rapidly and function smoothly with simple, easily accessible rider controls. It should be possible to push the bike backward without the rear wheel locking. The cyclist should be able to climb, accelerate, or pedal on the level with equal facility as with a standard gear-sprocket transmission.

▶ Retrofit—any transmission that is to be commercially successful should be able to be installed easily on a standard bicycle.

▶ Kinetic energy conservation—any energy fed into the system to accelerate the legs or the mechanical parts should be recovered sometime during the pedaling cycle. For example, muscular energy should not be required to retard leg movement at the end of a power stroke. A circular crank motion satisfies this requirement.

It may be possible to overlook one or two of these criteria and still succeed, depending on the application. But if any of the critical requirements (such as efficiency or reliability) are ignored, the transmission is doomed to fail in the marketplace.

Instead of the emergence of a revolutionary new system that replaces the chain drive, the past century has seen a continual improvement of the chain drive that has made it even harder to replace. Better derailleurs, chains, and gears, plus index shifters, have made chain-sprocket drives more efficient than ever.

One alternative drive system created in the late 1980s, the Shimano Biopace, met most of the mentioned criteria and achieved short-term commercial success, probably because of an intense advertising campaign and not because it was an improvement. The Biopace used oval drive sprockets that sped up the pedal travel by 7 to 17% in the power region. Unfortunately, there was no evidence that the system was in any way superior to a standard drive. In fact, in climbing hills the Biopace tended to bog down because of the slower pedal travel over the top and bottom of the crank cycle. Although it was an acceptable alternative transmission, the Biopace was withdrawn from the market by Shimano.

In theory, it should be possible to improve the combined metabolic and mechanical efficiency of a bicycle drive system by 1 or 2%, but so far this has proved impossible or impractical. This will not stop inventors from trying. New drive systems still appear every year at bicycle shows. We can hope that a breakthrough will occur before another hundred years have passed.

Instruments

At present, small bicycle computers are available that display performance variables such as speed, average speed, cadence, distance, time, and heart rate. They are inexpensive, accurate, and easy to use and are a valuable training aid. Like all electronic devices, they will be subject to continual improvement (Sargeant 1990).

What new functions should we expect in cycling computers in the next few years? The future of microelectronics is clear. Everything will get smaller. As this happens, the power of small computer chips will slowly improve, allowing higher-performance designs for the same cost and size (Sargeant 1990).

Let's list the functions that might be measured by a sophisticated bike computer that could be useful for training, research, or analysis to the coaches, trainers, athletes, and scientists who need to define cycling performance precisely. Some functions are already common in bike computers, but most are not. All are possible with today's technology. As electronic devices improve, more and more functions will be standard options on tomorrow's bike computers:

- Speed, average speed, maximum speed
- Cadence, average cadence, maximum cadence
- Trip distance, split distance, total distance
- Trip time, split time, clock time
- Power, average power, maximum power
- Hill slope in percent, average slope, maximum slope
- Elevation, trip gain or loss in elevation, maximum elevation
- Wind velocity and direction relative to the bike
- Air temperature
- Compass direction, map location, route selection
- Heart rate, average heart rate, maximum heart rate
- Breathing rate, average breathing rate, maximum breathing rate
- Body core temperature

From this list, you can see that to display more than a few of the functions would be impractical and would make a bike computer as complex as an aircraft instrument panel. Such a complicated bike computer would be nearly impossible for the average person to operate without continual reference to an instruction manual. Any more than two buttons on a cycle computer becomes confusing. However, for research purposes, most of the functions could be stored in memory. The handlebar display could be simplified to include perhaps speed, time, distance, power, and heart rate, and the additional stored information could be fed to a computer for later analysis.

Probably the most valuable instrument that has yet to succeed on the mass market is a power meter. If cyclists could read average power, updated every few seconds, they could maintain a constant power without regard to wind conditions, weather, or terrain. They could systematically plan workouts and be certain of an absolute gauge of their performance. This is not a simple task for instrument designers. To compute power, one must accurately measure force and velocity. Velocity is easy, but force is not. As a rider pedals, the thrust force and therefore the power varies unevenly from zero to maximum during each pedal cycle, meaning that the power must be integrated and averaged over several pedal cycles.

The SRM crank dynamometer system (Schoberer Rad Messtechnik, Welldorf, Germany) is a successful and accurate crank dynamometer used for research. It consists of an instrumented chain ring that transmits strain gauge readings by telemetry to a handlebar microprocessor or to a central computer, along with crank rpm and bicycle speed. Although extremely useful for training and research, it is quite expensive and not really adaptable to the mass market.

Currently two power meters are available commercially. One by Polar, the S710, works on chain tension. Another, Power Tap, has strain gauges in the rear hub. Whether they will be successful remains to be seen.

Comparing Road and All-Terrain Bicycle Technology

Only a decade or so ago in the United States, most commuting and touring bicycles were carbon copies of racing bicycles. As such they were not well suited for general use, and the public freely registered their complaints. These bikes required too much maintenance. The saddles were too narrow, too hard, and too uncomfortable. The high-pressure tires had too many flats. The tires gave a rough ride and were hard to steer over uneven pavement or in sand or gravel. The racing drop handlebars were uncomfortable and caused sore necks, hands, and shoulders if the cyclist rode on the drops. The brakes were hard to keep in adjustment and didn't give good stopping power on steep slopes. The wheels were too flimsy and kept slipping out of true. Potholes would bend the rims and cause pinch flats. There weren't enough gears to climb hills easily.

All of these complaints were valid. It takes a fair amount of skill and knowledge to keep a racing bike adjusted, and the bikes just aren't designed for comfort or convenience—they are designed for speed. It takes training to become comfortable on a racing bike.

Then came mountain bikes and their cousins, the hybrid city bikes. This new breed of machines used an upright riding position, comfortable grips, better saddles, and wide, rugged tires, plus a strong frame and wheels. In fact, they cured almost all of the complaints about racing-style touring bikes.

The sales of racing-style touring bicycles soon plummeted, and mountain and hybrid bikes captured about two thirds of the bicycle market in the United States. Mountain bikes were no doubt more fun—they could be ridden off road, and they were very comfortable on pavement. They could be ridden off curbs or over railroad tracks without fear, and cracks in the pavement were no problem. Suspensions were available that absorbed ride shocks.

In spite of their loss in popularity, road bikes won't disappear just yet; they are still a necessary but specialized breed. However, cyclists who want a general purpose bicycle can put smooth tires with side lugs on a mountain bike and ride almost anywhere with safety, comfort, efficiency, and convenience. They won't go as fast as a racing style bike, but that is a small price to pay considering the advantages. The mountain bike has become the equivalent in the United States of the European utility bike.

Technology transfer between road and mountain bicycles is a lively and continuous process that has already improved both types. There are mountain bikes with aero bars and slick tires, and road bikes with suspensions and 27 speeds. This technology transfer is a healthy trend that will continue to benefit all cyclists.

References

Berglund, L. 1987. *Evaporative weight loss as a measure of absorbed radiation in the human.* Paper presented at the 8th Conference of Biometeorology and Aerobiology, American Meteorological Society, Boston, Mass.

Brownlie, L.W., Gartshore, I., Chapman, A., and Banister, E.W. 1991. The aerodynamics of cycling apparel. *Cycling Science* 3(3-4): 44-50.

Coggan, A.R. 1990. Carbohydrate feeding during prolonged cycling to improve performance. *Cycling Science* 2(1): 9-13.

Coyle, E.F. 1989. Carbohydrate and cycling performance. *Cycling Science* 1(1): 18-21.

Danh, K., Mai, L., Poland, J., and Jenkins, C. 1991. Frictional resistance in bicycle wheel bearings. *Cycling Science* 3(3-4): 28-32.

Hoerner, S.F. 1965. *Fluid dynamic drag.* Hoerner Fluid Dynamics, 7528 Straunton Place N.W., Albuquerque, New Mexico 87120.

Jeukendrup, A.E., and Martin, J. 2001. Improving cycling performance. *Sports Med* 31(7): 559-569.

Kyle, C.R. 1973. *Factors affecting the speed of a bicycle.* Long Beach, Calif.: California State University.

Kyle, C.R. 1986. Athletic clothing. *Scientific American* 254: 104-110.

Kyle, C.R. 1988a. How friction slows a bike. *Bicycling* 180-185.

Kyle, C.R. 1988b. The mechanics and aerodynamics of cycling. In E.R. Burke and M.M. Newsom (eds.) *Medical and scientific aspects of cycling.* Champaign, Ill.: Human Kinetics. pp. 235-251.

Kyle, C.R. 1988c. Sunrayer, wheels, tires and brakes. *Lecture 3-3, G.M. Sunraycer Case History.* Warrendale, Penn.: Society of Automotive Engineers.

Kyle, C.R. 1989. The aerodynamics of handlebars and helmets. *Cycling Science* 1(1): 22-25.

Kyle, C.R. 1990. Wind tunnel tests of bicycle wheels and helmets. *Cycling Science* 2(1): 27-30.

Kyle, C.R. 1991a. Alternative bicycle transmissions. *Cycling Science* 3(3-4): 33-38.

Kyle, C.R. 1991b. The effect of crosswinds upon time trials. *Cycling Science* 3(3-4): 51-56.

Kyle, C.R. 1991c. Ergogenics for bicycling. In D. Lamb and M. Williams (eds.) *Perspectives in exercise science and sports medicine*. Indianapolis: Brown & Benchmark. pp. 373-412.

Kyle, C.R. 1991d. New aero wheel tests. *Cycling Science* 3(1): 27-30.

Kyle, C.R. 1991e. Wind tunnel tests of aero bicycles. *Cycling Science* 3(3-4): 57-61.

Kyle, C.R. 1997. Wind Tunnel Tests of Road Bicycles, Wichita State University, September 29-October 1, 1997. Report to United States Cycling Federation.

Kyle, C.R., and Berto, F. 2001. The mechanical efficiency of bicycle derailleur and hub-gear transmissions. *Human Power* 52: 3-10.

Kyle, C.R., and Burke, E.R. 1984. Improving the racing bicycle. *Mechanical Engineering* 109(6): 35-45.

Kyle, C.R., and Caiozzo, V.J. 1986a. The effect of athletic clothing aerodynamics upon running speed. *Med Sci Sports Exerc* 18(5): 509-515.

Kyle, C.R., and Caiozzo, V.J. 1986b. Experiments in human ergometry as applied to human powered vehicles. *Int J Sports Biomech* 2: 6-19.

Kyle, C.R., and Edelman, W.E. 1975. Man powered vehicle design criteria. In H.K. Sachs (ed.) *Proceedings of the Third International Conference on Vehicle System Dynamics*. Amsterdam: Swets & Zeitlinger. pp. 20-30.

Margaria, R., Cerretelli, P., Aghemo, P., and Sassi, G. 1963. Energy cost of running. *J Appl Physiol* 18: 367-370.

Moore, R.C. 1987. Rolling resistance performance, small tire. General Motors Report, General Motors Proving Ground, Warren, Michigan, April 13, 1987, pp. 1-15.

Noakes, T. 1990. The dehydration myth and carbohydrate replacement during prolonged exercise. *Cycling Science* 2(2): 23-28.

Okajima, S. 1990. Development of Shimano Pedaling Dynamics (SPD). *Cycling Science* 2(3): 7.

Padilla, S., Mujica, I., Angulo, F., and Goiriena, J.J. 2000. Scientific approach to the 1-h cycling world record: A case study. *J Appl Physiol* 89: 1522-1527.

Peronnet, F., Bouissou, P., Perrault, H., and Ricci, J. 1991. The one hour cycling record at sea level and at altitude. *Cycling Science* 3(1): 6-20.

Pugh, L.G.C.E. 1971. The influence of wind resistance in running and walking and the mechanical efficiency of work against horizontal or vertical forces. *J Physiol* 213: 255-276.

Sargeant, B. 1990. An overview of cycling instrumentation. *Cycling Science* 2(3): 13-18.

Sjogaard, G., Nielsen, B., Mikkelsen, F., Saltin, B., and Burke, E. 1982. *Physiology in bicycling*. Ithaca, N.Y.: Mouvement.

Swain, D., Coast, J.R., Clifford, P.S., Milliken, M.C., and Gundersen, J.S. 1987. Influence of body size on oxygen consumption during bicycling. *J Appl Physiol* 62(2): 668-672.

Whitt, F.R., and Wilson, D.G. 1982. *Bicycling science*. Cambridge, Mass.: MIT Press.

2

Bicycle Suspension Systems and Mountain Bike Technology

John Olsen

Bicycle suspension and disc brakes are two of the hottest subjects in bicycling. This chapter is an overview of some of the physics, engineering, and performance issues involved in suspension and disc brakes, not necessarily to allow you to proceed to design such systems with no further research, but to get potential designers and intelligent users thinking about concepts arrived at over a century of work in other vehicular fields.

Any subtopic in suspension design would require an entire book to cover in detail. Almost the same is true of disc brakes. This chapter is not intended to provide academic rigor, but rather to introduce and explain concepts that may be new to many in the bicycling community.

Suspension Without Suspension

To understand how suspensions work, it may be best to start with an unsuspended bike. Once you understand how such a bike responds to bumps and road roughness, you will more easily understand the function of suspension systems.

First of all, there is no such thing as an unsuspended bike; all bikes offer some ride-improving features. For most "unsuspended" bikes, some of that shock absorption comes from the flex of the tires and from enveloping, another feature of the pneumatic tire.

A rigid wheel rolling up to a rigid sharp-edged obstacle much smaller than the radius of the wheel begins to rise when the wheel contacts the obstacle. This occurs before the axle is directly above the obstacle. Some time passes between the initial contact and the point at which the axle is over the edge. Many simple analyses of wheeled-vehicle ride model the wheel and tire as "point followers"—the wheel is actually a rigid rod directly beneath the axle with no contact curvature or length. Such a point follower striking a sharp object would introduce high frequencies into the system, basically a Fourier transform of a step function. A rigid wheel, however, rises more gently, filtering out the higher frequencies extant in a sharp step.

Tires contact the ground over a span of several inches, depending on tire pressure and wheel diameter. A stone, say one eighth of an inch in diameter, would impress the tread that rested on it but would have little effect on the overall tire–ground contact area. The stone would be swallowed up by the tire, and the axle would lift much less than one eighth of an inch as a result. This is called *enveloping*, and all wheels do it. Enveloping is an averaging effect: The roughness of the ground under the contact patch is averaged out by the tire, greatly reducing the effect of small, peaky bumps. The larger the tire diameter, and the softer the tire pressure, the greater the enveloping effect. Tire enveloping works like a low-pass filter, again screening out higher-frequency input.

Larger obstacles, such as an expansion joint between uneven concrete slabs, are at least partially eaten by the flex of the tire's sidewall, again depending on the wheel diameter, tire pressure, and tire construction. Tires running at low pressures swallow bumps better than do those at higher pressures, and larger tires can swallow bigger bumps without pinch flats. The details of tire construction clearly have an effect on small-bump/high-frequency vibration isolation. (Switch from Continental GP3000s to Vredestien Fortezza Pro Race road tires of identical size and pressure and note the difference in vibration isolation over a chip-sealed surface, an experiment recently conducted unscientifically by the author.)

Bumps large enough to survive the passage through the tire also have to find their way through the flexible rim and spokes, up the flexible fork blades and steerer tube, and out the flexible handlebars before they can work on the rider's hands. If the bump strikes the rear wheel, then the path that the bump's energy must traverse includes the tire, rim, spokes, rear frame triangle, seat post, and saddle. Let us not forget the beneficial effect of relaxed, flexible arms—a loose set of arms provides marvelous shock and vibration protection to the upper body, saving the rider valuable energy. The rider's body is not, nor can it be modeled as, a rigid component.

On an efficient road bike, all of the mechanical components are relatively stiff, even the tire. Yet a sensitive and experienced cyclist can tell the difference in ride from one tire type to the next. Many claim that they can tell from one spoke lacing pattern to the next, from one fork bend and blade material to the next, and even from one frame material to the next. The vibration-absorption capabilities of the spokes, fork, and frame are topics of great debate in the cycling science community, and sufficient research has not yet been done to answer the question, say, of the detectability of the frame's effect on vibration transmission, once and for all.

The "Why" of Mountain Bike Suspension

What happens when you take the bike, designed for nothing worse than Belgian pavé, and subject it to the woods, deserts, and mountains—sans paving? Suspension advocates say you get pinched tubes, bent rims, wrist injuries, crashes, broken frames, and general mayhem.

© Bongarts/SportsChrome USA

An offroad bike must be compatible with the uneven surfaces and obstacles inherent in offroad racing.

Mountain bikes were originally unsuspended—not rigid, but unsuspended. Many riders felt, and a very few still feel, that the big, soft tires that equip serious mountain bikes offer all of the isolation you really need, and that any attempt at suspension is just so much extra weight.

Unfortunately, the wonderful challenge of mountain biking comes from the fact that the surfaces that are not as flat and smooth as possible. There are bumps—big ones, small ones, sharp ones, dull ones. These bumps are often so big that they overwhelm the flexibility of the tire and the rest of the bicycle. The rider becomes the suspension system, and this extra job exacts costs in oxygen consumption, reduced concentration, reduced control, and fatigue.

Of course, a rider can increase the fraction of obstacles that the tires can swallow by lowering tire pressure, but that goes only so far before pinch flats result. One can opt for forks and bars of greater flexibility, but these are minor, incremental improvements that may have other costs, such as reduced fatigue life, loss of handling precision, or brake chatter. In the end, virtually all riders would now agree that mountain bikes really would be better with perfect suspension, suspension that worked well enough to offset the inevitable increase in weight, cost, and complexity—a suspension that is a net improvement, not a net loss!

Suspension Goals and Components

Any suspension system has four basic goals. The first goal is to isolate the rider from the roughness of the road or trail, reducing fatigue and discomfort while leaving the rider with enough feel for acceptable control. This goal requires the isolation of relatively small-sized, medium-, and high-frequency bumps. An example would be a rider comfortably traversing a fire road with many small, exposed rocks.

The second goal is to absorb the energy and shock that comes from hitting larger obstacles and bumps, and dissipate this effect before it does too much damage to the equilibrium of the rider. This function requires the absorption of higher-amplitude, low-frequency bumps.

The third goal is to keep the wheels on the ground over rough terrain, where they can provide useful functions such as driving, braking, and steering.

The fourth goal is to avoid adding to the bicycle undesirable characteristics such as "pogoing"—the bicycle suspension working either as a direct effect of chain tension during pedaling or as an effect of acceleration—or pedal feedback, a change in the rotational velocity of the pedals when the rear suspension compresses over a bump.

In the first years of the full suspension revolution, systems that did well with goals 1, 2, and 3 were difficult to implement without violating goal 4. The challenge of any suspension design is to accomplish all four goals simultaneously, and suspension design has improved in the last 10 years to the point that many current suspension designs come very close (or at least, *acceptably* close) to the ideal.

Suspension designers strive to meet these goals using a combination of springs, dampers, levers, and linkages. Current designs cover the spectrum of mechanical complexity, and although the most complex solutions come close to meeting all of the goals of suspension, there are some less complex effective solutions as well.

Springs

We've already seen that the deflection of tires and components provides some suspension benefits. If some deflection is good, why not add more? To do so, we have to design controlled vertical flexibility into the frame— somewhere. A bump hitting a wheel has to be able to harmlessly compress something in the system somewhere before the violence gets to the rider. This "suspension travel" can be located in the front fork, in the down tube, in the seat support structure, in the stem, or in the rear triangle, or it can be in more than one location. All of these options have strengths and weaknesses, proponents and opponents.

As an example, let's assume for now that the suspension travel will occur in a telescopic front fork. If we simply provide a sliding joint in our fork, the fork will collapse, so we need to add a device that will provide some kind of restoring force to hold up the bicycle's front end.

This device is a spring. Springs come in a variety of types. You can choose a steel or titanium or carbon fiber coil spring, a spring that works by twisting a strong solid material. Gas springs trap air or some other gas in a cylinder that compresses the pressurized gas as the suspension travels. Elastomer springs compress, stretch, shear, or otherwise work rubber. Liquid springs compress a pressurized liquid. All springs provide more restoring force (if you push on them, they push back) the more they are compressed.

These spring types differ in several respects, including complexity, linearity, and energy storage efficiency. Some spring types (steel leaf springs, for example) store very little energy for their weight, whereas other springs (certain types of elastomer springs, or liquid springs) weigh very little for the amount of energy they store. Some springs, such as steel coil springs, are inherently linear; that is, they provide force in strict proportion to the amount that they are compressed. If a linear spring gives you 100 lb when it is compressed 1 in., it will give you 200 lb when it is compressed 2 in. The spring rate (stiffness) for a linear spring is the force you get at a certain amount of spring compression divided by the amount of compression in units of pounds per inch. Linear springs can be described by a single spring-rate number.

Other springs, such as piston-in-cylinder gas springs, some elastomer springs, and taper-wire coil springs, provide an inherently rising rate—the spring rate is higher at full compression than it is at the start of compression. Such springs get stiffer as they are compressed. This is generally good. Suspensions using such springs can be soft for small bumps but stiff enough at the end of travel to avoid bottoming on the big bumps. Such nonlinear, rising-rate springs provide a smoothly increasing range of spring rates.

You can make a linear spring provide a nonlinear force at the rear wheel through the use of a nonlinear mechanism. Such mechanisms are often employed in motorcycle suspension design, allowing a rising rate from basically linear steel coil springs.

Elastomer springs are usually not made of rubber—the material comes from a beaker, not the inside of a rubber tree. They are usually solid or foam blocks of some sophistication in shape, density, and material. The right combination of shape, material, and density can provide a rising-rate spring effect, helping to avoid bottoming in much the same way as a gas spring does.

It is important to understand that springs (except elastomer springs) do not absorb energy. They merely store it and give it back with little loss. Some people talk about springs as absorbers, but they are not. A pure spring, by itself, is a pogo stick. To avoid getting all of that stored energy back when you don't want it, the energy stored in the spring has to be converted from mechanical energy to some other kind of energy, usually heat. Springs do the work of holding you up, but they are unruly beasts with a mind of their own. It is necessary, or at least strongly desirable, to ally springs with some energy dissipation mechanism to keep them from returning all that energy at inopportune times.

Travel

How much suspension deflection, called *travel*, should a suspension system have? Imagine a rider attacking a rough course. The faster the rider goes, the harder the bumps try to compress the suspension. Most suspension systems are designed so that it takes a force equaling two to three times the normal weight on the suspension system (2 or 3 g) to fully compress the spring. If you have lots of travel available, the spring can be softer than is the case when travel is limited.

If there is a static load of 100 lb on a fork, then we might design the fork to bottom (run out of travel) at a load of 300 lb. If we have 10 in. of travel, we need a total linear spring rate of only 30 lb/in.; if we have only 2 in. of travel, we need a linear spring rate of 150 lb/in. to bottom on the same bump as did the long-travel spring.

All other factors being equal, the softer, longer-travel spring provides much better isolation from small, repetitive, or sharp bumps than does the short-travel spring. Thus, long travel lets us use soft springs to store a given amount of energy. If we are employing a nonlinear spring, then we can get tricky, starting soft but ending stiff, even with limited travel.

Preload

If you have a total spring rate of only 30 lb/in., and if the fork is going to carry a static load of 100 lb, then the fork will collapse more than 3 in. when you sit on the bike. In fact, off-road motorcycles, blessed with copious travel

(12 in. is not uncommon), do sag almost this much when supporting the weight of the rider. If you, a bicyclist with little travel, don't want some of your precious suspension travel used up in supporting the load even when you aren't moving (this load is called the *static load*), then you have a choice. You can opt for a very stiff spring, or you might employ *preload*.

Take a linear coil spring with a rate of 100 lb/in., a spring that will be forced to be 10 in. long when trapped inside the structure of the fork. What if we make that spring 11 in. long when it is lying on your workbench? Then we will have to compress the spring 1 in. when we install it. Since it is already compressed when it is waiting for action in the uncompressed suspension, it will have a preload of 100 lb. It will be able to support the static load with no deflection. Thus, the suspension won't collapse at all when it takes its designed load, even though the spring rate is only 100 lb/in.

If we preload the spring 2 in., what happens? The spring will push against the fully extended fork structure with a force of 200 lb, while the static load is applying only 100 lb. The fork won't compress at all until you hit a bump with enough vigor to generate an additional force of more than 100 lb. This means that the fork will be ineffective in dealing with small bumps because the bicycle may not generate that much force as it rolls over them. The forces from these smaller bumps will go right into the rider, just as they did with the unsuspended bicycle, if they aren't eaten by the tire, fork, and so on. The lesson is that big preload means poor protection from small bumps.

Remember that preloading a coil spring does nothing to change the spring's rate. If the spring is a linear spring, it will have the same spring rate no matter how much we compress or preload it.

Gas springs and elastomer springs can have preload too. To change the preload in a gas spring (a RockShox SID, for instance), you merely increase the gas pressure. The preload is proportional to the initial gas pressure. However, the spring rate of a gas spring also increases as you add initial pressure. This usually works out well, since those who need more preload often need more stiffness as well.

Both gas springs and elastomer springs can be designed to have almost infinite spring rates at full compression, making them very difficult to bottom completely. Figure 2.1 illustrates the change in spring rate that comes with a change in the preload of a typical air spring.

Damping

What do we do with all of the energy stored up in the spring? If we let it come bombing back out unimpeded, it might come out at a bad time and throw the rider flat on his or her back. It may bounce the tire off the ground, spoiling traction for climbing, turning, or braking. As you will see later, repetitive bumps may drive the undamped suspension into resonance, producing a huge response from a small input.

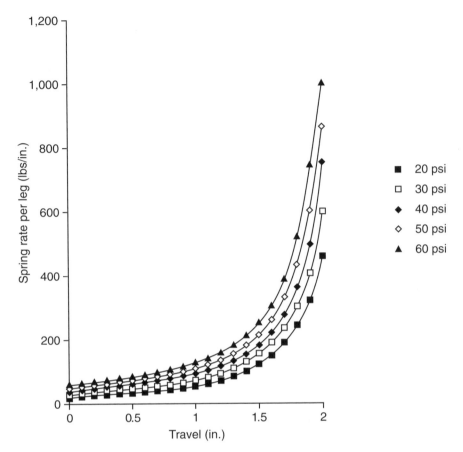

FIGURE 2.1   Change in spring rate due to a change in the preload of a typical air spring.

We need to convert some of that stored mechanical energy in the spring into heat. One way to do that is via friction. If our fork has some stickiness built into it (and all have some), then some of the stored energy will be lost to that friction and converted to heat. The downside to this simple remedy is that friction also locks up the fork for small bumps, which get transmitted to the rider. A suspension system with both a lot of preload and a lot of friction is not able to deal with small bumps, and the bike is basically unsuspended over such bumps.

All suspension systems have friction, but conventional wisdom would have a suspension designer work very hard to minimize it. Pivots instead of telescoping joints and careful bearing and bushing design help minimize friction. At least one clever suspension design (the front fork on the out-of-production Monolith bicycle) employed designed-in friction to help the suspension resist moving in response to the bobbing of the rider's body.

This bobbing created friction-enhancing side loading on the suspension bushings, preventing easy movement. Yet the suspension broke free relatively easily when a larger bump struck the front wheel and created a force vector pointing nearly straight up the axis of the fork. This design gave a feel like that of an unsuspended bike in routine maneuvering, but large bumps disappeared nicely. I offer this bicycle as evidence that friction isn't always bad in suspension. Just usually.

We also could choose a spring material that has inherent energy loss built into it. Elastomer springs have this property to varying degrees; when they are compressed and released, they heat up. This energy is stolen from the mechanical energy that they store when they are compressed.

This type of energy loss has some advantages. It is simple, with no moving parts; it can deal with small bumps (unlike friction), given that the suspension unit isn't set up with too much preload; and it is light in weight for the amount of energy it can absorb. Negatives include a large temperature sensitivity, fairly rapid breakdown with repeated loading, and problematic repeatability—matching spring rates can be challenging.

The energy loss scheme favored by the vast majority of motor vehicles is hydraulic damping. It is used on most cars, motorcycles, trucks, and airplanes because it can be very strong. Hydraulic damping can provide lots of force to control strong springs. Most hydraulic dampers work like pumps. They pump special oil through a small hole (an orifice), and the oil resists this flow. In a nonlinear way, the resistance depends on the velocity with which the pump is moving, and thus, the amount of oil that needs to flow. This resistance can be very strong, and it can be customized to provide different amounts of force in different directions through the use of various types of one-way valves and spring-loaded blow-off valves in the piston.

If the compression-damping orifice is forced to stay closed or highly restricted, the suspension unit can be locked out. The nearly incompressible hydraulic oil is trapped, rendering the suspension unit inoperative. If the rider can perform this lockout on the fly, he or she can choose to disable the suspension while climbing to keep the bike from bobbing up and down in response to the rider's torso motion during standing climbing, for instance. A number of suspension units (forks and shocks) offer lockouts. The necessity of a lockout provision is a matter of rider preference. Many riders who initially use lockout eventually stop using it, having gotten accustomed to the motion of the suspension in response to torso movements on climbs.

Damping can also help the spring prevent bottoming. Any compression damping provides a force that works with the spring to slow the plunge toward full travel. Compression damping can be tailored to get stronger as the suspension unit nears full travel. This is called hydraulic snubbing. Hydraulic snubbing could also be employed near full extension to prevent the clunking that happens when most current suspension systems top out, or return to full extension.

Hydraulic damping also has a dark side. A suspension with substantial compression damping that strikes a sharp-edged bump will strongly resist the rapid motion of the wheel as it tries to climb the bump. The spring can accommodate this rapid movement; it is only a slight exaggeration to say that springs aren't sensitive to velocity, they just care about how much they are compressed. The compression damping, however, produces a force the magnitude of which depends on how fast the wheel is rising, and thus how much oil the fork is trying to pump through the small, restrictive orifice. At some velocity, the orifice can't accommodate any more flow rate, and the column of oil lifts the bicycle, transmitting shock. Unless the valving that controls the damping is arranged to let a big hole open up under these circumstances, such a hydraulically damped suspension system can be harsh on sharp bumps. Such a big hole is called a *blow-off valve*. All good hydraulic dampers incorporate them in some form in the compression valving.

If the damping is too strong, it can also transmit little bumps since rapidly repeating bumps also want the wheel to move quickly, as will be shown in the next section.

Finally, if rebound damping is too strong compared to the stiffness of the spring, a suspension system can pump down. If strong rebound damping prevents the suspension from coming back to its normal ride height before the next bump comes along, and if a series of bumps occurs at the right spacing, then the suspension can pump itself down until there is no suspension travel left. This can happen to a hydraulically damped suspension unit with rebound damping very strong relative to the spring's stiffness.

Frequency Response

If you rest a mass on a spring in such a way that the mass can move only up and down with no friction, and if you give the mass a sharp whack with a hammer, you will notice that the mass moves up and down at a certain frequency. (Frequency is the number of cycles per second, a unit called hertz, abbreviated Hz.) The frequency at which the mass naturally bobs, called the *natural frequency*, depends on the amount of mass and the spring rate of the spring. A larger mass means a lower natural frequency; a smaller mass means a higher natural frequency. A stiffer spring means a higher natural frequency; a softer spring lowers the natural frequency.

Figure 2.2 shows how a simple mass sitting on a spring behaves if the bottom of the spring is shaken up and down steadily at a constant frequency and amplitude. If you shake the bottom of the spring up and down very slowly, the mass moves almost the same distance as does the bottom of the spring. This is analogous to a suspended bike riding over long-wavelength whoop-de-dos at a slow speed. If you slowly increase the frequency at which the spring base is shaken (imagine the rider on the whoops slowly speeding up), eventually you reach a frequency at which the mass goes wild, smashing up and down a great deal farther than the base of the spring is moving. This is called resonance, and it happens at the natural frequency.

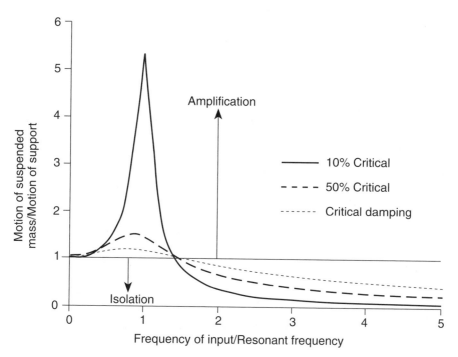

FIGURE 2.2   The frequency response of a mass resting on a spring with damping. Critical damping is the amount of damping that just keeps the mass from oscillating when the spring is compressed and the mass released.

This is, of course, bad news for the rider on the whoop-de-dos, unless that rider's suspension has lots of damping. Notice in figure 2.2 how much less the mass moves at resonance if damping is present. Much of that mechanical energy is being converted into heat.

You can avoid tremendous mass motion at the natural frequency by doing all the things that at other times are bad to do with a suspension system: using lots of preload, limiting the travel, and introducing friction. At resonance, a suspension system with lots of preload may not even know that it is being shaken at its natural frequency if the bumps are small enough that the spring doesn't see more than the preload force. At resonance, a suspension system with limited travel will simply slam into its travel stops, making lots of noise and fuss but at least not achieving a low orbit. A lot of friction will keep the mass on the planet—but controllable damping is better.

If you shake the base of the spring at a frequency higher than the natural frequency (our valiant rider has survived his resonance problem and accelerated through it), the behavior of the mass calms down. Soon, at a frequency roughly 1.4 times the natural frequency, the mass will be moving no more than the base of the spring once again, just as it did at very low frequencies. As you shake the base of the spring faster and faster, the mass moves less and less. When the spring is being shaken at a frequency much higher than the resonant frequency, the mass barely moves at all. The mass is now enjoying excellent isolation. High-input frequencies are generated by riding at speed over small bumps and by striking sharp edges.

However, if the suspension has lots of damping, the very damping that helped so much at resonance hurts at high frequencies, passing force into the mass that reduces isolation. At high frequencies, the oil column transmits substantial force to the bike and rider, reducing the amount of isolation that the suspension can provide at these frequencies and increasing the suspension's harshness. Ideally, a suspension system would offer strong damping at low frequencies, and especially at resonance, for good control, and yet provide very little damping above the natural frequency, for good isolation.

What does all of this mean? If you want to design a suspension system for an environment consisting of numerous small, repetitive bumps (a chip-sealed road, say, or perhaps the Paris-Roubaix course), you would want a soft suspension system working with the mass of the rider to provide a low natural frequency relative to the spacing of the bumps, with little preload and very little damping. This would provide maximum isolation, maximum comfort, and minimum fatigue. This is the "father's Oldsmobile" school of suspension design, typified by the Allsop Softride beam and stem. This approach to suspension is very rare.

If you aren't sure about the frequencies you will encounter but fear that you will have a wide range of bump spacings to contend with, remember that you will inevitably be operating around resonance some of the time. It would be disastrous to have little damping in this circumstance, so you have to add damping. If you are also concerned about absorbing the energy from big bumps and impacts, and if you have limited travel to work with, then you will want a stiffly sprung system with lots of damping and preferably a rising spring rate. You won't get much isolation over those small bumps, but you will survive the resonance-causing bumps and be far better off than without suspension when hitting the big stuff. This is the minimalist school of suspension design, typified by shorter-travel racing forks such as the RockShox SID and Manitou Mars. Such forks typically offer 70 to 80 mm of travel.

These days, a more common configuration is the recreational long-travel type of fork and/or rear suspension, offering 100 to 125 mm of travel. Such suspensions can be set up more softly with less harsh compression damping for greater comfort (isolation) over small bumps plus increased large-bump absorption capability. The increased weight that inevitably accompanies longer travel, plus increased bike motion during hard climbing from all that soft travel, means that these longer-travel bikes are not often used for cross-country racing.

Finally, very long travel mountain bikes aimed at either the downhill racing or the free-ride market are commonly available. Such bikes feature upwards of 150 mm of suspension travel at both ends. Weight and efficient climbing are not factors. The absorption of very large impacts and the maintenance of control over violent terrain taken at speed are paramount. These bikes commonly weigh more than 40 lb and are basically used only downhill.

Effect of Unsprung Weight: Why Less Is More

Remember our mass resting on a spring? What if another, smaller mass (we'll call it unsprung weight) is added to the bottom of the spring, and then another spring is added below the new mass? Instead of one mass on a spring and one natural frequency, we now have two masses free to vibrate, and two natural frequencies to worry about and to cause resonance.

This is a simple model of a bicycle with unsprung weight. The top mass represents the weight of the rider and whatever portion of the bicycle rests on the springs of the suspension system. The stiffness of the top spring represents the stiffness of the suspension spring(s). The new, bottom mass stands for the mass of the bicycle that lies below the suspension system. The lowest spring is the stiffness of the tire(s). Impact one mass or the other, and both masses will vibrate at different frequencies at the same time. The motion of one mass will, through the interconnecting spring and damper, affect the motion of the other mass. In fact, if we could build such a simple bicycle with only two masses connected like this, there would be a certain speed over a given wavelength of bump at which the unsprung mass would resonate. At this speed, this resonance would make for a bumpy ride on the sprung mass—the tail would be wagging the dog.

If there is enough damping between the unsprung and sprung masses to control the resonance of the much heavier sprung mass, then the resonance of the relatively light unsprung mass will be very heavily damped, and very little resonance will occur.

Rear Suspension

To all of the intricacies of front suspension design, rear suspension systems add an additional challenge: the pulsatile force transmitted by the chain to the rear wheel. The reaction of this drive force into the rear suspension, coupled with the inertial reaction of the bike and rider, causes a potential coupling of the tension in the chain and the force in the suspension spring that can result in several forms of disruptive and unpleasant behavior.

Despite its design challenges, a successful rear suspension system can be extremely valuable. Like front suspension, rear suspension can help a rider maintain control on hard, fast, bumpy descents, but can also be an ally to speed up a bumpy climb, even more than front suspension.

Every time an unsuspended bike's rider sees a 3-in. bump coming along, he or she must do a pull-up on the handlebars as the rear wheel approaches the bump, getting the heavy torso out of the way of the soon-to-be-rapidly-rising saddle. Failure to do so means pain, pinch flats, and perhaps an unplanned halt. A compliant rear suspension system can absorb much of that destructive energy, allowing the rider to remain seated and relaxed, concentrating on maintaining the best line up the hill and putting out a smooth flow of power. Some rear suspension designs actually use the increased chain tension that occurs during a pedaling pulse to force the rear wheel into the ground harder, increasing the traction limit temporarily.

Chain-Suspension Interaction

Imagine a motorcycle-like suspension system, with a swing arm pivoted right behind and slightly below the bottom bracket and a spring/shock unit with little preload (the suspension sags when the rider is in position; see figure 2.3a). Every time the rider pushes on the pedals, the chain compresses the suspension system by creating a torque that makes the suspension close, making the bike squat. Such a bike would inchworm down the trail, squatting every time the chain pulled on the rear cogs, unless the suspension spring was so stiff or so heavily preloaded that the sum of the static weight and the pedaling forces couldn't compress it. Such a stiff suspension would move only in response to very big impacts, say, on a fast downhill, but it would help little on a climb.

Now imagine that you have the ability to raise the swing arm pivot relative to the frame and chain line. At some point, the net force vector from the rear tire's contact patch will point directly at the swing arm pivot. With the pivot in this position, the tension in the chain cannot create any torque to extend or compress the suspension, and the suspension and drivetrain will be decoupled. Near this ideal location, the suspension could be set up with minimal preload, allowing maximal suspension effectiveness without resulting in pogoing. Unfortunately, the location of this decoupled point varies from gear to gear, so that a totally decoupled bicycle design with derailleurs would require a moving pivot.

Move the pivot above this point, and chain tension will cause the suspension to move in the opposite sense, extending with tension rather than compressing. The bike would "antisquat." If the static load on the suspension was enough to compress the spring, then chain tension pulses could pull the suspension unit to its maximum length with every stroke. The suspension would top out on hard pedal strokes, possibly causing a clunking noise if no provision for topping out gently was designed into the unit. This, again, is pogoing, only in the opposite direction.

In a sense, the suspension extension that comes with any pivot location above the neutral point can be valuable. It jams the rear tire into the dirt just as the pedal stroke calls for the maximum traction, mimicking the action of skilled climbers. However, most riders find any noticeable pogoing alarming and unpleasant; most feel that it must waste energy. And it may, at least on smooth surfaces; we just don't know how much or how significant that loss is.

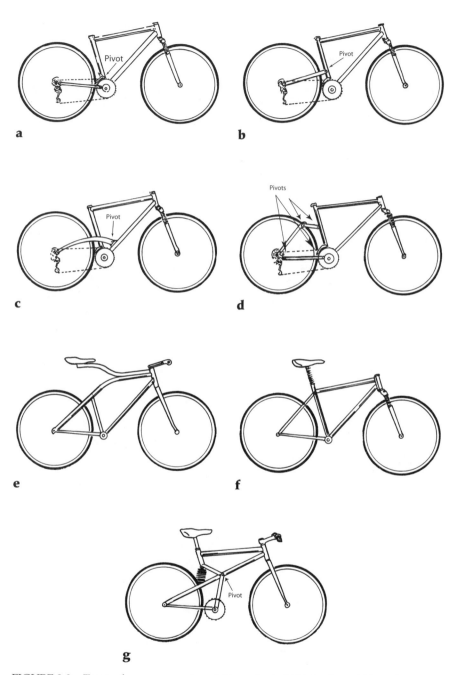

FIGURE 2.3 Types of rear suspension: *(a)* low pivot; *(b)* high pivot; *(c)* low-forward pivot; *(d)* four-bar linkage; *(e)* cantilevered beam suspended saddle (Allsop); *(f)* telescopic seat post suspended saddle; *(g)* unified rear triangle.

Pogoing in a high-pivot rear swing arm suspension can be totally avoided by running so much preload that the suspension can support its static load with no compression; that is, it is always topped out except when in the act of absorbing a big impact. In fact, most older high-pivot bikes were designed this way, with lots of preload. However, as mentioned previously, substantial preload means efficient transmission of small bumps, and a suspension that is active only during big hits.

Where does the ideal pivot point lie? Papadopoulos (1993) showed that the neutral point's location can be approximated by extending a ground reaction line at a 45° angle up and forward from the rear tire's contact point to the intersection with the top run of the chain, and extending another line forward from the rear axle through this intersection point (see figure 2.4). If the swing arm pivot lies along this line, then for the gear and chain location the tension in the chain will have very little effect on the rear suspension. A shift from one chain ring to another causes more change in this ideal location than does a shift from one rear cog to another. The pivot location would have to move when the chain changed chain rings to maintain neutrality. For the normal, fixed pivot location, the amount and perhaps even the sense of pogoing will vary from one chain ring to the next.

Since maximum torque and acceleration occur when the bike is in the small chain ring, it probably makes sense to optimize the pivot location for

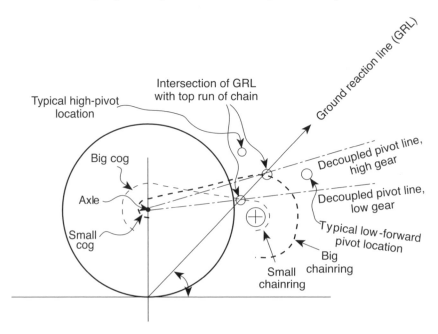

FIGURE 2.4 Finding a swing arm pivot point that will decouple chain forces from suspension.

From Papadopoulos 1993.

the lower range of gears. This means a relatively low pivot location, somewhere close behind the intersection of the top run of the chain and the small chain ring. On most bikes, the front derailleur cage can be in the way, so a short, simple, motorcycle-like swing arm is moderately challenging to implement. (The Trek Fuel is a good example of a well-implemented, simple swing arm system with a pivot in this location.)

A decreasing number of suspended bikes get around this issue by curving the swing arm up and over the front derailleur, coming down to a pivot ahead of the front derailleur and seat tube, just above the chain wheels. Most bikes with this configuration are close to neutral in the middle chain ring and exhibit moderate extensional pogoing in the small chain ring.

Multilink suspension systems, such as the Fisher RS-1 and the Specialized FSR, are four-bar linkages with the rear axle carried not by the swing arm but by the second vertical link. They can be designed to put the instant center—the imaginary point in space about which the link holding the rear axle initially rotates—in just the right place for a chosen chain ring, even if the front derailleur is there. This four-bar system with the axle carried by the second link is protected by the Horst Leitner patent, a patent now owned by Specialized.

Many simple swing arm bikes (the rear axle is clamped by the swing arm) appear at first glance to be four-bar or Horst patent designs since they have multiple links running from the rear swing arm above the axle to actuate the forward-mounted rear shock. However, the trajectory of the rear axle on bikes such as these is controlled purely by the swing arm. They are simple swing arm designs. Such bikes include the Kona Stinky series and the Trek Fuel.

Possibly it is simpler to understand rear suspension/pedaling interactions by looking at the rear axle trajectory. If the suspension constrains the rear axle to move perpendicular to the top run of the chain, then the tension pulsations in the chain can have no direct effect on the forces in the suspension. Simple swing arm bikes can be designed to achieve this goal in one gear, at one point in the suspension's travel. Four-bar designs can be designed to achieve this decoupling in more gears and at more points in travel since the axle's trajectory is no longer a simple arc but a complicated curve. Some suspension designs of even more complexity, such as the Santa Cruz Blur VPP, achieve even more complex axle trajectories that make the suspension almost perfectly decoupled, at least in the two smaller chain rings where chain tension is highest.

Also note that an axle trajectory perpendicular to the top run of the chain does not account for the suspension compression forces that arise when the rear tire contact patch forces the rider/bike combined center of gravity to accelerate with each pedal pulse. This acceleration causes a rearward pitch moment that compresses any suspension that isn't designed to extend slightly to compensate for acceleration. Again, large accelerations are created only in the lowest gears, so efforts aimed at countering this acceleration effect are best focused at the small chain ring.

Bump-Pedal Feedback

The second major chain-induced phenomenon that troubles in-frame rear suspension systems is bump-pedal feedback. When a bike with rear suspension strikes a bump with the rear wheel and the bump is large enough to cause the suspension to deflect, some rear suspension geometries will tug on the chain, producing a very noticeable deceleration or acceleration of the pedals. In extreme cases (for instance, a high-pivot bike with little preload), this behavior can be very annoying and distracting.

Papadopoulos (1993) showed that the rear swing arm pivot point that minimizes bump-pedal feedback is not the same point that minimizes pogoing. He pointed out that bump-pedal feedback is minimized by a fairly low swing arm pivot design that places the effective line of the swing arm tangent to a circle coaxial with, but somewhat smaller than, the smallest chain wheel. It is my experience that placing the pivot location close to that chosen by low-pivot designs (see figure 2.3a and 2.3c) would offer relatively little bump-pedal feedback.

Another simpler way around the chain-to-spring coupling problem is to avoid the issue altogether by suspending the rider above the frame, leaving the frame rigid. Whether by an Allsop Softride composite beam (see figure 2.3e) or by a sprung seat post (see figure 2.3f), the chain tension has no direct effect on the suspension system. Because they are totally decoupled, these suspension systems can be very soft, giving excellent isolation from small, high-frequency bumps and sharp-edged steps, at the expense of increased unsprung weight.

Disc Brakes

Rim brakes on mountain bikes subjected to muddy use are often the most maintenance-intensive components on the bicycle. It is possible to wear through a set of rim brake pads in a four-hour muddy ride, depending on soil conditions and elevation change. It is also possible to wear through a rear rim in three months of such riding. Rim brakes also heat the rim and can even cause blown latex tubes on a long enough descent.

The advent and perfection of disc brakes in the last five years has revolutionized mountain bike braking. Discs, usually stainless steel, 6 to 8 in. in diameter, provide the braking surface, a braking surface much farther from the mud and grit than the rim. Since the disc is most often rigidly mounted to a special hub, it has less lateral runout than a typically used mountain bike rim, so pad-to-disc clearance can be much smaller than typical pad-to-rim clearance. This means that very high lever ratios can be applied, sufficient to more than make up for the braking disadvantage caused by the 1:4 brake surface acting radius (roughly 3 in. versus 12 in.).

Also helping make up for the leverage disadvantage of the small disc are the pads. Since the disc is wear-resistant stainless steel, very aggressive automotive/motorcycle disc pad friction materials can be used, usually organic or organic with metallic particles.

The high lever ratios required between the rider's hands and the friction materials are delivered either by hydraulic systems (either closed or open) or mechanical systems. The open hydraulic systems use a master cylinder with an associated reservoir and a bleed hole designed to allow fluid to flow into the system from the reservoir if lever travel becomes excessive due to pad wear, or to leave the system if prolonged braking heats the fluid and expands it. Closed systems have no reservoir and depend on special low-coefficient of expansion fluids to cope with thermal effects. Arguably, the open systems have been the most successful. Most of these either use DOT-3 or DOT-4 brake fluid or less corrosive mineral oil.

The lever ratio of these hydraulic systems is determined by a combination of mechanical leverage and piston area ratio. Most hydraulic brakes employ a piston on both sides of the disc, plumbed to create the same hydraulic pressure. The pistons move more or less equally to the fixed disc. The caliper containing the pistons must be adjustable to center on the disc. The lack of friction in a hydraulic system gives a noticeable advantage—both in brake force realized and in sensitivity and control—over a cable system that has seen an equivalent amount of real-world use.

Mechanical systems have to create the same lever ratio as that easily created by a hydraulic system. Any losses in these mechanical systems cause noticeable degradation in braking force. The most successful designs are those with ramp and ball features, in which a rotating, screw-shaped ramp forces a ball up into a piston, which in turn pushes the brake pad into the disc.

Most mechanical discs feature a single piston and a sliding caliper, or a single piston that flexes the thin disc into a fixed pad on the far wheel side of the disc. These mechanical systems can be very effective as long as the cable is clean and lubricated and the mechanism is well greased, so that mechanical losses are minimal.

Well-designed disc brake systems can add as little as 150 g to the whole bike per wheel. Very good mechanical systems are found on bikes priced as low as $700. Although riders in relatively dry and clean areas may not need superior mechanical systems, they rank with suspension systems as one of the biggest improvements to come along in mountain biking.

Directions for Future Research

Front suspension systems have been around for more than a decade. These systems are accepted by all but the most conservative mountain bikers and road riders. In general, rear suspension designs have been ironed out well enough that they offer little pedal-suspension interaction or bump-pedal feedback. In fact, the only disadvantages to the best rear suspension designs are the inevitable ones: slight increases in weight, not-so-slight increases in cost, and some increase in maintenance.

A majority of the time spent riding mountain bikes involves relatively slow climbing and traversing level surfaces. In my experience, a full suspension bike with little or moderate coupling between chain tension and suspension forces, equipped with a moderately damped, relatively soft spring, can aid overall efficiency and speed in these conditions if the surfaces traversed are rough enough. This seems to be partially due to more uniform contact between the rear tire and the ground, to decreased fatigue since the rider can relax on the saddle even when hitting fairly large obstacles, and to the overall physiological benefits of a smoother ride.

These benefits decrease with very stiff suspension systems. If the riding surfaces are very smooth, an active full suspension bike will be measurably slower than an unsuspended bike, in my experience. Fast, high-intensity descents are aided by almost any well-damped suspension design. In fact, many of the early full suspension designs—in particular, high-pivot designs—are intended to function primarily in this regime. Limited work has been done in the area of cycling efficiency versus suspension type, primarily Berry and colleagues (1993).

Suspension design is a rich area for research, as many questions remain unanswered. Can rear suspension help overall efficiency on a climb? What type of suspension optimizes climbing efficiency? Do all active suspension designs reduce efficiency on smooth surfaces? Can rear suspension increase grip on a steep, loose, or slippery climb? What is the best trade-off between climbing efficiency and grip augmentation?

Design and tuning issues could also be investigated, including questions such as these: What is the optimum travel front and rear for full suspension bikes in different circumstances? What is the optimum damping scheme to maximize high-speed control, big-bump energy absorption, and high-frequency isolation?

As full suspension mountain bikes take more and more of the market and move down the price scale, these questions will be relevant to more and more of the cycling public. Industry and academia cannot currently answer all of these questions, so a very interesting rapid evolution process is playing itself out before our eyes. In the few years that full suspension bikes have been available, rapid progress has already been made. Some designs have already evolved out of existence. High pivots, for example, were becoming rare by the 1994 Anaheim bike show, whereas low-pivot designs and unified rear triangle designs (see figure 2.3g) were conspicuous. A decade later, URTs have, in turn, all but disappeared. Well-conceived research will help clarify and guide this process.

References

Berry, M., Woodward, M., Christopher, D., and Pittman, C. 1993. The effects of a mountain bike suspension system on metabolic energy expenditure. *Cycling Science* 5(1): 8-14.

Papadopoulos, J. 1993. Designing bicycle rear suspensions to reduce pedal interaction. Manuscript submitted for publication. [Personal communication]

3

Body Positioning for Cycling

Edmund R. Burke • Andrew L. Pruitt

For the cyclist interested in performance and comfort, proper position on the bicycle is paramount. A properly fitted cyclist will be efficient, powerful, comfortable, and injury free on the bike. An efficient and powerful position is one that enables the cyclist to pedal the bicycle effectively without a lot of wasted energy and improper pedaling mechanics. Being comfortable on the bicycle allows for the athlete's weight to be distributed among the saddle, pedals, and handlebars so the skeletal system bears the weight instead of the muscles of the back and arms.

A good bike fit, then, is imperative not only for comfort but also for minimizing potential for injury. Improper positioning can often lead to overuse injuries and premature fatigue while riding. For the past 20 plus years, Dr. Andy Pruitt has been describing cycling as "a marriage between the somewhat adaptable human body and a somewhat adjustable machine." The goal is to adjust the bicycle to the cyclist so that the cyclist has to adapt as little as possible (Burke 1994; Pruitt and Matheny 2001).

Types of Bicycles

Choosing among the plethora of bicycle styles currently available can be confusing. In this chapter, we will focus only on describing the proper positioning of a cyclist on a road racing bike, a mountain bike, and time trial bike.

Road Racing Bike

The most important angle on a bicycle is that formed by the seat tube and the ground (see figure 3.1). As we will see, an important fitting dimension requires that the knee be over the pedal spindle (KOPS) of the forward foot when the crank arms are horizontal. The seat tube angle is usually designed to accomplish this. The most common angles for road racing frames are from 72 to 74°, which will allow for an average-sized cyclist to position his or her knee over the pedal spindle with only minor adjustments to fore and aft movement of the saddle.

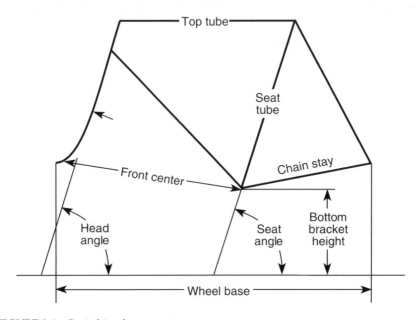

FIGURE 3.1   Basic bicycle geometry.

Consequently, the seat tube angle is related to femur length. The longer the femur, the shallower (smaller) the angle; a shallower angle tends to move the cyclist back on the bicycle. If someone has a short femur, the seat tube angle would have to be steeper (larger) to position the knee far enough forward. In general, the smaller the bicycle, the steeper the seat tube angle. More and more professional cyclists who are riding long road races with many climbs are also opting to use bicycles with a 72° seat tube angle. The steeper the seat tube, the harsher the ride, thus limiting the bicycle to shorter events.

Head tube angle, meanwhile, is based on frame size, top tube length, seat tube angle, pedal clearance in relation to the front wheel, and desired steering characteristics. It is commonly 73 to 75°. The steep head tube angle is usually combined with a relatively short fork rake, creating a reasonable amount of calculated steering trail for stability at high speed. This allows for the least amount of frame flex and a minimum tendency to stray when the cyclist is riding on straight stretches or descending a steep mountain.

Chain stay length is about 16 in., which reduces frame flex and keeps the overall wheelbase to somewhere between 38 and 40 in. A short wheelbase increases steering responsiveness.

When selecting a frame, see that about 4 to 5 in. of seat post is showing once saddle height is established (we will consider saddle height later). Select the smallest possible frame that affords a good mix of comfort and handling. As a rule, a smaller frame is lighter and stronger and handles better than a larger one. However, the frame should not be too small; this will cause the top tube to be short or will cause the seat post to be set past its maximum extension line.

Another method for determining bike frame is to measure your inseam. Stand on the floor in your stocking feet and measure from the floor to your pubic bone. Take two thirds of this number (multiply by 0.66) to determine an approximate estimate of your seat-tube length. Seat tubes are traditionally measured from the center of the bottom bracket to the center of the lug at the top of the seat tube. The lug is the piece of tubing that the tubes fit into at the joints. Most steel bikes have lugs. Note that some manufacturers measure to the top of the lug or seat tube.

Recently, the compact geometry frame has become popular with some cyclists. Its sloping top tube allows for a smaller, stiffer frame. This type of frame design has been used with mountain bikes for many years. To determine the size of a compact road frame, measure from the center of the bottom bracket in an upward vertical line to a point where, on a traditional road frame, it would intersect the top tube that extends horizontally from the head tube to the seat tube.

Mountain Bike

As with road bikes, mountain bike sizes usually are determined by seat tube length. Some models have sloping top tubes that result in extremely short seat tubes. In these cases, smaller frame sizes fit larger cyclists. The clearance between crotch and top tube when the rider straddles the top tube in cycling shoes should be a minimum of 3 in., enough to allow quick, painless dismounts. A mathematical formula for selecting frame size is based on inseam length minus 14 in. For a cyclist with a 36-in. inseam, the formula would be 36 − 14 = 22-in. frame.

Whereas many road bike frames are measured from the center of the crank spindle to the center of the top tube, many mountain bike frame builders measure from the center of the crank spindle to the *top* of the top tube. If the bike has a sloping top tube, then measure to the top of where it would be if it were level with the horizon.

The seat tube angle on most mountain bikes is around 71 to 73°. With a few variants this has been the norm in the industry in the last few years. Entry-level bikes usually have similar head tube angles to allow for slower and more predictable steering. Recently, head tube angle has become progressively steeper so the steering is more immediate and responsive.

Most racing cyclists will have the same position relative to saddle height and reach for both their mountain and road bikes. This is because many mountain bike cyclists also put in plenty of miles on their road bikes and want to have the identical position on the two bikes to eliminate the chance of injury.

Lastly, there is a large variation (from 11 3/4 to 13 in.) in the bottom bracket height of most mountain bikes. A bike with an 11-in. bottom bracket height and one with a 12-in. bottom bracket height would have a difference in stand-over height of 1 in. If using a higher bottom bracket, some cyclists prefer to lower their saddle height slightly so as to not have too high a center of gravity. A lower position will allow for greater stability with minimal cost to efficiency. Cyclists should carefully review their position when lowering saddle height, since this may cause them to throw their knees out at the top of the pedal stroke and could put undue stress on the anterior and lateral aspect of the knee.

In addition, if your mountain bike's crank arms are longer than your road bike's, you should lower the saddle an amount equal to the difference in crank arm length. This is necessary to give you the correct amount of bend in your knee at the bottom of the stroke. For example, if you run 172.5-mm crank arms on your road bike but 175-mm crank arms on your mountain bike, lower your mountain bike's saddle 2.5 mm.

Time Trial Bike

Positioning on the time trial bicycle is one of the more exciting topics of discussion among cyclists because there is still so much experimenting and refining taking place with the seat tube angles and aero arm positioning. More and more we are seeing steeper seat tube angles, with these angles ranging from 75 to 90°. Chris Boardman's hour-record-setting bicycle had an effective seat angle of 80° and an effective head tube angle of 74°. Positioning for the time trial will be discussed in greater detail later in the chapter.

Proper Fit to the Bicycle

There are several things to consider when fitting a bicycle. Let's review the latest findings on what will provide comfort, prevent injury, and improve cycling performance.

Optimal Saddle Height

Optimal saddle height for cycling has been estimated on the basis of power output (Hamley and Thomas 1967) and caloric expenditure (Hamley and Thomas 1967; Nordeen and Cavanagh 1975; Shennum and DeVries 1975). These reports generally agree that oxygen consumption is minimized at approximately 100% of trochanter height (from greater trochanter [boney points at widest parts of the hips] of femur to the floor while standing barefoot), or 106 to 109% of pubic symphysis height (measured from the ground to the pubic symphysis [bony prominence, middle of pelvis in the crotch area] while standing barefoot). Experienced cyclists generally choose a saddle height close to optimum simply by adjusting the seat height for maximum performance (Gregor, Green, and Garhammer 1982).

Muscle activity patterns (Desipres 1974; Ericson, Nisell et al. 1985; Gregor, Green, and Garhammer 1982; Jorge and Hull 1986), joint forces and moment patterns (Browning et al. 1988; Ericson 1986; Ericson et al. 1986; Ericson, Ekblom et al. 1985; Ericson, Nisell et al. 1985), and pedaling effectiveness (Broker et al. 1988) also have been reported to vary across seat heights. These relationships, however, have not been used to suggest optimal saddle heights.

Over the years, several formulas have been developed through use of the metabolic or empirical data mentioned to set saddle height for the cyclist on both the sport/tour and racing bicycle. Whenever fitting the bike to the cyclist, always recommend that the person wear the shoes he or she expects to wear the most when riding. This approach will allow for proper fit and comfort while riding.

Method 1   The simplest and usually the quickest method for determining seat height requires that the cyclist mount the bicycle on a wind-load resistance trainer and pedal comfortably while centered squarely in the saddle. The rider then unclips his or her feet, putting the heels on the top of the pedal, and pedals backward (see figure 3.2). The saddle height should

FIGURE 3.2   Estimating seat height from leg length.

be set at the point where the heels maintain contact with the pedals without the hips rocking from side to side as the cyclist reaches the bottom of the pedal stroke. This usually leads to a lower saddle height than that obtained with the other formulas we will review. When the cyclist is properly clipped into the pedals, there should be a slight knee flexion when the pedal is at the bottom of the stroke.

Method 2   One of the more common methods for determining seat height requires the subject to stand wearing cycling shoes with the feet about 2 in. apart on a hard floor and to hold a book or broomstick in a horizontal position while pulling it up firmly between the legs (see figure 3.3). Measure the distance (floor to crotch) and then multiply by 1.09 to get the distance from the center of the pedal spindle (axle) to the top of the saddle (see figure 3.4) when the crank arm is parallel to the seat tube (Hamley and Thomas 1967). This will give an upper limit to saddle height. Remember that the top of the saddle is the cupped part where one actually sits, not the front tip or the lip on the back of the saddle.

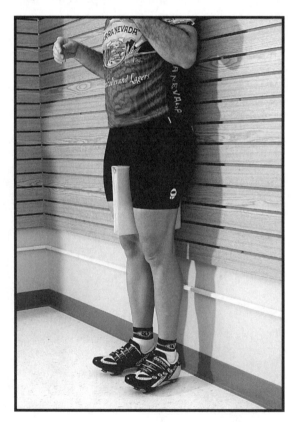

FIGURE 3.3   Measuring inseam length to estimate saddle height.

FIGURE 3.4   Saddle height is the distance between the top of the saddle and the center of the pedal axle, measured when the pedal is down and the crank arm is in line with the seat tube. LeMond measures from the saddle to the center of the bottom bracket.

Method 3   A third formula, recommended by Greg LeMond (LeMond and Gordis 1987), is to multiply the inseam measurement (floor to crotch as shown in figure 3.3) by 0.883 to get the distance from the center of the bottom bracket to the top of the saddle (see figure 3.4). This works out to be about 1/4 to 1 in. lower than with the first method for most people. This formula was determined years ago by Cyrille Guimard, LeMond's former coach, using wind tunnel tests and power tests. LeMond also recommends that you subtract 3 mm from the final figure when using clipless pedals (Matheny 1992). There are five more important qualifiers to this formula (Pruitt and Matheny 2001):

▶ This method was developed in the early 1980s when cycling shoes had thicker soles and pedals with toe clips and positioned the foot higher above the axle than modern clipless pedals do. These factors mean that the 0.883 multiplier may be too high when the cyclist is using modern equipment. Still, it's a good starting point for ballparking saddle height.

▶ Riders with feet that are long for their height may find that this formula produces a saddle that's too low. Long feet have the effect of lengthening legs beyond standard proportions.

▶ Cyclists with excessive soft tissue over their sit bones may find the saddle too low. When the cyclist sits for a while, the soft tissue compresses.

▶ Adding shoe thickness—in the form of insoles or cycling orthotics that extend under the ball of the foot—has the effect of lengthening the legs. This requires a higher saddle.

▶ Adding thickness between the crotch and saddle—such as when wearing thick winter cycling tights—effectively shortens the legs and requires a slightly lower saddle.

Method 4   Holmes, Pruitt, and Whalen (1994) recommend that the correct saddle height for an individual with no knee pain allows for 25 to 30° of flexion of the extended leg when the pedal is at bottom dead center (see figure 3.5). This angle is formed from the greater femoral trochanter to the lateral condyle to the lateral malleolus of the extended leg. Measure with a goniometer, which can be purchased at a medical supply store or can be made from a ruler and a protractor. Line up the instrument along the femur and the tibia, with the axis at the midpoint of the lateral condyle. Flexion of 25 to 30° allows for adequate decompression of the knee to prevent

FIGURE 3.5   Saddle height is evaluated by measuring degrees of knee flexion at the bottom dead center of the pedal stroke. Knee flexion should be 25 to 30 degrees.

anterior knee injuries and avoids the dead spot at the bottom of the pedal stroke. This position also decreases anterior knee stress by reducing patellar compression. Saddles that are too high can result in posterior knee pain, and saddles that are too low can result in anterior knee pain.

Remember that all of these formulas are estimates. After the initial setup, the cyclist may need to slightly readjust the saddle height (and other measurements listed later in this chapter). Any initial changes and readjustments should be accomplished in small increments of approximately 1/4 in. every few riding sessions.

The saddle height on a cyclist's mountain bicycle (one that will be used primarily off road) will be the same as the saddle height on that cyclist's road bicycle or slightly lower. Because of the higher bottom bracket on mountain bikes, duplicating the same position as on a road bicycle from pedal spindle to top of the saddle may result in a center of gravity that is too high. A lower position will allow for greater stability and maneuverability, with minimal cost to efficiency (Burke 1994). One also needs to take into account changes in crank arm length. If a cyclist's road bike has 172.5-mm crank arms and his or her mountain bike has 175-mm cranks, the seat can be set 2.5 mm lower.

Leg Length Discrepancies

Leg length inequalities that may be tolerable with walking can become problematic with cycling because of the cyclist's fixed position on the bike and because of the high number of repetitions completed each minute on the bicycle. Determine whether inequalities are functional or static, because corrections are specific for the type of discrepancy. Functional length differences that are due to foot mechanics (i.e., that occur at the ankle or foot) can be corrected primarily with orthotics and bicycle fit adjustments. Static inequalities can be treated with spacers or saddle or foot position adjustments.

Static length discrepancies may be present in the femur or the tibia. A scanogram (see figure 3.6), which provides static segmental measurements and location of length differences, can reveal these discrepancies.

Functional length discrepancies can result from faulty foot mechanics. Radiographic evaluation with a standing anterior-posterior view of the pelvis can be used to detect functional length differences. In order for a radiographic evaluation to be accurate, the floor the cyclist is standing on must be perfectly level. Good radiological technique needs to be followed to ensure that the image is not magnified or shortened.

The saddle height for cyclists with leg length discrepancies should always be adjusted to the long leg. Length corrections are then made on the shoe or pedal of the short leg, or with the fore/aft positioning of the feet if the length discrepancy occurs at the femur.

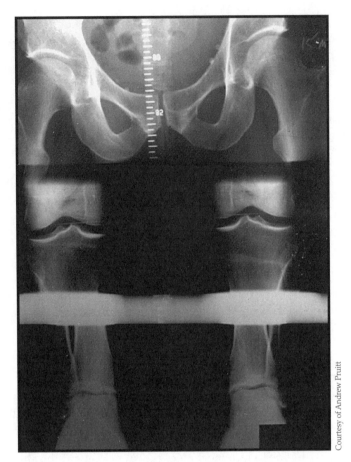

Courtesy of Andrew Pruitt

FIGURE 3.6   Scanogram of the static segmental measurements of a cyclist.

Then there are tibial and femoral length discrepancies. Tibial length discrepancies can be treated easily by using spacers to equalize the lengths. Spacers can be placed between the shoe and the cleat, or in the shoe of an off-road cyclist. Femoral length discrepancies are more difficult to treat. One method, though anecdotal, is to use a combination of spacers and an adjustment in the foot position on the pedal to provide correction. For example, a 6-mm difference could be treated by placing a 3-mm shim between the shoe and the cleat and by moving the foot of the short leg back 1 mm on the pedal and the foot of the long leg forward on the pedal.

Corrections for length should always slightly undercompensate the total difference, since many cyclists slightly correct with "ankling" (exaggerated plantar or dorsiflexion of the foot). Length discrepancies of 4 mm or less do not need correction unless the cyclist is symptomatic.

Fore and Aft Saddle Position

The rule of thumb for saddle fore and aft placement specifies that your knees should be vertically positioned over the pedal spindles when the pedals are forward and horizontal with the ground. This rule is widely regarded as a good starting position for proper weight distribution on the bike. It also promotes good pedaling style. This allows for the center of rotation of the knee to be located over the center of the rotation of the pedal spindle. As we will see later, there are several reasons to alter the position. Nevertheless, it is a good place to begin.

With the cranks horizontal to the ground (3 and 9 o'clock position), place a straightedge (yardstick) on the front of the patella of the forward knee and extend it down to the end of the crank arm (see figure 3.7). Make sure that the ischial tuberosities are bearing the weight on the saddle. Loosen the bolt (under the saddle) that holds the rails to the seat post and slide the saddle fore and aft until the straightedge is perpendicular to the ground. This is often referred to as the neutral knee position.

FIGURE 3.7   In the neutral fore/aft position, with the pedal at 90°, a straightedge is placed on the front of the knee and should fall to the end of the crank arm. The straightedge should be vertical.

Some triathletes prefer to have the front of the knee up to 3 cm in front of this neutral position. The more forward position will probably require a frame with a significantly steeper seat tube angle than comes standard on most road bikes. Remember, though, that any time you move the saddle forward, you are effectively lowering the saddle height, so you may have to adjust the saddle height again.

On rare occasions, some off-road specialists prefer to have their mountain bike seat set back from their road bike's seat position. The front of the knee should fall about 1 cm behind the end of the crank arm as indicated by a straightedge. A cyclist who is climbing a steep hill while seated on a mountain bike often sits as far back on the saddle as possible; this allows for greater traction on the rear wheel.

You will see professional road cyclists using this same position (with the saddle pushed back all the way on the rails) because they sit relatively far behind the bottom bracket in order to push bigger gears while sitting on long climbs. This position will be hard on a cyclist with low back pain or hamstring problems. As with the mountain bike rider, this type of setup is also very rare. This position is only right for a cyclist with a long femur coupled with a flexible lower back.

Saddle Tilt

The saddle should be set either level or with a slightly elevated front end. To determine the proper saddle tilt, a carpenter's level may be placed along the longitudinal axis of the saddle to indicate that the saddle is level or slightly angled with the front end higher. Some women prefer that the front of the saddle be angled slightly downward to prevent pressure on the perineal area. A number of men will also prefer their saddle angled down if riding in an aero position on a time trial bike. Some men will opt to have their saddle tilted slightly upward, but this may lead to urologic and neuropathic problems. When the nose points up, it also has ramifications for the lower back. The normal curvature is changed, often resulting in pain.

Despite these risks, there are two exceptions to the level-saddle rule (Pruitt and Matheny 2001):

1. People with unusual pelvic tilts or lumbar postures (swayback, for instance) sometimes require a slight upward tilt (1 to 3°) so they can get their weight on their sit bones rather than on soft tissue. Posture irregularities don't have to be so pronounced that people notice. For example, you could have a very subtle swayback syndrome that tilts your pelvis forward as you lean over to hold the handlebar. But usually a simple adjustment—raising the handlebar slightly—will let you level the saddle and still get the pressure off the pudendal nerves in your crotch.

2. In rare instances, the saddle should be tilted down slightly. This is appropriate mainly when in a low time trial position with aero bars.

Upper Body Position

Cyclists typically will adjust reach length according to what is comfortable, what is consistent with their level of back conditioning, and what can be maintained for desired distances. To find the proper stem length (reach), the cyclist should sit on the bicycle with the arms bent comfortably (about 15°), the hands in the drops, and the head facing forward. The next step is to drop a plumb line from the tip of the rider's nose; it should bisect the handlebar in the center at the stem (see figure 3.8).

Some determine stem length by assuming the position described and judging the stem length to be correct when the transverse part of the handlebar blocks out the view of the axle of the front wheel. Again, make sure that the cyclist is positioned on the drops and that the elbows are bent as for riding in a racing position. Greg LeMond recommends a position in which the elbow and knee are separated by about 1 to 2 in. (lengthwise), at their closest point, while the cyclist is riding in the drops of the handlebar with the arms bent at a 65 to 70° angle. Handlebar stems can be re-

FIGURE 3.8   When the bicycle is equipped with the proper stem length, a plumb line dropped from the top of the rider's nose would bisect the handlebar in the center of the stem.

Different cyclists have different needs, and each cyclist's individual characteristics should be taken into account when equipment is selected or adjusted.

placed to give proper extension. With the new threadless headsets, one should err on cutting the steerer tube longer to start with in the fitting process. This will allow for greater ability to adjust the steam height in the fitting process.

The height of the bars should be 1 to 2 in. below the top of the saddle for a small cyclist, and as much as 4 in. for a tall cyclist. If the cyclist is complaining of hand numbness (cyclist's palsy) or pain in the neck, arms, or shoulders, he or she may want to raise the stem to take weight off the hands. In addition, cyclists should use well-padded cycling gloves to absorb road shock and vibrations and should attempt to keep their wrists in a neutral position. Individuals with tight hamstrings or low back problems may require a shorter and/or higher stem and a normal saddle height or slightly lower.

The width of the bars on a road bicycle should be the same as the width of the shoulders (see figure 3.9); measure from the end of one acromion to the corresponding acromion across the front of the chest. Handlebar widths on a mountain bike generally range from 20 to 24 in. A wide bar is best for slow speed control, whereas a narrow bar allows for quicker turning and makes it easier to squeeze through wooded single-track trails. Most mountain bike specialists prefer riser handlebars that are around 22 to 24 in. wide.

FIGURE 3.9   Proper handlebar width.

Upper body position is the least exact part of the bicycle fit because it tends to be a function of comfort, experience (years of riding), hamstring and back flexibility, back problems, and ability to rotate the hips. It may take time and patience to get a cyclist into the "ideal" position.

On a mountain bike, upper body position will in most cases be more extended. A more extended position on a mountain bike allows enough room for lots of body English on climbs and descents and no overlap of knees and elbows. As on the road bicycle, the top of the stem should be 1 to 2 in. below the imaginary horizontal line extending from the top of the saddle. Too high a position on the bike raises the center of gravity and unevenly distributes the cyclist's weight between the front and rear wheels. Too small a frame forces the cyclist to lean over too far since the handlebars are so far below the saddle. Too large a frame will stretch the rider out too far.

Handlebar Position

The bottom of the handlebar on a road bicycle should be level or angled down slightly toward the rear wheel hub. Place each brake lever so that the tip just touches a straightedge extended forward from under the handlebar. The best all-around riding position is with the hands placed around the top of the brake level hood; this provides for good steering, quick access to brake levers, and good grip for out-of-the-saddle climbing. This is the favorite position of most cyclists. Many cyclists using bicycles equipped with Shimano STI or Campagnolo Ergo brake levers mount the levers a little higher on the curve of the bars. This is because the levers add about 1 cm in reach to the cyclist's extension when riding with the hands around the top of the brake lever hoods. Mounting them higher shortens the effective reach of the cyclist. One can also shorten the stem by 1 cm. Compared to Campagnolo brake levers, Shimano models have a more abrupt transition from the lever body to the handlebar. Some riders find one brand or the other to be more comfortable.

It's fine to position one brake lever slightly different from the other. Remember, the bike should look like you. Some riders have one arm that's slightly shorter than the other thanks to a broken bone or congenital factors. A broken collarbone can cause the same effect. In these cases, you'll want to have the brake lever higher on the short-arm side.

One signal that you need an asymmetrical reach is a stabbing pain behind one shoulder blade or on one side of your neck. Check by riding a trainer. Have a friend look from the front and from behind to see whether your shoulders are level. Adjust your brake levers until they are level.

Crank Arm Length

The consensus is that crank arm length should match the cyclist's leg length. The standard crank arm length of 170 mm suits cyclists of average proportions between 5 ft 5 in. and 6 ft. Shorter cyclists should consider crank arms of 165 or 167.5 mm. Cyclists under 5 ft should consider 160-mm crank arms. Cyclists 6 ft to 6 ft 2 in. might try 172.5-mm crank arms; 6 ft 2 in. to 6 ft 4 in., 175-mm crank arms; taller cyclists, 180- or 185-mm crank arms. Two cyclists may be of the same height with one having disproportionately longer legs. The cyclist with the longer legs may want to opt for slightly longer crank arms.

Crank arm length determines the size of the pedal circle, which relates to the vertical distance the rider's feet rise from the bottom of each pedal stroke to the top. This may affect comfort and does affect knee and hip flexion. For example, if a short rider uses long crank arms, the hips and knees may flex uncomfortably at the top of the pedal stroke even though the saddle is at the proper height. Crank arm length also influences the leverage and rpm rate that one produces while cycling. Long crank arms are good for pushing large gears and climbing at lower rpms, and shorter crank arms are good for low-gear, high-rpm pedaling. Most mountain bikes come with longer crank arms (172.5 to 175 mm).

Most bicycles come with proportionally sized crank arms. If the cyclist needs a different arm length, a bicycle dealer can change crank arms. Remember, when crank arms are changed, saddle height may have to be readjusted.

Foot Position

Position the feet so that the widest part of the foot (ball of the foot, metatarsal head of the great toe) is directly over the pedal axle. To prevent knee pain, adjust cleats so the angle of the foot on the pedal is neutral, as anatomically arrived at by the cyclist's own natural foot position on the pedal. In the past, before most of the pedals on the market where "floating pedals," the most efficient method of providing an accurate placement of the foot was to use a special instrument called the Rotational Adjustment Device (RAD). However, today most pedals offer more than 5° of float in either direction and have removed the need for a RAD adjustment.

Under certain circumstances, some cyclists prefer to mount their cleats on their cycling shoes so that the ball of the foot is ahead of or behind the pedal axle. When the ball of the foot is ahead of the axle, the effective lever arm from the ankle to the pedal axle is shortened. This requires less force to stabilize the foot on the pedal and puts less strain on the Achilles tendon and calf. Some triathletes, individuals with large feet, and time trial specialists use this position because it allows them to produce more force when using large gears. These cyclists must adjust both feet and lower the saddle the same amount. This will limit their ability to pedal at high cadences. A cyclist who is experiencing some soreness in the Achilles tendon or calf muscles should consider moving the ball of the foot forward a few millimeters on the pedal. Some cyclists with shoe sizes smaller than size 9 may consider moving the ball of the foot slightly behind the pedal axle. Cyclists with a shoe size larger than size 11 may consider moving the ball of the foot slightly in front of the pedal axle.

Placing the ball of the foot behind the pedal axle effectively lengthens the lever arm from the ankle to the pedal axle and makes it harder to keep the foot as a rigid lever. Consequently, the calf muscles and Achilles tendon need to do more work to stabilize the foot on the pedal. Track cyclists often use this position because it allows for higher rpms during fixed-gear events. But such a cyclist may be flirting with potential injury, especially if using large gear ratios.

Long-distance riders (Race Across America, etc.) often find that they can avoid painful numbness and "hot foot" by sliding their cleats all the way back. This puts the ball of their feet as far ahead of direct pedal pressure as possible. In fact, some ultramarathon riders go so far as to drill the shoe soles so they can move their cleats even farther to the rear.

Most important, cleat position should reflect any anatomic variants that may be noted on an examination. For example, a cyclist with external tibial rotation should be placed in a slightly externally rotated or toed-out cleat position. This is especially critical for cyclists using fixed rather than floating cleat systems because there is no rotation to compensate for anatomic variants. Cyclists who have marked pronation, excessive toeing out, or varus alignments (bowleg) may benefit from adding spacers between the pedal and the crank arm (see figure 3.10) or using orthotics. This can alleviate trauma to the medial malleolus for cyclists with excessive pronation and can improve hip-to-foot alignment for varus individuals.

FIGURE 3.10   Spacers (washers) between the pedal and the crank arm.

Clip-On Handlebars

In recent years, with the continued growth of the triathlon, time trial cycling, and ultra distance cycling events, we have seen an increased use of aero bars or clip-on type bars. These bars were developed to reduce the aerodynamic drag of the cyclist. Using clip-on (aero) handlebars effectively requires mastering four elements of positioning: narrowing the arms, riding with a flat back, lowering the chin, and keeping the knees in while cycling.

Narrowing the Arms   By narrowing the arms, the cyclist reduces the body's frontal area and allows for the wind to be directed around the body. The cyclist begins by gradually bringing in the armrest pads closer on the handlebar (see figure 3.11) until he or she can ride comfortably with the forearms almost touching for long periods of time. This may take several weeks or months. Once someone can ride like this comfortably and in a powerful position, he or she will have reduced aerodynamic drag greatly. It is also

FIGURE 3.11   Reducing the frontal area by bringing the arms close together.

more important to try to narrow one's elbows than to lower the stem to reach a more effective aerodynamic position.

Riding With a Flat Back   The next task is to work on riding comfortably with a flat back (see figure 3.12). Rotate the pelvis forward on the saddle and work on lower back and hamstring flexibility. The saddle should be level and the stem length long enough to get the proper back stretch. This will eliminate the hump that you see in many cyclists' backs when viewing them from the side. If one were to drop a plumb line from the front of the shoulder, it should touch the back of the elbow; this will keep the cyclist from overreaching. In other words, the upper arm should be fairly vertical with the elbow just ahead of the shoulder. Cyclists should not attempt this until they have been able to ride with the forearms positioned closely together for long periods of time. Caution should also be taken to prevent compression of the genital area.

a

b

FIGURE 3.12 The key to a flat back is pelvic rotation. *(a)* The cyclist sits with the pelvis turned under, as though sitting on a chair, and cannot flatten out his back. *(b)* With the pelvis rotated forward, the hump in the back can be reduced, as shown, or eliminated.

Lowering the Chin   Third, the cyclist will need to lower the chin to fill in the gap between the arms and to help streamline the aerodynamic shape further (see figure 3.13). Riders need to remember not to drop the chin so low that they cannot safely look down the road. Lowering the chin will also lower the shoulders and make a more perfect aerodynamic object. It is important not to bury the head. Safety and comfort are key concerns while time trialing or while riding off the front of a group.

FIGURE 3.13   Lowering the head and lowering the chin are not the same. The cyclist lowers the chin to help fill the hole between the upper arms.

Keeping the Knees In   In addition to accomplishing these three changes in upper body position, cyclists also need to be careful to keep their knees in while pedaling. If the other positional changes cause the cyclist to throw out the knees while pedaling to avoid hitting the arms, he or she may have to raise the stem or shoulders slightly to allow the knees to stay in while pedaling. Keeping the knees in while pedaling is just as important in air drag reduction as keeping the forearms together, keeping a flat back, and lowering the chin. Research on pedaling rpm in the wind tunnel has shown no correlation between pedaling rate and reduction in air resistance (Kyle 1989). Never move the feet closer on the pedals (closer to the crank arm) since reducing stance width is dangerous. In addition, varus knee cyclists will have a hard time keeping their knees in for effective aerodynamics.

Adjusting the tilt of the bars helps a cyclist accomplish these steps to get in comfortable position on the bicycle. Most athletes keep the tilt of the bars upward somewhere between 15 and 30° to achieve optimum comfort, performance, and power.

Questions have arisen about the effect of this position on breathing and oxygen consumption. Research completed at the University of Utah (Johnson and Shultz 1990) showed that using aerodynamic bars in this position had no measurable physiological cost on cycling. In the laboratory under two different submaximal conditions, 15 highly trained subjects rode a bicycle ergometer fitted with either dropped road bars or the same bars fitted with clip-on style bars. There was no evidence in the study to suggest that aero or clip-on bars interfered with breathing (ventilatory) mechanics. Not only was ventilation unaffected, but there was also no significant difference in oxygen consumption when the athletes worked at 80% of maximum during the 10-min steady state ride. Therefore, there is no foundation for concerns that the severely crouched position required with the use of an aerodynamic type handlebar will interfere with breathing. Work by Origenes and others (Origenes, Blank, and Schoene 1993) also has shown that riding in an aerodynamic position does not impair physiologic responses to high-intensity exercise.

As with any new piece of equipment, the more practice a cyclist has riding the bicycle with the aero bars before a long ride or race, the more familiar he or she will become with all aspects of riding technique and comfort. Not using aero bars or clip-ons is sure to put a cyclist at a disadvantage in certain events because of the lack of an optimum aerodynamic position on the bike.

Directions for Future Research

Future research will see more interaction of the clinician, biomechanist, and cyclist in determining proper position on the bicycle. For example, although a particular position will dramatically reduce the aerodynamic drag on the cyclist or increase power output, or both, it could lead to overuse injuries if practiced for many thousands of miles. The study of cycling biomechanics needs to be a more interdisciplinary science not only to lead to increases in performance, but also to reduce the incidence of injury.

Injury research is beginning to look into compensating for length differences through the use of a combination of asymmetrical crank arms. These systems are in the developmental stages and to date have not been evaluated for their effect on pedaling mechanics in cyclists with leg length discrepancies. Work also needs to be continued on the effects of force application to the pedals, with "static" versus "floating" pedals. Along with this research, it is necessary to look at the effect of shoe design on the loading of the lower leg and on overuse injuries. Research has been conducted showing that shoes designed to correct orthopedic imbalances can improve cycling performance (lower oxygen cost, improved heart rate) when riding at intensities replicating lactate threshold.

Lastly, future research on the effects of maintaining an aerodynamic position for extended periods of time needs to review the fatigue patterns in the lower and upper body musculature. This work is important to establish whether pathomechanical problems develop after several hours on the bicycle.

References

Broker, J., Browning, R., Gregor, R., and Whiting, R. 1988. Effects of seat height on force effectiveness in cycling. *Med Sci Sports Exerc* 20:583.

Browning, R., Gregor, R., Broker, J., and Whiting, R. 1988. Effects of seat height changes on joint force and movement patterns in experienced cyclists. *J Biomech* 21:871.

Burke, E. 1994. Proper fit of the bicycle. In *Clinics in sports medicine: Vol. 13(1). Bicycle injuries: Prevention and management,* edited by M.B. Mellion and E.R. Burke. Philadelphia: Saunders. pp 1-14.

Desipres, M. 1974. An electromyographic study of competitive road cycling conditions simulated on a treadmill. In *Biomechanics IV,* edited by R.C. Nelson and C. Morehouse. Baltimore: University Park Press. pp. 349-355.

Ericson, M. 1986. On the biomechanics of cycling: A case study of joint and muscle load during exercise on a bicycle ergometer. *Scand J Rehabil Med* 16:1-43.

Ericson, M., Bratt, A., Nisou, R., Nemeth, G., and Eicholm, J. 1986. Load moments about the hip and knee joints during ergometer cycling. *Scand J Rehabil Med* 18:165-172.

Ericson, M., Ekblom, J., Svensson, O., and Nisell, R. 1985. The forces on the ankle joint structures during ergometer cycling. *Foot Ankle* 6:135-142.

Ericson, M., Nisell, R., Arborelius, U., and Ekholm, J. 1985. Muscle activity during ergometer cycling. *Scand J Rehabil Med* 17:53-61.

Gregor, R., Green, D., and Garhammer, J. 1982. An electromyographic analysis of selected muscle activity in elite competitive cyclists. In *Biomechanics VII,* edited by A. Morecki and K. Fidelus. Baltimore: University Park Press. pp. 537-541.

Hamley, E., and Thomas, V. 1967. Physiological and postural factors in the calibration of a bicycle ergometer. *J Physiol* 191:55-57.

Holmes, J., Pruitt, A., and Whalen, A. 1994. Lower extremity overuse in bicycling. In *Clinics in sports medicine: Vol. 13(1). Bicycle injuries: Prevention and management,* edited by M.R. Mellion and E.R. Burke. Philadelphia: Saunders. pp. 187-206.

Johnson, S., and Shultz, B. 1990. The physiologic effects of aerodynamic handlebars. *Cycling Science* 2(4): 9-12.

Jorge, M., and Hull, M. 1986. Analysis of EMG measurement during bicycle pedaling. *J Biomech* 19:683-694.

Kyle, C. 1989. The aerodynamics of handlebars and helmets. *Cycling Science* 1(1): 22-25.

LeMond, G., and Gordis, K. 1987. *Greg LeMond's complete book of bicycling.* New York: Perigee Books. pp. 118-145.

Matheny, F. 1992. Finding perfect saddle height. *Bicycling Magazine* December: 46-50.

Nordeen, K., and Cavanagh, P. 1975. Simulation of lower limb kinematics during cycling. In *Biomechanics V-B,* edited by P. Komi. Baltimore: University Park Press. pp. 26-33.

Origenes, M., Blank, S., and Schoene, R. 1993. Exercise ventilatory response to upright and aero-posture cycling. *Med Sci Sports Exerc* 25(5): 608-612.

Pruitt, A., and Matheny, F. 2001. *Andy Pruitt's medical guide for cyclists.* Chapel Hill, NC: RBR Publishing Company.

Shennum, P., and DeVries, H. 1975. The effect of saddle height on oxygen consumption during bicycle ergometer work. *Med Sci Sports Exerc* 8:119-121.

4

Optimizing the Crank Cycle and Pedaling Cadence

Alejandro Lucía • Conrad Earnest •
Jesús Hoyos • José L. Chicharro

Before we begin our discussion of optimizing the crank cycle and pedaling cadence, we should address some important issues you would do well to keep in mind as you read this chapter. First, it is important to understand that we cannot really be sure that the often recommended normal (i.e., circular) crank system is the optimal one. In fact, other possibilities—such as eccentric and elliptical chain rings—may improve crank cycle dynamics. Preliminary studies have shown that these systems deserve some attention.

The second issue to bear in mind is the question of whether an optimal pedaling cadence actually exists. After decades of research, this question has yet to be answered. The topic of optimizing pedaling cadence grows more controversial when you consider that new research has been conducted using cyclists who are not highly trained. We will try to show that perhaps an optimal cadence doesn't exist. Instead, experienced cyclists probably spontaneously choose the cadence that works best for them, making it difficult to give advice based on scientific knowledge.

Crank Cycle

In the last two decades, cycling has been the subject of thorough research, although several basic questions have yet to be conclusively answered, including what really happens during the pedaling cycle itself. How do the phases of the crank cycle influence circulatory dynamics? Which is the optimal combination of pedaling cadence and muscle force application? Is the pedaling pattern humans, both cyclists and noncyclists, spontaneously adopt really optimal?

Limited Blood Flow During the Crank Cycle

Takaishi and colleagues (2002) adopted an integrative approach to the pedaling cycle using surface electromyography (EMG) and near infrared spectroscopy (NIRS) to estimate muscle fiber recruitment and blood flow, respectively, in the main quadriceps muscle involved in the pedal thrust, the vastus lateralis. Their results showed that, in noncyclists exercising at moderate to high power outputs (~ 200 W) and at low cadences (50 rpm), blood flow and oxygenation to the vastus lateralis (and most likely to all quadriceps muscles) is significantly restricted during the first third of the crank cycle. At this point in the pedal stroke, knee flexion and quadriceps contraction is the greatest as the leg moves through the pedal stroke and leg extension. Blood flow occlusion presumably occurs in the microcirculation (arterioles and venules) and is attributable to the increase in intramuscular pressure that occurs during muscle contraction (see figure 4.1). Their data also revealed a compensatory, transient increase in blood supply and oxygen transport after the pushing phase, when the vastus lateralis recovers from the contraction.

All professionals involved in training cyclists should keep in mind that muscle blood flow is first occluded and then overcompensated for following the compression period. Cycling is an aerobic sport (except sprint or short velodrome events) in which top-level performance largely depends on the amount of oxygen transported to the working muscles. Interestingly, oxygen appears to be most readily available to the main muscles only 50% of the time, when they are in their relaxation phase during the pedal upstroke. Besides the blood flow restriction caused by increased intramuscular pressure suggested by Takaishi's findings, blood flow through the iliac arteries, which irrigate all leg muscles, can be reduced during hip flexions, particularly when cyclists adopt aerodynamic positions, such as during time trials (Schep et al. 1999).

Regardless of other factors such as economy/efficiency, neuromuscular fatigue, or lactate washout, fast pedaling cadences (> 90 rpm) probably have an important advantage in that the duration of restricted blood flow to quadriceps muscles is shorter. In addition, for a given power output, the force applied on the pedals is reduced at fast cadences, and the required muscle contractions are less forceful (Faria 1992). At these

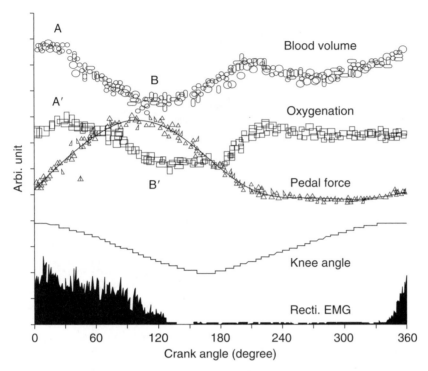

FIGURE 4.1   Changes in blood flow and oxygenation to the quadriceps muscle across the different angles of the crank cycle. Both variables are markedly reduced during2 most of the downstroke phase. *Recti EMG* refers to the electromyographic activity of the vastus lateralis muscle. It indicates the involvement of the vastus lateralis (i.e., muscle fiber recruitment) for each angle of the cycle. Data show that the vastus lateralis is not working during most of the upstroke phase, and it must contract while blood flow and oxygenation are decreased.

Reprinted, with permission, from T. Takaishi, T. Sugiura, K. Katayama, Y. Sato, N. Shima, T. Yamamoto, and T. Moritani, 2002, "Changes in blood volume and oxygenation level in a working muscle during a crank cycle," *Med Sci Sports Exerc* 34:520-528.

faster cadences, one would expect less blood flow occlusion in microvessels caused by intramuscular pressure. Finally, Takaishi and coworkers found blood flow occlusion to occur at low absolute power outputs (~ 200 W). However, elite cyclists are often required to generate much higher power outputs (> 350 to 400 W) and perform more forceful muscle contractions during the most important phases of professional road races (Lucia, Hoyos, and Chicharro 2001a). It follows that blood flow occlusion to quadriceps muscles might be even more marked in those with the best-trained muscles with a higher reliance on blood oxygen supply. This phenomenon might help explain the use of unusually fast cadences by the first Tour de France winner of the 21st century, Lance Armstrong (see page 114).

Blood Flow

Oxygen supply to the main muscles involved in cycling (knee extensor muscles) is greatly limited when needed the most—that is, when the muscles work harder during the pedal thrust. Blood flow to working muscles is a serious factor to keep in mind in optimizing pedaling cadence.

We all know that pedal movement during each crank cycle defines a perfect circle, but is it necessarily the best option?

During the last decade, several studies have been devoted to optimizing the biomechanical features of the pedal crank cycle. For instance, it is known that highest peak torques can be obtained with increased crank arm length during the downstroke phase of the duty cycle (Faria 1992). The length of the crank arm can be increased using noncircular, eccentric chain rings. In the last decade, the International Cycling Union (Union Cycliste Internationale or UCI) approved the use of noncircular chain rings by professional cyclists, and some teams, such as the French team Française des Jeux, used this new system (the so-called Harmonic chain rings or the Biopace system from Shimano) during training and competition.

Several studies have analyzed the effects of noncircular chain rings on cycling performance compared to conventional, round chain rings (Cullen et al. 1992; Henderson et al. 1977; Hue et al. 2001; Hull et al. 1994; Neptune and Herzog 2000). No improvement was observed in cycling performance during exhaustive tests or long-duration exercise. Apparently, these results are inconsistent with the theoretical benefits from a biomechanical perspective of these new chain rings. One explanation could stem from the fact that only trained cyclists, those adapted to the conventional, circular chain rings, were recruited as subjects for these studies. Perhaps the eccentric chain ring induced changes in the normal biomechanical and neuromuscular patterns (motor unit recruitment) adopted by the subjects after many years of training with the conventional system. This, in turn, may increase the metabolic cost of pedaling and mask the expected mechanical advantages of the new design. With eccentric chain rings, the pedal follows an elliptical path, which changes the usual pattern of force application and could induce the recruitment of different muscle fibers. These newly recruited fibers are likely to be less trained and less efficient than those involved in the normal pedaling pattern of experienced cyclists.

It is difficult to come up with a good experimental design to resolve the question since any cyclist is likely to be more efficient when using the system he or she is accustomed to, whether circular or noncircular. Further research on trained cyclists is needed. Perhaps Lance Armstrong could have won the Tour de France using a noncircular chain ring provided he was adapted to the system after years of training.

In contrast, Hue and colleagues (2001) recently showed the biomechanical advantage of noncircular chain rings—increased crank arm length and higher peak torque during the downstroke and decreased crank length during the upstroke. They noted a significant improvement in simulated all-out, 1-km tests performed by trained cyclists who were not used to the new noncircular system. During their test, absolute power output rather than efficiency was the main determinant of performance.

With eccentric chain rings, the elliptical shape of each pedal cycle changes when the cyclist applies maximal vertical force during the downstroke and upstroke (see figures 4.2 and 4.3). This increases the angular velocity of the pedals during the dead spots of the duty cycle when both cranks are vertical and reduces the length of the phase during which the force applied to the pedal is lowest. However, these changes in angular velocity during each crank result in a certain perception of acceleration and deceleration in the working limbs, and can lead to a less smooth, somewhat uncomfortable pedaling pattern during longer events.

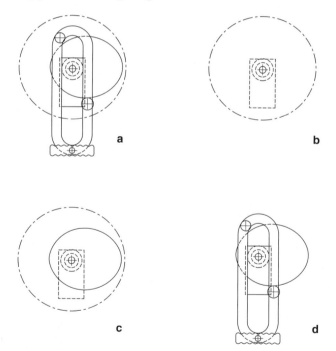

a

b

c

d

FIGURE 4.2   How an eccentric chain ring works. (*a*) Two crank arms slide into each other. (*b*) The inside crank arm is fixed on the center of the circular chain ring. (*c*) The outside crank arm revolves around an elliptical cam; (*d*) it is not fixed.

Reprinted, with permission, from O. Hue, O. Galy, C. Hertogh, J.F. Casties, and C. Prefaut, 2001, "Enhancing cycling performance using an eccentric chainring," *Med Sci Sports Exerc* 33:1006-1010.

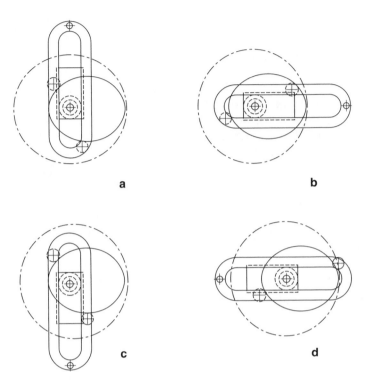

a   **b**

c   **d**

FIGURE 4.3   The eccentric chain ring during different angles of the crank cycle. *(a)* At 0°, the length of the crank arm is the same as that of a conventional, circular chain ring (e.g., 175 mm). *(b)* During the downstroke phase (0 to 180°), the crank arm length increases and reaches its maximum value of 200 mm at 90°. *(c)* At 180°, it returns again to its original length of 175 mm. *(d)* During the upstroke phase (180 to 360°), it decreases. Its minimum value (150 mm) corresponds to 270°.

Clearly, more research is needed to assess whether eccentric chain rings are more suitable than conventional ones. In any case, the aforementioned studies tell us that we cannot answer even the most apparently obvious question: Should the pedal crank really describe a perfect circle in each revolution? Furthermore, what is good for short, all-out events (noncircular chain rings) does not seem to be appropriate for endurance races. With all of these unresolved questions in mind, it becomes clear that cycling cadence optimization is a complex issue. Moreover, the recent launching on the market of yet another new method—the Rotor system—further complicates issues and adds to the existing controversy.

Rotor System

The UCI has certified the use of a new pedal crank system, the Rotor, developed by Pablo Carrasco. The Rotor adds four elliptic gears to the bottom brackets of the bicycle frame (see figure 4.4). This system makes each pedal independent of the other, so that pedal cranks are no longer fixed at 180° (see figure 4.5). Instead, the angle between both cranks varies during the pedal duty cycle, which could theoretically allow the rider more efficient motion in biomechanical terms by eliminating the dead spots that occur with the conventional system, when both cranks are in the vertical position. The work performed by the leg during the upstroke phase (during which less force is applied to the pedals) can be facilitated by the work of the other leg, which at the same time is involved in the more forceful downstroke phase (for an example, see the right and left pedal cranks during upstrokes and downstrokes, respectively, in figure 4.5). This sort of cooperation between both legs during the duty cycle could theoretically minimize the energy expended by recruited fibers and delay the occurrence of fatigue in these fibers. In addition, this enhanced cooperation between both legs seems to result in a smooth, round pedaling pattern, as opposed to noncircular chain rings.

The Rotor is commercially available and has gained popularity not only in the general sport market but also in elite sports such as triathlon, mountain biking, and cycling. All the riders of a professional cycling team—Relax-Fuenlabrada, Spain—used this device during the 2002 season, and

Rotor

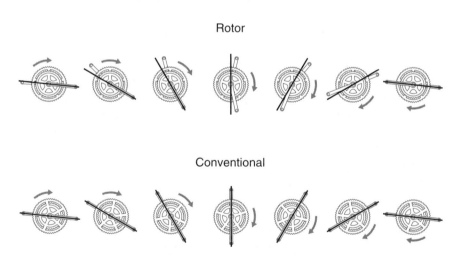

Conventional

FIGURE 4.4   Comparison between the mechanical performance of the Rotor and the conventional crank pedal system. With the conventional system, both pedals are constantly fixed at 180° from each other. With the Rotor system, each pedal is independent from the other, so that cranks are no longer fixed at 180°, except when both cranks are in the horizontal position. Instead, the angle between both pedals varies during the different phases of the duty cycle, which eliminates the dead spots that occur with the conventional system (i.e., when both pedal cranks are vertical). Arrows indicate the direction of the pedal movement.

Courtesy of Alejandro Lucía

FIGURE 4.5 Visual aspect of the Rotor system.

one cyclist from this team won the 2002 Vuelta a Andalucía, an important five-day tour race. Several top-level teams have conducted pilot tests using the Rotor during the preseason. To the best of our knowledge, however, only one scientific study independent of the Rotor company has tried to establish the possible effects of this new system on cycling performance. A preliminary study from our laboratory suggests an increase in efficiency at moderate to high workloads in physically active noncyclists who are not adapted at all to any type of pedal crank (Santalla et al. 2002). More research is needed, but, again, this new design might change our perspectives.

Anecdotal reports by trained cyclists using the Rotor for the first time show that the new system appears to be especially suitable and comfortable for pedaling at high cadences (> 90 rpm). We have also learned from personal reports of competitive mountain bikers that the Rotor system can bring some performance improvement during hill ascents of high slope (> 15%), in which riders are forced to remain seated. The main problem is that Rotor users complain of increased muscle soreness after several months of use. This could represent a major disadvantage for professional cycling, a sport in which muscle recovery, particularly during three-week races, is crucial.

Pedal Crank Optimization

The normal (circular) pedal crank system was developed by Pierre Michaux in 1861. Some 140 years later, we cannot be really sure that it is the optimal system. Therefore, we should be cautious when speaking of cadence optimization. Perhaps we should refer to pedal crank optimization in the first place!

Optimal Pedaling Cadence in Laboratory Studies

Most studies examining pedaling cadence have focused on pedal optimization in terms of economy/efficiency and local muscle stress. In this section, we will summarize the findings of the numerous laboratory studies that have attempted to identify which cadence is optimal. Unfortunately, few investigations have analyzed the question in well-trained cyclists riding their own bikes, making it difficult to apply the findings to actual cycling.

Optimal Cadence and Oxygen Cost: Economy/Efficiency

The two main messages to emerge from the numerous studies published since the beginning of the 20th century are as follows:

1. Low cadences (50 to 60 rpm) tend to be more economical/efficient than high pedaling cadences (> 90 rpm)
2. Paradoxically, most individuals prefer to pedal at high, theoretically inefficient/uneconomical cadences (examples include Boning, Gonen, and Maassen 1984; Cathcart, Richardson, and Campbell 1924; Chavarren and Calbet 1999; Coast, Cox, and Welch 1986; Croissant and Boileau 1984; Gaesser and Brooks 1975; Garry and Wishart 1931; Gueli and Shephard 1976; Jordan and Merrill 1979; MacIntosh, Neptune, and Horton 2000; Marsh and Martin 1997; Marsh and Martin 1998; Seabury, Adams, and Ramey 1977; Takaishi, Yasuda, and Moritani 1994; Takaishi et al. 1996; Takaishi et al. 1998).

A detailed look at the published studies suggests that both general conclusions need to be approached with caution. Several factors may alter the optimal and preferred pedaling cadence, including absolute and/or relative power output (i.e., watts or percentage maximal oxygen uptake [$\dot{V}O_2max$], respectively), duration of exercise, test mode (cycle ergometer tests versus riding a bicycle on a treadmill), fitness level of the subject (cyclist or noncyclist), and the high interindividual variability, even among trained cyclists of similar fitness levels, reported by most authors.

In general, during laboratory tests performed by noncyclists at constant power outputs (usually ≤ 200 W), pedaling at low rates (~ 50 to 70 rpm) resulted in lower oxygen uptake ($\dot{V}O_2$) than pedaling at higher rates (> 90 rpm). In any case, such a generalization is of little practical value. First, one questions the benefit of optimizing pedaling cadence in subjects whose power output rarely surpasses 200 W, those who cycle for fitness or recreation. Second, elite cyclists are the ones interested in optimizing cadence and making it more economical/efficient, and they are able to generate much higher power outputs during long periods. The average power output of Bjarne Riijs during the 1997 Amstel Gold Race, a World Cup classic lasting over seven hours, was close to 300 W (data from www.srm.de). During the most important stages of professional road cycling races, riders are often required to generate power outputs of over 400 W (Lucia, Hoyos, and Chicharro 2001a), not to mention the one-hour record in a velodrome (Bassett et al. 1999).

Bassett and colleagues (1999) estimated that the mean power outputs required to break the one-hour world records in a velodrome during the last years (53.0 to 56.4 km) ranged between 427 and 460 W. The average power output of Miguel Indurain during his 1994 one-hour record averaged 510 W (Padilla et al. 2000). Probably most pro riders are so economically below 200 W, that pedaling cadence hardly changes anything. Below 200 W, Lance Armstrong's human engine is probably similar to that of the last rider in the overall classification of the Tour de France in recent years, and pedaling cadence does not have a significant effect on either one. The picture is likely to be different above 400 W, but there are scarce data in the literature related to the oxygen cost of generating power outputs over 400 W for 20 or more minutes (Lucia, Hoyos, and Chicharro 2000), and no data exist on how pedaling cadence could alter this variable. This is the type of information needed in cycling science.

We should therefore be cautious when applying the findings of previous research concerning cadence optimization to highly trained cyclists. The most economical of cadences tends to increase with absolute power output, that is, with watts (Boning, Gonen, and Maassen 1984; Coast and Welch 1985; Hagberg et al. 1981; Seabury, Adams, and Ramey, 1977). For instance, Coast and Welch (1985) showed that the cadence eliciting the lowest $\dot{V}O_2$ at 100 and 330 W was 50 and 80 rpm, respectively. Thus, absolute power output is a key factor of cadence optimization and precludes any simple answer to the problem. On the other hand, trained cyclists are more effective than recreational riders at directing pedal forces perpendicular to the crank arm (Faria 1992). Such an ability carries a biomechanical advantage and probably allows trained riders to pedal at high cadences with no major loss of efficiency.

Instead of speaking of an inverse relationship between cadence and economy/efficiency, maybe it would be more correct to speak of a U relationship during constant-load exercise. There may be an optimum pedaling cadence below and above which oxygen cost increases significantly. Yet, can we assign a value to this theoretical optimum cadence at the bottom of the U? Probably not, given the great variability among cadence studies involving trained cyclists yielding the lowest $\dot{V}O_2$, from ~ 60 to ~ 90 rpm (Chavarren and Calbet 1999; Coast and Welch 1985; Hagberg et al. 1981).

It is generally accepted that the theoretical optimal cadence in terms of oxygen cost for most humans is generally lower than that preferred by trained cyclists (> 90 rpm). This generalization requires some specification. First, the gap between the most economical or efficient and preferred cadence is usually narrower in trained cyclists. For instance, Hagberg and colleagues (1981) found both to be close to 90 rpm in trained cyclists. Second, few data in the scientific literature concern the preferred cadence of trained cyclists during actual cycling, although it is consistently assumed to be higher than 90 rpm. Indeed, the latter is only really true for one-hour records in the velodrome. Besides, fixed gears are used in velodrome events. Fixed gears are designed so the rider is constantly forced to move the pedals and might elicit different physiological responses than normal, free gears.

Only one report addressed the preferred pedaling cadence of professional cyclists during three-week races (Lucia, Hoyos, and Chicharro 2001b). Among other findings, the mean preferred cadence of the subjects was shown to range from 70 to 90 rpm, and high variability was shown between subjects and the type of terrain (flat versus uphill). High interindividual variability has also been reported for the preferred cadence of trained cyclists (72 to 102 rpm) during laboratory testing (Hagberg et al. 1981).

Finally, irrespective of the cadence adopted, the oxygen cost of pedaling is largely determined by the percentage distribution of efficient type I fibers in the main muscles involved in cycling—the knee extensor muscles, particularly the *vastus lateralis*—at least in trained cyclists (Coyle et al. 1991, 1992). We could speculate that, in subjects with a particularly high percentage distribution of type I fibers in the knee extensor muscles, the choice of theoretically inefficient/uneconomical cadences (too low or too high) would have a lower impact on the metabolic cost of cycling than would that choice in cyclists with a smaller proportion of this fiber type.

Cadence Optimization

To date, no conclusive statement about cadence optimization in terms of oxygen cost can be made, at least in the case of trained cyclists able to generate high power outputs. More research is needed.

Optimal Cadence and Lactate Production and Clearance

Lactic acid (or more correctly speaking, lactate) is by no means a noxious metabolite of the body or a waste product, as has been erroneously assumed. Lactic acidosis is no longer considered to be a major cause of fatigue in strenuous exercise. So as not to disturb the cyclist's movements during laboratory or field tests, lactate concentration is usually determined in capillary blood through a small puncture in the fingertip or earlobe. Ideally, lactate should be measured in leg muscle fibers through a muscle biopsy obtained with a needle or at least in the femoral vein, which returns the venous blood coming from all the leg muscles back to the heart. The problem is that not many cyclists would enjoy these invasive measurements. More important, however, are the questions, What does blood lactate concentration mean? and, Where does lactate come from or go to?

At least in endurance cycling, lactate is a molecule produced mainly in the fast fibers (or more correctly speaking, type II fibers) of the knee extensors via a fast metabolic pathway, anaerobic glycolysis. The cyclist's legs start to rely on type II fibers and anaerobic glycolysis when the slower aerobic pathways, which operate mainly in type I fibers, are unable to provide all the energy required to generate high power outputs (> 350 or 400 W in trained cyclists). Lactate molecules released into venous blood from type II fibers can reach the heart, which sends them back to the leg muscles via arterial blood. Type I fibers of trained leg muscles have the ability to take up lactate and incorporate it as a fuel for aerobic pathways. During submaximal cycling, blood lactate concentration is an indicator of the balance between lactate production, which occurs in type II fibers, and lactate clearance by type I fibers. It is also an indirect estimator of the recruitment of inefficient type II fibers. In theory, the lower the blood lactate concentration for a given submaximal power output, the better the performance and efficiency, not because of the effects of lactate per se, but rather because of the physiological phenomena it reflects.

Consequently, if high pedaling cadences were less efficient than lower ones for a given power output, one would expect blood lactate to increase with cadence. Some data seem to confirm this. Cox and colleagues (1994) reported that when cadence was increased from 50 to 70 rpm during an incremental test, the power output eliciting a blood lactate concentration of 4 mmol/L of blood was reduced. This finding can be interpreted as an increase in lactate production and in the recruitment of inefficient type II fibers at faster cadences. Other reports seem to confirm that muscle lactate production increases at high cadences for a given power output (Löllgen, Graham, and Sjogaard 1980). Alternatively, a transitory increase in blood lactate at high cadences might reflect the enhanced blood flow associated with high cadences caused by improved venous return to the heart. In this case, increased lactate might not necessarily reflect a decrease in performance. This may suggest an improvement in blood flow and hemodynamics brought about by high cadences.

Optimal Cadence and Hemodynamics/Blood Flow

While numerous studies have analyzed the effects of varying pedaling cadences on oxygen cost, little data exist on the changes in hemodynamics induced by different pedaling cadences. Heart rate (HR) has been frequently monitored and usually shows the same pattern as $\dot{V}O_2$ (Coast and Welch 1985; Michielli and Stricevic 1977; Seabury, Adams, and Ramey 1977). If $\dot{V}O_2$ increases with pedaling cadence, so does HR. In fact, increased HR might explain the higher $\dot{V}O_2$ sometimes associated with fast cadences compared to slower ones, at least at low absolute power outputs. Increments in pedaling cadence activate mechanoreceptors—nerve afferents especially sensitive to limb movement frequency—in working limbs (Rowell and O'Leary 1990). This results in a direct ascending message from mechanoreceptors to cardiorespiratory centers located in the central nervous system aimed at increasing HR and pulmonary ventilation, particularly respiratory frequency. Consequently, $\dot{V}O_2$ also increases since this variable is partly determined by HR and pulmonary ventilation. Increased HR and pulmonary ventilation can explain the feeling of breathlessness and central cardiorespiratory fatigue that some cyclists experience at high cadences, particularly during mountain ascents.

Only one investigation has explored the effects of different cadences on cardiac output, the amount of blood pumped by the heart per minute of exercise, in adult humans (Gotshall, Bauer, and Fahrner 1996). Before explaining the results of this report, we must emphasize that assessing cardiac output is important since this variable determines blood flow, and quadriceps muscles undergo marked blood flow occlusion during the downstroke phase of the crank cycle (Takaishi et al. 2002). Any pedaling cadence, slow or fast, capable of maximizing blood flow to working muscles for a given power output could overcome, at least partly, the inevitable blood restriction brought about by quadriceps muscle contractions and might represent an important physiological advantage. However, which pedaling cadence pattern is able to offer such an advantage?

Gotshall, Bauer, and Fahrner (1996) addressed this question and found that, for a fixed power output of 200 W, the cardiac output of cyclists and blood flow to their quadriceps muscles increases with cadence, from 70 to 110 rpm. Why would high pedaling cadences favor cardiac output and hemodynamics? At higher pedaling cadences, leg muscles contract and relax at a higher frequency. This, in turn, might enhance the effectiveness of the skeletal-muscle pump. Contractions of muscles around leg veins exert a pumping action on these vessels, which have thin walls and facilitate venous blood return. The blood returning to the heart has to overcome the force of gravity. Thus, the faster the pumping effect of skeletal muscles around leg veins is, the quicker the blood returns to the heart. The heart itself is a greatly efficient pump, at the service of exercising muscles. In essence, the more venous-deoxygenated blood the heart receives from muscles at high cadences, the more arterial-oxygenated blood it sends back to them. Although more research is needed, the pioneer findings of Gotshall and coworkers are to be considered, especially by those who work with elite cyclists. If maximal cardiac output and blood availability to working muscles constitute a limiting threshold for top-level performance, then the hemodynamic advantage brought about by fast cadences might compensate for their higher metabolic cost.

Optimal Cadence and Muscular Fatigue

As mentioned, for a given power output, the peak force generated per pedal thrust decreases with increasing pedal frequencies (Faria 1992). This is why high pedaling cadences minimize peripheral muscle fatigue, even if efficiency could actually fall. Though not without its scientific limitations, surface electromyography (EMG) is the best available method for noninvasively estimating muscle fatigue and muscle fiber recruitment during pedaling exercise without disturbing a cyclist's movement. This technique consists of placing surface electrodes on the skin over the working muscles (e.g., the quadriceps) to detect muscle electrical activity. Using this approach, Takaishi and colleagues (1996) showed that those cadences eliciting the lowest peripheral fatigue (80 to 90 rpm) were different from the most economical ones (60 to 70 rpm).

Both factors—lower muscle stress and improved hemodynamics—could contribute to the choice of higher cadences by some trained cyclists, regardless of metabolic cost. In subjects who are not highly trained, minimization of local fatigue rather than economy/efficiency is the main factor determining preferred pedaling cadence (Takaishi, Yasuda, and Moritani 1994). In any case, independent of the cadence pattern adopted, elite cyclists can reduce the work performed by knee extensors by pulling up the pedal crank of the opposite leg (Coyle et al. 1988). This, in turn, might reduce muscular fatigue in knee extensor muscles. The main findings of laboratory research on pedaling cadence is summarized in figures 4.6 and 4.7.

High Cadences

Improved blood flow to working limbs and the minimization of local muscle stress are possible advantages of higher cadences, especially at high absolute power outputs. Both of these advantages could compensate for the theoretically higher oxygen cost of fast cadences and explain the preference for high cadences shown by some trained cyclists.

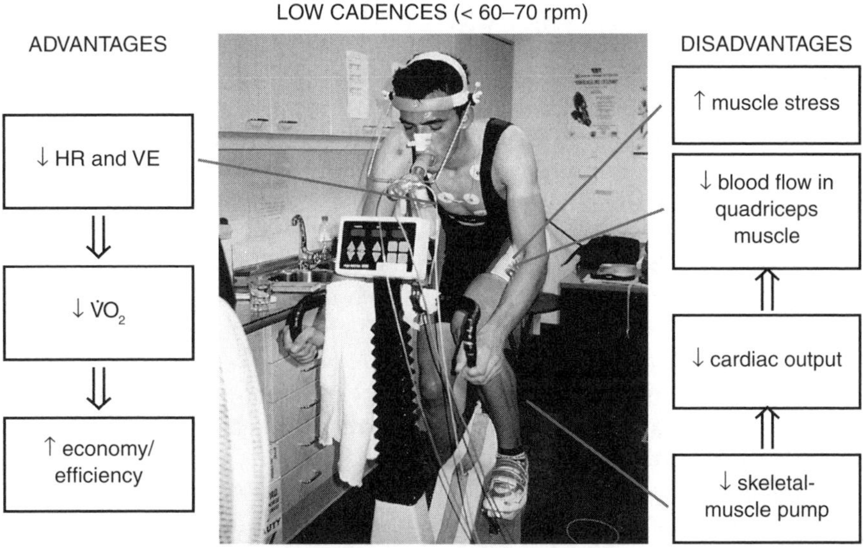

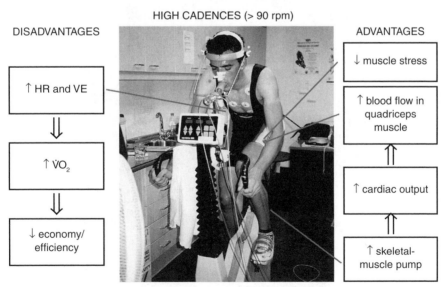

LOW CADENCES (< 60–70 rpm)

ADVANTAGES

- ↓ HR and VE
  ⇓
- ↓ V̇O₂
  ⇓
- ↑ economy/ efficiency

DISADVANTAGES

- ↑ muscle stress
- ↓ blood flow in quadriceps muscle
  ⇑
- ↓ cardiac output
  ⇑
- ↓ skeletal-muscle pump

FIGURE 4.6   Theoretical advantages and disadvantages of low cadences in most individuals. The conclusions shown here are based on research conducted mostly on cyclists not highly trained. HR = heart rate; VE = pulmonary ventilation, that is, the amount of air that is inspired or expired (in L/min).

Photo courtesy of Alejandro Lucía.

HIGH CADENCES (> 90 rpm)

DISADVANTAGES

- ↑ HR and VE
  ⇓
- ↑ V̇O₂
  ⇓
- ↓ economy/ efficiency

ADVANTAGES

- ↓ muscle stress
- ↑ blood flow in quadriceps muscle
  ⇑
- ↑ cardiac output
  ⇑
- ↑ skeletal-muscle pump

FIGURE 4.7   Theoretical advantages and disadvantages of fast cadences in most individuals. The conclusions shown here are based on research conducted mostly on cyclists not highly trained. HR = heart rate; VE = pulmonary ventilation, that is, the amount of air that is inspired or expired (in L/min).

Photo courtesy of Alejandro Lucía.

From the Lab to the Bike

Most studies designed to explore cycling cadence are limited by the fact that subjects were tested in a laboratory setting, in which they rode a stationary cycle ergometer. In the best cases, subjects were tested while riding their own bikes on an ergometer or treadmill. In addition, tests at fixed power outputs have been the exercise model of choice in most field studies. Any cyclist would agree that constant-power tests performed under lab conditions can hardly mimic the continually changing conditions of actual cycling, such as wind resistance, inertia characteristics, level versus uphill roads, or big peloton riding versus drafting behind one or a few cyclists versus riding alone against wind resistance. Not to mention the continual rapid accelerations and decelerations that occur during mass-start races.

In lab studies, cyclists usually are required to remain seated, although many cyclists, especially climbing specialists of low body mass such as Marco Pantani, frequently stand during mountain ascents and constantly switch from sitting to standing. Most early work on preferred cadence was based on untrained or well-trained subjects but not elite cyclists, and even less (or should we say nothing) is known about cadence optimization for

© Jim and Mary Witmer

The changing conditions of an actual road race are difficult to mimic in a laboratory setting.

competitive power outputs above 400 W. What do we know about cadence optimization for standing? What about cadence optimization for the aerodynamic position that elite cyclists typically adopt during time trials?

For these reasons, we should be cautious when trying to extrapolate the often controversial findings of previous lab studies to the real world and when giving advice about cadence patterns to competitive cyclists. Before speaking of cadence optimization in trained riders, first we should establish their preferred cadence under real conditions. In theory, a trained cyclist will adopt spontaneously the optimal cadence. At least, this is the case in distance running: Trained runners spontaneously choose the best possible combination of both stride length and frequency (Anderson 1996). It would also be fair to postulate that given a different musculoskeletal framework, optimal pedaling cadence may differ between men and women.

Preferred Pedaling Cadence in Professional Road Cycling

Today it is quite simple to record pedaling cadence during actual cycling using instruments such as speed meters (some also measure cadence), the SRM power-meter system, or Polar heart rate monitors. The latter were used in a study designed to measure pedaling cadence in professional riders (Lucia, Hoyos, and Chicharro 2001b). Data were taken during the 1999 season from seven subjects participating in one and/or two of the main three-week races for professional cyclists (Giro, Tour, and Vuelta). We analyzed data (means of 15-s intervals) from each subject during the three principal stages of this type of tour race: mass-start flat stages (long, flat parcours ridden at average speeds higher than 40 kph within a large group of cyclists), individual time trials (40 to 60 km on an overall level terrain), and the ascent phases of mass-start mountain stages (high mountain ascents of 7% mean grade ridden at speeds lower than 25 kph either individually or within a small group).

The mean characteristics of the three phases are shown in figure 4.8. During time trials and flat stages, we recorded data throughout the entire stage from start to finish. During mountain stages, we specifically selected only those phases corresponding to the ascent of the mountain passes that are usually assigned to the second part of typical parcours in the Pyrenees, Alps, or Dolomites. (The latter include three to five high mountain passes and descents with some flat terrain between each pass.) This prevented us from obtaining data corresponding to phases (descents or level terrain) that do not reflect specific uphill performance. We selected the core (20- to 40-min duration) of the ascents to the most famous mountain cols in professional road cycling, classified as hors category by race organizations such as Galibier, Tourmalet, and Mortirolo. The proportion of level or low upgrade (< 4%) terrain in several of these mountain roads is null.

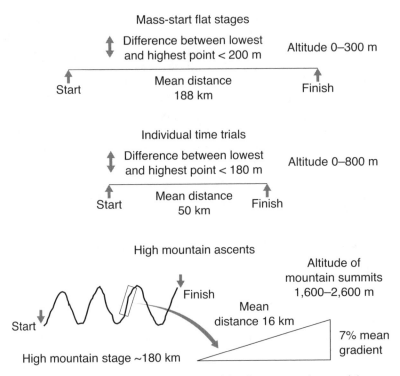

FIGURE 4.8 Average course characteristics of the three main phases of three-week classic stage races (Giro d'Italia, Tour de France, Vuelta a España) in which we studied pedaling cadence.

Adapted, with permission, from A. Lucía, J. Hoyos, and J.L. Chicharro, 2001,"Preferred pedaling cadence in professional cycling,"*Med Sci Sports Exerc* 33:1361-1366.

Mean cadence averaged ~ 70 rpm during mountain ascents and ~ 90 rpm during both flat stages and time trials (see table 4.1). Although it has been assumed that elite cyclists spontaneously adopt fast pedaling cadences (> 90 rpm), such an assumption is not based on actual data, at least when it comes to tour road races. In these competitions, preferred cadences ranged from 70 to 90 rpm. Let us take a closer look at the data.

TABLE 4.1 Average Cadence of Professional Cyclists

	Flat stages, mass start	Individual time trials	High mountain ascents
Pedal cadence (rpm)	89 (80 to 99)	92 (86 to 96)	71 (62 to 80)
Speed (kph)	44 (38 to 51)	47 (44 to 50)	17 (12 to 25)

Data collected during the 1999 season (Giro, Tour, and Vuelta). All values expressed as mean and range (minimum to maximum). The specific characteristics of the different parts of the races are shown in figure 4.8.

Flat Stages

Although mean cadence averaged ~90 rpm, there was high variability among cyclists and within the same cyclists, depending on the different parts of each particular stage. During approximately 16% of the total duration of the stage, cyclists did not have to pedal at all (cadence of 0 rpm). This included several short bouts of less than 1 to 2 min of freewheel cycling randomly interspersed throughout the stage—short descents or brief recovery periods following accelerations of the peloton. Pedaling rates above 110 rpm were recorded during short periods of less than 2 or 3 min and mostly corresponded to abrupt accelerations such as breakaways from the main group and attacks, the last kilometers of the stage, and sprints.

In general, pro cyclists spontaneously adopt fast pedaling rates during the flat stage of tour races. Despite this rather high mean cadence, they still have to push hard gears—53 × 13 to 14 on average to reach a mean speed well above 40 kph—for four or five hours to meet the high requirements of this particular competition phase. Selecting slower pedaling patterns such as 70 rpm would imply the use of extremely high gears (e.g., 55 × 11) for long periods, increasing the risk not only of acute muscle fatigue but also of muscle damage and long-term muscle soreness. In fact, some degree of muscle damage already occurs when pushing more reasonable, but still hard, gears (53 × 13 to 14 on average) at around 90 rpm.

Muscle damage is reflected when components of the muscle cells such as creatine-phosphokinase (CPK) or the protein myoglobin appear in the cyclist's blood. This is what occurs during three-week stage races (Mena, Maynar, and Campillo 1996), indicating that the membranes surrounding muscle cells are literally broken. This is a common finding after exhaustive running, an exercise model that largely involves eccentric muscle contractions. In this type of contraction, muscles try to shorten but are inevitably lengthened. It is what occurs to the quadriceps muscle when the foot hits the ground. Eccentric contractions cause great strain on the membranes and contractile and structural proteins of each muscle fiber.

Leakage of proteins from broken muscle cells would be expected to be uncommon in cycling because cycling involves mainly concentric contractions, which are less traumatic than eccentric ones. However, the speed at which flat stages are covered by the peloton today has increased so much compared to the past—partly because of the higher quality of road surfaces and partly because the peloton is composed of many more riders—that cyclists are forced to push very hard gears to keep the required velocity, independent of their preferred cadence pattern. Cumulative muscle damage from these flat stages, usually held in the first week of competition, may negatively impact performance later in the three-week period, particularly during the two most important race phases, high mountain and time trial stages.

Because fast pedaling rates (90 or more rpm) can require a greater $\dot{V}O_2$ than slower ones, pro riders might not necessarily choose the most efficient pedaling rates, per se. However some of these effects (for example, muscle damage and O_2 cost) are attenuated or exaggerated to some degree given the rider's position in the peloton. Those riding in the peloton would be spared both stresses because of the lower air resistance stress associated with drafting. Those taking the longest pulls or working in breakaway groups would encounter greater stresses. Therefore, optimal pedaling cadence and metabolic cost is further complicated by the rider's position within the team and the rider's goal during a particular stage. This is particularly true in regard to protecting team leaders during long stage events so that they may perform better during unprotected race stages such as climbs and time trials. In any case, the great aerobic endurance of professional riders—for example, their high resistance to fatigue of type I fibers (Lucia et al. 1998)—may partly compensate for the theoretically lower economy of using faster cadences.

Mass Starts

During mass-start flat stages, cyclists tend to pedal at around 90 rpm. This does not preclude that they still must push very hard gears, which greatly strains their quadriceps muscles. Some of these effects may be spared or exaggerated depending on peloton position. Regardless of efficiency considerations, minimizing muscle damage as much as possible by the use of high cadences seems to be a good strategy for these stages, aiding muscle recovery during the second and third weeks of the race.

Individual Time Trials

In individual time trials, mean cadence is approximately 90 rpm. Data were collected from cyclists with different roles on the team; some—for example, climbers or riders whose main role was to work for their leaders—were not required to perform maximally in this competition phase. Time trial specialists, including a former time trial world champion, adopted faster cadences of 90 to 100 rpm. Thus, in road cycling, the general assumption that elite riders prefer cadences between 90 and 100 rpm is only applicable to this specific case. Holders of the one-hour velodrome record over the last years have also adopted fast cadences of 90 to 105 rpm.

Because of technical advances in aerodynamics, time trialists today are able to maintain extraordinarily fast mean velocities, close to 50 kph. As with flat stages, selecting a slower pedaling rate implies the use of extremely high gears during long periods, increasing the risk of muscle damage and tendon injuries. In fact, if one considers the start from zero speed, the curves and short uphills along the course, or the stretches in which the riders must face a strong headwind, all of which tend to decrease mean velocity, it is easy to understand that those who are able to achieve an average performance of ~ 50 kph must ride at about 55 kph for long periods to compensate for these slower bouts. Such high speeds, unimaginable decades ago, can only be reached at pedaling rates greater than 90 rpm. Lower cadences would require the use of extremely hard gears, not to mention the gear needed to pedal at 50 to 60 rpm.

Blood flow in the iliac arteries, which irrigate all leg muscles, can be reduced during hip flexions when time trialists adopt the typical aerodynamic position. This additional limitation for oxygenated blood delivery to working muscles should be considered in further studies dealing with cadence optimization during individual time trials.

Cadence During Time Trials

The average cadence during flat individual time trials is similar to that of mass-start flat stages, that is, about 90 rpm. Top-level time trial specialists have the ability to pedal at a rate in excess of 90 rpm. Independent of efficiency or blood flow considerations, the choice of high cadences is unavoidable; at lower cadences, the strain on muscles and tendons would be very difficult to tolerate.

High Mountain Ascents

During mountain ascents, most riders, including former winners of the Tour de France, pedal at lower cadences (around 70 rpm on average) than during flat parcours. During ascents, cyclists frequently switch from the conventional sitting position to a theoretically less economical standing position that allows them to exert more force on the pedals. Scientific data related to cadence optimization when riding in the standing position is lacking. Given the probable flow restrictions of the iliac arteries in elite cyclists, one could speculate that the less efficient standing position temporarily increases oxygen delivery to working muscles since these arteries cease to be occluded during hip flexions since the angle between trunk and thighs is greater. This is a significant advantage in itself. It may also mean some degree of transient recovery for the muscle fibers that are specifically recruited in the conventional sitting posture.

Exercise intensity during mountain ascents might vary considerably depending on each cyclist's team role. Unlike team leaders or climbing specialists who must perform maximally or near maximally, cyclists with other roles are not required to perform maximally and can adopt more efficient cadences of 60 to 70 rpm at lower speeds. In contrast, the best climbers can attain cadences of 80 rpm, at least in the sitting position.

The physiological explanation for the choice of relatively low cadences during mountain ascents is not apparent. In fact, cyclists could generate similar climbing speeds of around 20 kph on average using light gears (39 × 23 to 25) and high cadences (90 or more rpm), but they usually tend to push harder gears (39 × 17 to 21 and rarely 39 × 23) at about 70 rpm. It could be that the specific conditions of climbing performance—the negative effect of both the force of gravity and rolling resistance—are too demanding for most cyclists to overcome the theoretically higher $\dot{V}O_2$ and HR associated with fast pedaling rates. In addition, it should be considered that the summit of many mountain passes lies at moderate altitude (~ 2000 m). At high altitude, the atmospheric partial pressure of oxygen (PO_2), the main force driving inspired oxygen into the blood after passing through the lungs, considerably decreases. This phenomenon, hypoxia, decreases the $\dot{V}O_2$max in most humans and limits the availability of oxygen to working muscles. This implies that, for the same absolute power output, the relative exercise intensity is higher at high altitude than at sea level. Interestingly, Lance Armstrong's $\dot{V}O_2$max does not seem to be diminished at high altitude, at least up to 1829 m, the height of Colorado Springs (personal observation by Dr. J.T. Kearney, U.S. Olympic Training Center, Colorado Springs). This peculiar physiological capacity could account for his ability to overcome the higher metabolic cost of the use of a much higher cadence than his counterparts.

Economy and Uphill Stages

In most pro riders, average cadence during mountain ascents (around 70 rpm) approaches the range shown to be most economical in previous laboratory studies. Economy may be a limiting factor for uphill performance—except, of course, for Lance Armstrong.

Lance Armstrong

Since 1999, Lance Armstrong has been the only professional cyclist to use very fast cadences (> 90 rpm) for both level and uphill terrains, at least during the most determinant phases of tour races. For example, let's look at his ascent of the Alpe D'Huez (a 14-km climb of 8% mean gradient) in the 2001 Tour de France. This was one of the greatest performances in the history of cycling: 38 min of near-maximal to maximal effort at an estimated mean power output as high as 475 to 500 W! His average speed was 22 kph, which he reached at a mean cadence of ~ 100 rpm using a 39 ×

23 gear. This is a really unusual pedaling pattern for a cycling champion during a mountain climb. During the same ascent, Jan Ullrich used a more common pedaling pattern: 41 × 17 at about 70 rpm (mean speed of 21 kph). Interestingly, Armstrong's position on the seat is more toward the front than the position usually adopted. This increases the angle between the thighs and trunk, which theoretically facilitates blood flow through the iliac arteries.

One of Armstrong's training consultants, Chris Carmichael, claims that Armstrong's muscles were so atrophied and weak after cancer treatment that it was easier for his body to learn cycling again using fast cadences (www.ridefast.com). As we know, fast cadences may be less efficient but they place less mechanical strain on leg muscles. Lance Armstrong's $\dot{V}O_2$max is so high (well above 80 ml/kg/min) (unpublished observations from previous physiological tests at the U.S. Olympic Training Center) that it probably allows him to tolerate the higher metabolic cost of fast cadences. Such a high $\dot{V}O_2$max means that his quadriceps muscles are extremely well trained and demand great amounts of oxygen. In this context, using low cadences at high power outputs is probably not the best strategy because it increases intramuscular pressure during the pedal thrust phase. This can shut off oxygen delivery to working muscles. Except in the determining competition stages, Armstrong's cadence is lower and not so different from that of other riders. This is probably the best approach for him: During the part of a stage or competition when oxygen demands are not high, he does not need to waste energy with inefficient, high pedaling patterns. When required to perform maximally (e.g., at the end of the stage), fast cadences probably offer him the best cost/benefit ratio (higher metabolic cost but lower muscle stress and blood occlusion).

Finally, is Lance Armstrong's approach to cycling optimization the best possible for all elite cyclists? Not necessarily. For example, consider the ascent of Hautacam, a typical mountain of the Tour de France in the Pyrenees, a 17-km climb of ~ 7% mean gradient. In 2000, Armstrong defeated the best climbers in the world, including Marco Pantani, with a pedaling pattern similar to the one he used in Alpe d'Huez a year later (39 × 23 at about 100 rpm). In 1996, Bjarne Riijs won the Tour de France and exhibited a similar, astonishing performance during the ascent of Hautacam. He also defeated the best climbers of the time, including Miguel Indurain. His pedaling pattern, however, was totally different—70 or less rpm. In fact, he used the large (53-tooth!) chain ring. Could anyone argue that the pedaling pattern of the best climber in that particular Tour was not optimal?

To sustain extremely high power outputs of close to 500 W, Lance Armstrong prefers to reduce the strain on his leg muscles at the expense of a higher metabolic cost. This is the cadence he is used to and probably the optimal one for him, given his unusually high $\dot{V}O_2$max. This does not mean that his cadence pattern is optimal for every elite cyclist.

Preferred Pedaling Cadence in Off-Road Cycling

To date, there is little information in the literature concerning the physiological demands of off-road cycling, at least when compared to road cycling. At the time of this writing, several interesting papers that deal with the physiological responses shown by elite mountain bikers (MTB) during actual racing have been submitted but still await publication. Therefore, most of what can be said about cadence optimization for MTB riders is largely speculative.

The exercise intensity of an elite cross-country race is very high and has a marked anaerobic component (unpublished data from physiologists of the MAPEI cycling team). Roughly speaking, the intensity of cross-country races (about two-hours' duration) is similar to that of time trials or mountain ascents for the best road cyclists, that is, at or above 90% of the maximal heart rate (see chapter 10). Furthermore, MTB riders must have the ability to produce very high power outputs during very short periods over the course (for instance, steep climbs). They also have to avoid obstacles constantly, such as ruts and rocks, along the way. Because of these constant, abrupt variations in power output, optimal cadence might vary considerably during the race. On the other hand, power output is likely to be high during actual competitions, and decreased muscle leg stress and optimal blood flow to working limbs are possible advantages associated with high cadences.

Unpublished studies on elite MTB riders show, however, that their average pedaling cadence is considerably lower than that of road cyclists, that is, around 60 rpm. MacRae, Hise, and Allen (2000), working on subelite MTB riders, reported a mean cadence of ~ 70 rpm on an uphill off-road course, similar to that adopted by pro riders in uphill road cycling. Future studies might provide us with clues on cadence optimization for off-road cycling. Compared to road cycling, researchers may encounter marked difficulties when simulating actual off-road cycling, and when transferring laboratory data to the real world. How might actual conditions, such as constant variations in course terrain or ground characteristics (grass versus rocks versus sand) be simulated in the laboratory? For instance, it could be that optimal cadence on grass surfaces is not the same as that required on sandy trails.

Directions for Future Research

Future studies dealing with crank cycle and pedaling cadence optimization should try to focus on elite riders able to generate high power outputs (400 or more W) during long time intervals (20 or more min). They should also mimic actual cycling conditions as closely as possible. Nowadays, this is already possible, since $\dot{V}O_2$ can be measured under field conditions using portable metabolic analyzers (such as the Cosmed or the Aerosport TEEM systems). EMG instruments can also be used during real cycling. And, as we know, power can be accurately measured with the SRM system. Even capillary blood lactate can be estimated using a number of portable lactate analyzers. Thus, cyclists could ride their own bicycles while their best possible cadence or crank pedal system is explored from an integrative perspective: efficiency/economy, muscle stress and muscle fiber recruitment, or lactate production and washout. In fact, one of the biggest challenges for sport scientists interested in elite athletes' performance is to transfer their laboratory data adequately to real conditions.

Finally, biomechanics plays a very important role in cycling studies (the biomechanical aspects of pedaling optimization have been scarcely mentioned in this chapter since they fall outside our field of expertise). Maybe it is time for physiologists and biomechanists to start working together and to speak the same language.

References

Anderson, T. 1996. Biomechanics and running economy. *Sports Med* 22:76-89.

Bassett, D.R., Chester, J.R., Passfield, L., Broker, J.P., and Burke, E.R. 1999. Comparing cycling world hour records, 1967-1996: Modeling with empirical data. *Med Sci Sports Exerc* 31:1665-1667.

Boning, D., Gonen, Y., and Maassen, N. 1984. Relationship between work load, pedal frequency, and physical fitness. *Int J Sports Med* 5:92-97.

Cathcart, E.P., Richardson, D.T., and Campbell, W. 1924. Studies in muscular activity: II The influence of speed on the mechanical efficiency. *J Physiol* 58:355-361.

Chavarren, J., and Calbet, J.A. 1999. Cycling efficiency and pedaling frequency in road cyclists. *Eur J Appl Physiol* 80:555-563.

Coast, J.R., Cox, R.H., and Welch, H.G. 1986. Optimal pedaling rate in prolonged bouts of cycle ergometry. *Med Sci Sports Exerc* 18:225-230.

Coast, J.R., and Welch, H.G. 1985. Linear increase in optimal pedaling rate with increased power output in cycle ergometry. *Eur J Appl Physiol* 53:339-344.

Cox, M.H., Miles, D.S., Verde, T.J., and Nessenthaler, G. 1994. Influence of pedal frequency on the lactate threshold of elite cyclists. *Eur J Appl Physiol* 26:S67.

Coyle, E.F., Coggan, A.R., Hopper, M.K., and Walters, T.J. 1988. Determinants of endurance in well-trained cyclists. *J Appl Physiol* 64:2622-2630.

Coyle, E.F., Feltner M.E., Kautz, S.A., Hamilton, M.T., Montain S.J., Baylor A.M., Abraham L.D., and Petrek G.W. 1991. Physiological and biomechanical factors associated with elite endurance cycling performance. *Med Sci Sports Exerc* 23:93-107.

Coyle, E.F., Sidossis, L.S., Horowitz J.F., and Beltz, J.D. 1992. Cycling efficiency is related to the percentage of type I muscle fibers. *Med Sci Sports Exerc* 24:782-788.

Croissant, P.T., and Boileau, R.A. 1984. Effect of pedal rate, brake load and power on metabolic responses to bicycle ergometer work. *Ergonomics* 27:691-700.

Cullen, L., Andrew, K., Lair, K.R., Widger, M.J., and Timson, B.F. 1992. Efficiency of trained cyclists using circular and non circular chainrings. *Int J Sports Med* 13:264-269.

Faria, I.E. 1992. Energy expenditure, aerodynamics and medical problems in cycling: An update. *Sports Med* 14:43-63.

Gaesser, G.A., and Brooks, G.A. 1975. Muscular efficiency during steady-rate exercise: Effects of speed and work rate. *J Appl Physiol* 38:1132-1139.

Garry, R.C., and Wishart, G.M. 1931. On the existence of a most efficient speed in bicycle pedaling and the problem of determining human muscular efficiency. *J Physiol* 72:425-437.

Gotshall, R.W., Bauer, T.A., and Fahrner, S.L. 1996. Cycling cadence alters exercise hemodynamics. *Int J Sports Med* 17:17-21.

Gueli, D., and Shephard, R.J. 1976. Pedal frequency in bicycle ergometry. *Can J Appl Sport Sci* 1:137-141.

Hagberg, J.M., Mullin, J.P., Giese, M.D., and Spitznagel, E. 1981. Effect of pedaling rate on submaximal exercise responses of competitive cyclists. *J Appl Physiol* 51:447-451.

Henderson, S.C., Ellis, R.W., Klimovitch, G., and Brooks, G.A. 1977. The effect of circular and elliptical chain wheels on steady-rate cycle ergometer work efficiency. *Med Sci Sports Exerc* 9:202-207.

Hue, O., Galy, O., Hertogh, C., Casties, J.F., and Prefaut, C. 2001. Enhancing cycling performance using an eccentric chainring. *Med Sci Sports Exerc* 33:1006-1010.

Hull, M.L., Williams, M., Williams, K., and Kautz, S. 1994. Physiological response to cycling with both circular and noncircular chainrings. *Clinical Sports Medicine* 13:39-73.

Jordan, L., and Merrill, E.G. 1979. Relative efficiency as a function of pedaling rate for racing cyclists. *J Physiol* 296:49-50.

Löllgen, H., Graham, T., and Sjogaard, S. 1980. Muscle metabolites, force, and perceived exertion bicycling at various pedal rates. *Med Sci Sports Exerc* 12:345-351.

Lucía, A., Hoyos, J., and Chicharro, J.L. 2000. The slow component of VO_2 in professional cyclists. *Br J Sports Med* 34:367-374.

Lucía, A., Hoyos, J., and Chicharro, J.L. 2001a. Physiology of professional road racing. *Sports Med* 31:325-337.

Lucía, A., Hoyos, J., and Chicharro, J.L. 2001b. Preferred pedaling cadence in professional cycling. *Med Sci Sports Exerc* 33:1361-1366.

Lucía, A., Pardo, J., Durantez, A., Hoyos, J., and Chicharro, J.L. 1998. Physiological differences between professional and elite road cyclists. *Int J Sports Med* 19:342-348.

MacIntosh, B.R., Neptune, R.R., and Horton, J.F. 2000. Cadence, power, and muscle activation in cycle ergometry. *Med Sci Sports Exerc* 32:1281-1287.

MacRae, H.S-H., Hise, K.J., and Allen, P.J. 2000. Effects of front and dual suspension mountain bike systems on uphill cycling performance. *Med Sci Sports Exerc* 32:1276-1280.

Marsh, A.P., and Martin, P.E. 1997. Effect of cycling experience, aerobic power, and power output on preferred and most economical cycling cadences. *Med Sci Sports Exerc* 29:1225-1232.

Marsh, A.P., and Martin, P.E. 1998. Perceived exertion and the preferred cycling cadence. *Med Sci Sports Exerc* 30:942-948.

Mena, P., Maynar, M., and Campillo, J.E. 1996. Changes in plasma enzyme activities in professional racing cyclists. *Br J Sports Med* 30:122-124.

Michielli, D.W., and Stricevic, M. 1977. Various pedaling frequencies at equivalent power outputs: Effect on heart rate response. *N Y State J Med* 77:744-746.

Neptune, R.R., and Herzog, W. 2000. Adaptation of muscle coordination to altered task mechanics during steady-state cycling. *J Biomech* 33:165-172.

Padilla, S., Mujika, I., Angulo, F., and Goiriena, J.J. 2000. Scientific approach to the 1-h cycling record: A case study. *J Appl Physiol* 89:1522-1527.

Rowell, L.B., and O'Leary, D.S. 1990. Reflex control of the circulation during exercise: Chemoreflexes and mechanoreflexes. *J Appl Physiol* 69:401-418.

Santalla, A., Manzano, J.M., Perez, M., and Lucia, A. 2000. A new pedaling design: The Rotor. Effects on cycling performance. *Med Sci Sports Exerc.* 34:1854-1858.

Schep, G., Bender, M.H.M., Kaandorp, D., Hammacher, E., and de Vries, W.R. 1999. Flow limitations in the iliac arteries in endurance athletes: Current knowledge and directions for the future. *Int J Sports Med* 20:421-428.

Seabury, J.J., Adams, W.C., and Ramey, M.R. 1977. Influence of pedaling rate and power output on energy expenditure during bicycle ergometry. *Ergonomics* 20:491-498.

Takaishi, T., Sugiura, T., Katayama, K., Sato, Y., Shima, N., Yamamoto, T., and Moritani, T. 2002. Changes in blood volume and oxygenation level in a working muscle during a crank cycle. *Med Sci Sports Exerc* 34:520-528.

Takaishi, T., Yamamoto, T., Ono, T., Ito, T., and Moritani, T. 1998. Neuromuscular, metabolic, and kinetic adaptations for skilled pedaling performance in cyclists. *Med Sci Sports Exerc* 30:442-449.

Takaishi, T., Yasuda, Y., and Moritani, T. 1994. Neuromuscular fatigue during prolonged pedaling exercise at different pedaling rates. *Eur J Appl Physiol* 69:154-158.

Takaishi, T., Yasuda, Y., Ono, T., and Moritani, T. 1996. Optimal pedaling rate estimated from neuromuscular fatigue for cyclists. *Med Sci Sports Exerc* 28:1492-1497.

5

Cycling Biomechanics: Road and Mountain

Jeffrey P. Broker

Biomechanics is a bridge discipline linking the life sciences of anatomy, physiology, and biology with the physical sciences of engineering mechanics. Perhaps because an individual riding a bicycle represents a pure integration of human and machine, biomechanists are often drawn to cycling. This attraction is heightened by the relative ease with which the cycling task can be used in a laboratory setting to study musculoskeletal function.

Today, advancements in cycling science continue to expose unique and fascinating aspects of this human/machine system. With the strong growth of mountain biking, the questions and issues surrounding the biomechanics of cycling have become more complex and multifaceted.

In this chapter, we will examine critical scientific findings related to the biomechanics of road and mountain cycling. First, a brief review of the critical foot-pedal interface is presented. Basic concepts of pedal loading will be reviewed, followed by a discussion of the major findings concerning pedaling mechanics over the past 10 years. A particular focus will be the concepts of pedaling quality, the interpretation of pedaling effectiveness, the differences between road and mountain bike pedaling patterns, and the effects of climbing on pedaling technique.

Next, the discussion will turn to the characteristics of the human engine. First, an apparent paradox in how muscles act during pedaling will be introduced. The paradox will be solved by visiting muscle activation patterns and joint moment (torque) profiles, with a close look at the unique and disparate roles played by single-joint (uniarticular) and dual-joint (biarticular) muscle. The discussion concludes with a joint moment comparison of climbing in and out of the saddle followed by some final comments regarding many of the peripheral issues surrounding cycling biomechanics.

The Pedal: A Critical Rider/Bicycle Interface

Bicycle pedals represent two of only five attachment sites between the body and the bicycle. Because the pedals are the primary site of energy transfer from rider to bicycle, and because pedal motion and pedal loading largely establish how a cyclist's legs move and are stressed during pedaling, the pedal naturally becomes a focal point for cycling scientists.

Instrumented Bicycle Pedals

Instrumented force pedals have become the tool of the trade for modern cycling biomechanists. Instrumented pedals were first described by Sharp in 1896. Sharp's unique pedal contained springs mounted between two plates, which deformed under load during pedaling. This deformation caused a marker to scribe an ink trace on a strip of circulating paper mounted below the pedal. Normal forces, those perpendicular to the pedal surface, were recorded, probably for the first time.

Modern-day instrumented pedals are generally of three types: pedal-body strain gauge designs, piezoelectric-based designs, and fixed-shaft strain gauge designs (see figure 5.1). The pedal-body strain gauge design measures pedal loading through extensometric (strain) gauges attached to deformable structural elements in the pedal body (Cavanagh and Sanderson 1986; Hull and Davis 1981; Miller and Seirig 1977; Newmiller, Hull, and Zajac 1988; Soden and Adeyefa 1979). These pedals measure normal (perpendicular) and tangential (fore/aft) forces applied to the pedal surface. Depending on design complexity, they also may provide medial/lateral (side-to-side) forces, the point of load application, and applied moment (or torque) about a vertical axis running through the pedal. More recent variations contain adjustable pedal body elements that permit the evaluation of how pedal cant, rotation, and platform height affect performance and musculoskeletal loading (Wooten and Hull 1992).

Piezoelectric designs contain piezoelectric transducers between two rigid plates within the pedal body (Broker and Gregor 1990; Ericson,

a

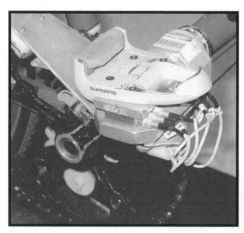

b

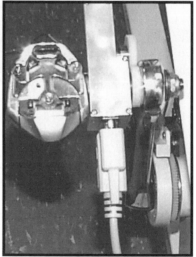

c

FIGURE 5.1   Instrumented pedals for performing biomechanical analyses of cycling. Common variations include the (a) pedal-body strain gauge, (b) piezoelectric transducer, and (c) fixed-shaft strain gauge designs.

Photos courtesy of Jeffrey Broker.

Nissell, and Ekholm 1984). The two transducers permit the determination of the location of the applied load in the medial-lateral plane and applied torque about a vertical axis, in addition to the normal and tangential components of pedal loading. Piezoelectric pedals offer the advantage over strain gauge pedals of higher response to applied loads, simpler calibration capability, and minimal cross sensitivity, meaning that loads applied in one direction do not affect the measurement of loads applied in another direction. These designs, however, require complex signal processing and are more expensive.

Finally, the fixed-shaft strain gauge measures pedal loading at the pedal spindle shaft (Alvarez and Vinyolas 1996; Reiser 2000; Rowe, Hull, and Wang 1998). The pedal spindle is fixed to the pedal body, and strain gauges are placed on the spindle just outboard of the crank. Pedal rotation relative to the crank is maintained by replacing the normal threaded engagement to the crank with a smooth shaft and roller bearing pressed into the crank body. The instrumented pedal and attached spindle remain fixed relative to each other, with rotation occurring at the crank interface. These pedals appear reasonably simple to instrument and calibrate, yet they may be unsuitable for high-load situations because of the crank bearing configuration, and do not currently provide medial-lateral load patterns.

The three instrumented pedal design types offer variable shoe-pedal options, including conventional toe straps, as well as Look, Time, and Shimano clipless interfaces. One design provides for multi-interface compatibility (Wheeler, Gregor, and Broker 1992). Finally, forces measured at the pedal are relatively meaningless if the orientation of the pedal in space or relative to the bike frame is unknown. Therefore, all instrumented pedal designs incorporate some method of measuring pedal angle with respect to the crank. Potentiometers mounted lateral to the pedal body or beneath the pedal body are the customary options. An additional potentiometer is typically mounted near the bottom bracket to measure crank position, usually via a matched set of gears mounted on the left crank arm and fixed to the potentiometer shaft.

Before discussing the information provided by today's instrumented bicycle pedals, it is worth noting a couple of inherent limitations of the common designs. First, all designs incorporate wire bundles that transmit the force and position data from the pedal to the bicycle frame or off the frame to nearby data acquisition modules. These wire bundles are often free hanging (umbilical-like) or attached to the rider's legs.

Second, instrumented pedals are invariably more bulky than actual bike pedals; this is due more to the position-sensing potentiometer requirement than the force-sensing gauges. Potentiometers usually hang below the pedal body or project laterally away from the bike frame. These features and the on-board signal processing requirements render them poorly suited to nonlaboratory applications. Imagine the face of a cycling scientist as his expensive and delicate instrumented pedal slams into the surface of a banked velodrome during banked cornering or strikes a rock on a single-track, off-road trail. Nevertheless, the instrumented pedals developed by Alvarez and Vinyolas (1996) and Rowe, Hull, and Wang (1998) do have on-board data acquisition capabilities and are designed to collect on- and off-road pedaling mechanics data, respectively.

Creative mechanical and electrical engineers are continually challenged to design and build rugged instrumented pedals with miniature force- and position-sensing elements, wireless data transmission (from pedal to frame at least), and lightweight on-board signal processing and storage capabilities.

Basic Concepts of Pedal Loading

A discussion of the more complex interactions between rider and bicycle and their variants across conditions and cycling disciplines would be premature without a basic understanding of pedal loads and their scientific description. Pedal forces are typically measured and described in component terms. The normal force component acts perpendicular to the pedal surface, and the tangential force component acts along the surface of the pedal in the fore/aft direction.

By knowing the pedal angle relative to the bicycle crank, the normal and tangential components can be mathematically resolved into *effective* and *ineffective* components. The effective component acts perpendicular to the bicycle crank and thus drives the crank around in its circle. The ineffective component acts parallel to the crank, and thus performs no useful external work.

Typical normal and tangential force profiles during pedaling are shown in figure 5.2a. Pedal angles measured in combination with these forces are shown in figure 5.2b. The effective and ineffective components associated with these normal and tangential forces are shown in figure 5.3. Focusing on the effective patterns, it becomes clear that effective forces and thus crank torque vary substantially throughout the pedal cycle. Peak torque during level cycling, numerically equal to the product of peak effective force and crank length, occurs roughly when the crank is level and forward, about 100° past top dead center. Further, torque is generally negative during the upstroke, as the effective force acts downward on the rising pedal in this region. Finally, torque is low when the pedal is either at the top or bottom of the pedal cycle, as forces applied to the pedal are low and/or are not directed toward crank rotation.

A more powerful way to see the manner in which pedal forces vary throughout the pedal cycle is in a clock diagram format (see figure 5.4). Here forces applied to the pedal are shown as force vectors (arrows), with lengths proportional to magnitude and directions representative of the manner in which they are applied. The clock diagram clearly shows why crank torque peaks about 100° after top dead center. The forces are very large and are directed nearly perpendicular to the crank. The diagram also highlights the low torque regions at the top and bottom of the pedal cycle (forces are small or are not directed perpendicular to the cranks), as well as the negative torque region during the upstroke.

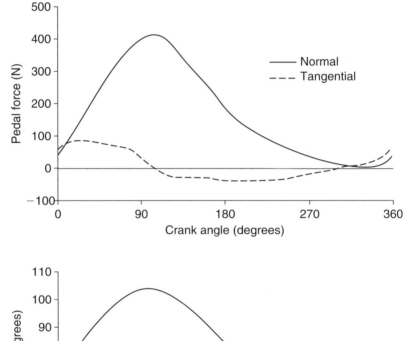

a

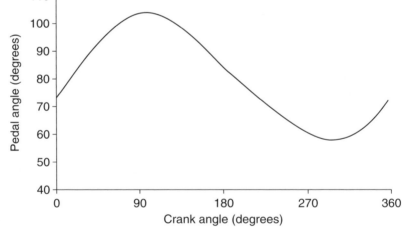

b

FIGURE 5.2 (a) Average normal and tangential components of pedal loading recorded during cycling at 350 W, 90 rpm (n = 17 road riders). Crank angles of 0 and 360° correspond with the pedal at top dead center. The normal and tangential components act perpendicular and parallel to the pedal body surface, respectively. (b) Pedal angle associated with the same riding condition, with 90° representing a flat pedal and angles greater than 90° describing a "heel-down" pedal position.

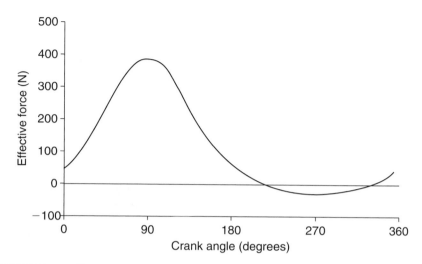

FIGURE 5.3   Effective component of pedal loading, derived from the normal and tangential components. Cyclists are riding at 350 W, 90 rpm ($n = 17$ road riders). The effective always acts perpendicular to the crank, and thus is responsible for generating crank torque. Negative effective forces (between 220 and 320° crank angle) occur during the upstroke as the load on the rising pedal is downward.

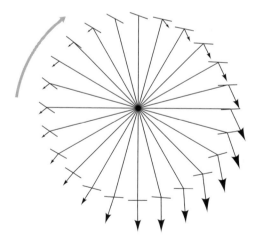

FIGURE 5.4   Cycling clock diagram depicting the direction and magnitude of pedal loading as well as pedal orientation. Note the direction of the arrows through the top and bottom of the pedal cycle. Forces here provide little contribution to developing crank torque.

The Concept of Net Torque

Because the two pedals on a bicycle are connected to each other and the chain ring, net crank torque must be thought of as the combined effect of the forces applied to each pedal. Net crank torque varies during the pedal cycle (see figure 5.5). Two distinct peaks are evident, corresponding to the right and left pedal downstrokes, respectively. Peak net torque usually is slightly less than single-pedal peak torque, as the upstroke pedal exhibits negative torque while its upstroke counterpart experiences its greatest torque. Two distinct minima in net crank torque also are evident, occurring shortly after the pedals pass through their respective top dead centers. These minima occur because effective forces on both pedals, acting forward on the higher pedal and rearward on the lower pedal, are typically low.

At first glance, it is easy to misinterpret the net torque pattern shown in figure 5.5. Recall that the net torque pattern during the first half of the pedal cycle (the left side of figure 5.5) represents the combined effect of the right pedal force pattern during its downstroke plus the left pedal force pattern during its upstroke. When one of the two net crank torque peaks is larger than the other, it could mean that the forces applied to the pedal during the downstrokes are larger on one side than they are on the other (the traditional, or lay, interpretation). However, the peak torque difference may also be due to different pedal force magnitudes during the upstrokes. In other words, the apparent asymmetry could be an upstroke imbalance instead of a downstroke imbalance.

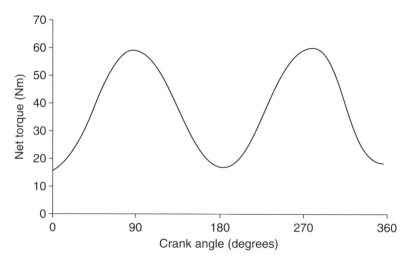

FIGURE 5.5   Average total crank torque (combined, both pedals) at 350 W, 90 rpm ($n = 17$ road riders). Distinct peaks correspond with the right and left pedal downstrokes. Minima occur when the cranks are near vertical, as forces driving the cranks around in this region are small.

Asymmetry interpretation may seem trivial, but several commercially available devices for both indoor training and outdoor riding advertise the ability to assess pedaling technique asymmetry. Quantification of net crank torque derived from chain ring, rear hub, or chain tension measurements seemingly opens the door to such assessments, as do measurements of torque oscillation on indoor trainers. Figure 5.6a shows a hypothetical net crank torque profile for a cyclist riding at 250 W (90 rpm). The first peak, which

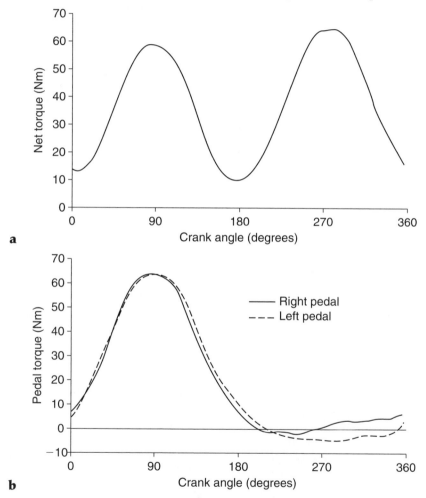

FIGURE 5.6   *(a)* Hypothetical total crank torque profile (both pedals) for a given cyclist riding at 350 W, 90 rpm. Note the different magnitude of the two torque peaks—the first peak occurs during the right pedal downstroke, and the second peak occurs during the left pedal downstroke. At first glance, this would appear to suggest a right leg weakness in the downstroke. *(b)* Independent crank torque profiles used to generate the total profile in 5.6a, showing the asymmetry to be an upstroke effect. Because the negative torque on the left pedal during the upstroke is so great, the combined torque (right plus left) in this region of the pedal stroke is reduced.

occurs during the right pedal downstroke, is noticeably smaller than the second. Does this indicate a relative weakness of the right leg extensors? Should the cyclist being tested train the right side harder to correct the imbalance?

No. Examination of the independent pedal torques (figure 5.6b) reveals that the asymmetry does not originate from an imbalance in downstroke applied forces. Rather, the cyclist is actually more active during the upstroke on the right pedal (which occurs during the downstroke on the left). As such, the negative torque developed on the right pedal during the left pedal downstroke (right side of figure 5.6b) counteracts the positive left pedal torque less than the negative torque developed on the left pedal a half revolution later counteracts the right pedal downstroke torque. If a weakness-based imbalance does exist, it is in the left leg (hip and knee flexors) during the upstroke, and not in the right leg. The source of an apparent net crank torque asymmetry cannot be isolated by measuring only net crank torques or externally measuring bicycle power output. Instrumented pedals or independent measurement of both right and left cranks (e.g., using strain gauges on both crank arms) are required to fully isolate pedaling asymmetries.

Cycling Power Versus Net Crank Torque

Cycling power will be discussed in more detail in chapter 6, but let's briefly examine the relationship between net crank torque and bicycle power. Mathematically, instantaneous bicycle crank power (P_c), or that derived from the leg muscles and delivered to the pedal, is the product of the instantaneous crank torque (T_c) and instantaneous crank angular velocity (ω_c).

$$P_c = T_c \times \omega_c$$

Both of these quantities can be measured using instrumented pedals. Net crank torque T_c equals the sum of the two independent pedal torques, each calculated by multiplying the dual pedal effective force magnitudes by the crank arm lengths. Crank angular velocity is determined by differentiating crank angle with respect to time.

Practically speaking, crank angular velocity is reasonably constant during steady state cycling at cadences above 80 rpm. Under such conditions, instantaneous crank power can be estimated by multiplying the instantaneous crank torque by the average crank angular velocity in radians per second. If the cadence (CAD) in revolutions per minute is known, the equation takes the following form:

$$P_c = T_c \times CAD \times 2\pi/60$$

Figure 5.7 shows the instantaneous total power profile for road cyclists ($n = 17$) riding at an average power output of 350 W (90 rpm). Note that power oscillates between nearly 600 and 110 W during a single pedal revolution. These fluctuations of power delivery to the rear wheel characterize normal pedaling, create the often heard rhythmic beat of an indoor wind-

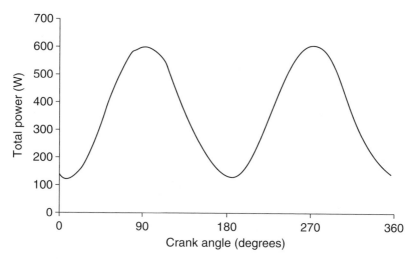

FIGURE 5.7   Average instantaneous crank power associated with riding at 350 W, 90 rpm (*n* = 17 road riders). Crank power varies substantially during the pedal stroke, with minima occurring when the cranks are near vertical.

load trainer, and are useful in comparing cycling disciplines and conditions and perhaps understanding pedaling quality.

Effective Versus Ineffective Forces

Many cycling coaching publications, magazines, and equipment manufacturers continue to directly or indirectly mischaracterize the dual role of the interactive forces between the pedal and foot. Therefore, we will visit this issue.

Researchers introduced the terms *effective forces* and *ineffective forces* to cycling in the 1980s, and subsequently began using them to describe pedaling quality (Cavanagh and Sanderson 1986; LaFortune and Cavanagh 1983). This seemed natural, given the direct relationship between the effective force profile and the work done at the pedal by the cyclist. These researchers suggested or implied that ineffective forces (those parallel to the crank) do no useful work and therefore represent wasted energy. More recently, although most cycling biomechanists have revised their interpretation of effective and ineffective forces, manufacturers of novel cycling transmission systems seem to have adopted the premise. The problem with this approach is that the spinning leg/foot/crank and pedal system generates forces independent of muscular work.

Consider a cyclist sitting on a bicycle with the pedals stationary. Both pedals will experience forces as the weight of the legs act downward through the pedal bodies. If the pedals are at the top and bottom of the pedal cycle, the forces largely would act along the axis of the cranks; the forces on the upper pedal would tend to compress the crank, and the forces on the lower pedal would tend to lengthen the crank. The question arises: Are these forces "wasted"? Since no muscular work is required to maintain the system in this configuration, the answer must be no.* The pedals actually serve to maintain the positions of the limbs in space, preventing them from extending toward the ground.

Now consider the normal pedaling condition, characterized in clock diagram form in figure 5.4 (page 125). Large downward-directed forces are applied to the pedal at the bottom of the pedal stroke. These forces, often labeled *ineffective* in that they act to lengthen the crank and do not assist in propelling the crank, are predominately generated by the interaction between the pedal and the lower limb. The pedal supports and changes the movement direction of the leg without active muscular contractions. If a cyclist were instructed to pedal in such a way that these forces were minimized or eliminated altogether, significant muscle work would be required and no additional bicycle power would result. Thus, these forces acting along the axis of the cranks at times are often highly functional.

Kautz and Hull (1993) presented a method to separate these naturally occurring components of pedal loading from the total (or measured) pedal load. Doria and Lot (2001) introduced a similar technique using "generalized torques" to separate the muscular-based torque applied to the bicycle cranks from measured torque. The natural component of pedal loading is generated by gravitational and inertial forces acting on the leg and thus is nonmuscular.

The measured, fundamental (nonmuscular), and muscular components of pedal loading computed for a cyclist pedaling at 400 W at roughly 120 rpm are presented in figure 5.8. The measured pedal load (figure 5.8a) exhibits the typical pattern described—downward during the downstroke and through the bottom of the pedal cycle and still downward (and thus opposing crank rotation) during the upstroke. Also, through the top of the pedal cycle, the measured pedal load is quite small here, directed nearly straight upward, and thus does not act to propel the crank.

Natural pedal loads that arise from gravitational and inertial effects are shown in figure 5.8b. A substantial portion of the measured downward loading at the bottom of the pedal cycle (figure 5.8a) is in fact due to gravity and inertia and not muscular actions. Later, during the upstroke, the measured forces that act downward on the pedal also are gravity and inertia based; that is, the cyclist is not actively pushing down.

---

* In actuality, it does take a very small amount of muscular energy to hold the cranks in a purely vertical orientation. The minimum potential energy state of the legs during the pedal cycle is achieved when the cranks are approaching vertical with the lower pedal 20 to 25° before bottom dead center and the upper pedal 20 to 25° before top dead center.

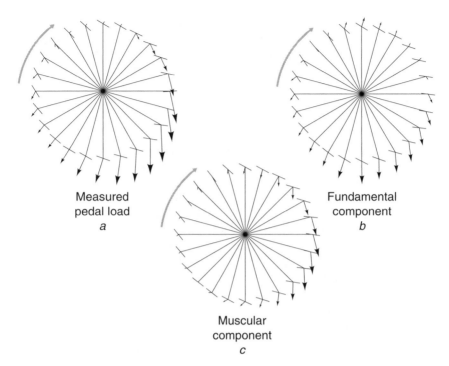

Measured
pedal load
a

Fundamental
component
b

Muscular
component
c

FIGURE 5.8   Clock diagrams illustrating the *(a)* measured, *(b)* natural (nonmuscular), and *(c)* muscular components of pedal loading for an elite U.S. National Team
cyclist. The muscular and natural components sum to create the measured load. The
natural component is derived from the inertial and gravitational effects present
during pedaling, and thus arises at no cost to the rider.

The muscular component of pedal loading (figure 5.8c) represents more
of what the cyclist perceives. Muscular actions drive downward during
the first half of the cycle, rearward through the bottom, and upward during recovery. Despite muscle actions, however, the gravitational and inertia-
based pedal forces produce the seemingly ineffective pedal forces. Note
that this particular cyclist generates virtually no forward-directed forces at
the top of the pedal cycle, and thus could benefit from improving this aspect of her pedaling.

Pedaling Mechanics—Observations From 10 Years of Testing

More than 150 pedaling mechanics tests have been performed by the U.S.
Olympic Committee since 1992. These tests have included more than 125
cyclists from road, track sprint, track endurance (e.g., pursuit), mountain,
triathlon, and even disabled sports (principally below-knee amputees). The
data set contains many riders at the peak of the international cycling community. Several important observations have been made.

Circular Pedaling. Cyclists may move their feet in circles during pedaling, but applied force and developed torque in no way appears circular. The clock diagram (figure 5.4, page 127) clearly illustrates how pedal forces and torque vary during a pedal cycle. However, as described in the discussion of gravitational, inertial, and muscular contributions to pedal loading, the muscular component of pedal force does somewhat represent pedaling circularity. The direction of pedal force application throughout the cycle, derived from muscle contributions, is nearly perpendicular to the crank throughout the entire pedal cycle. However, the magnitude of the forces applied at various stages within the cycle is far from equal.

To give cyclists a feel for greater torque production at the top and bottom of the pedal cycle, and so they can experience a "lighter" upstroke, we occasionally have them pedal with one leg on the laboratory simulator. Force application patterns become much more circular, as there is a mechanical necessity to truly lift the pedal during the upstroke and drive the pedal forward and backward through the top and bottom of the pedal stroke, respectively. Single-leg pedaling on fixed indoor trainers and during riding has often been recommended to cyclists who develop low crank torque (or low effective forces) through the top and bottom of the pedal stroke.

Power Cranks™ are specially designed bicycle cranks that contain a clutch at the connection to the bottom bracket spindle. They introduce an interesting circular version of pedaling. The right and left cranks essentially are independent of each other because of a slip-clutch that creates engagement between the cranks and the crank spindle only during forward pedaling. One pedal can be rotated forward while the other remains stationary. The cranks can be rotated at the same angular velocity but at various phasing relative to each other (other than the normal 180° separation). Or the cranks can be pedaled normally (180° apart). The clutch, however, eliminates the connection between cranks, and thus the descending pedal does not lift the ascending pedal. Simply put, the legs must apply positive torque throughout the pedal cycle to maintain the relative phasing between the two pedals.

Marketing claims surrounding these cranks include enhanced pedaling efficiency (work output/metabolic expenditure). However, the premise for enhanced efficiency appears partially based on the effective versus ineffective force argument. Elimination of forces not acting perpendicular to the cranks is not necessarily economical. The manufacturers also claim that the circular pedaling requirement associated with independent leg action is more natural. Scientific testing of these cranks under various experimental conditions will be required to evaluate these claims and isolate the true effects. Relative to the U.S. Olympic Committee's cycling service program, Power Cranks™ do create a pedaling environment that facilitates more effective use of the top and bottom of the pedal cycle in torque generation, as well as lightness (reduced counterproductive torque) during the upstroke. Whether cyclists should always train and compete on the Power Cranks™ has yet to be determined.

Elite Versus Recreational Cyclist Pedaling Technique.   Cyclists of all abilities exhibit negative effective forces (i.e., forces applied to the pedal perpendicular to the crank but in opposition to crank rotation) during the upstroke (180 to 360°) in steady state cycling (figure 5.4, page 125). As we have recognized at the Olympic training center, cyclists correctly sense that they lift or pull the leg up during recovery but do not lift the leg as fast as the pedal is rising. Thus, the pedal actually helps lift the leg.

Compared to recreational cyclists, elite cyclists generally have reduced negative force effectiveness during the upstroke, and typically the region of the upstroke during which they exhibit these negative effective forces is reduced. Usually, this counterproductive region is reduced by the cyclist generating positive effective force early in the upstroke (past the bottom of the pedal cycle) and before the pedal reaches the top of the cycle. The magnitude of the negative effective forces during the upstroke increases—gets more negative—as cadence increases (the pedal rises faster). Effective forces during the upstroke are less negative and less counterproductive at higher work rates (cycling power) for a given cadence, and may even be positive during sprinting and climbing.

© Empics

Elite cyclists display reduced negative force effectiveness during the upstroke, compared to recreational cyclists.

Aerodynamic Positioning Modifies Pedaling Style. Before the 1996 Olympics, U.S. cyclists participated in numerous wind tunnel and on-track evalua- tions of aerodynamic form. The testing sought to identify rider/bike con- figurations that minimized aerodynamic drag. Cyclists reported their comfort with various positions, as well as their perceived ability to deliver power effectively to the pedals.

These tests were supplemented with pedaling mechanics evaluations using the Olympic Committee's instrumented force pedals. Each athlete's sensitivity to aero positioning was evaluated. Many cyclists did not exhibit pedaling mechanics sensitivity to aero positioning—that is, their mechan- ics did not change as they moved from a traditional road racing position into a flat-back, time trial position. However, some cyclists did exhibit a degradation of their mechanics when moved into the aero position. These cyclists usually possessed limited hip flexibility or experienced contact between their thighs and their torsos when rotated into the flat-back posi- tion. If an athlete demonstrated sensitivity to aerodynamic position, coun- termeasures (typically geometry changes) were introduced to regain normal pedaling form.

Triathlon was added as a medal sport to the 2000 Olympics. We began working with triathletes to improve their overall pedaling form and inte- grate them more effectively with their bicycles. Part of this integration in- volved checking their sensitivity to aerodynamic positioning.

When pedaling mechanics sensitivity to aero positioning arises, it usu- ally takes the form depicted in figure 5.9. The most obvious effect is a re- duction in crank torque through the top of the pedal cycle. In essence, the flat-back position turns some cyclists into "mashers." This can be explained by the shortened position of the hip flexors, which are responsible for torque generation through the top of the pedal cycle, and passive resistance to hip flexion in the aero position. A related effect, for those demonstrating aero position sensitivity, is slightly larger counterproductive pedal forces on the upstroke pedal in the aero position.

For cyclists demonstrating sensitivity, our typical course of action is a small bicycle geometry change directed toward opening up the hip angle (i.e., moving the hip into a more extended position throughout the pedal cycle). This can be done by moving the saddle slightly forward and up, within rule restrictions.

As a final note, Browning (1991) studied the impact of fore/aft saddle positioning on joint torques in elite triathletes. Browning was particularly interested in the effect of the popular triathlon time trial position on mus- culoskeletal loading. As might be expected, the flat-back position accom- panied by a forward seat position shifted the work of pedaling slightly toward the knee extensors, and thus slightly away from the hip extensors. Therefore, aerodynamic positioning involves more than just a reorienta- tion of the body above the bicycle.

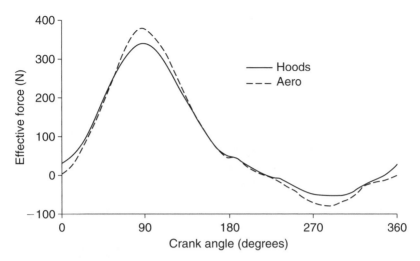

FIGURE 5.9   Average effective force profiles for an elite triathlete pedaling in two different positions: seated upright with his hands on the brake hoods and in an aerodynamic position employing aero handlebars and a flat-back posture. The cyclist is riding at approximately 250 W, 90 rpm. Differences are most evident through the top of the pedal cycle (0 and 360° crank angle) and during the upstroke (right). Greater force is required during the downstroke while in the aero position to offset the negative effects in the other regions.

Discipline Differences.   During our 10 years of pedaling mechanics testing, we noticed that some elite mountain bikers exhibited markedly more uniform pedaling (generating larger effective forces at the top and bottom of the pedal cycle) than cyclists in other disciplines. Similar observations of sprinters revealed the opposite—they seemed to employ a "mashing" style, generating the most torque during the downstroke. Recently we organized our large multiyear data set and set out to quantitatively test for differences in pedaling technique across five cycling disciplines: road, track sprint, track endurance (pursuit), mountain, and triathlon (Broker, Crawley, and Coughlin 2002).

Virtually every rider tested over the past 10 years was evaluated under a common cycling condition, 90 rpm and 250 W. Some riders also were tested at 90 rpm and 350 W. Included in the comparison data set were 86 riders (male and female)—20 road, 23 mountain, 15 track sprint, 8 track pursuit, and 20 triathlon. The following four measures were used to evaluate pedaling style differences:

1. Percentage of work performed in the top quadrant of the pedal stroke (45° before top dead center to 45° after top dead center)
2. Percentage of work performed in the bottom quadrant of the pedal stroke (45° before bottom dead center to 45° after bottom dead center)

3. Peak-to-peak power oscillation
4. Peak effective force

Measures 3 and 4 were expressed relative to average power output (W/W and N/W, respectively).

An analysis of variance with post hoc follow-up statistical testing exposed interesting differences among the disciplines. As expected, sprinters emerged as the mashers of the pedaling community, exhibiting greater downstroke peak effective forces than other disciplines. Road and mountain riders appeared to perform greater work in the top quadrant than riders in other disciplines, but these differences were only statistically significant in the 90 rpm/350 W condition (see figure 5.10). No significant differences were seen in work production through the bottom quadrant of the pedal cycle. Finally, peak-to-peak power oscillation differed among disciplines, with mountain and road riders exhibiting significantly lower-magnitude oscillations than sprint and triathlon riders at the high power condition (see figure 5.11).

The differences observed could be due to many factors. First, the groups are different anthropometrically. In particular, sprinters clearly have more massive leg musculature than road and mountain riders. Since gravitational and inertial components of pedal loading can be significant, leg mass differences among the riders of different disciplines may impact pedaling technique at the pedal.

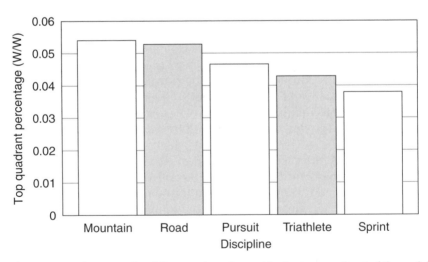

FIGURE 5.10 Amount of pedaling work performed in the top quadrant of the pedal cycle (45° before the top to 45° after), displayed across five different cycling disciplines. Cyclists at 350 W, 90 rpm. Road and mountain riders are more effective at delivering energy to the cranks through the top of the pedal cycle than are pursuers, triathletes, and sprint cyclists.

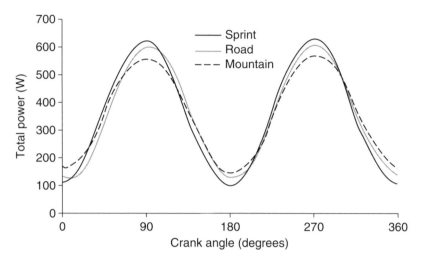

FIGURE 5.11   Average total (right plus left pedal) power oscillations for mountain, road, and sprint riders. Cyclists are pedaling at 350 W, 90 rpm. Mountain and road cyclists pedal more uniformly, resulting in lower peak-to-peak oscillations in total pedaling power.

Second, in general, triathletes were new to competitive cycling, often coming from swimming or running backgrounds. Lack of exposure to cycling, and possibly an interaction with their running muscular development, may explain why their technique differs from that of road cyclists.

Finally, mountain riders spend considerable time climbing in loose soil, which requires avoiding high oscillations in power delivery to the rear wheel. As such, more "circular" pedaling styles for mountain riders may represent a highly functional adaptation and skill. We now recommend off-road training to riders with poor pedaling skills.

Pedal Forces During Mountain Biking

Mountain racers exhibit more uniform pedaling technique (i.e., more constant net crank torque) than cyclists in other disciplines as measured in the laboratory. Whether mountain racers employ these techniques while riding on single-track trails is unknown. If the premise that mountain racers acquire these skills because of exposure to conditions requiring more uniform torque generation—such as climbing in loose soil—is true, then we would certainly expect these pedaling skills to emerge off road, and perhaps even more so.

Rowe, Hull, and Wang (1998) designed and fabricated an instrumented pedal incorporating a mountain bike shoe/pedal interface and on-board data acquisition and storage. Wire bundles carry the pedal force and position transducer signals up the rider's legs to a data logger in a fanny pack.

This pedal system effectively removes the instrumentation system from the laboratory, allowing the measurement of pedal forces during off-road riding.

Rowe, Hull, and Wang reported exemplary data describing mountain bike pedaling mechanics for level riding in the saddle at 90 rpm and 250 W. The data, although not resolved into effective and ineffective components, substantially resembles what has been measured in the laboratory under similar conditions. These researchers also presented pedal forces during coasting over a bumpy track. Future work with pedals such as these, including the evaluation of climbing in loose or hard-packed conditions, powered cornering, and even descents, will yield valuable information concerning the differences and similarities among road, track, and off-road cycling.

Climbing Versus Standing: Observations at the Pedal

So far our discussion of pedaling mechanics has focused solely on steady state cycling while in the saddle. An interesting question concerns the mechanics at the pedal during climbing, both in and out of the saddle. Caldwell and colleagues (1998) set out to evaluate the mechanics of climbing using an instrumented force pedal identical to that described by Broker and Gregor (1990). These researchers had cyclists pedal a Velodyne cycling simulator mounted on a stationary treadmill with an adjustable grade. Cyclists pedaled both in and out of the saddle during simulated climbing, at an average power level of 294 W up an 8% grade.

According to Caldwell and colleagues, standing climbing differed from seated climbing in several ways. First, as might be expected, cadences during climbing were lower than during level cycling at the same power level (65 versus 82 rpm). No significant differences in cadence were observed between seated and standing climbing. Second, standing cycling involved dramatically higher peak pedal forces and peak effective forces, which occurred later in the downstroke. Presumably because of forward positioning of the hips and full body weight application to the pedals during each downstroke, effective forces reached 131% of those seen in seated climbing. Third, forces during standing climbing within the upstroke were still counterproductive (opposed crank rotation) and larger in magnitude than those seen in seated climbing. Fourth, pedal angles were shifted by 15 to 35° depending on the point in the pedal cycle, in response to a more toes-down ankle posture. Finally, torque generation through the top and bottom of the pedal cycle was virtually nonexistent in standing climbing.

It should be mentioned that these standing climbing experiments were conducted on a fixed-fork simulator that did not allow the lateral bicycle motions commonly seen in real-world climbing. Nevertheless, as the researchers pointed out, pedal forces were substantially similar to those reported in a limited sample study involving on-road measurement of pedal forces (Alvarez and Vinyolas 1996). More testing will be required to fully evaluate the use of upper extremity forces and bicycle movement during climbing.

The Cycling Engine

Few would question the relative dominance of the legs in providing energy to propel a bike. To the attentive observer, the legs extend and flex in a rhythmic pattern during pedaling. As the legs extend during the downstroke, muscle power is presumably derived from the hip, knee, and ankle extensors. Half a cycle later, during the upstroke, muscle power is presumably derived from the hip, knee, and ankle flexors. And in the general sense, this is what occurs.

But a quick review of the muscles responsible for these actions brings to light an apparent pedaling paradox. In particular, the rectus femoris, a knee extensor, also flexes the thigh; the hamstrings, which extend the hip, also flex the knee; and the gastrocnemius, an ankle plantar flexor, also flexes the knee. These biarticular muscles seemingly act in curious ways during pedaling. When they act, they complement or provide the energy for one joint's action (e.g., hip extension during the downstroke, via action of the hamstrings), while simultaneously countering the action at an adjacent joint (e.g., the hamstrings acting to flex the knee in the presence of knee extension during the downstroke). Thus, mechanical energy production, management, and delivery to the pedal during cycling is not so straightforward. Since the energetic demands on the leg muscles are relevant to our understanding of muscle roles in cycling, as well as muscle training and injury, a further look into the demands on lower extremity muscles and their relationship to cycling energetics is warranted.

Muscles Drive the System

Perhaps the most straightforward method of determining the contributions made by muscles to pedaling is via electromyography (EMG). EMG involves monitoring the electrical activity of muscles, usually by attaching small electrodes to the surface of the skin. Muscle activation patterns measured in experienced cyclists (Ryan and Gregor 1992) have been used to define how single-joint (uniarticular) and two-joint (biarticular) muscles act during cycling. Specifically, Ryan and Gregor measured activity patterns (EMG) in 10 leg muscles in 18 experienced cyclists during cycling at 90 rpm and 250 W. The uniarticular muscles monitored were the gluteus maximus, vastus lateralis, vastus medialis, long head of biceps femoris, and soleus and tibialis anterior. The biarticular muscles monitored included the hamstrings (semimembranosus and semitendinosus), the rectus femoris, and the gastrocnemius.

Activation timing of these muscles is depicted in figure 5.12. For ease in interpreting the activation periods of these muscles, keep in mind a 22° right shift in actual muscle force generation when viewing the EMG data in figure 5.12. This shift accounts for a time delay (commonly termed electromechanical delay or EMD) between the initiation of measured electrical drive and the onset of muscle force. A delay of 40 msec has been used here, representing a range of EMD values reported for fast and slow muscle types under both concentric and eccentric actions. This delay corresponds to 22° of crank rotation at 90 rpm. Thus, figure 5.12 generally shows the electrical activation present 22° before the corresponding force-generating periods of the muscles indicated.

Ryan and Gregor noted that the uniarticular muscles (gluteals, vastii, and soleus) assume a relatively invariant role as primary power producers during cycling. Note how activation periods for these muscles correspond with the corresponding joint actions these muscles produce (hip extension for the gluteals, knee extension for the vastii, and ankle plantar flexion for the soleus). Conversely, the biarticular muscles (hamstrings, rectus femoris, and gastrocnemius) behave differently and with greater variability. These muscles appear to be active to transfer energy between joints at critical times in the pedaling cycle, much like guide wires in a multilink mechanical system.

A deeper understanding of muscle coordination in cycling can be gained by examining the joint moments or torques at the hip, knee, and ankle during pedaling (figure 5.13). These moments are derived through an inverse dynamic analysis of the rider/bicycle system. The dynamic analysis is termed "inverse" because external forces (at the pedal) and skeletal motions are measured, and then the resultant joint moments required to balance the lower extremity link-segment model are computed.

Several critical features should be gleaned from figure 5.13. First, during the downstroke (0 to 180°), the hip, knee, and ankle predominantly exhibit extensor moment patterns. That is, the hip, knee, and ankle extensor muscles act to forcefully extend these joints or counterbalance loads tending to flex these joints at the ankle as the pedal descends. Note that positive joint moments at the knee represent extensor moments, while positive moments at the ankle and hip represent flexor moments at these joints (plantarflexor at the ankle). This should not be a great surprise, particularly given the EMG patterns previously described and the obvious extension seen in the lower extremity during the downstroke. Note, however, that only the knee joint appears to exhibit a significant moment at the top and early in the pedal cycle.

Second, the extensor moment at the knee terminates and switches to a flexor moment roughly 125° into the pedal cycle, well before the leg is fully extended. Here, despite ongoing knee extension, the net effect of muscle actions about the knee is to oppose this extension. Still, the knee extends. This phenomenon was first described by Gregor, Cavanaugh, and LaFortune (1985) as a variant of Lombard's paradox.[*] Functionally, this flexor moment redirects the pedal load from downward to rearward, a more effective crank loading situation.

[*] Lombard's paradox originally referred to muscle actions during rising from a chair. The functions of the biarticular rectus femoris, hamstrings, and gastrocnemius appear paradoxical because of their conflicting actions at the hip, knee, and ankle during this movement (Lombard 1903).

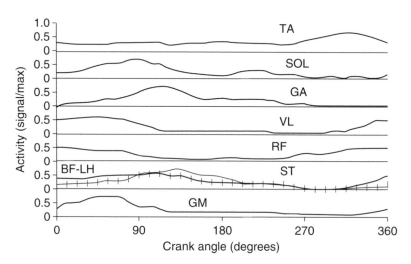

FIGURE 5.12   Muscle activation patterns for eight lower-extremity muscles monitored during cycling at 250 W, 90 rpm. Muscles represented include tibialis anterior (TA), soleus (SOL), gastrocnemius (GA), vastus lateralis (VL), rectus femoris (RF), the long head of the hamstrings biceps femoris (BF-LH), semitendinosis (ST), and gluteus maximus (GM).

Adapted, by permission, from Ryan, M.M. and Gregor, R.J. 1992, "EMG profiles of lower extremity muscles during cycling at constant workload and cadence," *J Electromyogr Kinesiol* 2(2):69-80.

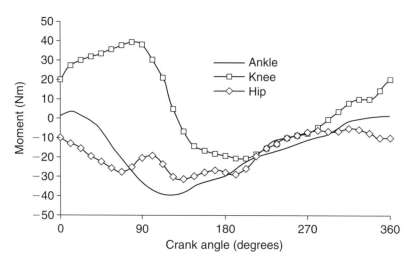

FIGURE 5.13   Average net joint moment (or torque) patterns at the hip, knee, and ankle for a cyclist riding at 250 W, 90 rpm. Positive torques are flexor at the hip, extensor at the knee, and dorsiflexor at the ankle.

Third, during the upstroke, moments at the hip are first extensor and then flexor as the pedal approaches the top of the pedal cycle. The hip moment acts counter to hip joint motion early in the upstroke. The reverse is true at the knee, where flexor moments are present early in the upstroke, followed by an extensor moment as the pedal nears the top. The knee moment in the upstroke generally acts in the same direction as the knee joint motion, first flexing early and then extending late. (The knee begins extending before the pedal reaches the top of the cycle, as the lower segment of the leg swings forward beneath a relatively stationary thigh.)

Finally, the ankle moment is plantar flexor throughout the upstroke until the last 35 to 45°, as it largely opposes, and thus controls, the slight dorsiflexor motion observed. The magnitude of this moment, however, becomes very small during the last 90° of the pedal cycle.

Comparing EMG and Joint Moment Patterns

By integrating the information gathered from EMG and dynamic analyses of cycling, the disparate roles of uniarticular and biarticular muscles now become clear. A suitable exercise is to compare the muscle activity periods shown in figure 5.12 with the joint moment patterns shown in figure 5.13.

Starting at the ankle, the activity of the soleus, a uniarticular ankle plantar flexor, corresponds precisely with the dominant extensor ankle moment region. Although not depicted in figure 5.12, the magnitude of the EMG signal peaks in the downstroke at nearly the same point in the cycle as the corresponding ankle moment peak. The active region of the gastrocnemius, a biarticular muscle that also plantar flexes the ankle, is slightly delayed relative to the soleus. Since this muscle also generates a flexor moment at the knee, the delay in peak gastrocnemius activity corresponds nicely with the sustained ankle plantar flexor moment and the switch at the knee from an extensor to a flexor moment, which occurs during the second half of the downstroke. Activity of both of these muscles extends into the early upstroke as well, contributing to the coincident plantar flexor moment at the ankle. Finally, the tibialis anterior, a uniarticular ankle dorsiflexor, contributes functionally to generate the dorsiflexor ankle moment in the last 45° before top dead center.

Up at the knee, the uniarticular vastii exhibit activity from about 45° before top dead center to 90° after top dead center. This region corresponds perfectly with the dominant knee extensor moment. Rectus femoris, a biarticular muscle that extends the knee and flexes the hip, displays similar activation timing. Although this may seem counterproductive during the early downstroke because the hip is extending at this time, relative actions at the knee and hip for this muscle (due to differing moment arms) are such that the muscle is isometric (not changing in length) or slightly shortening as it performs these dual roles (Broker 1991; Caldwell et al. 1999).

This is an excellent example of how a muscle acts as a guide wire to couple adjacent joint motions; here the powerful gluteals are extending the hip, allowing the rectus femoris to exert an extensor moment at the knee via its attachment from the pelvis to the tibia, via the patella.

The hamstrings, biarticular muscles that flex the knee and extend the hip, are principally active during the downstroke and again late in the upstroke. Peak activity for these muscles occurs when the hip extensor and knee flexor moments coincide late in the downstroke. However, these muscles are also active earlier in the downstroke, when their flexor contribution to the knee moment (extensor at the time) would seem counterproductive. Like the rectus femoris on the front of the knee, however, these muscles are shortening or are nearly isometric during this combined hip extension and knee extension because their moment arms are larger at the knee than at the hip. As such, they effectively couple these adjacent joint motions together, via the guide-wire effect.

Finally, the gluteus maximus, a large uniarticular hip extensor, is active during the downstroke, coincident with the large extensor moment discussed here. It becomes relatively silent during the upstroke, when the hip flexes despite a small extensor moment generated by the hamstrings and passive tissues surrounding the hip.

Joint Moments During Climbing

As cyclists shift from a seated to a standing posture during climbing, leg motion patterns, force application patterns, and thus muscular contributions to propel the cranks likely change. This shift often serves to redistribute effort among the many muscle groups.

Caldwell and colleagues (1999) extended their examination of pedaling mechanics during climbing to include the quantification of joint moments. Eight national caliber cyclists climbed in a seated or standing posture at an average power output of 294 W and 64 to 65 rpm. For comparison, they also pedaled level while seated at the same power output but at an average cadence of 82 rpm. Instrumented force pedals and high-speed film captured pedal forces and limb motions; joint moments were computed using the inverse dynamics procedure mentioned earlier.

The ankle moment during seated climbing was quite similar to level cycling, except that in seated climbing the peak moment was higher and occurred earlier in the downstroke. The principal reason for the greater ankle joint moment magnitude was the lower cadence seen in seated climbing, which necessitates higher pedal forces. Comparing seated to standing climbing, the ankle moment patterns were similar in shape, but standing exhibited a greater ankle moment peak much later in the pedal cycle (24° before bottom dead center). This finding would suggest a more rapid fatigue of the ankle plantar flexors (soleus and gastrocnemius) while standing.

At the knee, moment patterns between seated level and seated climbing were substantially similar, with the extensor and flexor moment peaks occurring 8 to 15° earlier when climbing. When standing, the knee extensor moment pattern became bimodal during the downstroke, such that the extensor to flexor moment shift, which normally occurs 125 to 130° past top dead center (see figure 5.13), was delayed until 10 to 15° before bottom dead center. The subsequent flexor region was dramatically shorter as well. Effort at the knee would thus appear to shift to the extensors (vastii) and somewhat away from the hamstrings during standing climbing.

Finally, the hip moment patterns across the seated level, seated climbing, and standing climbing conditions were remarkably similar both in magnitude and timing. Peak extensor moments were highest in the seated climbing condition, although this peak was only significantly different from the standing climbing condition.

Based on these findings, Caldwell and colleagues concluded that standing climbing brings the uniarticular muscles into play more heavily, as the legs must support body weight in addition to propelling the bike. Conversely, biarticular muscles appear to contribute to weight support as appropriate, while directing the pedal force vector to more effectively drive the cranks. Muscle roles are not that different from those during standard, seated cycling. The effects of lateral bike motion and vigorous upper extremity usage on lower extremity joint moments and coordination remain unstudied.

Directions for Future Research

Biomechanics is a broad scientific area. A comprehensive discussion of the many biomechanical issues of cycling could fill a thick book (for a review, see Gregor, Broker, and Ryan 1991). In this chapter, the focus has been on the fundamental features of pedaling—pedal interface dynamics and muscular function during pedaling. More advanced interpretations of pedaling quality have been introduced, interesting findings gathered from a decade of pedaling mechanics testing have been described, and the fascinating neuromuscular control involving uniarticular and biarticular muscles has been developed. Hopefully, the concepts discussed will complement the information in other chapters of this book and lead those interested to related issues of cycling.

From a biomechanist's perspective, several critical areas of cycling science demand further exploration. For example, current bike-fitting practices appear to be more art than science. Admittedly, some bicycle shops and specialty technical groups offer techy-looking bike-fitting services based on algorithms accounting for various body dimensions and riding postures. Devices are available to perform quick, qualitative assessments of pedaling form as frame configurations are modified. But effective integration of cyclist and bike probably cannot be achieved with simple algorithms and quick performance checks. Bike-fit techniques of the future will probably require more explicit characterization of the rider, with due consideration given to both performance optimization and injury minimization. Research directed at rider-specific optimization of frame geometry will be welcomed.

Another area of cycling biomechanics deserving further attention concerns nonstandard transmission systems. Although noncircular chain rings have largely faded from the cycling landscape—because of biomechanical studies that failed to identify any advantages—new devices continue to be developed and may indeed enhance cycling performance. Transmission systems that uncouple the right and left cranks offer a dramatic variant on the standard cycling task. The degree to which such pedaling may stimulate positive functional adaptations and the neuromuscular mechanisms involved with pedaling this way have yet to be evaluated. Pedals are now available that prevent forward rotation of the pedal bodies relative to the cranks. Anecdotal reports suggest that these pedals enhance power delivery. These devices also deserve a closer look.

Finally, as computer and instrumentation technologies continue to advance, our ability to provide useful information to cyclists and coaches improves. On-board measurement of cycling power (see chapter 6) is now within the reach of even recreational cyclists. Force-measuring pedals, while still mostly restricted to the laboratory, may emerge before long as viable training tools on the track, the road, and even on the trails. Instrumented shoes with an infrared communication port to home computers may exist in the future. Accurate interpretation and effective communication of the data provided by these devices will demand continued research into the many subtleties of pedaling. The process will never end. We should all stay tuned.

References

Alvarez, G., and Vinyolas, J. 1996. A new bicycle pedal design for on-road measurements of cycling forces. *J Appl Biomech* 12:130-142.

Broker, J.P. 1991. *Mechanical energy management during constrained human movement*. Unpublished doctoral dissertation, University of California at Los Angeles.

Broker, J.P., Crawley, J.C., and Coughlin, K. 2002. Pedaling mechanics differences across cycling disciplines: Observations over 10 years of testing. *Med Sci Sports Exerc* 34(5): S90.

Broker, J.P., and Gregor, R.J. 1990. A dual piezoelectric element force pedal for kinetic analysis of cycling. *Int J Sports Biomech* 6(4): 394-403.

Browning, R.C. 1991. *Lower extremity kinetics during cycling in elite triathletes in aerodynamic cycling*. Unpublished master's thesis, University of California at Los Angeles.

Caldwell, G.E., Hagberg, J.M., McCole, S.D., and Li, L. 1999. Lower extremity joint moments during uphill cycling. *J Appl Biomech* 15(2): 166-181.

Caldwell, G.E., Li, L., McCole, S.D., and Hagberg, J.M. 1998. Pedal and crank kinetics in uphill cycling. *J Appl Biomech* 14(3): 245-259.

Cavanagh, P.L., and Sanderson, D.J. 1986. The biomechanics of cycling: Studies of the pedaling mechanics of elite pursuit riders. In *Science of Cycling*, edited by Edmund Burke. Champaign, Ill.: Human Kinetics. pp. 91-122.

Doria, A., and Lot, R. 2001. The generalized torque approach for analyzing the results of pedaling tests. *J Biomed Eng* 123:33-39.

Ericson, M.O., Nissell, R., and Ekholm, J. 1984. Varus and valgus loads on the knee joint during ergometer cycling. *Scand J Sports Sci* 6:39-45.

Gregor, R.J., Broker, J.P., and Ryan, M.M. 1991. The biomechanics of cycling. *Exerc Sport Sci Rev* 19:127-169.

Gregor, R.J., Cavanaugh, P.R., and LaFortune, M. 1985. Knee flexor moments during propulsion in cycling: A creative solution to Lombard's paradox. *J Biomech* 18:307-316.

Hull, M.L., and Davis, R.R. 1981. Measurement of pedal loading in bicycling I. Instrumentation. *J Biomech* 14:843-855.

Kautz, S.A., and Hull, M.L. 1993. A theoretical basis for interpreting the force applied to the pedal in cycling. *J Biomech* 26:155-165.

LaFortune, M.A., and Cavanagh, P.R. 1983. Effectiveness and efficiency during bicycle riding. In *Biomechanics VIIB: International Series on Sports Science* 4B, edited by Matsui and Kobayashi. Champaign, Ill.: Human Kinetics. pp. 928-936.

Lombard, W.P. 1903. The action of two-joint muscles. *American Physical Education Review* 8:141-145.

Miller, N., and Seirig, A. 1977. Effect of load, speed, and activity history on the EMG signal from the intact human muscle. *J Bioeng* 1:147.

Newmiller, J., Hull, M.L., and Zajac, F.E. 1988. A mechanically decoupled two force component bicycle pedal dynamometer. *J Biomech* 21:375-386.

Reiser, R.F. 2000. Biomechanics of recumbent cycling: Instrumentation, experimentation, and modeling. Unpublished doctoral dissertation, Colorado State University at Fort Collins.

Rowe, T., Hull, M.L., and Wang, E.L. 1998. A pedal dynamometer for off-road bicycling. *J Biomech Eng* 120:160-164.

Ryan, M.M., and Gregor, R.J. 1992. EMG profiles of lower extremity muscles during cycling at constant workload and cadence. *J Electromyogr Kinesiol* 2(2): 69-80.

Sharp, A. 1896. *Bicycles and tricycles*. Longmans Green (reprinted M.I.T. Press, Cambridge, 1977).

Soden, P.D., and Adeyefa, B.A. 1979. Forces applied to a bicycle during normal cycling. *J Biomech* 12:527-541.

Wheeler, J.B., Gregor, R.J., and Broker, J.P. 1992. A dual piezoelectric bicycle pedal with multiple shoe/pedal interface compatibility. *Int J Sports Biomech* 8:251-258.

Wooten, D., and Hull, M.L. 1992. Design and evaluation of a multi-degree-of-freedom foot/pedal interface for cycling. *Int J Sport Biomech* 8:152-164.

6

Cycling Power: Road and Mountain

Jeffrey P. Broker

A decade ago, two high-tech cyclists comparing their training programs might have focused on weekly mileage, periodization phases, time to ride a given course, or percentages of recent rides spent in specific heart rate zones. A time trialist might have spoken of a new flat-back position he tried that resulted in reduced heart rate at a given speed. Heart rate monitors captured training bouts, allowing cyclists to track their relative effort levels across rides, days, and weeks within training phases. Heart rate monitors and stopwatches became the primary gauge of a cyclist's training program, and heart rate measures were used to maximize the training adaptation process.

In the past five years, the heart rate monitor has been replaced or supplemented by the cycling power meter, a new, perhaps more powerful, measurement device. Now, the high-tech cyclist describes a workout in terms of average or peak watts (W), percentage of rides spent in various power zones, or peak watts per kilogram during a climb or sprint effort. The cyclist knows his or her maximum steady state cycling power, understands the rise and fall of cycling power associated with climbing hills and drafting, and fine tunes the training process with workouts targeting specific power schedules.

Cycling power is the current hot topic. In this chapter, we begin with a definition of cycling power and its importance to cyclists and coaches. Then the nature of power will be outlined, including an equation of motion for cycling, power measurements on a bicycle, and power requirements of road and mountain biking events. The chapter will conclude with a discussion concerning how power measures might be used in training and with brief suggestions for future work in the area.

Power Defined

Power is the rate of doing work expressed in joules (J) per second or watts (W). To understand the nature of power, you must understand the concept of work. Work is performed when a force acts over a distance (work = force × distance) or when torque acts through an arc of rotation (work = torque × angular displacement).

Power is the rate of performing work or work performed per unit of time (power = work/time). Relevant variants of this equation are developed by substituting the two components of work into this equation and rearranging the parentheses:

$$\text{Power} = (\text{force} \times \text{distance})/\text{time} \quad (6.1)$$

$$\text{Power} = \text{force} \times (\text{distance}/\text{time}) \quad (6.2)$$

Or, for the rotational case,

$$\text{Power} = (\text{torque} \times \text{angular displacement})/\text{time} \quad (6.3)$$

$$\text{Power} = \text{torque} \times (\text{angular displacement}/\text{time}) \quad (6.4)$$

Recognizing that distance divided by time equals velocity, and angular displacement divided by time equals angular velocity, functional power equations for cycling become:

$$\text{Power} = \text{force} \times \text{velocity} \quad (6.5)$$

$$\text{Power} = \text{torque} \times \text{angular velocity} \quad (6.6)$$

Thus, if the force required to overcome rolling and air resistive forces are known for a given cycling speed, the associated cycling power can be calculated directly using equation 6.5. A rider overcoming total resistive forces of 6.7 lb (30 N) at a velocity of 18.6 mph (30 kph, or 8.33 m/sec^{-1}) requires an average power output of roughly 250 W.* For comparison, 1 horsepower (hp) is equivalent to 746 W; thus, our cyclist would produce roughly 1/3 hp to ride at 18.6 mph.

---

*Components of cycling power not included in this formulation are drivetrain losses and energy required to spin the wheels. These components increase the pedal power required to maintain constant bicycle velocity and will be discussed shortly.

The rotational variant of power (equation 6.6) comes into play when measuring cycling power. By measuring crank torque and crank angular velocity, crank power can be computed. Likewise, torque at the rear hub and rear wheel angular velocity can be combined to compute power.

Why Cycling Power?

All cycling coaches and most knowledgeable cyclists know that effective training programs are built on an appropriate balance of training duration, intensity, and frequency. Training duration represents the amount of time spent in a given training situation. Training intensity represents the physiological load associated with a training session. Finally, training frequency represents the repetition interval linked to a training regimen. Of these, training intensity is perhaps the most difficult to manage, particularly for cyclists.

Speed, or cycling velocity, is a poor measure of cycling intensity. In fact, measurements of heart rates and power outputs on bicycles during racing often expose negative correlations between bicycle speed and effort level (Jeukendrup 2002). This occurs because low cycling velocity usually is associated with strenuous hill climbing, and maximal velocity usually occurs during high-speed descent, when power output and physiological load are at relative minima. Further, rarely does a cyclist ride alone, in still wind, over uniformly flat terrain. Substantial variations in cycling effort occur in response to the effects of other riders (in drafting), mild to moderate winds, and variations in grade.

Heart rate measurements have long been used to estimate physical effort during cycling. Recent studies have used heart rates, compared with laboratory measures on the same subjects, to estimate the physiological demands of professional mass-start stage races in road cycling (Fernandez-Garcia et al. 2000; Lucia et al. 1999; Padilla et al. 2001), road time trials (Lucia et al. 1999; Padilla et al. 2000), and even mountain bike cross-country races (Gregory 2001; Martin 1997). Heart rates do respond nicely to variations in cycling power, or work rate, but they also exhibit substantial variation in response to environmental conditions such as temperature, humidity, and altitude. Heart rates also vary as a function of hydration, fatigue, and exercise duration. It is often said that heart rates best reflect the physiological stress experienced by an exercising individual rather than the true intensity of the effort.

Power is a better measure of exercise intensity. When measured at the cranks, power represents the quantity of energy delivered to the pedals by the cyclist per unit of time. When power levels double, it doesn't matter whether the increase resulted from a change in grade, wind direction, cycling speed, or a combination of these factors. In all cases, the rider delivers twice as much energy to the pedals per unit of time.

Measuring cycling power presents a better picture of cycling intensity.

Energy delivered to the pedals represents external work performed by the rider and is not equivalent to the physiological energy expended to perform the task. Humans are only 21 to 24% efficient in converting chemical energy to mechanical energy during cycling. A cyclist riding at 250 W is actually expending metabolic energy at a rate of nearly 1000 W (over 1 hp)!

Besides monitoring cycling intensity, measuring power has numerous other benefits. These include monitoring training, course characterization, aerodynamic assessments, and pacing. These benefits will be discussed after the nature of cycling power is explored more fully.

Nature of Cycling Power

Cycling power is probably best understood by examining an equation of motion for cycling. This equation describes the relationship between rider work and bicycle speed, and it can be developed by considering the five principal resistive elements: drivetrain friction, inertial forces associated with acceleration of the bike, gravitational forces in climbing, tire rolling resistance, and aerodynamic drag. A simplified functional equation of motion for cycling including these five elements takes the following form:

6.7
$$Pcyc = P_{dt} + mVAcyc + WVsin(ArctanG) + WVCrr_1cos(ArctanG) + NCrr_2V^2 + 1/2\rho C_dAV(V + V_w)^2$$

where *Pcyc* is the net instantaneous mechanical power produced by the rider, P_{dt} is power to overcome drivetrain friction, *m* is the mass of the rider and bicycle, *V* is bicycle velocity, *Acyc* is instantaneous acceleration or deceleration of the bicycle/rider system, *W* is the weight of the bicycle and rider, *G* is the grade, Crr_1 is the coefficient of static rolling resistance, *N* is the number of wheels (in case a tricycle is analyzed), Crr_2 is the coefficient of dynamic rolling resistance, C_d is the coefficient of aerodynamic drag, *A* is the frontal surface area of the rider and bicycle, ρ is the air density, and V_w is the velocity of the headwind or tailwind (positive for headwind).

Let's look at some of the critical features of equation 6.7. First, rider and bicycle mass (weight) figure linearly into the second, third, and fourth elements of the equation. Thus, a 10% increase in rider plus bicycle weight increases the power required to accelerate the rider and bicycle, power to overcome gravity, and power to overcome static rolling resistance by an equal 10%. Next, power to offset dynamic rolling resistance, the fifth term in equation 6.7, is not dependent on rider and bicycle mass, but increases as the square of bicycle velocity. Doubling bicycle speed increases the power to overcome dynamic rolling resistance by a factor of 4. Finally, and most critically, power to overcome aerodynamic drag increases as the cube (third power) of velocity, so doubling bicycle speed increases power to overcome aerodynamic resistance by a factor of 8. Since all elements figure into the power the rider must produce to maintain motion, these elements will be discussed individually.

Power at the Pedals

The left side of equation 6.7 approximates the power provided by the rider at the pedals. As described in chapter 5, forces are applied to the pedals in a characteristic manner. Through the top of the stroke, applied pedal forces are small and usually directed slightly forward. Crank torque through this region is generally low. When the cranks are nearly horizontal in their respective downstrokes, forces and crank torques are near their peak magnitudes. Forces through the bottom of the pedal stroke are largely downward, caused by gravity and inertia, so crank torque in this region is low. Finally, during the upstroke, forces are small and downward, generally opposite the direction of pedal motion. Thus, crank torque is negative during the upstroke.

The net effect of crank torque on both pedals is shown in figure 6.1, where total instantaneous power developed by the rider is plotted versus crank angle. Average power, or that associated with overcoming the various resistive elements of cycling, is 350 W. Considerable oscillations occur about the average power of 350 W. In fact, two distinct power peaks are evident, representing the separate peak torque regions for the right and left pedals, when they are nearly halfway through their respective downstrokes. The two power minima (or valleys) observed in the total power curve represent power-passive periods, which occur when the cranks are nearly vertical.

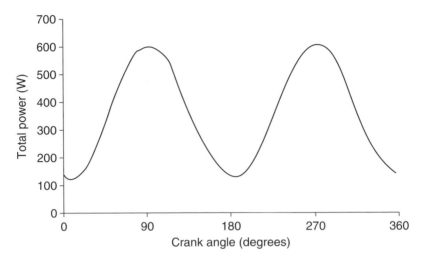

FIGURE 6.1 Average instantaneous crank power associated with riding at 350 W, 90 rpm ($n = 17$ road riders). Two distinct peaks are evident, with minima occurring when the cranks are near vertical.

Testing across the various disciplines of road, track, and mountain biking revealed that mountain bike racers have the lowest relative oscillations in total power during pedaling (Broker, Crawley, and Coughlin 2002). Low oscillations in mountain bike racing appear to be highly functional, as rear wheel traction on loose soil relies substantially on continuous power flow from the pedals to the rear wheel.

Drivetrain Power Losses

Mechanical energy is delivered from the chain ring to the rear wheel through the chain and transmission. Unfortunately, friction in the bottom bracket bearings, chain elements, and rear transmission consumes a small portion of this energy. Danh and colleagues (1991) and Kyle (1988) suggested that grease lubrication generates six to seven times the friction of light oil, cone and cup bearings have one-seventh the friction of cartridge bearings, and sealed cartridge bearings generate 10 times the friction of unsealed cartridges. Interestingly, slightly worn bearings and seals may have lower energy losses than new bearings.

As might be expected, power losses in the chain increase when the chain is significantly deflected, as when a large chain ring is used with large rear cogs or when a small chain ring is used with small rear cogs. When clean and slightly worn cup and cone bearings lubricated with light oil are used with a straight, clean chain, chain ring, derailleur, and rear cog set, drivetrain losses can be expected to be as low as 2 to 4% of the total energy input from the rider.

Rolling Resistance

As bicycle tires roll over the ground, the treads, casings, and enclosed tubes (if used) deform. Most of this deformation is elastic, occurring where the tire actually contacts the ground; that is, the rubber material springs back. A portion of this deformation, however, is inelastic and consumes energy. This energy loss, principally as heat, is often defined as rolling resistance and has both static and dynamic components. The static component does not vary with bicycle speed, whereas the dynamic component does. Rolling resistance is affected by casing and tread construction, tread design, and tube configuration. Generally, thinner and more flexible casings exhibit lower rolling resistance, as do lightweight natural rubber tubes with ultrafine or slick tread designs (Kyle 1996).

Rolling resistance also is affected by surface roughness, wheel loading, tire pressure, tire diameter, wheel diameter, tire temperature, steering, and acceleration. Rolling resistance increases with lower tire pressure and lower air temperature. Steering input and propulsive torque delivered to the rear wheel create casing deformations, increasing energy losses to rolling resistance. Rolling resistance can best be minimized by using lightweight, flexible, ultra-high-pressure tires with fine tread on smooth concrete. This is impractical for mountain bike riding, of course, where energy losses are intentionally compromised in exchange for enhanced traction.

Typical values for static rolling resistance coefficients (Crr_1 in equation 6.7) are listed in table 6.1. Resistive forces created at the tires are small but not insignificant. For calculations of cycling rolling resistance, dynamic coefficients (Crr_2) of 0.05 N $\times$ m $\times$ sec^{-1} are recommended until more test results become available (Kyle 1996).

Power of Climbing and Descending

Expensive bicycles are extremely light, for good reason. The effects of gravity on cycling power are substantial. Gravity naturally causes power to increase dramatically during hill climbs while reducing efforts on descents. Unfortunately, the energy saved on downhills never offsets the added energy of climbing because of aerodynamic effects. Consequently, hilly courses are slower than flat courses of the same length.

Bicycle power changes with grade or slope. Figure 6.2 shows the power required to climb (excluding the power to overcome aerodynamic drag and rolling resistance) as a function of bicycle velocity and grade. Required power is expressed in watts per pound, allowing any combination of rider and bicycle to be represented. For example, a rider climbing a 5% grade at 10 mph (16.1 kph) must deliver roughly 1.0 W/lb to the pedals just to overcome the effect of the grade. If the bicycle and rider weigh 176 lb (80 kg), the total power to overcome just the grade would be 176 W. Rolling resistance (a relatively small effect) and aerodynamic resistance (a moderate effect) add to the climbing power requirement. Given that maximum steady state power

TABLE 6.1 Static Rolling Resistant Coefficients for Select Bike Tires

Tubular

Tire type	Tire size (mm)	On linoleum	On concrete	On asphalt
Continental	686 × 19	0.19	0.17	0.22
Continental	610 × 19	0.26	0.23	0.27
Clement Colle Main	686 × 19	0.16		
Clement Colle Main	610 × 19	0.21		

Clincher

Tire type	Tire size (mm)	On linoleum	On concrete	On asphalt
Specialized Turbo S	700 × 19	0.26		0.29
Specialized Turbo S, Kevlar wall/latex tube	700 × 19	0.23	0.27	
Specialized Turbo S, Kevlar wall/butyl tube	700 × 19	0.28		
Specialized Turbo S, Kevlar wall/polyurethane liner	700 × 19	0.29		
Specialized Turbo S, Kevlar wall/polyurethane liner	700 × 19	0.54		

Crr^1 × 100. Tire pressures all were 100 psi. Static rolling resistance is determined by multiplying the total rider plus bike weight on each tire by the coefficient below divided by 100.

Adapted, by permission, from C.R. Kyle, 1996, Selecting cycling equipment. In *High Tech Cycling*, edited by E.R. Burke (Champaign, Ill: Human Kinetics), 14.

outputs for world-class cyclists are in the 400 to 450 W range, it is easy to see why cycling velocity decreases rapidly as grade increases. It is also clear why elite riders of small stature excel on hilly race courses.

Effects of Inertia

When average cycling power delivered to the pedals by the rider exceeds the sum of the aerodynamic, rolling, grade, and transmission resistances, bicycle acceleration occurs. This acceleration is directly proportional to the net force produced at the rear wheel contact patch, and inversely proportional to total rider plus bicycle mass. Thus, lighter bicycles with lighter riders accelerate more readily.

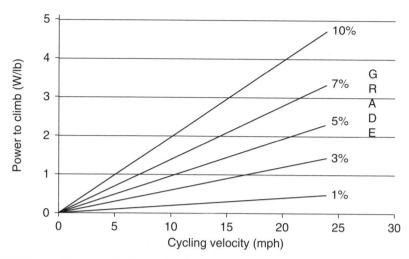

FIGURE 6.2 Power to climb as a function of cycling velocity and grade. Power to climb is expressed in watts per pound of total rider plus bicycle weight. Power to overcome aerodynamic drag and rolling resistance is not included.

A 176-lb (80-kg) rider plus bicycle, accelerating uniformly from rest over 200 ft (61 m) in 10 s, will accelerate at 4 ft/sec^{-2} (1.22 m/sec^{-2}). Velocity at the 200-ft mark will be 27.3 mph (44.7 kph). The same propulsive force developed by a rider and bike weighing an additional 5 lb (181 lb total) will result in the cyclist being 5.25 ft behind at the 200-ft mark. This demonstrates how a rider on a lightweight bike will have an advantage in a race with many decelerations and accelerations.

When bicycles accelerate, both wheels are angularly accelerated. The wheels have a certain amount of rotational inertia (I), or resistance to angular acceleration, dictated by their mass and the distribution of their mass about their hubs. Light wheels with their mass concentrated closer to the hub are easier to accelerate than are wheels with the mass located closer to the rims.

Aerodynamics

At cycling velocities exceeding 20 mph, roughly 80% of the total resistive forces on a cyclist and bike is due to aerodynamic drag. Traditional racing bikes are responsible for roughly 35% of the total aerodynamic drag; the remainder is attributed to the rider's body. Streamlined time trial bicycles may reduce the aerodynamic drag to 20% of the total. Nevertheless, when compared to the other elements resisting rider and bicycle motion, aerodynamic forces on the rider and bicycle create the vast majority of resistance to forward progression, and thus attention to managing and reducing aerodynamic drag from all sources is highly encouraged.

Bicycle Frame.   Before the Union Cycliste Internationale (UCI) regulated the shape and form of racing bicycles shortly before the 2000 Olympics, radical versions of the modern bicycle had evolved. Perhaps the most striking characteristic of these superbikes was the shape and configuration of their major frame structural elements. Traditional round head tubes, down tubes, seat tubes, and top tubes were replaced by ovalized, airfoil-like elements. Further, the frames departed substantially from the look of a traditional racing bicycle. Figure 6.3 illustrates the frame designs incorporated in many of the bicycles developed in the years leading up to the 2000 Olympics.

The importance of airfoil section frame elements is understood by considering the manner in which air flows around these shapes. A round cylinder in an airstream creates a turbulent wake with a trailing low pressure region that generates high drag. The coefficient of drag (C_d in equation 6.7) for such a cylinder, if smooth, is roughly 1.2. By contrast, an ovalized airfoil in an airstream creates a smooth surface over which the air flows with minimal turbulence. The airfoil can have 1/10th the drag of the cylinder given the same frontal area (C_d = 0.1 or less).

The arrangement of frame elements on a bicycle also affects airflow and drag. For a conventional double-diamond frame bicycle, the airstream

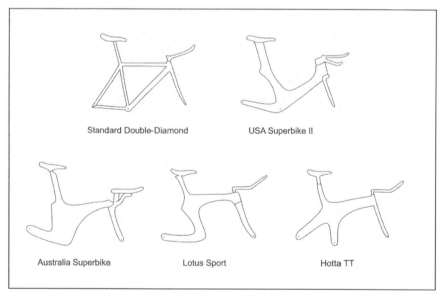

Standard Double-Diamond   USA Superbike II

Australia Superbike   Lotus Sport   Hotta TT

FIGURE 6.3   Bicycle frame configurations designed for time trial events. The now illegal superbike geometries attempted to minimize the number of times the airstream crossed frame members, limit drag-inducing interactions between the airstream and the rider's legs, and use smooth transitions between connecting frame members.

passes over four frame elements at a level just above the axles: the fork, the down tube, the seat tube, and the rear seat stays. Looking at the superbike frame arrangements in figure 6.3, it becomes clear that there are many ways to reduce the number of times the airstream passes over frame elements. Designers also strive to cleanse the airstream interactions with the frame, incorporating very narrow frame elements with smooth transitions between adjacent structural members.

A critical feature of aerodynamic bicycles is their interaction with the rider. Wind tunnel tests have demonstrated that some bicycles appear aero-dynamically superior (have very low drag) when tested in a wind tunnel without a rider, but perform comparatively worse when a rider is added. The reason appears to be that some frame configurations cause obstructions or deviations of the airstream between the rider's legs at certain points in the pedal cycle. This effect depends on the rider's leg muscular development, limb lengths, and the arrangement of frame elements. As such, drag-producing interactions between riders and their reportedly aerodynamic bicycles should not be overlooked.

Bicycle Components and Wheels. Careful selection and installation of bicycle components can significantly reduce aerodynamic drag. Table 6.2 lists the aerodynamic consequences of specific bike components in terms of their resulting drag reduction at 30 mph (48.4 kph). Many of these component modifications produce time savings well within typical separations between competitors in international events, have become standard features on today's racing bicycles, and are relatively inexpensive to incorporate. Incidentally, approximately 10 g of drag is produced by holding half a pencil perpendicular into an airstream at 30 mph. Consider how many components on standard bicycles resemble pencil-like shapes (cables, water bottle cages, etc.).

Wind tunnel experiments have evaluated and quantified the aerodynamic advantages and disadvantages of bicycle wheels, both in headwind and crosswind conditions. Because a rider is responsible for providing the energy to both rotate the wheels and propel the bicycle through the air, wind tunnel tests are usually performed to determine both the aerodynamic drag on a spinning wheel (spinning at wind tunnel air speed) and the energy required to actually keep the wheel spinning. Kyle (1995) reported the following general conclusions concerning the aerodynamic characteristics of bicycle wheels:

▶ Disk wheels or three-spoke composite wheels are aerodynamically superior to any spoked wheel. Also, disk wheels in the shape of a lens (thicker at the hub than at the rim) are superior to flat disks.

▶ Narrow 18-mm tires significantly reduce aerodynamic drag on wheels.

▶ Aerodynamic drag decreases as the diameter of the wheel decreases.

▶ Aero-bladed and oval spokes dramatically reduce aerodynamic drag; fewer spokes are better.

TABLE 6.2 Estimated Aerodynamic Advantages of Various Bike Components

Pedal Systems

Component/system	Drag force (lb)
Clipless pedals, Shimano/Look-type system (reference)	0
Shimano pedals, toe clips and straps	+0.165
Campagnalo pedals, toe clips and straps	+0.165

Cranks and chain rings

Component/system	Drag force (lb)
Custom crank w/ solid disk, 52 T sprocket (reference)	0
Same crank w/ normal 52 Y sprocket	+0.027
Standard Shimano crank w/ one 42 T sprocket	+0.075
Standard Shimano crank w/ one 52 sprocket	+0.096
Standard Shimano crank w/ 52 and 42 T sprockets	+0.145

Miscellaneous components

Component/system	Drag force (lb)
Aero shifters on down tube (reference)	0
Normal down tube shifters (levers up)	+0.054
Normal down tube shifters (levers down)	+0.027
Sheathed cable, perpendicular to airstream	+0.106*
Bare cable, perpendicular to airstream	+0.033*
Water bottle on down tube (reference)	0
Water bottle behind seat	+0.551
Aero water bottle and cage	+0.089

* Per foot.
Each category has a reference upon which components are compared. Drag forces are for a 30-mph test condition.

Adapted, by permission, from C.R. Kyle, 1995, Bicycle aerodynamics. In *Human Powered Vehicles*, edited by A.V. Abbott and D.G. Wilson (Champaign, Ill: Human Kinetics), pp. 141-155.

▶ Aero rims provide a smooth, tapered trailing edge that reduces turbulence and thus drag.

▶ Contrary to what one might think, the aerodynamic drag of disc wheels and three-spoke composite wheels actually decreases in mild crosswinds. This effect is due to aerodynamic lift.

Effect of Rider Position.   Racing bicycles are responsible for roughly 20 to 35% of total aerodynamic drag; the remainder is attributed to the rider's body. Experiments in wind tunnels and controlled tests using on-board power-measuring devices have shown that a cyclist riding with a flat back, a tucked head, and forearms positioned parallel to the bicycle frame (on clip-on bars, for example) experiences dramatically less aerodynamic drag than a less streamlined rider.

Tests of U.S. National Team riders in the General Motors wind tunnel in 1995 exposed the tremendous opportunity for performance enhancement with even minor adjustments in rider positions. For example, one 4000-m individual pursuit specialist was positioned in the wind tunnel atop his bicycle in two slightly different positions. One position was labeled his fatigued position, representative of a posture he often adopted during the last few laps of his 4.5-min event. His aerodynamic drag in this position, measured at a wind speed of 30 mph (48.3 kph), was 5.28 lb (23.57 N). When he lowered his head, extended his aerodynamic handlebars an inch, and dropped his handlebar stem an inch, his drag decreased to 5.0 lb (22.28 N). The effect of this 0.28-lb difference on a 4000-m individual time trial, at constant mechanical power output, was calculated to be 201 ft, or 3.91 s at the finish line! Most international events are decided by fractions of this difference.

Some riders have difficulty achieving the flat-back position. This position involves forward rotation of the pelvis, which tends to place the hip in greater flexion at the top of the pedal stroke. Increased hip flexion effectively lengthens the hip extensor muscles (gluteals and hamstrings) while shortening the hip flexor muscles (rectus femoris and iliopsoas), relative to their normal operating conditions. These changes in muscle operating conditions sometimes compromise a rider's ability to pedal the bicycle effectively. The effect, observable with force-measuring pedals, is most noticeable in the upstroke and across the top of the pedal cycle.

The increased hip flexion created by the forward rotation of the pelvis, in conjunction with the forward position of the torso, also can cause interference problems between the thighs and chest. A solution to avoid compromising pedaling mechanics in favor of enhanced aerodynamic positioning is slight forward and upward motion of the saddle. Such saddle motion effectively opens up the hip angle to better replicate the standard riding position. This is the reason triathletes and time trialists often ride bicycles with steeper seat tubes.

The UCI currently limits the fore/aft position of the saddle such that the nose of the saddle is positioned at least 5 cm behind the bottom bracket spindle. This rule, which discourages extreme forward positioning on the bicycle, can be waived for anthropomorphic reasons.*

Research findings are largely inconclusive in determining the best arm position, whether to place the arms together or apart on aerodynamic handlebars. Anecdotal evidence suggests a combination of factors may dictate whether the arms should be together or apart. With the arms together, a large portion of the airstream is presumably directed around the rider's body. With the forearms separated, a significant portion of the airstream passes over the handlebars, beneath the rider's chest, between the legs, and across the seat tube toward the rear wheel.

The arms-together position may be more appropriate for the rider who has difficulty achieving a narrow and rounded position of the shoulders with the elbows and forearms apart and/or rides a bike with a round seat tube and a non-aero spoked rear wheel. In this case, the rider effectively directs a significant portion of the airstream around the body and away from the high-drag frame and rear wheel. Conversely, the latter position may be appropriate for the rider who can become narrow through the shoulders even with the arms apart and rides an aero bike with an aero rear wheel. Additional research will hopefully establish optimal combinations for riders and bicycles of various aerodynamic characteristics.

Significant changes in body position on the bicycle should be made slowly and incrementally because the flat-back position places greater stress on the lower back and neck, and the aero position places more weight on the front wheel and thus may compromise bicycle stability and handling. Training time should be devoted to experimenting with more forward positions to adapt to the modified skeletal loads and gain familiarity with alterations in bicycle handling.

Drafting. No discussion of cycling power would be complete without addressing drafting. Drafting simply means riding inside the wake of riders ahead. What are the effects of drafting on power output? Four methods have been used to study the phenomenon. Wind tunnel tests were used nearly 20 years ago to test the effects of drafting on cycling aerodynamics, and are still used today. Riders are positioned in a wind tunnel in various numbers and arrangements, and the drag on select riders within the group is measured.

A less expensive yet still scientific method of determining the effects of drafting involves coastdown tests. Rider plus bicycle deceleration is mea-

---

* Shorter riders have difficulty meeting the 5-cm UCI rule because it forces them to ride with exceptionally shallow seat tube angles. Short riders are often allowed to ride with their saddles forward of the 5-cm limit.

sured while coasting in zero wind. Deceleration rates are compared in drafting and nondrafting conditions. As might be imagined, bicycle spacing must be carefully managed to achieve accurate results with this method.

A third method to quantify drafting effects was pioneered by physiologists who measured oxygen consumption while riders cycled on the road in various drafting configurations (see Hagberg and McCole 1996). A boom-mounted oxygen breathing system allowed researchers riding in a car beside a pace line or small peloton to collect expired gases from one of the cyclists. Since this method involves physiological response to various drafting situations, it has practical application. Using this method, Hagberg and McCole reported energy savings of 26 ± 7% associated with riding in a pace line in the second, third, or fourth positions behind a lead rider. The middle-back riding position in an eight-rider peloton resulted in a 39 ± 6 % reduction in energy expenditure.

The fourth method for studying the effects of drafting requires on-board instrumentation to measure power output. Such systems are widely available today, allowing the recreational cyclist a chance to see and fully appreciate the effects of drafting.

Wind tunnel and velodrome tests with U.S. National Team cyclists preparing for the 1996 Olympics in Atlanta provided a unique look at the effects of drafting. Drag was measured on each rider as the pace line was "rotated" about them, allowing us to determine the drag in each of the four positions. The wind tunnel data were compared to power measurements made with on-board power-measuring systems (SRMs) mounted on bicycles in a four-member pace line as they circled two different velodromes.

Power to ride in each of four positions in a pace line is shown in figure 6.4, expressed as a percentage of lead power for the wind tunnel and velodrome tests. Two velodrome tests are depicted, one (Adelaide) involving the U.S. Superbike-I bicycles on an indoor wood velodrome in Australia, and the other involving the competition U.S. Superbike-IIs, ridden on the Olympic track in Atlanta just months before the 1996 Olympics. As indicated, power to ride in the second position was roughly 61 to 66% of the lead power, over a one-third reduction in cycling effort! The rider in the third position benefited even more, generating only 57 to 62% of the lead power. In the fourth position, the benefit was nearly identical to that of the third position.

Additional interesting features of drafting should also be appreciated from figure 6.4. First, the wind tunnel tests resulted in superior drafting advantages when compared to the track tests. This finding makes sense, as riders in the wind tunnel were placed in what should be considered an "idealized" drafting position. Spacing and alignment were nearly perfectly controlled.

Second, the U.S. Superbike-I bicycles ridden in the indoor velodrome tests experienced greater power savings than the U.S. Superbike-II bicycles

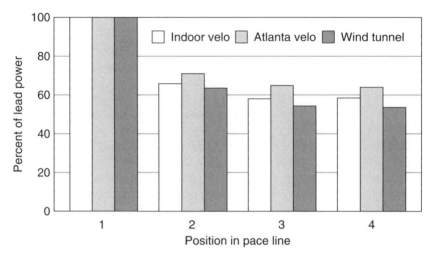

FIGURE 6.4   Effect of drafting on cycling power. Riders in the drafting positions (2-4) generate over one third less power to maintain velocity than the lead rider.

ridden on the outdoor Atlanta track. This finding may be due to three factors. Although winds at the outdoor velodrome in Atlanta were estimated to be less than 5 mph during testing, the effect of mild winds on drafting are likely to be reductions in power savings. Since the Adelaide testing was performed on an indoor track, winds were absent, and thus the superior drafting effect was somewhat expected.

Next, the Atlanta track testing was performed on the first day the national team riders had ridden their new Superbike-II bicycles (after a warm-up). Unfamiliar handling characteristics of the Superbike-II bicycles may have resulted in poorer pace line alignment during testing, causing drafting power savings to decrease. Finally, riders felt the Superbike-II bicycles, aerodynamically superior to the Superbike-I bicycles, were difficult to draft in the first place. If aerodynamic rider plus bicycle systems create smaller wakes, drafting will be less effective for the trailing riders. Herein lies a functional advantage of having aerodynamic equipment and positioning: riders following behind will benefit less.

Measuring Cycling Power Outside the Laboratory

For years, scientists have used laboratory-based cycling simulators and ergometers to study human performance. These devices offered researchers the ability to control cycling power (or work rate) while measuring other variables such as heart rate, perceived exertion, oxygen consumption, pedal forces, and muscle recruitment patterns. In the past 10 years, however, commercially available devices have been developed to measure cycling power outside the laboratory. These power meters, employing various measurement schemes, have revolutionized cycling training and testing.

In general, three different power-measuring systems for road and mountain bike use are available today. The first system, the SRM (Schoberer Rad Messtechnik, Welldorf, Germany), gained widespread popularity among cycling scientists and high-level coaches in the years preceding the 1996 Olympics. SRM systems were used to track training intensity, fine-tune aerodynamic positioning, characterize race course demands, and even quantify the demands of racing (Golich and Broker 1996).

The SRM (see figure 6.5) employs metallic strain gauge sensors attached to deformable structural elements embedded inside a sealed custom chain ring assembly. Also contained inside the sealed chain ring assembly is a reed switch that detects crank revolutions to determine cadence. Signals representing crank torque and crank revolutions are telemetered to a sensor on the frame, which connects to a power control unit mounted on the handlebars (see figure 6.5b). A standard wheel speed sensor mounted on the front fork provides bicycle speed, and the SRM control unit contains a Polar heart rate receiver. The control unit computes and stores cycling power using a variant of equation 6.6 for intervals ranging from 1/10 s up to 10 s. Data are downloaded via cable to a computer for subsequent analysis. A typical graph representing a ride stored on an SRM includes heart rate, bicycle speed, cadence, and power.

Advantages of the SRM system are high accuracy, general robustness under rough operating conditions (a version is available for triple chain ring mountain bikes), adaptability to various bicycles, and simplicity. Disadvantages include weight, commitment to a given drive-side crank length (unless additional cranks are purchased), and cost. Further, because the

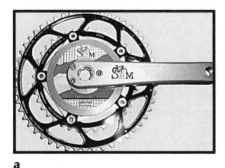

a **b**

FIGURE 6.5 SRM cycling power-measuring system: (*a*) strain gauge chain ring assembly and (*b*) handlebar-mounted control/display unit.

Photos courtesy of Jeffrey Broker.

SRM determines power at the chain ring, energy losses caused by drive-train friction are not included in the power calculation. These losses typically represent 2 to 4% of the total power output.

A second device currently available for measuring power outside the laboratory is the Power Tap (see figure 6.6). This device measures torque applied at the rear wheel hub. Like the SRM, torque is measured using strain gauges that deform under applied torque. Cadence is determined from fluctuations in torque at the rear hub. Signals representing torque, cadence, and bicycle speed are transmitted to a control unit mounted on the handlebars. Power is computed using a variant of equation 6.6, and data representing up to seven hours of riding are stored every 1 to 2 s.* The data can be downloaded to a computer for subsequent review and analysis.

The Power Tap is less expensive than the SRM system. Also, it is generally simple to install and use, and like the SRM, incorporates heart rate monitoring and data storage. Because it measures power at the rear hub, drivetrain losses are included in the power calculation. Disadvantages include the weight of the rear hub sensor assembly (heavier than that of the SRM) and a commitment to a specific (instrumented) rear wheel.

A recently introduced power-measuring device is the Polar Power Output Sensor (see figure 6.7). This system uses a unique power-measuring scheme. A sensor mounted to the drive-side chain stay detects high-frequency chain vibrations. Knowing the length and mass of the tensioned chain (inputs determined by the user from charts and measurements), chain vibration frequency is used to compute chain tension. A second sensor mounted to the lower derailleur pulley detects the passage of each chain link (see figure 6.7b). Since power equals the product of force and velocity, chain tension, or force, is multiplied by chain velocity to determine instantaneous power.

Like the other power-measuring devices, the Polar system transmits signals to a handlebar-mounted receiver for data storage and display. Polar, however, employs a custom watch (Polar S710 with heart rate function) to perform the function of the control unit. The watch is mounted to a cradle on the handlebars (see figure 6.7c). Advantages of the Polar system are its ease of installation (only the rear derailleur idler pulley bolt is changed), low weight, and low cost. Disadvantages include more wires than the SRM and Power Tap systems, the need to remove and weigh the chain for accurate determination of setup parameters, and possible sensitivity to certain frequencies of road or trail vibration.

Accuracy levels of the three power-measuring devices vary. Currently, the more expensive SRM is viewed as the gold standard, with claimed mea-

---

*Storage intervals of 2 s permit data collection for seven hours. Storage intervals of 1 s permit data storage up to three and a half hours.

FIGURE 6.6   Power Tap cycling power-measuring system: (a) strain gauge rear wheel hub; (b) frame-mounted sensor for receiving torque, velocity, and cadence data from the rear wheel and hub; and (c) handlebar-mounted control/display unit.

Photos courtesy of Jeffrey Broker.

FIGURE 6.7 Polar cycling power-measuring system: *(a)* chain tension sensor; *(b)* rear pulley sensor for measuring chain velocity; and *(c)* handlebar-mounted control/display unit.

Photos courtesy of Jeffrey Broker.

sured power accurate to within ± 0.5 to ± 5% of the actual value, depending on the model.* However, consumer testing of the Power Tap suggests that its accuracy may approach that of the SRM under most conditions. Testing of the Polar system is in the very early stages, and insufficient information concerning accuracy is available. Future testing under a wide array of operating conditions will be required to fully characterize the ability of all of these systems to provide accurate data repeatedly. Naturally, continued refinements in the systems will improve their function as well.

Power Output Levels of Road and Mountain Bike Racing

The actual power produced by elite cyclists in competition has long interested scientists, physiologists, coaches, and cycling enthusiasts. Before the advent of on-board power-measuring devices, power outputs during racing were indirectly estimated from physiological measures (principally heart rate) linked to work rates measured in the laboratory. Power outputs also have been indirectly estimated using variants of the cycling equation of motion (equation 6.7), using published data for rolling resistance and wind tunnel tests to provide critical coefficients of drag.

As power-measuring devices became popular, so too did research directly characterizing the power required to race bicycles. The results of such research—which must be applied with some caution as individual rider plus bicycle weight, frontal surface area, and power capacity vary significantly—are fascinating.

Power Requirements During Mass-Start Road Races

The mass-start road race represents a long-duration, highly variable effort for cyclists. During a single stage, riders may spend hours pedaling lightly in the moving air of a tightly packed peloton. They may encounter steep hills or participate in breakaways or chases that demand higher power outputs. For those at the front, the final sprint to the finish represents an all-out, peak power effort.

To quantify the unique demands of road racing, Golich and Broker (1996) mounted SRM systems on the bicycles of four members of the U.S. National Team competing in the 1994 Tour DuPont. Data were collected during a single three-and-a-half-hour stage. First, the results confirmed that heart rate and power output were not well correlated. As the event progressed, heart rates gradually increased despite relatively uniform power outputs. Second, the percentage of time spent in various power and speed

---

* The amateur version contains only two strain gauges and has a claimed accuracy of ± 5%. The professional version contains four gauges, with a claimed accuracy of ± 2%. A science version, using eight gauges, has a claimed accuracy of ± 0.5%.

ranges during the event was interesting (see table 6.3). Cyclists spent nearly half the time riding at power levels less than 150 W. This reflects the extended period of time spent drafting within the peloton. Roughly one quarter (23%) of the time was spent at power levels between 240 and 360 W, but surprisingly little time was spent above 360 W (1% of the total time). Closer examination of the data, synchronized with various phases of the stage, revealed that power outputs during hill climbing were not particularly high; cyclists appeared to reduce cycling speed to maintain effort level at or near their individually attainable steady state levels.

TABLE 6.3   SRM Measured Power and Velocity Distribution

Recorded for one rider in a 3-hour, 37-minute stage race (1991 Tour DuPont).

Cycle power (W)	Percent of ride	Cycle velocity (mph)	Percent of ride
0–120	51%	0–7.5	3%
120–240	17%	7.5–15.0	15%
240–360	23%	15–22.5	19%
360–480	4%	22.5–30	30%
480–600	1%	30–42.5	21%

Adapted, by permission, from D. Golich, and J. P Broker, 1996, "SRM instrumentation and the power output of elite male cyclists during the Tour DuPont," *Performance Conditioning for Cycling* 2(9): 6-8.

Similar characterizations of road racing power have been reported by Grazzi and colleagues (1999), Jeukendrup (2000), Martin (1997), Padilla and colleagues (2000), and Schoberer (1998). Table 6.4 provides racing power data from Schoberer (1998) and Martin (1997), including race length, duration, maximum power, and average power levels. These data clearly show that average power levels during road racing are relatively moderate, despite short periods of high power (well over 500 W).

At the highest level of competition, Bjarne Riis, champion of the 1996 Tour de France, rode a one-day race (260 km) with an SRM mounted to his bike. The data were reported by Mantell (1998), who identified 20 isolated "surges" in effort during the race, during which Riis produced 530 W of power. A solo breakaway during the last 40 km involved an average power output of 390 W. Similarly, Jeukendrup (2000) reported average power levels for a six-hour stage of the Tour de France to be just above 240 W, with an associated energy expenditure of 5700 Kcal.

TABLE 6.4   Road Racing Power

	Schoberer (1998)	Schoberer (1998)	Martin (1997)
Race length (mi)	167	128	77
Race duration (h:min)	7:14	5:02	3:19
Maximum power (W)	517	603	1,109
Average power (W)	249	202	300

Data from Schoberer 1998 and Martin 1997.

Power Requirements During Individual Time Trial Events

Unlike the mass-start stage race, the individual time trial (ITT) demands a relatively steady state power output. Drafting is not allowed, and tactical challenges are limited.

Power measures during ITTs validate the demanding steady state nature of this event. Padilla and colleagues (2000) reported power outputs for 12 to 19 riders during 28 ± 8.6 km long ITTs, competed as stages of the Tour de France, Giro d'Italia, and Vuelta a España. Average power outputs of 347 to 380 W were reported, depending on race length. As would be expected, an inverse relationship between ITT length and average power output emerged—the shorter the race, the higher the average power output. In the shortest race, a 7.3-km prologue, average power was 380 W. Isolated efforts involving exceptionally high power outputs were absent.

Importantly, Padilla and colleagues (2000) also reported ITT power outputs referenced to the athlete's individual peak power outputs, measured on a laboratory cycling ergometer. When expressed relative to peak power output, cyclists in these races produced 89 ± 6%, 84 ± 7%, and 79 ± 6% of their peak power outputs during time trials of 7.3 km, 28 km, and 49.3 km, respectively.

Power Requirements During Mountain Bike Cross-Country Races

Given the extreme variations in terrain encountered during mountain bike racing, relatively wide variations in cycling power are expected in these events. On the other hand, mountain bike races are traditionally shorter in duration than road races, permitting more intense efforts. Recent research has exposed the unique demands of such racing.

Schoberer (1998) reported maximum, minimum, and average power outputs for mountain bike racing over a 50-km cross-country course (2 hours, 48 minutes). Average power was 233 W, and peak power reached 794 W. Compared to road racing, these numbers suggest that mountain bike racing is performed at lower intensity levels, at least in an average sense.

Martin (1997) reported similar results. He compared the power distribution of a road racer and a mountain bike racer during races of 125 km (3 hours, 19 minutes) and 39 km (1 hour, 51 minutes), respectively. Compared to a mass-start road race, Martin concluded (admittedly based on a small sample size) that mountain bike racing involved power outputs 100 W lower than road racing (198 ± 140 W versus 300 ± 177 W), despite the shorter duration. Interestingly, Martin stressed that his road racer spent 10% of his race above 500 W, whereas the mountain bike racer spent only 1% of his race above this level.

More recently, Gregory (2001) conducted a more comprehensive evaluation of the physiological and physical determinants of mountain bike racing. Gregory tested nine cyclists performing cross-country mountain bike time trial races on an 8.5-mile (13.8-km) course with a 2119-ft (646-m) elevation gain. Over the two-hour, 20-minute race, the cyclists averaged a power output of 306.8 ± 14 W, pedaling at an average cadence of 68.3 ± 4.3 rpm. The efforts were accomplished with heart rates roughly 90% of their individual max heart rates. Gregory's data suggest that the mountain bike racing environment is an intermittent and high-intensity task, which, because of the need for significant technical skills, elicits lower-intensity power outputs than road time trials.

Using Power to Control Training

Measurement of cycling power is an excellent way to control training. Actually, coaches have been attempting to control effort levels during cycling training for decades. Today, systems such as the SRM, Power Tap, and Polar power-measuring devices provide the means to truly track and control effort. Cyclists and their coaches can establish targeted power level zones in which a given effort or set of efforts must fall (e.g., 200 to 250 W for 30 min; 350 to 400 W for 1-min intervals). The cyclist checks the on-board power-measuring system for feedback to keep the cycling effort in the target zone. This is particularly helpful when riding conditions cannot be accurately controlled. In the presence of a strong headwind or tailwind, for example, the power meter simply directs the rider to modify cycling speed to maintain the effort within the targeted zone.

Coaches can use power data downloaded from a cycling power meter as a critical tool to track training status and design training programs. Imagine a cyclist using a power meter reporting generalized fatigue and lackluster performance during a recent training ride. The coach, in examining the power and heart rate data, may find the cyclist is indeed underperforming relative to his or her usual level. Heart rates may be high despite moderate to low power levels.

Alternatively, perhaps the ride involved shifting winds, a moderately difficulty hill, and limited opportunities to rest in a drafting position. Power levels during this ride would be higher than normal, somewhat validating the cyclist's perception of effort, but also explaining the elevated yet understandable sense of fatigue.

Another way to use power measurements to direct training concerns performance targeting. For example, a rider wishing to complete a flat 40-km time trial in one hour (average speed of 40 kph) can establish in training the average power level required to maintain such a pace. Then, the training program can focus on the maintenance of this target power level for longer and longer periods, eventually reaching the hour goal. If during the 40-km race the wind blows, and power is measured, effort can be modified to maintain that sustainable power level developed in training.

Course characterization and pacing development are two other applications of power meter data. Riding a course in advance of a race (preferably early in training) permits each section of the course to be described in terms of effort level, speed, and even desired cadence. Uphill sections requiring high power output, for example, can be characterized in terms of length, duration, cycling speed, power, and perhaps cadence. Once the course is characterized section by section, training can be adapted to prepare the cyclist for the planned or scheduled effort profile.

Research examining pacing strategies suggests that maintaining a relatively constant power output during sustained efforts such as individual time trials results in superior performance. Power-measuring devices provide riders with immediate feedback describing their current effort levels. Effort levels can be adjusted to adhere to a prescribed racing strategy. This is particularly helpful when conditions change caused by wind, hills, or even drafting in non-time-trial events.

Finally, power-measuring devices, when used in a systematic manner, permit the aerodynamic assessment of equipment and rider position.* Ideally, a cyclist rides the bicycle on an indoor velodrome, increasing velocity every two or three laps. Data are downloaded, and a power-versus-velocity relation is developed (see figure 6.8). Adjustments to bicycle componentry, geometry (particularly handlebar setup), rider position, and/or clothing (including helmet) are then made, and the test is repeated. A new power-versus-velocity relation is created and compared to the original. The goal is to shift the power-versus-velocity relation to the right (see figure 6.8) so that for any given velocity, less power is required. This procedure provides direct information describing the performance enhancements in cycling speed achievable via improved aerodynamics.

---

* Accurate calibrations of power-measuring devices are essential if accurate aerodynamic assessments are to be attempted.

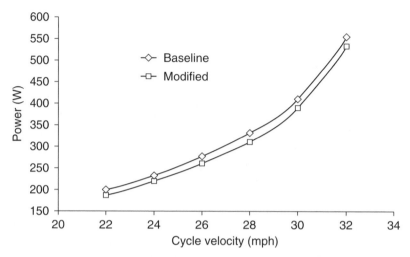

FIGURE 6.8   Sample power-versus-velocity data recorded during velodrome tests aimed at improving cycling aerodynamics. Baseline data clearly illustrate how power increases nonlinearly with cycling velocity. After a handlebar and seat position adjustment, data were recollected (modified curve). The power-versus-velocity curve shifted to the right, meaning that the rider in the modified position achieved a similar velocity at a lower power level, or could ride at increased velocity for the same power output.

Directions for Future Research

Cycling power will continue to be a critical performance factor for coaches, scientists, and high-tech cyclists. Given the rapidly growing popularity of cycling power-measuring devices, techniques for using the information provided by these devices to effectively control training and racing will improve. So too will the technology supplying the information.

In the next five years, the reliability, accuracy, simplicity, and effectiveness of commercially available power meters undoubtedly will increase. A lightweight racing version of the Power Tap is currently under development. Polar plans an upgrade to its signal-processing procedures to account for the potentially confounding effects of road vibration and to address sensor-spacing issues. SRMs are probably being further refined to address minor technical issues. The data analysis and presentation programs used by these power-measuring systems continue to evolve as well, offering more powerful tracking of performance and training status. Hopefully, the cost of these devices will fall too, providing more cyclists the opportunity to benefit from their use.

Research employing cycling power and power-measuring devices is in the early stages, and future work in this area is expected. Continued monitoring of cyclists in racing situations will more completely characterize the unique demands of each event at many levels of competition. Analyses of the physical determinants of success for cyclists in each of the many disciplines will broaden, based substantially on cycling power output and physiological correlates.

Finally, it is not hard to imagine a cycling training system in the near future that uses on-road measurement of cycling power and speed, perhaps with altitude change, to simulate a given course on an indoor trainer. A cyclist would ride a given real course, allowing the on-board cycling computer to track variations in speed, power, and elevation (although elevation change could be estimated from speed and power). Data from the device would then be downloaded to an indoor, electromagnetic trainer that would store the course profile. Upon request, the indoor trainer would then reproduce the course by adjusting load to match velocity-specific power requirements, permitting idealized training for racing or more real-world conditions for cyclists training during the cold winter months. Perhaps the trainer could change configuration to match grade variations. With today's technology, a video of the course, projected on a large, flat screen monitor, could accompany the simulation. Or maybe just a bike ride without any wires, sensors, and computers is in order.

References

Broker, J.P., Crawley, J.C., and Coughlin, K. 2002. Pedaling mechanics differences across cycling disciplines: Observations over 10 years of testing. *Med Sci Sports Exerc* 34(5): S90.

Danh, K., Mai, L., Poland, J., and Jenkins, C. 1991. Frictional resistance in bicycle wheel bearings. *Cycling Science* 3(3-4): 44-50.

Fernandez-Garcia, B., Perez-Landaluce, M., Rodriguez-Alonso, M., and Terrados, N. 2000. Intensity of exercise during road race pro-cycling competition. *Med Sci Sports Exerc* 32:1002-1006.

Golich, D., and Broker, J.P. 1996. SRM instrumentation and the power output of elite male cyclists during the Tour DuPont. *Performance Conditioning for Cycling* 2(9): 6-8.

Grazzi, G., Alfieri, N., Borsetto, C., Casoni, I., Manfredini, F., Mazzooni, G., and Conconi, F. 1999. The power output/heart rate relationship in cycling: Test standardization and repeatability. *Med Sci Sports Exerc* 31:1478-1483.

Gregory, J. 2001. The physiological and physical determinants of mountain bike cross country cycling. Unpublished master's thesis, Department of Anatomy and Physiology, University of Tasmania.

Hagberg, J., and McCole, S. 1996. Energy expenditure during cycling. In *High-tech cycling*, edited by E.R. Burke. Champaign, Ill.: Human Kinetics. pp. 167-184.

Jeukendrup, A.E. 2000. Nutrition in sport. In *Cycling: IOC encyclopedia of sport and exercise*, edited by R.J. Maughan. Oxford: Blackwell Science. pp. 562-573.

Jeukendrup, A.E. 2002. Power output. In *High performance cycling*, edited by A.E. Jeukendrup. Champaign, Ill.: Human Kinetics. pp. 69-102.

Kyle, C.R. 1988. How friction slows a bike. *Bicycling* June: 180-185.

Kyle, C.R. 1995. Bicycle aerodynamics. In *Human powered vehicles*, edited by A.V. Abbott and D.G. Wilson. Champaign, Ill.: Human Kinetics. pp. 141-155.

Kyle, C.R. 1996. Selecting cycling equipment. In *High tech cycling,* edited by E.R. Burke. Champaign, Ill.: Human Kinetics. pp. 1-44.

Lucia, A., Hoyos, J., Carvajal, A., and Chicarro, J.L. 1999. Heart rate response to professional road cycling: The Tour de France. *Int J Sports Med* 20:167-172.

Mantell, M. 1998. Riis's pieces. *Velonews* 27:32.

Martin, D. 1997. Road vs. mountain bike. *Bicycling Australia* October: 37-42.

Padilla, S., Mujika, I., Orbananos, J., and Angulo, F. 2000. Exercise intensity during competition time trials in professional road racing. *Med Sci Sports Exerc* 32:850-856.

Padilla, S., Mujika, I., Orbananos, J., Santisteban, J., Angulo, F., and Goiriena, J. 2001. Exercise intensity and load during mass-start stage races as a professional road cycling. *Med Sci Sports Exerc* 33:796-802.

Schoberer, U. 1998. Operating Instructions (SRM), Welldorf, Germany.

7

The Cycling World Hour Record

Chester R. Kyle • David R. Bassett, Jr.

Simply put, the world hour record is the distance a cyclist can pedal a bicycle in one hour on a flat circuit course. Hour records have been kept faithfully since 1876, when F.L. Dodds of England pedaled a penny farthing, or ordinary bike, 25.508 km (15.8 mi) in one hour. The bike bore almost no resemblance to a modern bicycle; it had an enormous front wheel with radial spokes, a small rear wheel, and hard rubber tires.

When the chain-driven safety bicycle with pneumatic tires was first introduced in 1886, the hour record took an immediate leap. The record has more than doubled since the days of the high wheeler. Except for the lack of a seat tube, the revolutionary 1886 Rover safety bicycle incorporated almost all of the elements of a modern track bicycle. The most remarkable hour record was set in 1996 by Chris Boardman of England at 56.375 km. Boardman rode an exotic composite aerodynamic bicycle, now illegal to race. See table 7.1 and figure 7.1.

TABLE 7.1 UCI Cycling World Hour Records, 1870 to Present

Date	Cyclist	Bike	Location	Distance (km)
3/25/1870	J.T. Johnson, England	High wheeler	Aston Cross, Birmingham	22.785
3/25/1876	F.L. Dodds, England	High wheeler	Cambridge	25.508
8/02/1882	H.L. Cortis, England	High wheeler	Surbiton	32.484
8/31/1888	H.E. Laurie, England	Classic track	Long Eaton, England	33.913
5/11/1893	Henri Desgranges, France	Classic track	Paris-Buffalo	35.325
10/31/1894	Jules Dubois, France	Classic track	Paris-Buffalo	38.220
7/30/1897	M. van den Eynde, Belgium	Classic track	Paris-Municipale	39.240
9/7/1898	W.W. Hamilton, USA	Classic track	Denver, Colorado	40.781[a]
8/24/1905	Lucien Petit-Breton, France	Classic track	Paris-Buffalo	41.110
6/20/1907	Marcel Berthet, France	Classic track	Paris-Buffalo	41.520
8/22/1912	Oscar Egg, Switzerland	Classic track	Paris-Buffalo	42.122
8/7/1913	Marcel Berthet, France	Classic track	Paris-Buffalo	42.742
8/21/1913	Oscar Egg, Switzerland	Classic track	Paris-Buffalo	43.525
9/20/1913	Marcel Berthet, France	Classic track	Paris-Buffalo	43.775
6/18/1914	Oscar Egg, Switzerland	Classic track	Paris-Buffalo	44.247
8/29/1933	Maurice Richard, France	Classic track	Saint-Trond	44.777
10/31/1935	Giuseppe Olmo, Italy	Classic track	Milano-Vigorelli	45.090

TABLE 7.1 (continued)

Date	Cyclist	Bike	Location	Distance (km)
10/14/1936	Maurice Richard, France	Classic track	Milano-Vigorelli	45.325
9/29/1937	Franz Slaats, Holland	Classic track	Milano-Vigorelli	45.558
11/3/1937	Maurice Archambaud, France	Classic track	Milano-Vigorelli	45.840
11/7/1942	Fausto Coppi, Italy	Classic track	Milano-Vigorelli	45.871
6/29/1955	Jacques Anquetil, France	Classic track	Milano-Vigorelli	45.159[b]
9/19/1956	Ercole Baldini, Italy	Classic track	Milano-Vigorelli	46.393
9/18/1957	Roger Rivière, France	Classic track	Milano-Vigorelli	46.923
9/23/1958	Roger Rivière, France	Classic track	Milano-Vigorelli	47.346
9/27/1962	Jacques Anquetil, France	Classic track	Milano-Vigorelli	47.493
10/30/1967	Ferdinand Bracke, Belgium	Classic track	Rome-Olympic Vel.	48.093
10/10/1968	Ole Ritter, Denmark	Classic track	Mexico City Olympic Vel.	45.653[a]
10/25/1972	Eddy Merckx, Belgium	Classic track	Mexico City Olympic Vel.	49.431[a]
1/19/1984	Francesco Moser, Italy	Aero bike (AB)	Mexico City Sports Center	50.808[a]
1/23/1984	Francesco Moser, Italy	Aero bike	Mexico City Sports Center	51.151[a]
9/9/1985	Hans-Henrik Oersted, Denmark	Aero bike	Balsano Dell Grappa	48.144
8/8/1986	Francesco Moser, Italy	Aero bike	Milano-Vigorelli	48.543
8/20/1986	Francesco Moser, Italy	Big wheel AB	Milano-Vigorelli	49.801

(continued)

TABLE 7.1 (continued)

Date	Cyclist	Bike	Location	Distance (km)
5/21/1988	Franceso Moser, Italy	Big wheel AB	Stuttgart (indoors)	50.644[c]
7/17/1993	Graeme Obree, Scotland	Obree aero superbike (ASB)	Hamar (indoors)	51.596[c]
7/23/1993	Chris Boardman, England	Aero bars ASB	Bordeaux (indoors)	52.270[c]
4/27/1994	Graeme Obree, Scotland	Superman pos. ASB	Bordeaux (indoors)	52.713[c]
9/2/1994	Miguel Indurain, Spain	Aero bars ASB	Bordeaux (indoors)	53.040[c]
10/22/1994	Tony Rominger, Switzerland	Aero bars, standard bike, disc wheels	Bordeaux (indoors)	53.832[c]
11/5/1994	Tony Rominger, Switzerland	Aero bars, standard bike, disc wheels	Bordeaux (indoors)	55.291[c]
9/6/1996	Chris Boarman, England	Superman pos. ASB	Manchester (indoors)	56.375[c]
10/27/2000	Chris Boardman, England	Classic track	Manchester (indoors)	49.441[d]

All records are outdoor records unless specified as indoor records.

[a] High altitude records; all others are sea level records.

[b] Unofficial record. Anquetil refused to submit to drug testing after the ride.

[c] Indoor sea level record; all others are outdoor.

[d] Indoor sea level record; similar to Merckx's bike in 1972.

During the past century, some of the most famous cyclists have either held or attempted the prestigious hour record, including five Tour de France winners—Lucien Petit-Breton of France, Fausto Coppi of Italy, Jacques Anquetil of France, Eddy Merckx of Belgium, and Miguel Indurain of Spain. These five cyclists have won the Tour de France 19 times.

In this chapter, we will discuss the reasons behind the most dramatic increases in the hour record over its long history, most importantly the rapid improvement in equipment technology, both early and modern, and better athletic performance due to improved training and technique. Ad-

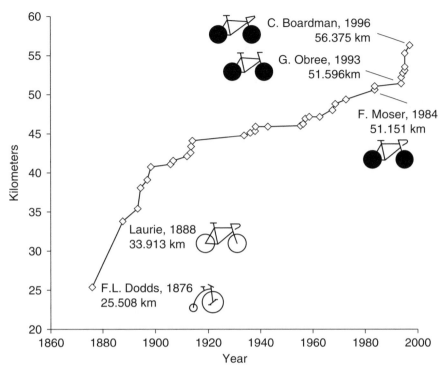

FIGURE 7.1   World cycling hour record, 1876-2000.

vances in cycling physiology and nutrition have also contributed to cycling performance. Better equipment technology combined with improved athletics have yielded the most rapid increase in the hour record since the introduction of the safety bicycle.

This chapter includes a math model that illustrates the effect of human power output and bicycle equipment on hour records. The model predicts the required power to pedal at a certain velocity given the rider's body size and height and the equipment used. The model also includes the influence of environmental factors such as altitude and track conditions. Since a cyclist's oxygen uptake varies with altitude, we will also discuss this effect on cycling performance.

At racing speeds, aerodynamic drag is about 90% of the retarding force against a bicycle (see figure 7.2). We will review the historical influence of cycling aerodynamics and the Union Cycliste Internationale (UCI), the international governing body of bicycle racing. Without UCI regulations regarding aerodynamics, the bicycle could have taken a far different form, as illustrated by the incredible performance of streamlined human-powered bicycles illegal in standard bicycle racing. On a level course with no wind,

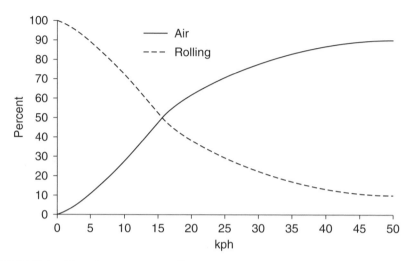

FIGURE 7.2   Air resistance versus rolling resistance.

these completely enclosed recumbent pedal-powered vehicles have reached top speeds of over 130 kph and have covered distances of over 82 km in one hour.

Historic Influences on the Hour Record

From 1876 to 1898, the early days of the bicycle, speeds increased rapidly due to improvements in racing bicycles and equipment. Drop handlebars, ball bearings, toe clips, high-pressure tubular tires, lightweight steel tubular diamond frames, and lightweight wheels were introduced before 1900. After 1898, the track racing bicycle remained essentially unchanged for the next 86 years.

From 1898 to 1984, the hour record improved by small increments, due mainly to better athletes and training and occasionally to intense competition. For example, in 1907 Marcel Berthet of France set a new hour record of 41.520 km, beginning one of the most dramatic duels in cycling history. Berthet's record was broken by Oscar Egg of Switzerland in 1912. Between 1912 and 1914, Berthet and Egg exchanged the hour record five times. Not until 1933 was Egg's 1914 record of 43.725 km broken, a span of 19 years.

Due to World War I and World War II, no new records were set from 1914 to 1933 or from 1942 to 1955. In 1972, another event discouraged attempts—Eddy Merckx of Belguim, five-time winner of the Tour de France, set a record of 49.431 km at high altitude in Mexico City (2300 m), where air density is 20% lower and human power requirement is lower than at sea level. At the time, Merckx's record was considered unbeatable, so for 12 years cyclists did not attempt the hour record.

In 1984, Francesco Moser of Italy used an entirely different approach to breaking the record. Riding a unique aerodynamic bicycle at high altitude (Mexico City, 2300 m), he decisively broke Merckx's record by riding 50.808 km in an hour. Four days later he covered 51.151 km. The bicycle, designed by exercise physiologist Antonio Dal Monte of Rome, had disk wheels and a sloping top tube that permitted Moser to ride in a low crouched position using cow horn handlebars. It was the first time since 1914 that disk wheels had been used in competition (they were used in a streamlined bicycle race in Berlin, Germany, on April 14, 1914). Moser wore a slick, tight-fitting jersey and full-length tights. Instead of the usual leather helmet, he covered his hair with what looked like a swim cap. Moser's whole racing system was designed by Dal Monte for low wind resistance. The surprise was that the UCI permitted these innovations. The question was, Why?

Aerodynamics and the UCI

In 1913, Parisian Etienne Bunau-Varilla was granted patents on streamlined enclosures for a bicycle. In track demonstrations, he proved that the dirigible-shaped shell made bicycles at least 6 kph faster than the best standard racing bicycle. In response, the UCI passed its historic Rule 31, forbidding

any device on a bicycle intended to reduce air resistance (Kyle 2001).

UCI Rule 31 seemed clear and was not challenged until about 1978, when bicycles with airfoil-shaped tubing and other aerodynamic innovations such as teardrop-shaped tubing, streamlined frame fillets, streamlined helmets, shoes with covered laces, and streamlined handlebars began to appear. In 1980, Shimano introduced a complete line of aerodynamic components. The grupo was

The UCI has vacilated in its opinion of special aerodynamic equipment, such as the aerodynamic helmet worn by this rider.

not popular and was discontinued after a few years, although the equipment was effective.

When Dal Monte introduced modern disk wheels in 1984, the technical committee of the UCI seemed to reinterpret Rule 31 to mean that if a bicycle component had a structural or functional purpose, streamlining was legal. By the 1996 Olympics, almost all time trial competitors had bicycles with exotic streamlined monocoque carbon graphite frames and disk wheels and complete aerodynamic cycling systems including bicycles, shoes, helmets, and clothing. Riders used the exaggerated superman time trial position that is now illegal (see figure 7.3). France, the United States, Germany, Italy, Russia, and others rode these "superbikes" in the Atlanta Olympics.

With this equipment, every major cycling time trial record in the world was broken. For example, in 1996 Chris Boardman of England set a 4,000-m individual pursuit record of 4:11.114 (57.34 kph), more than 24 s faster than the world record in 1984 when cycling aerodynamics first became a significant factor in international bicycle racing. Incredibly, Boardman's 4,000-m time was more than 6 s faster than the four-man team pursuit world record of 1984. Also in 1996, Boardman set a new world hour record of 56.375 km.

After 1984, the UCI vacillated in its interpretation of aerodynamics Rule 31. From 1984 to 2000, it made and rescinded more than a dozen rules regarding aerodynamics (Kyle 2001). In 1986, the United States proposed a

FIGURE 7.3 Bicycle racing positions: (*a*) traditional racing position, standard track bike; (*b*) standard aero bars; (*c*) the Obree position; (*d*) the superman position.

composite monocoque time trial bike designed by engineers Don Guichard and Chester Kyle, which the UCI technical committee summarily rejected. But in 1991, the UCI reversed its decision and allowed Boardman to race a similar Lotus bike in the 1992 Olympics.

The availability of aerodynamic bikes and new riding positions had an immediate effect on the hour record. Between 1993 and 1996, the record was broken six times and the distance increased by over 5 km, the most rapid increase since 1888 when racers switched from the high wheeler to the chain-driven safety bicycle. In 1993 and 1994, the hour record was broken twice by an unknown amateur, engineer Graeme Obree of Scotland. The first time Obree broke the record on a bicycle of his own design using a riding position he invented (see figure 7.3). When the UCI outlawed Obree's unique riding position, he invented the superman position and broke the record again. (In the interim, Chris Boardman surpassed Obree's first record.) Obree has the distinction of having had his legal innovations banned twice by the UCI.

In 1996, when Boardman set his extraordinary individual pursuit record and new hour record by using an exotic aerodynamic monocoque bicycle and Obree's superman position, panic ensued in the UCI. The organization felt that time trial racing was becoming a contest among engineers, designers, and scientists instead of between athletes.

The UCI's response was to outlaw monocoque bikes beginning in 2000 (UCI 2002a). For general time trials, the new ruling requires a diamond frame, limits frame tubing cross-sectional dimensions, and in effect rolls back bicycle design to about 1986. The UCI also outlawed the superman aero riding position and required bicycles to have two wheels of the same size. Still, for time trialing, UCI regulations are fairly liberal. Disk wheels, standard aero bars, aero tubing sections, and other innovations are still legal for individual or team time trials on road or track.

The UCI was not nearly so liberal with its new hour record regulations (UCI 2002b). The UCI 2000 rulings for the hour record require a standard track bicycle with triangular frame, much like Eddy Merckx's 1972 machine. The bike must have round tubing, traditional style drop bars, and two spoked wheels of equal diameter with 16 to 32 spokes. The spokes cannot exceed 2 mm in cross section, although oval spokes are permitted. The wheels must have shallow rims, not to exceed 2.2 cm in dimension. The bike cannot weigh less than 6.8 kg. The rider must use a safety helmet with no part intended to lower wind resistance. In other words, for the hour record, the UCI rolled bicycle design standards back 30 years.

In 1972, the UCI rule book had less than a page governing racing bicycles; the current UCI rule book has 12 pages. In general, the UCI has tried to create racing regulations that will prevent racers from having an unfair advantage in equipment. Because it also specifies that bicycles used in racing must be commonly available commercially, this goal appears within reach.

UCI and Recumbent Bicycles

The UCI's negative reaction to recent technological innovations is certainly not unique in its history. In 1933, another crisis precipitated a UCI ruling that permanently changed the course of bicycle design. Charles Mochet of France invented a practical recumbent bicycle called the Velocar. On a recumbent bike, the rider pedals from a low reclining position, decreasing wind resistance and increasing speed with the same power. Mochet contracted second category rider François Faure to race the Velocar on the tracks of Europe. By 1933, Faure was beating the best professional European racers. The recumbent Velocar was obviously faster than a standard racing bicycle. On July 7, 1933, Faure broke Oscar Egg's long-standing hour record of 44.247 km with a distance of 45.055 km. This created a storm of newspaper publicity.

Unfortunately for Mochet, the hour record was broken in August 1933 by a conventional bicycle racer, Maurice Richard, at 44.777 km. In February of 1934, the UCI temporarily recognized Faure's record and referred the matter of the Velocar to a special commission. In April of 1934, the commission ruled that the Velocar was not a bicycle; they rescinded Faure's record and recognized Richard's. They also passed a series of rules banning recumbents from competing in UCI-sanctioned races. With the 1934 UCI ruling, the brief racing history of recumbent bicycles ended and didn't begin again for over 40 years (Kyle in press).

Recumbent Bicycle Hour Record

If bicycles of unlimited design were permitted to compete against traditional bicycles, there would be no contest. In occasional exhibitions, single streamlined recumbent bicycles have lapped an elite four-man pursuit team of conventional bicycle track racers twice in 4000 m, posting times of about 3 min 30 s. These machines, called human-powered vehicles (HPVs), are often less than 3 ft high and resemble the fuselage of a jet aircraft without wings. The wheels, rider, and bicycle are completely enclosed in a streamlined shell.

The current HPV world record for the 200-m sprint on a straight, level course with a flying start and no wind is 130.435 kph (81.048 mph). This is nearly 60 kph faster than the fastest conventional sprint track bicycle ridden by the world's most powerful cycle athlete. The current HPV sprint record was set by Canadian amateur Sam Whittingham at Battle Mountain, Nevada, in 2001 (see figure 7.4). So far, HPV records have been set by amateur cyclists, whereas standard cycling records are almost always set by professionals.

Formal HPV racing began in 1975 with the founding of the International Human Powered Vehicle Association (IHPVA). Vehicles of any design are

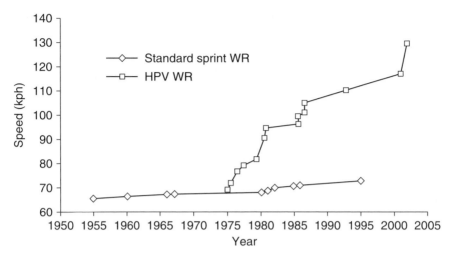

FIGURE 7.4   HPV 200-m world records versus standard bicycle 200-m sprint records, 1975 to 2002.

permitted in IHPVA races as long as they are human powered (Kyle in press).

In the hour, streamlined HPVs are nearly 25 kph faster than standard racing bicycles. The current HPV hour record is held by Lars Teutenberg of Germany at 82.601 km (51.326 mph), a record set in 2002 (see table 7.2 and figure 7.5). Ed Dempsey of Santa Ana, California, is currently offering a $25,000 prize for the first HPV to cover 90 km in one hour. As of this writing, the prize is unclaimed, although several unsuccessful attempts have been made. One low recumbent machine, designed by engineer Matt Weaver of Watsonville, California, is completely sealed from the outside except for controlled ventilation. There are no windows. Weaver steers using a video display. The bike has 20-in. wheels and weighs only 33 lb, including the carbon graphite frame and the computer-designed streamlined Kevlar shell.

Considering the speed handicap of traditional bikes, it is clear why the UCI banned recumbents and streamlining. If they hadn't, bicycle races would be outright contests of technology, with the athlete secondary to the machine. By banning recumbents in 1934, however, the UCI effectively halted the development of recumbent bicycles for more than 40 years. Only recently have these machines been commercially produced, and now recumbents are occasionally seen on the roads of Europe and the United States. At present there are about 80 small recumbent manufacturers worldwide who yearly produce a few thousand bicycles and tricycles. Recumbents are still only a very small fraction of the overall market. This might have been different had the UCI ruled in favor of Charles Mochet in 1933.

TABLE 7.2   HPV Hour Records

Date	Rider/ designer	Bike	Location	Distance (km)
7/7/1933	Francois Faure/ Charles Mochet (France)	Velocar, open recumbent	Paris	45.055
11/18/1933	Marcel Berthet/ Marcel Berthet (France)	Velodyne, streamlined bike	Paris	49.992
3/3/1939	Francois Faure/ Charles Mochet (France)	Velocar, streamlined recumbent bike	Paris	50.537
5/6/1979	Ron Skarin/ Chester Kyle (USA)	Teledyne Titan, streamlined bike	Ontario, Canada	51.306
5/4/1980	Eric Edwards/ Al Voight (USA)	Vector, streamlined recumbent trike	Ontario Canada	59.449
9/29/1984	Fred Markham/ Gardner Martin (USA)	Gold Rush, streamlined recumbent bike	Indianapolis	60.350
9/10/1985	Richard Crane/ Derek Henden (England)	Streamlined recumbent bike	Uknown	66.305
8/28/1986	Fred Markham/ Gardner Martin (USA)	Gold Rush, streamlined recumbent bike	Vancouver, British Columbia, Canada	67.013
7/15/1989	Fred Markham/ Gardner Martin (USA)	Gold Rush, streamlined recumbent bike	Adrian, Michigan	73.000
9/10/1985	Pat Kinch/ Miles Kingsbury (England)	The Bean, streamlined recumbent bike	Bedfordshire	75.575
7/27/1996	Lars Teutenberg/ Guido Martens (Germany)	Tomahawk II, streamlined recumbent bike	Munich	78.037
7/29/1998	Sam Whittingham/ George Georgiev (Canada)	Varna, streamlined recumbent bike	Blainville	79.136
8/7/1999	Lars Teutenberg/ Guido Martens (Germany)	Whitehawk, streamlined recumbent bike	Dudenhofen	81.158
7/27/2002	Lars Teutenberg/ Guido Martens (Germany)	Whitehawk, streamlined recumbent bike	Dudenhofen	82.601

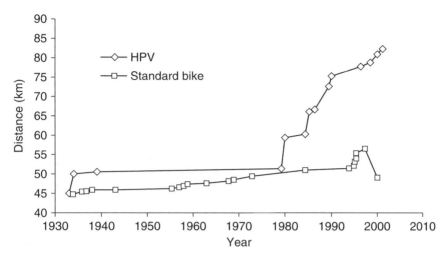

FIGURE 7.5   HPV hour records versus standard bike hour records.

Math Models of the Hour Record

During the past decade, crank dynamometers have enabled scientists to accurately measure the power required to cycle under race conditions. In 1994, physiologist Peter Keen measured record holder Chris Boardman's crank power at 442 W (0.59 horsepower or hp) for one hour (Keen 1994). An earlier measurement of hour record holder Eddy Merckx was done at the Sportshocsschule in Koln, Germany, on April 24, 1975. Merckx produced 455 W for one hour on a stationary bicycle ergometer (Kyle and Caiozzo 1986).

Bassett and colleagues (1999) developed a mathematical model of track cycling using field measurements of power. They used the model to compare cycling hour record holders under the same standardized conditions. The model predicts the crank power of cyclists pedaling at a steady speed, knowing the cyclists' height and weight as well as the altitude, cycling equipment, clothing, body position, track circumference, and track surface. They also developed a relationship between the decline in maximal aerobic power ($\dot{V}O_2$max) with increasing elevation. With the math model, Bassett and colleagues found that the estimated sea level power of the hour record holders from 1967 to 1996 varied from about 370 W to 460 W (see table 7.3).

According to the estimates in table 7.3, Eddy Merckx delivered the highest equivalent sea level power (429 W) of any of the earlier record holders until Miguel Indurain (436 W) in 1994. Merckx's record was set in the high altitude of Mexico City. He did not train at high altitude before his attempt, so his aerobic power was lower than it would have been had he been acclimated. Although our model took this into account, it should be noted that the effects of high altitude on $\dot{V}O_2$max vary according to the individual. In any case, the power of 429 W predicted by the model seems reasonable compared to

Merckx's stationary ergometer power of 455 W for an hour. After 1994, Tony Rominger at 460 W and Chris Boardman at 442 W were highest.

Starting with Moser and Antonio Dal Monte, hour record attempts have usually included support from physiologists and coaches, who prepare the cyclist prior to the record attempt. This scientific preparation and training has been remarkably successful.

Padilla and coworkers (2000) tested Miguel Indurain extensively before his record ride in 1994 with the intent of preparing him to maintain a record pace. Their estimate of Indurain's power during his record ride, 497 to 509 W, was much higher than the 436 W given in table 7.3. Padilla attributed this

TABLE 7.3 Power and Distance, Normalized to Manchester and Boardman's Equipment and Position

Rider	Track	Elevation (m)	Original record distance (km)	Power required at track elevation (W)	Power corrected to sea level (W)
F. Bracke	Rome	48	48.093	400	400
O. Ritter	Mexico	2338	48.653	336	376
E. Merckx	Mexico	2338	49.431	366	429
F. Moser	Mexico	2338	50.808	358	401
F. Moser	Mexico	2338	51.151	364	407
F. Moser*	Stuttgart	121	50.644	410	410
G. Obree	Hamar	124	51.596	369	369
C. Boardman	Bordeaux	73	52.270	409	409
G. Obree	Bordeaux	73	52.713	389	389
M. Indurain	Bordeaux	73	53.040	436	436
T. Rominger	Bordeaux	73	53.832	427	427
T. Rominger	Bordeaux	73	55.291	460	460
C. Boardman	Manchester	60	56.375	442	442
C. Boardmann**	Manchester	60	49.441	414	414

* 1988 sea level record using aero bike.
** Record set under UCI 2000 rules; bike essentially the same as Merckx's 1972 bike.

Adapted, by permission, from D.R. Bassett, C.R. Kyle, L. Passfield, J.P. Broker, and E.R. Burke, 1999, "Comparing cycling world hour records, 1967-1996: modeling with empirical data," *Med Sci Sports Exerc* 31(11):1665-1676.

higher estimated power output to Indurain's large body size (1.88 m, 82 kg; 6 ft 2 in., 181 lb) and the difficulty in evaluating the air drag of cyclists with larger than average body size. Padilla's group used a variety of methods to verify their power predictions including wind tunnel tests, stationary bicycle ergometer tests, and extensive physiological measurements. Although Padilla's group did not measure power using a crank ergometer as Keen (1994) did, Padilla's calculation of power for the smaller hour record holders such as Rominger and Boardman was close to the values given in table 7.3.

Considering the models of both Bassett and Padilla, there seems to be little doubt that elite cyclists can put out over 450 W (0.60 hp) for one hour. This extraordinary power is more than double what a fit recreational cyclist can do for an equal time period (150 to 200 W) (Kyle and Caiozzo 1986; Whitt and Wilson 1982).

Math Model of Track Cycling

The math model developed by Bassett and colleagues (1999) was based on tests using an SRM crank dynamometer system. The SRM crank dynamometer (Schoberer Rad Messtechnik, Welldorf, Germany) consists of an instrumented chain ring that transmits strain gauge readings by telemetry to a handlebar microprocessor or to a central computer, along with crank rpm and bicycle speed. From this, average power can be computed and stored.

The SRM tests were performed on USA Team cyclists by Jeff Broker of USOC Sports Sciences and on British Team cyclists by Louis Passfield of the University Medical School at Aberdeen and Peter Keen of the British Cycling Federation. These data were collected by coaches and technical staff for the purpose of preparing their athletes for national and international competition. A typical power curve is shown in figure 7.6.

This power series equation was used as a basis for the math model used by Bassett and colleagues (1999):

$$P = A_1V + A_2V^2 + A_3V^3$$

A_1 is a constant expressing the static rolling resistance of bicycle wheels and tires (a bicycle wheel has a frictional resistance to motion even when standing still). A_2 is a constant related to dynamic rolling resistance (rotating bicycle tires, wheels, and bearings increase frictional resistance as speed increases). A_3 is a constant that is a function of air density, the frontal area of the rider and bicycle, and the aerodynamic drag coefficient (related to the shape of the object and the efficiency with which it moves through the air). V is the velocity of the bicycle in kph.

The constant A_1 may be derived from experimental data (Bassett et al. 1999). Racing bicycle tire tests show that rolling resistance increases with the weight on the tire, the steering angle, the roughness of the surface, and other factors. Several things tend to cause the rolling resistance on a

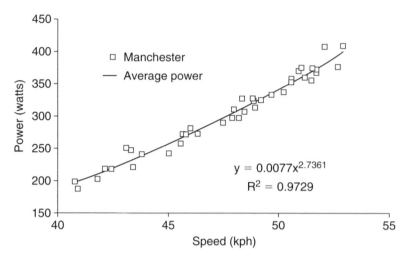

FIGURE 7.6   SRM crank power versus speed, Manchester velodrome, Lotus bike.

bicycle racing track to be higher than that measured on a straight, level test surface. First, in the curves of a track the centrifugal force at racing speeds raises the weight on the tire by over 1.5 times. Second, the steering angle of a bicycle at racing speed oscillates through about ±3° with every pedal stroke, causing increased rolling friction due to tire scrubbing. Scrubbing occurs when the tire contact patch acquires a slip angle with the pavement as the bicycle turns. Third, bicycle tracks are always cambered (banked) even on the straights. The fact that the bicycle is almost never perpendicular to the track means that a steering correction is required to hold the bicycle on a line, causing additional tire friction. Fourth, most racing tracks are not entirely smooth. Even though static rolling resistance can be as low as 0.22% of the down force applied to the tire, a more reasonable estimate for conditions on a bicycle track would be an average of 0.35% of the applied force on the tire (Bassett et al. 1999). This would give a value for A_1 of $(0.00953\ M_t)$ W/hr (kg/km)$^{-1}$ where M_t is the total mass of the bicycle and rider in kg.

A_2 is proportional to the increase in rolling resistance due to bearing friction, dynamic tire deformation, and the windage of a spinning wheel. It has been measured for a 17-in. Moulton bicycle wheel with wheel covers by Richard Moore of General Motors (Moore 1987). Since no other reliable data are available, the constant derived from Moore's report was used; A_2 equals 0.00775 W/km^{-2}/hr^2.

Since A_3 is a function of the aerodynamic drag of the bicycle and rider it may be expressed as

$$A_3 = 1/2\rho C_d A_f$$

where ρ is the air density, C_d is the aerodynamic drag coefficient, and A_f is the frontal area of the bicycle and rider.

Air Density

Air density varies with altitude according to atmospheric temperature and pressure. The air density ratio may be estimated from the following polytropic gas equation, which is used for calculating low-level density variation in the U.S. Standard Atmosphere (Olson 1973):

$$\rho_2/\rho_1 = [1 - g(n-1)(z_2 - z_1)/(nRT_1)]^{(1/(n-1))}$$

where ρ is the air density in kg/m^3, g is the acceleration of gravity 9.807 m/s^2 at sea level, n is a polytropic gas coefficient $n = 1.235$, z is the elevation above sea level in meters, R is the gas constant for air $R = 287.1\ Nm$(kg° K)$^{-1}$, and T is the absolute temperature in Kelvin $T = 288°$ K (15° C). For example: $z = 1829$ m for Colorado Springs, and the density ratio would be $\rho_2\rho_1 = 0.836$, compared to sea level. This means that the density, and therefore the air resistance, should be about 16.4% less in Colorado Springs than at sea level for the same rider and bicycle.

Frontal Area

The frontal area of the bicycle and rider may be found by photographing the cyclist and rider from the front with a telephoto lens along with a calibrated area for reference. By cutting out the outline of the rider and bicycle and weighing the outline and a cutout of the reference area, a simple proportion will yield the frontal area. However, this is not practical, so Bassett and colleagues (1999) developed an expression for frontal area using the cyclist's weight in kilograms (M) and height in meters (H):

$$A_f = 0.0293H^{0.725} M^{0.425} + 0.0604$$

Drag Coefficient and Other Factors

The drag coefficient as given in the equation for A_3 is generally unknown since it varies with the cyclist's position and equipment. However, it is not necessary to know the drag coefficient to find A_3. Bassett and colleagues (1999) used the average height and weight of five cyclists plus their average power measured by a crank dynamometer to derive an expression for A_3 in terms of the frontal area and other factors such as altitude, equipment type, position, and so on:

$$P = K(0.00953\ M_tV + .00775V^2 + K_1(A_f).007551V^3)$$

where K is a factor that allows adjustment for track roughness or other external conditions, and K_1 is an aerodynamic factor that incorporates a correction for altitude (the density ratio) and corrections for rider position, bicycle type, components, clothing, helmets, and so on. No correction for wind speed was included in either of the factors K or K_1 since on an oval racing track the effect of wind is unpredictable. K_1 can be expressed as

$$K_1 = K_d K_{po} K_b K_c K_h$$

where K_d is the density ratio compared to sea level (the polytropic gas equation), K_{po} is the effect of position, K_b is the effect of the bicycle and components, K_c is the effect of clothing and K_h is the effect of the helmet. Table 7.4 lists a few of the more important factors affecting aerodynamic drag. The correction factors listed in table 7.4 were obtained by tests of bicycles, cyclists, wheels, and helmets in the General Motors wind tunnel (Bassett et al. 1999). Obviously, by improving position, bicycles, wheels, components, clothing, helmets, and so forth, a time trial bicycle can be much faster. The factors listed in table 7.4 are valid in the range of racing speeds from 50 to 60 kph.

The power values shown in table 7.3 were calculated using the expression for A_3 that took into account frontal area and other factors. For example, let's use this equation to estimate the average power of Chris Boardman when he set an hour record in 2000 under the UCI's new rules. The UCI rule changes forced Boardman to use a retro bike. On an indoor track in Manchester on October 27, 2000, with equipment similar to Eddy Merckx's in 1972, Boardman broke Merckx's record of 49.431 by just 10 m. Boardman used wire-spoked wheels, simple drop handlebars, round steel frame tubing, and a safety helmet—it was a step back in time. The performance was really impressive since Merckx set his record at high altitude (2338 m) in Mexico City, whereas Boardman's track was near sea level (60 m). The constants in the equation are as follows:

Height and weight = 1.75 m and 68 kg

Mt = 68 + 6.8 = 74.8 kg

K = 1.0 (Manchester)

Af = 0.325 m^2

K_d = 0.994

K_{po} = 1.10

K_b = 1.07

K_c = 1.0

K_h = 1.01

$K_1 = K_d K_{po} K_b K_c K_h$ =1.182

V = 49.441 kph

The power from the equation is 414 W. This is lower than the 442 W Peter Keen measured for Boardman's 1996 record. However, Boardman retired just after this 2000 hour record ride because he had been suffering from a bone-wasting disease and was unable to take effective medicine for the illness because of the UCI's rigorous drug standards.

TABLE 7.4   Correction Factors to Cycling Aerodynamic Drag

Density ratio K_d

Sea level	1.0
Colorado Springs, 1829 m	0.836
Mexico City, 2340 m	0.794
Bogata/Duitama, Columbia, 2500 m	0.781

Rider position K_{po}

Standard position with aero bars, elbows in (inside body contour)	1.0
Standard position with aero bars, elbows wide (outside body contour)	1.07 to 1.11
Historic racing position with drop bars, varying torso and head angle	1.08 to 1.18
Obree position	0.96
Superman position	0.95

Bicycle and components K_b

Round tube standard track bike, aero bars, disk or composite wheels	1.0
Round tube standard track bike, drop bars, wire spoke wheels	1.07
Composite double triangular frame, oval frame members (Corima)	1.0
Aluminum aero tube bike (Hooker, USA-SBI)	0.93
Lotus composite aero bike (1992 Olympics, Boardman)	0.93
Advanced composite aero bike, USA SB2, 1996 Merckx (Boardman)	0.925

Bicycle clothing K_c

Short sleeves, 3/4 legs, nylon spandex skin suit	1.0
Same design, optimum weave material	0.98
Cotton jersey, separate shorts	1.02
Wool jersey, full tights, full sleeves	1.09

Bicycle helmets K_h

Aero time trial helmet (USA, England, Germany, France, Italy)	1.0
Modern slotted protective helmet	1.025
Historic leather strap helmet	1.04

These correction factors to the aerodynamic drag assume an average air drag for a rider and bicycle of approximately 2.5 kg (24.5 N) at 48 kph. By multiplying these factors together, an overall correction K_t may be obtained.

Effect of Altitude on Aerobic Power

From 1968 to 1984, four hour records were set at the high altitude of Mexico City (2300 m)—Ritter in 1968, Merckx in 1972, and Moser in 1984 (twice). When elite athletes perform at high altitude, their aerobic capacity and therefore their ability to produce mechanical power declines. The amount of the decline depends heavily on the amount of time they have trained at high altitude. Bassett and colleagues (1999) developed equations describing the percent decline in aerobic capacity versus altitude. They used published data from studies of elite runners before and after acclimatization at high altitude.

The percent decline in $\dot{V}O_2$max at various elevations is shown in figure 7.7. An equation describing the relationship between altitude and maximal aerobic capacity for unacclimated elite athletes is

$$Y = (0.1781)X^3 - (1.434)X^2 - (4.073)X + 100.352$$

where Y is the percent of $\dot{V}O_2$max measured at sea level, and X is the altitude in km. This equation predicts a $\dot{V}O_2$max in Mexico City (2338 m) that is 85.3% of the sea level value, or a 14.7% decline.

For acclimatized athletes, the equation expressing this relationship is

$$Y = (-1.122)X^2 - (1.8991)X + 99.921$$

where Y is the percent of $\dot{V}O_2$max measured at sea level, and X is the altitude in km (see figure 7.7). This equation predicts a 10.6% decline in $\dot{V}O_2$max at 2338 m for Ritter and Moser (89.4%), compared to a 14.7% decline (85.3%) computed for Merckx using the equation to find the relationship between altitude and maximal aerobic capacity for unacclimated elite athletes.

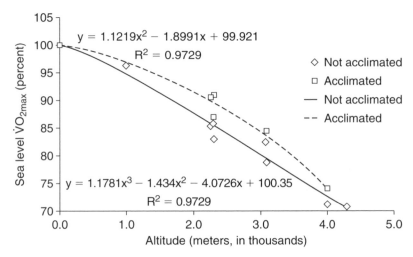

FIGURE 7.7 Maximal oxygen uptake versus altitude.

To estimate the sea level aerobic power capacity of an athlete, divide the power at high altitude by the fractional aerobic power. For example, Merckx produced 366 W in Mexico City. The equivalent power at sea level would be 366/0.853 = 429 W.

Optimum Elevation for Hour Records

Although there is a detrimental loss of aerobic power with altitude, there is a beneficial decrease in wind resistance; the two effects oppose each other. Bassett and colleagues (1999) estimated that up to about 2500 m elevation, distance in the hour would increase, but after that it would decline (see figure 7.8). At 2500 m, the decline in aerobic power begins to overpower the benefit of lower wind resistance. This is approximately the elevation of Mexico City. Consequently, there would be little reason to attempt an hour record at higher altitude. For shorter races, in which the aerobic power component is less, this optimum elevation would be higher.

In recent years, hour record attempts have been made on indoor tracks at near sea level (Stuttgart, Hamar, Bordeaux, Manchester). The variable winds and environmental conditions of outdoor tracks make such venues unattractive for record attempts, and there are no indoor cycling tracks at high elevation—the tracks in Mexico, Colorado, Colombia, Bolivia, Argentina, and so forth, are all outdoors. Boardman's last two records were set indoors, near sea level, at Manchester. This trend will no doubt continue.

The question arises, how much of the rapid improvement in hour records in the 1990s was due to aerodynamics and how much was due to improved training and coaching? Earlier record holders (Bracke, Ritter, and Merckx),

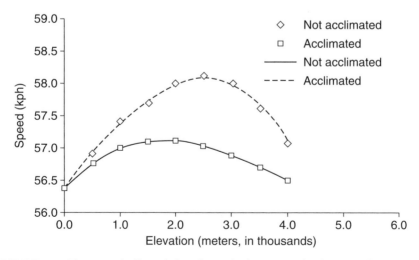

FIGURE 7.8   Theoretical effect of altitude on the hour record: Chris Boardman.

who all used round tube standard bikes, averaged about 402 W output during their record rides (Bassett et al. 1999). The next series of record holders (Moser, Boardman, Obree), who all used aerodynamic improvements, averaged powers of about 403 W, or about the same. The aerodynamic improvements during this time resulted in a distance increase of about 10%. The last three challengers (Indurain, Rominger, and Boardman) averaged 446 W, a very large increase. During this time, aerodynamic improvements did not change significantly. The increased power of these cyclists resulted in a distance increase of about 7%. In other words, since Bracke's era, about 60% of the improvement in hour record distance was due to aerodynamics and about 40% was due to higher power output (Bassett et al. 1999). The combination led to the most rapid rise in the hour record in more than a century.

Now that equipment has reverted to 1972, what will lead to greater hour record distances? There is still room for increased power and endurance, and this will bring the next wave of increases. The competition isn't over yet.

References

Bassett, D.R., Kyle, C.R., Passfield, L., Broker, J.P., and Burke, E.R. 1999. Comparing cycling world hour records, 1967-1996: Modeling with empirical data. *Med Sci Sports Exerc* 31(11): 1665-1676.

Keen, P. 1994. The truth behind the race of truth. *Cycle Sport* July: 46-50.

Kyle, C.R. 2001. Bicycle aerodynamics and the Union Cycliste Internationale: The conflict between technology and regulations. *Transactions, 11th Cycling History Conference, Osaka Japan, August 23-25, 2000.* San Francisco: Vanderplas Publications. pp 118-131.

Kyle, C.R. In press. A brief history of the international human powered vehicle association, 1976-1998. *Transactions, 12th Cycling History Conference, San Remo, Italy, September 25-28, 2001.* San Francisco: Vanderplas Publications.

Kyle, C.R., and Caiozzo, V.J. 1986. Experiments in human ergometry as applied to the design of human powered vehicles. *Int J Sport Biomech* 2: 6-19.

Moore, R.C. 1987. Rolling resistance performance, small tire. *General Motors Report*, General Motors Proving Ground, Warren, Michigan, April 13. pp. 1-15.

Olson, R.M. 1973. *Essentials of fluid mechanics.* New York: Intext Educational Publishers. pp. 71-72.

Padilla, S., Mujika, I., Angulo, F., and Goiriena, J.J. 2000. Scientific approach to the 1-h cycling world record: A case study. *J Appl Physiol* 89: 1522-1527.

Union Cycliste Internationale (UCI). 2002a. General organization of cycling as a sport. Ch. 3 Equipment. http://www.uci.ch/english/about/rules.htm.

Union Cycliste Internationale (UCI). 2002b. Track races, the hour record, Ch. 3, section 3.5.026.

Whitt, F.R., and Wilson, D.G. 1982. *Bicycling science.* Cambridge: MIT Press. p. 51.

8

Altitude Training in Preparation for Competition at Sea Level

Randall L. Wilber

Most of the current interest in altitude training can be traced back to the 1968 Summer Olympic Games, held in Mexico City at an elevation of 2300 m (7544 ft). At the 1968 Olympics, sprinters and jumpers in track and field set several world records in the "thin air" of Mexico City, whereas the distance runners ran markedly slower compared with 1968 world records. In addition, athletes from altitude-based countries such as Kenya and Ethiopia won a relatively high percentage of medals in the middle- and long-distance races.

The Mexico City Olympics clearly showed that to compete successfully in endurance events at altitude, an athlete had to either be a native of an altitude-based country such as Kenya or Ethiopia or have completed extensive altitude training before competition. Logically, the next question that many athletes, coaches, and sport scientists began asking was, What effect does living and/or training at altitude have on sea level performance?

Since the 1968 Summer Olympics, several scientific studies have been conducted for the purpose of answering that question and others that arose: What is the optimal altitude at which to train? How long do you need to train at altitude to gain physiological benefits? How long does the altitude effect last after return to sea level?

Whereas the original method of altitude training was to live high and train high, most contemporary athletes use some modification of "live high, train low" (LHTL) altitude training. The LHTL strategy proposes that athletes can improve sea level endurance performance by living high (2000 to 2700 m, 6560 to 8860 ft) while simultaneously training at low elevation (≤1,000 m or 3,280 ft).

Living at a relatively high altitude increases red blood cell (RBC) mass and hemoglobin, while simultaneous training at low altitude induces beneficial peripheral and neuromuscular adaptations. The hematological and neuromuscular improvements that result from LHTL lead to the enhancement of sea level maximal oxygen consumption ($\dot{V}O_2$max) and endurance performance (Levine and Stray-Gundersen 1997).

A modification of LHTL training currently being used in several countries is the nitrogen house, a normobaric hypoxic apartment that simulates an altitude environment. Another modification involves the use of supplemental oxygen to simulate sea level conditions during high-intensity workouts conducted at altitude. Finally, athletes use simulated altitude devices such as the Colorado Mountain Room and the Hypoxico Altitude Tent to enable them to sleep high and train low.

Potential Physiological Benefits of Altitude Training

Human physiology is affected in different ways at high altitude. In general, the various systems of the human body—pulmonary, cardiovascular, endocrine, skeletal muscles—respond and adjust in an effort to provide enough oxygen to survive in the hypoxic environment of high altitude. Some of these life-supporting physiological responses may also enhance athletic performance, particularly in endurance sports.

Hematological

The scientific rationale for using altitude training for the enhancement of aerobic performance is based on the body's response to changes in the partial pressure of inspired oxygen (P_IO_2) and the partial pressure of oxygen in the arterial blood (P_aO_2). P_IO_2 at sea level is equal to 149 mmHg. At Mexico City (2300 m, 7544 ft), P_IO_2 drops to approximately 123 mmHg. At the summit of Mt. Everest (8852 m, 29,035 ft), P_IO_2 is approximately 50 mmHg or only about 30% of sea level P_IO_2.

Because of the altitude-induced decrease in P_IO_2, there is a decrease in P_aO_2, which leads to a drop in renal P_aO_2 and renal tissue oxygenation (Ou et al. 1998; Richalet et al. 1994). It is hypothesized that this reduction in renal tissue oxygenation stimulates the synthesis and release of erythropoietin (EPO) (Porter and Goldberg 1994; Richalet et al. 1994), the principal hormone that regulates erythrocyte (RBC) and hemoglobin production. In turn, an increase in serum EPO concentration stimulates the synthesis of new RBCs in the red bone marrow by promoting the cellular growth of immature erythrocytes, specifically the colony-forming unit-erythroid (CFU-E). Erythropoietin receptors are present on the surface of CFU-E. Binding of EPO to CFU-E receptors initiates the production of cellular transcription factors, synthesis of membrane and cytoskeletal proteins, synthesis of heme and hemoglobin, and the terminal differentiation of cells (Bell 1996). The RBC maturation process takes five to seven days from the initial altitude-induced increase in serum EPO (Bell 1996; Flaharty et al. 1990).

These hematological changes may significantly improve an athlete's $\dot{V}O_2$max by enhancing the blood's ability to deliver oxygen to exercising muscles. It has been shown that improvements in RBC mass, hemoglobin concentration, and $\dot{V}O_2$max enhance aerobic performance (Berglund and Ekblom 1991; Birkeland et al. 2000; Ekblom and Berglund 1991). Essentially, many athletes and coaches view altitude training as a natural or legal method of blood doping.

Research by Chapman, Stray-Gundersen, and Levine (1998) suggests that some athletes experience a better hematological response at altitude than others do. Female and male collegiate runners who completed either LHTL or traditional "live high, train high" altitude training were classified as responders or nonresponders based on their performance in a postaltitude 5-km run. On average, responders demonstrated a significant 4% improvement (37 s) in the postaltitude 5-km run versus their prealtitude performance; nonresponders were approximately 1% slower (14 s). Hematological data showed that responders had a significantly larger increase in serum EPO (52%) compared with nonresponders, who demonstrated a 34% increase in serum EPO. Similarly, postaltitude RBC mass for responders was 8% higher ($p < 0.05$), but nonresponders' RBC mass was only 1% higher (not statistically significant) compared with prealtitude values. A breakdown of responders indicated that 82% came from the LHTL group, and 18% came from the "live high, train high" group. The authors concluded that each athlete may need to follow an altitude training program that places the athlete at an individualized, optimal altitude for living and another altitude for training, thereby producing the best possible hematological response.

Skeletal Muscle

As described, the primary reason endurance athletes train at altitude is to increase RBC mass and hemoglobin concentration. In addition, they may gain secondary physiological benefits as a result of altitude exposure. For example, altitude training has been shown to increase skeletal muscle capillarity (Desplanches et al. 1993; Mizuno et al. 1990). In theory, this physiological adaptation enhances the exercising muscles' ability to extract oxygen from the blood.

Other favorable skeletal muscle microstructure changes that occur as a result of training at altitude include increased concentrations of myoglobin (Terrados et al. 1990), increased mitochondrial oxidative enzyme activity (Terrados et al. 1990), and a greater number of mitochondria (Desplanches et al. 1993), all of which serve to enhance the rate of oxygen utilization and aerobic energy production.

Nevertheless, scientific data in support of altitude-induced skeletal muscle adaptations are minimal, particularly among well-trained athletes. Only Mizuno and colleagues (1990) examined elite athletes; Desplanches and colleagues (1993) and Terrados and colleagues (1990) examined the effect of altitude training on the skeletal muscle characteristics of untrained individuals. Additional studies conducted on elite athletes failed to demonstrate significant changes in skeletal muscle microstructure caused by altitude training (Saltin et al. 1995; Terrados et al. 1988). Furthermore, Desplanches and colleagues (1993) conducted their study at impractical simulated elevations (4100 to 5700 m, 13,450 to 18,700 ft), an altitude too high for athletes to train at. Thus, based on the current scientific literature, it is unclear whether altitude training, as practiced by most elite athletes at moderate elevations of 1800 to 3050 m (6000 to 10,000 ft) improves oxygen extraction and utilization via favorable changes in skeletal muscle capillarity, myoglobin, mitochondrial oxidative enzyme activity, and mitochondrial density. Additional research is warranted.

Another important physiological adaptation that may occur as a result of exposure to moderate altitude is an improvement in the capacity of the skeletal muscle and blood to buffer the concentration of hydrogen ions (H^+). High concentrations of H^+ are known to contribute to skeletal muscle fatigue by impairing actin-myosin crossbridge cycling, reducing the sensitivity of troponin for calcium (Ca^{2+}) and inhibiting the enzyme phosphofructokinase (PFK) (McComas 1996). Thus, an enhanced H^+ buffering capacity may have a beneficial effect on aerobic and anaerobic performance.

In support of this, Mizuno and colleagues (1990) reported a significant 6% increase in the buffering capacity of the gastrocnemius muscle of elite male cross-country skiers who lived at 2100 m (6890 ft) and trained at 2700 m (8860 ft) for 14 days. Significant improvements in maximal O_2 deficit (29%) and treadmill run time to exhaustion (17%) were observed after the athletes returned to sea level. In addition, a positive correlation ($r = 0.91$, $p < 0.05$) was demonstrated between the relative increase in buffering capacity of the gastrocnemius muscle and treadmill run time to exhaustion.

Gore and colleagues (2001) reported that skeletal muscle buffer capacity increased 18% ($p < 0.05$) in male triathletes, cyclists, and cross-country skiers following 23 days of living at 3000 m (9840 ft) and training at 600 m (1970 ft). Furthermore, they found that mechanical efficiency significantly improved during a 4 × 4-min submaximal cycling test following the 23-day LHTL period.

The precise mechanisms responsible for enhanced skeletal muscle buffering capacity following high altitude training are unclear but may be related to changes in creatine phosphate and/or muscle protein concentrations (Mizuno et al. 1990). Improvements in blood buffering capacity may be due to increases in bicarbonate (Nummela and Rusko 2000) or hemoglobin concentration. The potential physiological benefits of altitude training are summarized in figure 8.1.

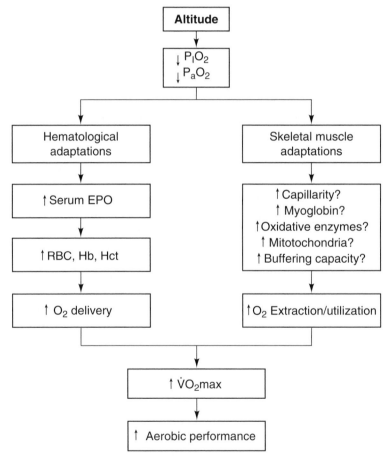

FIGURE 8.1 Summary of the purported physiological benefits of using altitude training for the enhancement of aerobic performance. EPO = erythropoietin, Hb = hemoglobin, Hct = hematocrit, P_IO_2 = partial pressure of inspired oxygen, P_aO_2 = partial pressure of oxygen in the arterial blood, RBC = red blood cells, $\dot{V}O_2$max = maximal oxygen consumption.

Physiological Responses at Altitude: Considerations for Training

In general, athletes experience greater physiological stress when competing and training at altitude compared with similar training at sea level. At altitude, many athletes undergo a number of physiological changes that may limit their ability to compete and/or train. Two of the most important physiological changes that occur are altitude-induced decrements in arterial oxyhemoglobin saturation (S_aO_2) and $\dot{V}O_2$max. These physiological limitations may force athletes to reduce their daily training volume and/or training intensity and modify their competition strategy from what they would normally do at sea level.

Arterial Oxyhemoglobin Saturation

Partial pressure of inspired oxygen (P_IO_2) decreases upon exposure to altitude. This decrease in P_IO_2 leads to a reduction in the partial pressure of oxygen at the alveolar level of the lungs (P_AO_2), the site where oxygen diffuses through the pulmonary capillaries to the blood. A decrement in P_AO_2 subsequently leads to a reduction in the partial pressure of oxygen in arterial blood (P_aO_2), resulting in fewer oxygen molecules binding to hemoglobin, decreasing S_aO_2.

At rest, P_aO_2 and S_aO_2 are slightly reduced at high altitude (Banchero et al. 1966; Huang et al. 1984) despite an increase in pulmonary ventilation. During submaximal and maximal exercise at altitude, P_AO_2 and S_aO_2 are markedly lower compared with similar exercise at sea level (Gale et al. 1985; Hartley, Vogel, and Landowne 1973; Sylvester et al. 1981; Wagner et al. 1986). This effect may be because the altitude-induced reduction in P_AO_2 results in a decrease in pulmonary capillary diffusion time (Dempsey, Hanson, and Henderson 1984; Torre-Bueno et al. 1985; Wagner et al. 1986). In other words, since P_AO_2 is reduced at altitude, pulmonary capillary diffusion time is not long enough to allow for optimal oxygenation of the pulmonary arterial blood, resulting in a lower S_aO_2.

Interestingly, this exercise-induced decrement in S_aO_2 appears to be more pronounced in well-trained athletes versus untrained individuals at both sea level and high altitude. Lawler, Powers, and Thompson (1988) evaluated untrained and trained males who performed incremental cycle ergometer exercise at sea level and at a simulated altitude of 3000 m (9840 ft). Arterial oxyhemoglobin saturation was measured indirectly via pulse oximetry (S_pO_2), as opposed to directly from arterial blood (S_aO_2). The trained group experienced a significantly greater decrement in S_pO_2 compared with the untrained group at both sea level (trained 90.1%, untrained 95.5%) and simulated altitude (trained 77.3%, untrained 86.3%), suggesting that trained aerobic athletes experience greater impairment of arterial oxyhemoglobin saturation upon exposure to altitude than do untrained individuals. It has been suggested that the reduced pulmonary capillary transit time experienced at altitude—combined with the relatively high cardiac output, pulmonary blood flow, and hemoglobin content of endurance athletes—serves to widen the P_AO_2–P_aO_2 diffusion gradient, resulting in a greater S_aO_2 reduction in trained versus untrained individuals (Dempsey 1986; Gore et al. 1996; Torre-Bueno et al. 1985; Wagner et al. 1986).

Furthermore, decrements in S_aO_2 have been demonstrated in endurance athletes at elevations as low as 580 m (1902 ft). Gore and colleagues (1997) evaluated trained male and female cyclists and triathletes during a 5-min maximal cycle ergometer exercise test in a hypobaric chamber in conditions simulating sea level and low altitude (580 m, 1902 ft). Arterial oxyhemoglobin saturation decreased significantly in both the men (sea level 92.0%, low altitude 90.1%) and women athletes (sea level 92.1%, low altitude 89.7%) upon acute exposure to the simulated low altitude (Gore et al. 1997). Similar findings were reported by Gore and colleagues (1996) in well-trained male cyclists whose S_aO_2 fell significantly at a simulated altitude of 580 m (1,902 ft) (86.5%) compared with sea level (90.4%).

Maximal Oxygen Consumption

It is well-documented that exposure to altitude reduces maximal oxygen consumption. In a classic study, Squires and Buskirk (1982) evaluated the effect of acute exposure to hypobaric hypoxia (simulated altitude via a reduction in barometric pressure) on $\dot{V}O_2$max in male recreational runners ($\dot{V}O_2$max averaged 60.1 ml · kg^{-1} · min^{-1}). Each runner performed a maximal treadmill test in a hypobaric chamber at simulated altitudes of 363 m (1190 ft), 914 m (3000 ft), 1219 m (4000 ft), 1524 m (5000 ft), and 2286 m (7500 ft). Maximal oxygen uptake at 362 m averaged 4.35 L · min^{-1} and was significantly reduced by 5%, 7%, and 12% at 1219 m, 1524 m, and 2286 m, respectively. Several additional studies involving athletes and physically fit soldiers demonstrated that $\dot{V}O_2$max declines in a curvilinear manner as altitude increases from 580 to 8848 m (1902 to 29,021 ft). Fulco, Rock, and Cymerman (1998, 2000) summarized these data.

Robergs and colleagues (1998) have suggested that $\dot{V}O_2$max is reduced by approximately 9% for every 1000-m (3280-ft) increase in elevation above 1050 m (3444 ft). However, recent evidence suggests that trained endurance athletes may experience decrements in $\dot{V}O_2$max at relatively low elevations. Peak oxygen consumption decreased significantly in both male (–6%) and female endurance athletes (–4%) upon acute exposure to a simulated altitude of 580 m (1902 ft) (Gore et al. 1997). Similar findings were reported in well-trained male cyclists whose $\dot{V}O_2$max dropped 7% ($p < 0.05$) at a simulated altitude of 580 m (1902 ft) (5.10 L · min^{-1}) compared with sea level (5.48 L · min^{-1}) (Gore et al. 1996).

Peronnet, Thibault, and Cousineau (1991) proposed a mathematical model that describes the potential effect of acute altitude exposure on

$\dot{V}O_2$max. According to the model, an athlete's maximal oxygen consumption at altitude, expressed as a percentage of sea level $\dot{V}O_2$max (% SL $\dot{V}O_2$max) at a given barometric pressure (P_B, expressed in Torr), can be approximated using the following quadratic equation:

$$\% \text{ SL } \dot{V}O_2\text{max} = a_0 + a_1 P_B + a_2 (P_B^2) + a_3 (P_B^3)$$

where $a_0 = -174.1448622$, $a_1 = 1.0899959$, $a_2 = -1.5119 \times 10^{-3}$, and $a_3 = 0.72674 \times 10^{-6}$.

This equation was developed from data obtained between 0 and 4000 m (13,120 ft) (760-462). Using the Peronnet, Thibault, and Cousineau (1991) equation, for example, at an altitude of 2000 m (6560 ft) ($P_B \sim 600$), an athlete's maximal oxygen consumption would be approximately 93% of sea level $\dot{V}O_2$max. At an altitude of 3000 m (9840 ft) ($P_B \sim 525$), $\dot{V}O_2$max would be approximately 86% of the sea level value, whereas at 4000 m (13,120 ft) ($P_B \sim 462$), $\dot{V}O_2$max would be approximately 78% of the sea level maximal oxygen uptake.

Athletes exposed to altitude exhibit great individual variability in the decrement in $\dot{V}O_2$max . In an effort to explain this decrement, Koistinen and colleagues (1995) reported that the decrease in maximal oxygen consumption in trained athletes at a simulated altitude of 3000 m (9840 ft) was significantly correlated ($r = 0.61$) to sea level $\dot{V}O_2$max. In other words, the largest reduction in $\dot{V}O_2$max at altitude was observed in the most aerobically fit athletes. Several additional studies involving athletes and soldiers demonstrated that relatively fit individuals ($\dot{V}O_2$max > 63 ml $\cdot$ kg$^{-1} \cdot$ min^{-1}) generally experience a greater decrement in $\dot{V}O_2$max at altitude than less fit individuals ($\dot{V}O_2$max < 51 ml $\cdot$ kg$^{-1} \cdot$ min^{-1}) (Fulco, Rock, and Cymerman 1998, 2000).

The greater decrement in $\dot{V}O_2$max seen in aerobically fit versus unfit individuals at altitude has been associated with pulmonary gas exchange limitations, which in turn result in a decrease in S_aO_2 and a reduction in oxygen availability to the exercising muscles. This physiological response is known as exercise-induced arterial hypoxemia (EIAH). Findings by Chapman, Emery, and Stager (1999) suggest that the decrement in $\dot{V}O_2$max seen in well-trained endurance athletes training at altitude may be related more to EIAH than to their level of fitness or $\dot{V}O_2$max.

Aerobic Performance and Training Capacity

Scientific data and mathematical models suggest that aerobic performance is negatively affected by exposure to altitude. Several studies examined the effect of altitude on either well-trained or elite aerobic athletes evaluated on aerobic performance within the initial days of exposure to actual or simulated elevations ranging from 580 to 5200 m (1902 to 17,056 ft). Performance measures in these studies included sport-specific time trials, work capacity tests conducted on sport-specific ergometers, and endurance time during an exhaustive incremental exercise test. All investigations reported decrements in aerobic performance on acute exposure to altitude (Bailey et al. 1998; Brosnan et al. 2000; Buskirk et al. 1967; Daniels and Oldridge 1970; Dill and Adams 1971; Faulkner, Daniels, and Balke 1967; Faulkner et al. 1968; Gore et al. 1997; Jensen et al. 1993; Roberts et al. 1998; Roi, Giacometti, and Von Duvillard 1999; Vallier, Chateau, and Guezennec 1996). Performance decrements ranged from 2 to 34%, depending on altitude. Decrements in aerobic performance at altitude have been associated with altitude-induced reductions in $\dot{V}O_2$max secondary to reductions in S_aO_2 (see figure 8.2).

In addition to decrements in aerobic performance, athletes exposed to altitude also experience a decrease in training capacity. Because of altitude-induced decrements in S_aO_2 and $\dot{V}O_2$max, endurance athletes have difficulty maintaining sea level training intensity at higher elevations. Although some athletes attempt to replicate the absolute training load of their sea level workouts, they do so at the risk of becoming ill, injured, or overtrained. Both anecdotal and scientific evidence suggest that most ath-

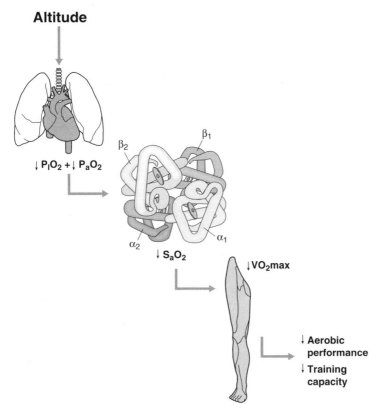

FIGURE 8.2   Sequence of physiological responses that occur at high altitude leading to reductions in aerobic performance and training capacity.

letes find it difficult to maintain sea level intensity during altitude training workouts, especially in the initial days at altitude.

Levine and Stray-Gundersen (1997) quantified the effect of altitude exposure on training intensity in competitive distance runners who were divided into three groups: a "low-low" group that lived and trained at sea level (150 m, 492 ft), a "high-low" group that lived at moderate altitude (2500 m, 8200 ft) and trained at low altitude (1250 m, 4100 ft), and a "high-high" group that lived and trained at moderate altitude (2500 m, 8200 ft). Table 8.1 shows the differences in training intensity among the three groups during base/overdistance training as well as interval training (1000-m intervals). Collectively, the data suggest that absolute training intensity during base and interval workouts is significantly reduced at low and moderate altitude in well-trained competitive distance runners.

Preliminary evidence suggests that altitude-induced decrements in training capacity can be offset through the use of supplemental oxygen, which

TABLE 8.1 Altitude Effect on Absolute Training Intensity in Competitive Distance Runners During Base Training and Interval Training Workouts (1000 m)

	BASE TRAINING	
	Running velocity (% sea level, 5000-m time)	**$\dot{V}O_2$ (% sea level $\dot{V}O_2$max)**
Low-low (n = 13)	82	72
High-low (n = 13)	77*	67
High-high (n = 13)	76*	64*

	INTERVAL TRAINING	
	Running velocity (% sea level, 5000-m time)	**$\dot{V}O_2$ (% sea level $\dot{V}O_2$max)**
Low-low (n = 13)	111	92
High-low (n = 13)	104*	86
High-high (n = 13)	96*	74*

* Significantly different versus low-low ($p < 0.05$).

Low-low: lived and trained at sea level (150 m, 490 ft)
High-low: lived at moderate altitude (2500 m, 8200 ft) and trained at low altitude (1250 m, 4100 ft)
High-high: lived and trained at moderate altitude (2500 m, 8200 ft)

Adapted, by permission, from B.D. Levine and J. Stray-Gundersen, 1997."Living high-training low: effect of moderate-altitude acclimatization with low-altitude training on performance," *J Appl Physiol* 83: 102-112.

can be used to simulate either normoxic (i.e., sea level) or hyperoxic conditions during high-intensity workouts conducted at altitude (Morris, Kearney, and Burke 2000; Wilber et al. 2002a). Supplemental oxygen training is described in more detail later in this chapter.

Heart Rate

Within the first few days of altitude exposure, heart rate at rest and during submaximal exercise is elevated compared with sea level (Grover et al. 1976; Grover, Weil, and Reeves 1986; Klausen 1966; Vogel, Hansen, and Harris 1967; Vogel et al. 1974; Welch 1987), whereas heart rate during maximal exercise at high altitude may be similar or lower versus that at sea level (Bouissou et al. 1986; Stenberg, Ekblom, and Messin 1966). Changes in resting and exercise heart rate in the initial few days at high altitude do not appear to alter after several days of altitude acclimatization (Wolfel et al. 1994). Given that many coaches and athletes use heart rate as a reference of workout intensity, it is imperative that the appropriate adjustments be made to heart-rate-based training zones to attain an optimal training effect and avoid overtraining. Most of the knowledge we currently have regarding cardiovascular responses at high altitude comes from the classic studies conducted at relatively high elevations (>3100 m, 10,168 ft) using either untrained or moderately trained subjects. Nevertheless, it is probably safe to assume that similar but perhaps attenuated cardiovascular responses occur in well-trained or elite athletes upon exposure to more moderate elevations where altitude training typically takes place.

Respiratory and Urinary Water Loss

The maintenance of proper fluid balance is a concern for athletes at sea level, especially for those involved in sports conducted in hot and humid environments. The need for proper hydration is even more important for athletes training at altitude. Within the first few days at altitude athletes tend toward dehydration because of increased *respiratory* water loss (Kayser 1994) secondary to enhanced pulmonary ventilation (Dempsey and Forester 1982; Laciga and Koller 1976; Moore et al. 1986) and increased *urinary* water loss secondary to down regulation of the renin–angiotensin–aldosterone mechanism (Hogan et al. 1973; Maher et al. 1975). At moderate altitudes of 2500 to 4300 m (8200 to 14,110 ft), respiratory water loss may be as high as 1900 ml per day in men (Butterfield et al. 1992) and 850 ml per day in women (Mawson et al. 2000). Urinary water loss may average approximately 500 ml per day (Butterfield 1996).

Given the potential for performance-limiting dehydration, athletes training at altitude need to maintain fluid balance through regular hydration. This should be done in conjunction with daily workouts, as well as during the nonworkout period of the day. Fluid intake in the form of water, juices, and carbohydrate-electrolyte drinks should be increased to as much as 5 L per day to ensure adequate hydration. Caffeinated beverages (coffee, tea, soda), which act as diuretics, should be reduced or eliminated.

Blood Lactate Response and Acid-Base Balance

The blood lactate response at altitude is often referred to as the "lactate paradox." Reeves and colleagues (1992) described the lactate paradox as a physiological response in which blood lactate concentration during submaximal and maximal exercise is *increased* upon acute high altitude exposure, but is *decreased* with altitude acclimatization. Kayser (1996) hypothesized that the acclimatization-induced reduction in lactate accumulation during submaximal and maximal exercise is mediated by at least two potential mechanisms:

1. A decrease in the maximum substrate flux via aerobic glycolysis caused by the reduction in $\dot{V}O_2$max experienced at altitude
2. Alterations in the metabolic control of glycogenolysis and glycolysis at the cellular level, which may be caused by changes in sympathetic nervous system responses that occur with acclimatization

A recent study by Lundby and colleagues (2000) showed that among a group of mountaineers, peak blood lactate concentration was lower after one and four weeks of acclimatization of approximately 5400 m (17,712 ft), but after six weeks of acclimatization had returned to a level that was similar to that observed at sea level and during acute exposure to simulated high altitude. These data suggested that the lactate paradox may be a temporary phenomenon that is reversed during a prolonged period at altitude lasting six or more weeks.

As described in the lactate paradox model, blood lactate response during submaximal and maximal exercise in the first few hours and days at high altitude may be more pronounced compared with similar exercise at sea level. Coaches and athletes should be aware of this potential physiological limitation as they design individual workouts. High blood lactate levels and accompanying high concentrations of hydrogen ions are known to contribute to skeletal muscle fatigue by mechanisms previously described in this chapter (McComas 1996).

In addition, H^+ buffering capacity may be adversely affected in the initial hours and days at altitude. One of the first physiological responses that occurs upon exposure to altitude is an increase in pulmonary ventilation. This higher ventilatory rate results in an increase in CO_2 exhalation and thus a decrease in the partial pressure of carbon dioxide (PCO_2) (Dempsey and Forester 1982; Laciga and Koller 1976). In addition, there is an increase in H^+ removal via hyperventilation, which results in an increase in blood pH (Hansen, Stetler, and Vogel 1967). This acid-base imbalance stimulates the kidneys to increase renal bicarbonate excretion within hours of arriving at altitude (Hansen, Stetler, and Vogel 1967). Given that bicarbonate

(HCO$_3^-$) serves as one of the primary metabolic buffers of H$^+$ produced during exercise, a reduction in bicarbonate may result in a reduced H$^+$ buffering capacity and thus may adversely affect training, particularly maximal or supramaximal exercise.

Carbohydrate Utilization

Initial studies that evaluated the effect of altitude exposure on substrate utilization suggested an increased reliance on lipids for energy (Young et al. 1982, 1987). This finding was supported by the fact that serum-free fatty acid and glycerol levels increased upon acute exposure to 4300 m (14,110 ft), and were further increased after 18 days at altitude (Young et al. 1982). This effect was observed at rest and during submaximal exercise. In addition, a reduction in muscle glycogen utilization and serum lactate occurred during submaximal exercise following 18 days at altitude (Young et al. 1982). Taken together, these data suggested that acute altitude exposure and subsequent acclimatization promotes greater utilization of fat and less dependence on carbohydrate as an energy substrate both at rest and during exercise.

In contrast, more recent studies using very accurate radioactive tracers suggest an alternative substrate utilization pattern, that is, that carbohydrate utilization is enhanced and lipid utilization is reduced at altitude (Brooks et al. 1991; Roberts et al. 1996a, 1996b). Within four hours of arriving at 4300 m (14,110 ft), fatty acid consumption of the leg muscles was not different versus the consumption at sea level when measured at rest and during submaximal exercise (Roberts et al. 1996a), but glucose rate of appearance and glucose oxidation percent were significantly greater compared with sea level at rest and during exercise (Roberts et al. 1996b). After 21 days of altitude acclimatization, resting and exercise fatty acid consumption was significantly lower compared with sea level values (Roberts et al. 1996a), whereas the glucose rate of appearance and glucose oxidation percent remained significantly greater compared with sea level at rest and during exercise (Roberts et al. 1996b). Collectively, these findings suggest an increased dependence on blood glucose, the most oxygen-efficient fuel, as an energy substrate during acute and chronic altitude exposure (Brooks et al. 1991; Roberts et al. 1996b). However, a couple of recent studies (Beidleman et al. 2002; Braun et al. 2000) showed that this substrate utilization pattern may be less dominant in women than in men.

The scientific investigations on carbohydrate utilization reviewed in this section were conducted at an impractical elevation, one too high for athletes to train at. However, it is possible that the significant increase in glucose utilization at 4300 m (14,110 ft) that was reported in several of these studies may occur to a lesser degree at moderate altitude where athletes typically live and train. Therefore, it is imperative that athletes make a concerted effort to replenish their carbohydrate stores through high glycemic food and drink when training at altitude.

Iron Metabolism

Ferritin, the storage form of iron, is a requisite component for RBC synthesis. As such, endurance athletes must maintain adequate iron levels, particularly during increased training periods. This is even more important for athletes training at altitude because of the potential increase in erythropoiesis (RBC production) that may occur in the hypoxic environment. Stray-Gundersen and colleagues (1992) reported that altitude-induced erythrocythemia did not take place in endurance athletes diagnosed as "iron deficient" (serum ferritin < 20 ng $\cdot$ ml^{-1} for females; < 30 ng $\cdot$ ml^{-1} for males) before completing a four-week altitude training camp at 2500 m (8200 ft) (see figure 8.3). The data suggest that athletes need to normalize and closely monitor iron status *before* attempting altitude training if they expect to increase RBC mass. In addition, recent studies have shown decrements in endurance performance in "iron-depleted, nonanemic" athletes, suggesting that low iron may negatively affect performance by other iron-dependent physiological mechanisms such as the cytochrome-c oxidase reaction of the electron transport system (Friedmann et al. 2001; Hinton et al. 2000).

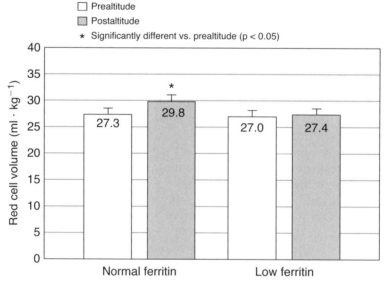

FIGURE 8.3   Effect of four weeks of living and training at 2500 m (8200 ft) on RBC volume in trained female and male distance runners who had normal or low serum ferritin prealtitude. Low serum ferritin was defined as <20 and <30 ng $\cdot$ ml^{-1} for the female and male runners, respectively.

Reprinted, by permission, from J. Stray-Gundersen, C. Alexander, A. Hochstein, D. deLemos, and B.D. Levine, 1992," Failure of red cell volume to increase to altitude exposure in iron deficient runners,"*Med Sci Sports Exerc* 24 (suppl 5): S90.

Potential Physiological Problems

Many athletes experience upper respiratory tract infections (URTI) and/ or gastrointestinal infections at altitude. This increase in URTI and gastrointestinal infections may be due to an altitude-induced suppression of the immune system caused by increased serum levels of neuropeptides and endogenous glucocorticoids, such as cortisol (Bailey et al. 1998; Wilber et al. 2000). Some researchers reported that exposure to altitude leads to an increase in free radical concentration, which in turn results in increased lipid peroxidation (Bailey and Davies 1997; Simon-Schnass 1994; Vasankari et al. 1997). Vasankari and colleagues (1997) speculated that exposure to higher levels of ultraviolet radiation may be responsible for the increase in lipid peroxidation (destruction of cell membranes). Supplementation with the antioxidant vitamin E (400 mg per day for 10 weeks) may offset hypoxia-induced peroxidation and may attenuate decrements in aerobic performance at moderate altitude (Simon-Schnass and Pabst 1988).

An individual's body composition may be altered upon exposure to high altitude. Initially, total body weight may decrease slightly because of increased respiratory and urinary water loss. Chronic exposure to high altitude may lead to body weight reduction resulting from decrements in fat mass and muscle mass (Boyer and Blume 1984; Hoppeler et al. 1990; MacDougall et al. 1991; Rose et al. 1988). These decrements in fat and muscle mass may be due to increases in basal metabolic rate (Butterfield et al. 1992) and activity level (Kayser 1992) combined with decreased caloric intake. However, Kayser (1992) indicated that up to altitudes of approximately 5000 m (16,400 ft), weight loss from fat and muscle can be prevented by maintaining an adequate, varied caloric intake. This is encouraging to athletes since most altitude training camps are at elevations well below 5000 m. Svedenhag and colleagues (1991) found that the postaltitude body composition of Swedish elite male distance runners was not significantly different compared with their prealtitude value following two weeks of training at 2000 m (6560 ft). Gore and colleagues (1998) observed similar results in Australian elite male track cyclists following three weeks of training at 2690 m (8820 ft). Still, athletes training at altitude need to make a concerted effort to maintain optimal body weight and body composition through proper nutrition and hydration.

Athletes who are exposed to an altitude environment may experience some degree of sleep disturbance. This is particularly true for athletes training at altitude for the first time. Sleep disturbances may be defined as an increase in the number of awakenings throughout the sleep period, periodic labored breathing, and a decrease in slow-wave sleep and REM sleep (Goldenberg et al. 1992). Although most of these symptoms have been documented in alpine climbers involved in high altitude expeditions (e.g., Mt. Everest with an elevation of 8852 m or 29,035 ft), athletes who are engaged in training at moderate or low altitude may experience milder forms of sleep disturbance. It appears that altitude acclimatization helps to reduce the negative effects of sleep disturbance (Goldenberg et al. 1992).

Acute mountain sickness (AMS) is an altitude-induced illness with clinical symptoms of headache, nausea, vomiting, and weakness. Although AMS is more prevalent at high altitude (>5000 m, 16,400 ft), it is not uncommon for athletes training at moderate or low altitude to experience mild AMS. The prescription drug acetazolamide has been shown to be effective in reducing the symptoms of AMS, primarily by increasing arterial oxygen levels and reducing peripheral edema (Bradwell et al. 1992). Nonprescription aspirin has also been shown to be effective in reducing some of the symptoms of AMS. Physical rest is considered the principal nonpharmacological treatment for moderate AMS (Bartsch 1992).

Aerodynamic Benefits for Cyclists at Altitude

In cycling, where aerodynamics plays an important role, competitive performance at altitude may be enhanced because of reduced air density and decreased aerodynamic resistance. It has been suggested that the optimal altitude for cycling time trials of 2 km to 40 km is 3200 to 3500 m (10,500 to 11,480 ft), with times estimated to be 4 to 4.5% faster compared with sea level performances (Olds 1992, 2001).

A model proposed by Capelli and di Prampero (1995) suggests that the optimal elevation for breaking the world record for one-hour unaccompanied cycling is approximately 4000 m (13,120 ft). At this elevation, $\dot{V}O_2max$ is significantly reduced, but there is a greater reduction in the amount of power dissipated by the cyclist against air resistance. In other words, cycling competition at altitude features less aerodynamic drag due to the decrease in air density (see figure 8.4). This improvement in cycling aerodynamics exceeds the decrement in $\dot{V}O_2max$ and results in greater cycling velocity at altitude than at sea level.

For the one-hour cycling time trial, the model proposed by Capelli and di Prampero (1995) suggests that at 4000 m (13,120 ft) the optimal aerodynamic–$\dot{V}O_2max$ trade-off is achieved. Beyond this elevation, the decrement in maximal oxygen uptake may exceed aerodynamic gains and lead to a reduction in cycling velocity. The highest velodrome in the world is located in La Paz, Bolivia (3417 m, 11,210 ft) and, interestingly, the current one-hour world record (56.375 km), held by Chris Boardman of Great Britain, was set on an indoor track at sea level (Hahn and Gore 2001).

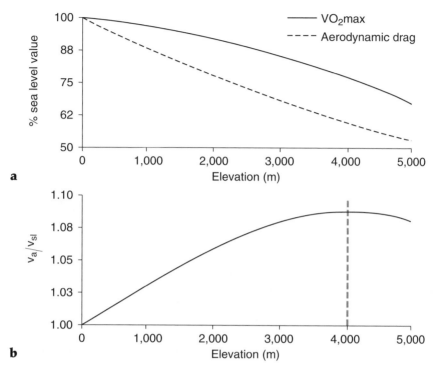

FIGURE 8.4   The effect of altitude on cycling performance in the one-hour time trial. (a) Although $\dot{V}O_2$max (solid line) decreases as one ascends from sea level to 5000 m (16,400 ft), the amount of aerodynamic drag (broken line) is reduced to a greater degree and thus allows the cyclist to ride faster at altitude despite the drop in $\dot{V}O_2$max. (b) The $\dot{V}O_2$max decrement versus aerodynamic benefit is optimized at an elevation of approximately 4000 m (13,120 ft), at which point the decrement in $\dot{V}O_2$max exceeds the beneficial effects of reduced aerodynamic drag. $V_a V_{sl}$: velocity at a given altitude relative to velocity at sea level; $\dot{V}O_2$max: maximal oxygen consumption

Reprinted, by permission, from Capelli, C. and di Prampero, P.E., 1995, "Effects of altitude on top speeds during 1 h unaccompanied cycling," *J Appl Physiol* 71:469- 471.

Altitude Training and Sea Level Performance

Numerous scientific studies have been conducted since the 1960s to determine the effect of altitude training on athletic performance at sea level. To review all of the scientific studies on this topic is beyond the scope of this chapter. For more detailed information on altitude training and athletic performance at sea level, see the review articles by Bailey and Davies (1997); Boning (1997); Fulco, Rock, and Cymerman (1998, 2000); Hahn (1991); and Wolski, McKenzie, and Wenger (1996). Despite years of research, we are still not able to say conclusively whether high altitude training leads to improvements in sea level performance.

Altitude Training Does Enhance Sea Level Performance: Summary of Studies

In general, the subjects recruited for these studies were either well-trained or elite aerobic athletes who lived and/or trained for 11 to 70 days at actual or simulated elevations ranging from 2300 to 4000 m (7544 to 13,120 ft). In each of these investigations, the athletes were evaluated within five days after completion of altitude training; in a few studies the athletes were evaluated at additional time points during a postaltitude period lasting two to three weeks. Performance measures in these studies included sport-specific time trials (runs of 1 mi, 3 km, 5 km, 10 km; cycling for 4000 m, 40 km); work capacity tests conducted on sport- and nonsport-specific ergometers; and endurance time during an exhaustive incremental exercise test.

Only two of these investigations reported a significant increase in hemoglobin concentration, and less than half reported an improvement in $\dot{V}O_2$max as a result of altitude training. However, all studies indicated that sea level endurance performance was enhanced following altitude training. Improvement in sea level endurance performance ranged from 1 to 33%. It should be emphasized that nearly 60% of the studies did not include a sea level control group, making their conclusions regarding performance debatable. For those studies that did not include a sea level control group, the question remains, "Was the improvement in sea level endurance performance due to high altitude training or to some other variable independent of high altitude training?" Therefore, the investigations that did include a sea level control group (Asano et al. 1986; Burtscher et al. 1996; Levine and Stray-Gundersen 1997; Terrados et al. 1988) should be considered the most credible. Table 8.2 presents a summary of the scientific literature whose results support the use of altitude training for the enhancement of sea level endurance performance in trained aerobic athletes.

Altitude Training Does Not Enhance Sea Level Performance: Summary of Studies

In general, subjects recruited for these studies were either well-trained or elite aerobic athletes who lived and/or trained for 11 to 63 days at actual or simulated elevations ranging from 1500 to 4000 m (4920 to 13,120 ft). In most investigations, athletes were evaluated within seven days after completion of altitude training; in a few studies, athletes were evaluated at additional time points during a postaltitude period lasting two to three weeks. Performance measures in these studies included sport-specific time trials (rowing for 2500 m; runs of 880 yd, 1000 m, 1 mi, 2 mi, 3 mi, 5 km; swimming for 200 yd, 500 yd); work capacity tests conducted on sport- and nonsport-specific ergometers; and endurance time during an incremental exhaustive exercise test.

TABLE 8.2 Scientific Studies That Support the Use of Altitude Training to Enhance Sea Level Performance in Trained Aerobic Athletes

Studies listed by ascending altitude.

	Mizuno et al. 1990	Daniels and Oldridge 1970	Terrados et al. 1988	Burtscher et al. 1996	Levine and Stray-Gundersen 1997
Altitude (m/ft)	Live 2100/6890 Train 2700/8860	2300/7544	2300/7544[c]	2315/7590	Live 2500/8200 Train 1250/4100
Subjects	Male elite CC skiers (n = 10) Danish NT	Male elite runners (n = 6) U.S. NT	Male elite cyclists (n = 8)	Male recreational runners (n = 10)	Female and male collegiate runners (n = 13)
SL control	No	No	Yes	Yes	Yes
Altitude exposure (days)	14	14/14/7[b]	21 to 28	12	28
Postaltitude SL test (day)	2	1 to 5	1 to 2	3 16	3
Change in Hb (%)	NR	NR	4 NSD	NR/NR	9*
Change in V̇O₂max (%)	NSD	5[#]	3 NSD	1 NSD/10*	5*
Performance test	Treadmill run time to exhaustion	1) 3-mi TT 2) 1- and 3-mi SC	1) Work capacity (kJ) in exhaustive cycling test 2) Cycling maximal power output (W)	Work capacity (kJ) in exhaustive cycling test	5-km TT
Change in performance%[a]	17*	1) 3[#] 2) 14 PRs, 1WR	1) 33* 2) 12*	8* 16*	1*
Additional results/comments					• 1% improvement in 5-km TT = 13.4 s • 5-km TT on SL day 7, 14, 21 NSD vs. SL day 3 • 5-km TT improvement correlated to V̇O₂max increase (r = 0.65; p < 0.01)

(continued)

[a] Positive value represents an improvement in postaltitude versus prealtitude sea level endurance performance.

[b] 14-day and 7-day training periods at altitude were separated by 5-day periods at sea level during which time subjects raced in sanctioned competitions.

[c] Hypobaric chamber.

[d] Normobaric hypoxic apartment (nitrogen house)

[e] "Mechanical efficiency" (%) was determined from the ratio of power outut (kJ/min⁻¹) to energy expended (kJ/min⁻¹) as calculated from V̇O₂ and respiratory exchange ratio (RER).

TABLE 8.2 (continued)

	Gore et al. 1998	Stray-Gundersen et al. 2001	Matilla and Rusko 1996	Gore et al. 2001	Dill and Adams 1971	Asano et al. 1986
Altitude (m/ft)	2690/8820	Live 2500/8200 Interval train 1250/4100 Base train 2500/8200	Live 3000/9840[d] Train SL	Live 3000/9840 Train 600/1970	3090/10,135	4000/13,120[c]
Subjects	Male elite cyclists (n = 8) Australian NT	Female and male elite runners (n = 22) U.S. NT	Male competitive cyclists (n = 5)	Male triathletes, cyclists, and CC skiers (n = 13)	Male champion high school runners (n = 6)	Male elite runners (n = 5)
SL control	No	No	No	Yes	No	Yes
Altitude exposure (days)	31	28	11	23	17	70
Postaltitude SL test (day)	4, 9, 21	3	5	2	1	"after"
Change in Hb (%)	NSD	8*	NR	NSD	NR	NSD
Change in $\dot{V}O_2$max (%)	NSD	3*	NR	-6*	4#	NSD
Performance test	4000-m TT	3-km TT	40-km TT	Mechanical efficiency[e] during 4 x 4-min submaximal cycle ergometer bouts (corresponding to 36, 52, 68, and 84% $\dot{V}O_2$peak)	Treadmill run time to exhaustion	10-km TT
Change in performance[a]	4*	1*	4*	1*	24#	5*
Additional results/ comments	4% improvement based on the best time recorded by each athlete on any one of the three PA days	1% improvement in 3-km TT = 5.8 s		Skeletal muscle buffer capacity increased 18%*		

* Significant difference versus prealtitude (p < 0.05)

Statistical analysis not reported.

CC = cross-country; Hb = hemoglobin (g/dL); NR = not reported/measured; NSD = no statistical difference; NT = national team; PA = postaltitude; PR = personal record; SC = sanctioned competition; SL = sea level; TT = time trial; WR = world record

216

Does training at altitude lead to success in races at sea level?

A few investigations reported significant improvement in hemoglobin concentration following altitude training; however, most reported no improvement in sea level $\dot{V}O_2$max. All studies indicated that sea level endurance performance was not enhanced after altitude training; a few reported worse endurance performance. Approximately 65% of these investigations included a sea level control group in the experimental design, thereby enhancing their credibility.

It should be noted, however, that several factors may have affected the physiological and performance results of studies that failed to demonstrate a beneficial effect of altitude training on sea level endurance performance. One factor may be the iron status of the athletes who participated in the investigations. As described earlier, Stray-Gundersen and colleagues (1992) reported that altitude-induced erythropoiesis did not take place in endurance athletes who were diagnosed as iron deficient (serum ferritin <20 ng · ml^{-1} for females; <30 ng · ml^{-1} for males) prior to completing a four-week altitude training camp at 2500 m (8200 ft). It is possible that some of the athletes involved in altitude training had abnormally low ferritin levels before living and training at altitude, and thus may not have experienced an increase in RBC mass and hemoglobin. In turn, this may explain why some of those studies failed to demonstrate improvements in $\dot{V}O_2$max and/ or endurance performance subsequent to altitude training.

The training stimulus at altitude may be another factor that affected the results of these scientific studies. In some studies (e.g., Buskirk et al. 1967), athletes were forced to markedly reduce their workout intensity because of the hypoxic conditions of 4000 m (13,120 ft). Consequently, the decrease in workout intensity may have resulted in the athletes being detrained when they returned to sea level, and thus may have adversely affected $\dot{V}O_2$max and performance.

Overtraining may also have confounded the performance results of some altitude training studies. For example, Vasankari and colleagues (1993) evaluated elite cross-country and biathlon skiers following a 14- to 18-day training and racing period at 1650 m (5400 ft). They reported a significant 29% increase in serum cortisol in the skiers following altitude training. Elevated serum cortisol has been associated with overtraining symptoms such as skeletal muscle catabolism (Hakkinen et al. 1989) and immunosuppression (Nieman 1997; Nieman et al. 1994, 1995a, 1995b). Moreover, serum cortisol and other stress hormones may suppress erythropoiesis (Berglund 1992). Training-induced (or nontraining-induced) injury or infection may also inhibit RBC production via an increase in inflammatory cytokines (Fandrey and Jelkmann 1991). Thus, it is possible that some athletes failed to demonstrate an improvement in $\dot{V}O_2$max and performance because they returned to sea level in an overworked or overtrained state.

A final factor to consider when evaluating performance results is the individual response of athletes to altitude training. Chapman, Stray-Gundersen, and Levine (1998) speculated that each athlete may need to follow an individualized altitude training program that allows for optimal physical training and physiological adaptation. One athlete may obtain the best physiological and performance results by following a LHTL program, whereas another athlete may get similar results by using a traditional "live high, train high" program or no altitude training program at all. Some of the athletes in these studies may not have been exposed to an altitude training regimen that allowed for the optimal development of physiological and performance-enhancing benefits. Individual responses may also be a factor in postaltitude performance. Gore and colleagues (1998) reported that postaltitude cycling performance (4000-m time trial) was individualistic among elite track cyclists when evaluated on days 4, 9, and 21 postaltitude, suggesting that optimal performance for each athlete may occur at a different time point following altitude training.

Table 8.3 summarizes the scientific literature whose results do not support the use of altitude training for the enhancement of sea level endurance performance in trained aerobic athletes.

TABLE 8.3 Scientific Studies That Do Not Support the Use of Altitude Training to Enhance Sea Level Performance in Trained Aerobic Athletes

Studies listed by ascending altitude.

	Bailey et al. 1998	Bailey et al. 1998	Telford et al. 1996	Jensen et al. 1993	Chung et al. 1995
Altitude (m/ft)	1500/4920	1640/5380	1760/5770	1822/5980	1890/6200
Subjects	Male elite runners (n = 14) British NT	Male elite runners (n = 10) British NT	Male elite runners (n = 9) Australian NT	Male elite rowers (n = 9) Italian NT	Female and male elite swimmers (n = 10) South Korean NT
SL control	Yes	Yes	Yes	Yes	Yes
Altitude exposure (days)	28	28	28	21	21
Postaltitude SL test (day)	20	10 20	1 to 7	"within 7"	7
Change in Hb (%)	4 NSD	9 NSD/5 NSD	3 NSD	NR	F = 10#; M = 4#
Change in $\dot{V}O_2$max (%)	NR	1 NSD/-1 NSD	3 NSD	NSD	F = 0; M = 5#
Performance test	1000-m TT	1000-m TT	3200-m TT	6-min rowing ergometer test	Swimming NC; 100- to 200-m events
Change in performance%[a]	NSD	NR -2*	NSD	NSD	0.1 to 0.7#
Additional results/comments	Lactate threshold and running economy NSD		3200-m TT was 10 s faster after altitude training but identical to improvement in SL control group		Swimming NC held 6 weeks postaltitude

(continued)

TABLE 8.3 (continued)

	Ingjer and Myhre 1992	Svedenhag et al. 1991	Faulkner et al. 1967	Faulkner et al. 1968	Adams et al. 1975[b]
Altitude (m/ft)	1900/6230	2000/6560	2300/7544	2300/7544	2300/7544
Subjects	Male elite CC skiers (n = 7) Norwegian NT	Male elite runners (n = 5) Swedish NT	Male collegiate swimmers (n = 15)	Male collegiates runners (n = 5)	1) Male trained runners (n = 6) 2) Male trained runners (n = 6)
SL control	No	Yes	No	No	Yes
Altitude exposure (days)	21	14	14	42	1) SL 20, altitude 20 2) Altitude 20, SL 20
Postaltitude SL test (day)	1 14	6 12	1	3 to 6	1 to 3 1 to 3
Change in Hb (%)	5*/1	2 NSD/1 NSD	1 NSD	NR	NR/NR
Change in $\dot{V}O_2max$ (%)	1 NSD/1 NSD	NSD/NSD	1 NSD	2[#]	−1 NSD/−4*
Performance test	NR	Treadmill run time to exhaustion	1) 200-yd TT 2) 500-yd TT	1) 1-mi TT; 2) 2-mi TT; 3) 3-mi TT	2-mi TT
Change in performance%[a]	NR	1 NSD −5 NSD	1) NSD 2) 1 NSD	1) 0 to 2[#]; 2) −1 to 1[#] 3) 2 to 3[#]	1 NSD −1 NSD
Additional results/comments	Significantly lower blood lactate during 6-min treadmill run at 90% $\dot{V}O_2max$ on postaltitude day 1, but not postaltitude day 14				1) 7 s faster (9:03 vs. 9:10) 2) 7 s slower (9:22 vs. 9:15)

TABLE 8.3 (continued)

	Levine and Stray-Gundersen 1997	Rahkila and Rusko 1982	Hahn et al. 1992	Buskirk et al. 1967	Vallier et al. 1996
Altitude (m/ft)	Live 2500/8200	2600/8530	3100/10,170[c]	4000/13,120	4000/13,120[d]
Subjects	Female and male collegiate runners (n = 13)	Male trained CC skiers (n = 6)	Female and male elite rowers (n = 8) Australian NT	Male collegiate runners (n = 6)	Female and male elite triathletes (n = 5) French NT
SL control	Yes	Yes	Yes	No	No
Altitude exposure (days)	28	11	19	63	21
Postaltitude SL test (day)	3	"after"	1 (Hb, $\dot{V}O_2$max) 6 (performance)	3 to 7; 10 to 15; 3 to 7; 10 to 15; 3 to 7; 10 to 15	7
Change in Hb (%)	9*	5*	–1 NSD	NR	–3 NSD
Change in $\dot{V}O_2$max (%)	5*	–3 NSD	NSD	0; 0; 0; 0; 0; 0	2 NSD
Performance test	5-km TT		2500-m rowing ergometer TT	880-yd TT; 880-yd TT 1-mi TT; 1-mi TT; 2-mi TT; 2-mi TT	Maximal power output (W) during cycling exercise
Change in performance%[a]	NSD		1 NSD	0; –6 to –4[#]; –6 to –4[#]; –6 to –3[#]; –4 to 0[#]; –8 to –4[#]	NSD
Additional results/comments	• 5-km TT slower by 3.3 s • 5-km TT on•SL days 7, 14, 21 NSD vs. SL day 3			No improvement in performance for any athlete in any TT	

[a] Positive value represents an improvement in postaltitude versus prealtitude sea level endurance performance.
[b] Refer to text for explanation of study design.
[c] Supplemental hypoxic training (15.2% O_2).
[d] Hypobaric chamber.
* Significant difference versus prealtitude (p < 0.05)
[#] Statistical analysis not reported.

CC = cross-country; F = female; Hb = hemoglobin (g/dL); Male = male; NC = national championship; NR = not reported/measured; NSD = no statistical difference; NT = national team; SL = sea level; TT = time trial

Current Practices in Altitude Training

In recent years endurance athletes have begun to use several novel approaches and modalities for altitude training, including normobaric hypoxia via nitrogen dilution (in a nitrogen apartment), supplemental oxygen, hypoxic sleeping devices, and intermittent hypoxic exposure. For a detailed review of current trends in high altitude training, see Wilber (2001).

Nitrogen Apartments

Nitrogen apartment describes a normobaric hypoxic apartment that simulates an altitude environment equivalent to approximately 2000 to 3000 m (6560 to 9840 ft). *Normobaric hypoxia* refers to simulated altitude via a reduction in oxygen concentration, but no change in barometric pressure.

The nitrogen apartment was originally developed by Finnish sport scientists in the early 1990s for the purpose of simulating an altitude environment. In Finland, the nitrogen house is in fact a series of well-furnished hotel rooms that provide a high level of comfort and privacy. In several countries, elite athletes have individual nitrogen apartments within their homes.

Athletes who use a nitrogen apartment adhere to the LHTL approach. Typically, they live and sleep in the nitrogen apartment for 8 to 18 hours a day, but train at sea level or approximate sea level conditions. The nitrogen apartment simulates moderate altitude by manipulating the oxygen concentration in the apartment. The barometric pressure in the nitrogen apartment is equivalent to sea level (approximately 760 mmHg), but the concentration of inspired O_2 within the nitrogen apartment (fraction of inspired oxygen [F_IO_2] approximately 0.1530) is less than at sea level or outside the nitrogen apartment (F_IO_2 approximately 0.2093). Figure 8.5 illustrates how F_IO_2 is reduced to 0.1530 in a hypoxic apartment. A ventilation system pulls in ambient air, composed of approximately 20.93% O_2 and 79.0% N_2. Simultaneously, a gas of 100% N_2 is introduced into the ventilation system, resulting in an internal gas composition of approximately 15.3% O_2 and 84.7% N_2. This normobaric hypoxic environment simulates an altitude of about 2500 m (8200 ft).

Data from several studies suggest that using a nitrogen apartment may produce beneficial changes in serum EPO, reticulocyte count, and RBC mass, which in turn may lead to improvements in postaltitude endurance performance (Laitinen et al. 1995; Mattila and Rusko 1996; Piehl-Aulin et al. 1998; Rusko et al 1995, 1999). Mattila and Rusko (1996) evaluated five male competitive cyclists who completed an 11-day training block in which they lived 18 hours a day at a simulated altitude of 3000 m (9840 ft) (normobaric hypoxia) and completed two separate workouts at sea level (ambient normobaric normoxia) during the other six hours of the day. Details of the training sessions were not reported. Blood tests conducted on the fifth day

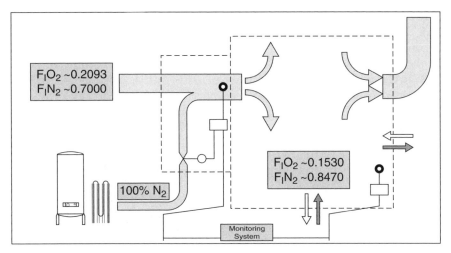

FIGURE 8.5   Schematic illustration of a normobaric hypoxic apartment.
F_IN_2: fraction of inspired nitrogen; F_IO_2: fraction of inspired oxygen

after the athletes began the training period indicated significant increments in serum erythropoietin (47%) and reticulocyte count (98%). Compared with prealtitude values, 40-km time trial performance was 4% faster ($p < 0.05$) when assessed on the fifth day following the 11-day "high-low" training block. Although these data supported the use of a nitrogen apartment for the enhancement of hematological variables and sea level endurance performance, they must be interpreted with caution because of the lack of a sea level control group.

Other studies have failed to demonstrate significant changes in RBC indices as a result of normobaric hypoxic exposure (Ashenden et al. 1999a, 1999b, 2000). The discrepancy in these findings may be due in part to methodological differences used to measure total hemoglobin and RBC mass (i.e., Evans blue dye technique versus carbon monoxide rebreathing technique). In addition, differences in the hypoxic stimulus that the subjects were exposed to (i.e., elevation and duration of exposure), and/or the training status of the subjects (trained versus elite national team athletes) may account for the inconsistent results. A limited number of studies have suggested that anaerobic capacity and performance are enhanced as a result of using a normobaric hypoxic apartment (Nummela and Rusko 2000).

Supplemental Oxygen

Supplemental oxygen is used to simulate either normoxic (sea level) or hyperoxic conditions during high-intensity workouts conducted at altitude. This use of supplemental oxygen is a modification of LHTL in that athletes live in a natural terrestrial altitude environment but train at "sea level" with the aid of supplemental oxygen. This system is used effectively at the U.S. Olympic Training Center in Colorado Springs, where U.S. National Team athletes live at 1860 m (6100 ft) or higher, but can train at "sea level" with supplemental oxygen (see figure 8.6). The average barometric pressure in Colorado Springs is approximately 610 mmHg, which yields a P_IO_2 of approximately 118 mmHg. By inhaling a certified medical gas composed of 26.5% O_2, athletes can complete high-intensity training sessions in a sea level environment at a P_IO_2 equivalent to 149 mmHg (760 mmHg; F_IO_2 approximately 0.2093).

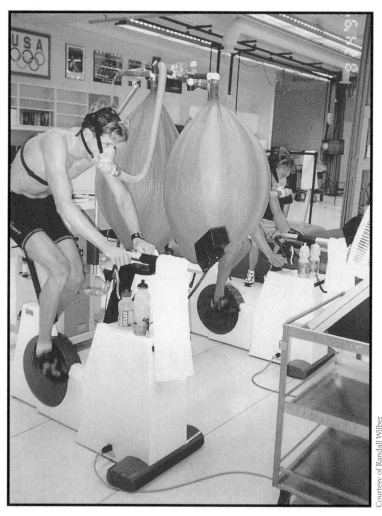

Courtesy of Randall Wilber

FIGURE 8.6 Supplemental oxygen training by U.S. National Team triathletes at the U.S. Olympic Training Center in Colorado Springs (1860 m, 6100 ft).

Only a few studies have evaluated supplemental oxygen as a method of altitude training conducted over a period of several weeks. Morris, Kearney, and Burke (2000) evaluated the efficacy of living at 1860 m (6100 ft) while doing high-intensity training at "sea level" with the aid of supplemental oxygen. Eight male junior cyclists, members of the U.S. National Team, completed a 21-day training period during which they lived and completed their base workouts at 1860 m (6100 ft), but performed their interval training in simulated sea level conditions using a gas mixture consisting of approximately 26.5% O_2. Interval workouts were done three days per week and required the athletes to complete 5×5-min cycling efforts at 105% to 110% of maximal steady state heart rate. A control group of eight male cyclists completed the same training program at 1860 m using a normoxic gas mixture (F_IO_2 approximately 0.2093). Athletes using supplemental oxygen were able to train at a significantly higher percentage of their altitude lactate threshold (126%) than their counterparts who trained in normoxic conditions (109%). Following the 21-day training period, the athletes performed a 120-kilojoule (kJ) cycling performance time trial in simulated sea level conditions. The cycling performance test showed improvements of 2 s and 15 s for the normoxic-trained and hyperoxic-trained cyclists, respectively. The 15-s improvement in cycling performance seen in the hyperoxic-trained group was significantly better than their pretraining performance.

The findings of Morris, Kearney, and Burke (2000) demonstrate that high-intensity workouts at moderate altitude (1860 m, 6100 ft) are enhanced through the use of supplemental oxygen that simulates sea level conditions. In addition, these researchers showed that postaltitude sea level endurance performance is enhanced when supplemental oxygen is used in conjunction with LHTL altitude training.

Wilber and colleagues (2002a) reported similar results. Trained male cyclists and triathletes who lived at moderate altitude (1600 to 1900 m, 5280 to 6230 ft) were evaluated to determine the effect of supplemental oxygen used in conjunction with a strenuous cycling interval workout. Testing was conducted at 1860 m (6100 ft). The athletes performed three trials, completing 6×100 kJ (1:1.5 work-to-rest ratio) while inspiring a medical-grade gas composed of 21.0% (control), 26.5%, or 60.0% O_2. Figure 8.7 shows the important results of this study. Collectively, the data of Wilber and colleagues (2002a) suggest that supplemental O_2 (26.5 or 60.0%) produced significant increases in arterial oxyhemoglobin saturation (S_pO_2) and power output contributing to a significant improvement in exercise performance during intense interval training at moderate altitude. In terms of practical application, these data provide support for the use of supplemental O_2 as an altitude training strategy that allows athletes to live at moderate altitude and effectively "train low" with minimal travel and inconvenience.

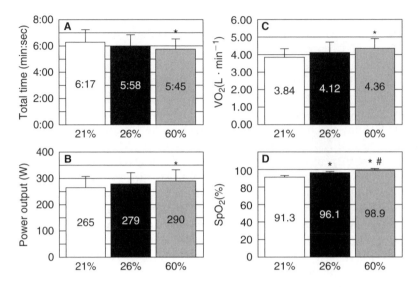

FIGURE 8.7   Effect of supplemental oxygen (26.5% O_2, 60.0% O_2) on (a) average total time, (b) power output, (c) oxygen uptake, and (d) oxyhemoglobin saturation in trained male cyclists during an interval training workout conducted at 1860 m (6100 ft). The interval workout consisted of 6 × 100 kilojoule (kJ) using a work-to-rest ratio of 1:1.5.

Adapted, by permission, from R.L. Wilber, P.L. Holm, D.M. Morris, G.M. Dallam, and S.D. Callan, 2002," Effect of F_IO_2 on physiological responses and power output in trained cyclists at moderate altitude," *Med Sci Sports Exerc* 34(Suppl. 5):S269.

Hypoxic Sleeping Devices

Endurance athletes have recently started to use hypoxic sleeping devices as part of their altitude training programs. These modalities include the Colorado Altitude Training (CAT) Hatch, the Hypoxico Altitude Tent, and the Colorado Mountain Room, all of which are designed to allow athletes to sleep high and train low. The CAT Hatch is a cylindrical hypobaric chamber that allows one person to lie in a supine or prone position and can simulate altitudes up to approximately 4575 m (15,006 ft). It creates a simulated altitude environment by reducing the barometric pressure inside the chamber (i.e., hypobaric hypoxia). The CAT Hatch is commercially available at a cost of approximately $14,000 U.S. (2002 price). At present, no scientific studies have been conducted to determine the efficacy of the CAT Hatch on RBC production, $\dot{V}O_2$max, and/or performance in elite athletes.

Another unique simulated altitude device that endurance athletes are currently using is the Hypoxico Altitude Tent (see figure 8.8). The tent can be installed over a standard double or queen-sized bed and simulates elevations up to approximately 4270 m (14,005 ft). The Hypoxico Altitude Tent uses an oxygen filtering membrane that "scrubs" or reduces the concentration of O_2 from the air outside the tent. The oxygen-reduced air is pumped inside the tent, resulting in a normobaric hypoxic environment. The Hypoxico Altitude Tent is commercially available at a cost of approximately $7500 U.S. (2002 price).

The Colorado Mountain Room uses similar technology to the Hypoxico Altitude Tent, but it is designed to convert an entire bedroom into a normobaric hypoxic living/sleeping environment. A standard-sized bedroom converted to the Colorado Mountain Room costs approximately $15,000 U.S. (2002 price).

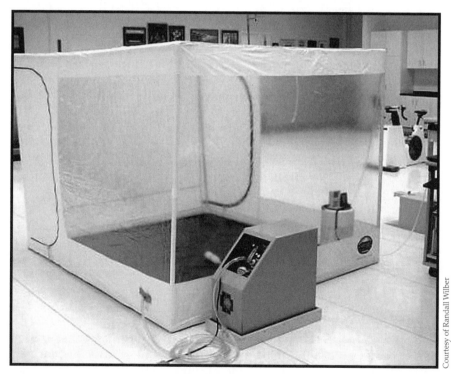

Courtesy of Randall Wilber

FIGURE 8.8   The Hypoxico Altitude Tent creates a normobaric hypoxic environment that simulates altitudes up to 4270 m (14,000 ft).

No scientific studies have been published to document the efficacy of the Hypoxico Altitude Tent or the Colorado Mountain Room on RBC production, $\dot{V}O_2$max, and/or performance in elite athletes. Preliminary research suggests that simulated altitude tents are relatively safe and comfortable normobaric hypoxic environments (Shannon, Wilber, and Kearney 2001; Wilber et al. 2002b), but do not significantly alter RBC levels (Ingham et al. 2001).

Intermittent Hypoxic Exposure

The use of intermittent hypoxic exposure (IHE) to enhance athletic performance is based on the fact that brief exposures to hypoxia/ high altitude (1.5 to 2.0 hours) stimulate the release of erythropoietin (Eckardt et al. 1989; Knaupp et al. 1992). These findings suggest that intermittent hypoxic exposure is sufficient to significantly increase serum EPO and RBC concentration and ultimately enhance $\dot{V}O_2$max and endurance performance. Athletes typically use intermittent hypoxic exposure at rest or in conjunction with training, referred to as intermittent hypoxic training (IHT). In effect, IHE and IHT allow the athlete to live low and train high. Athletes use a hypobaric chamber or a Hypoxicator device for IHE and IHT sessions.

At present, it is unclear whether IHE or IHT improve RBC and hemoglobin production despite increments in serum EPO (Frey et al. 2000; Rodriguez et al. 2000). Data are equivocal regarding the claim that IHE or IHT enhance $\dot{V}O_2$max and endurance performance in well-trained athletes (Meeuwsen, Hendriksen, and Holewijn 2001; Rodriguez et al. 1999; Terrados et al. 1988; Vallier, Chateau, and Guezennec 1996). Preliminary data suggest that anaerobic power and anaerobic capacity may improve as a result of IHT (Meeuwsen, Hendriksen, and Holewijn 2001). A few studies demonstrated potentially beneficial changes in activity of the oxidative enzyme citrate synthase in the vastus lateralis muscle in untrained subjects following eight weeks of IHT (Green et al. 1999; Melissa et al. 1997). Whether similar changes occur in well-trained or elite athletes is unknown.

Ethical Considerations

Some of the altitude training strategies described in this chapter have raised issues regarding the ethical integrity of their use to enhance athletic performance. In the International Olympic Committee's (IOC) most recent position statement on the use of banned substances, the IOC defined *doping* as "the use of an artifice, whether substance or method, potentially dangerous to athletes' health and/or capable of enhancing their performances, or the presence in the athlete's body of a substance, or the ascertainment of the use of a method on the list annexed to the Olympic Movement Anti-

Doping Code" (de Merode 2000). Moreover, *blood doping* is defined as "the administration of blood, red blood cells, artificial oxygen carriers and related blood products to an athlete" (de Merode 2000). Based on these definitions, some have objected to the use of normobaric hypoxic apartments, supplemental oxygen, altitude tents, and so on, on ethical and legal grounds, claiming they provide an unfair advantage to the athletes who use them in preparation for competition. In light of this controversy, the IOC Medical Commission recently indicated that it will evaluate the safety and ethical issues related to the use of simulated high altitude devices.

Recommendations and Guidelines

Based on scientific data as well as experiential evidence from athletes and coaches, the following recommendations and guidelines are offered for effective high altitude training in preparation for sea level performance. It must be reemphasized that each athlete responds differently to living and training at altitude. Therefore, these general recommendations and guidelines should serve as a starting point from which to design an individualized altitude training program for each athlete.

- *What is the optimal altitude at which to live?*

  The optimal altitude at which to live appears to be somewhere between 2100 and 2500 m (6888 to 8200 ft). In general, living below 2100 m (6888 ft) may not be high enough to stimulate an increase in RBC production, whereas living above 2500 m (8200 ft) may lead to training and recovery problems (Witkowski et al. 2001). Ideally, athletes would live and sleep high between 2100 and 2500 m (6888 to 8200 ft) and train low. Use of simulated altitude devices (nitrogen apartments, altitude tents) or supplemental oxygen make LHTL a viable option for athletes as opposed to traditional "live high, train high" altitude training.

- *How long do I need to stay at altitude to gain physiological benefits?*

  Athletes should spend a minimum of four weeks at altitude if they expect to derive some of the hematological and muscle buffering benefits associated with altitude training (Gore et al. 2001; Levine and Stray-Gundersen 1997; Stray-Gundersen, Chapman, and Levine 2001). Again, the best scenario would be for the athlete to live between 2100 and 2500 m (6888 and 8200 ft) either naturally or via simulated altitude and train at a relatively low elevation. If the athlete is using a nitrogen apartment or an altitude tent, exposure to the simulated altitude environment should be a minimum of 8 to 10 hours per day.

- *How long does the "altitude effect" last after returning to sea level?*

  As we would expect, there appears to be tremendous individual variability in the duration of the "altitude effect" after returning to sea level. As previously described, Gore and colleagues (1998) reported that postaltitude cycling performance (4000-m time trial) was individualistic among elite track cyclists when evaluated on days 4, 9, and 21 postaltitude, suggesting that optimal performance for each athlete may occur at a different time point in the weeks following altitude training. In another study (Levine and Stray-Gundersen 1997), 5-km running performance in trained distance runners who completed four weeks of LHTL was similar on days 7, 14, and 21 postaltitude compared with day 3 postaltitude, suggesting that the beneficial effects of LHTL on running performance may last for up to three weeks postaltitude. Athletes and coaches should perform several dry runs well in advance of major competitions to determine the optimal timing of return to sea level following a high altitude training phase.

Training Modifications

Exposure to altitude leads to decrements in P_IO_2, P_aO_2, S_aO_2, and $\dot{V}O_2$max. These altitude-induced physiological responses have a significant impact on an athlete's ability to train and compete at altitude, especially in the first two weeks of exposure. Consequently, it is imperative that modifications be made to the athlete's training volume and training intensity to ensure that the athlete does not overtrain. Figure 8.9 shows the recommended

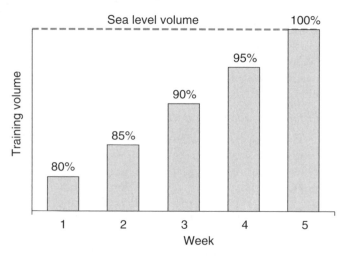

FIGURE 8.9   Modifications to training volume at moderate altitude (1800 to 3050 m, 6000 to 10,000 ft) during the initial five weeks of training. As a general rule, sea level training volume should be reduced by approximately 10 to 20% initially.

modifications to training volume at moderate altitude (1800 to 3050 m, 6000 to 10,000 ft) during the initial five weeks of training. As a general rule, training volume should be reduced by approximately 10 to 20% initially.

Figure 8.10a shows the recommended modifications to training intensity during interval workouts at moderate altitude during the initial five weeks of training. As a general rule, sea level interval workout training intensity should be reduced by approximately 5 to 7% initially.

Finally, figure 8.10b shows the recommended modifications to recovery during interval workouts at moderate altitude during the initial five weeks of training. As a general rule, sea level recovery during interval

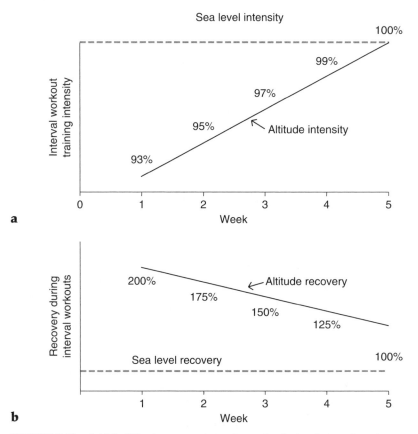

FIGURE 8.10 *(a)* Modifications to training intensity during interval workouts at moderate altitude (1800 to 3050 m, 6000 to 10,000 ft) during the initial five weeks of training. As a general rule, sea level interval workout training intensity should be reduced by approximately 5 to 7% initially. *(b)* Modifications to recovery during interval workouts at moderate altitude (1800 to 3050 m, 6000 to 10,000 ft) during the initial five weeks of training. As a general rule, sea level recovery during interval workouts should be doubled initially.

TABLE 8.4 Recommendations for Nontraining Altitude Issues That Should Be Addressed by Athletes and Coaches to Ensure a Productive Altitude Training Program

	Effect of altitude	Recommendations
Heart rate	May be higher vs. sea level at rest and during submaximal exercise. May be similar or lower vs. sea level during maximal exercise.	Adjustments to heart-rate-based training zones may be necessary in order to avoid undertaining or overtraining.
Hydration level	Increased respiratory and urinary water loss at altitude. Potential dehydration.	A concerted effort should be made to increase fluid intake by 4 to 5 L per day. Restrict intake of caffeinated beverages.
Carbohydrate metabolism	Increased carbohydrate utilization at altitude. Potential glycogen depletion.	A concerted effort should be made to replace carbohydrate prior to, during, and after workouts via carbohydrate replacement drinks and solid carbohydrate.
Iron	Decrease in iron stores (ferritin) upon altitude exposure. Potential iron deficiency. Potential non-erythropoietic response.	Have iron status evaluated via a blood test several weeks prior to altitude. Normal iron status is serum ferritin > 20 ng/ml in females and > 30 ng/ml in males. If iron status is abnormally low prior to high altitude exposure, consult physician regarding iron supplementation.
Immune system	Potential for immunosuppression and increased chance of illness.	Ensure adequate rest and recovery. Ensure adequate postexercise carbohydrate intake to modulate training-induced stress hormone response. Ensure adequate dietary intake of the vitamins folate, B6, and B12 and the minerals zinc, selenium, and copper, which affect the immune system.
Oxidative stress	Increased vs. sea level	Antioxidant supplementation (vitamins A, C, or E).
Ultraviolet radiation	Increased vs. sea level	Ultraviolet sunscreen and sunglasses; antioxidant vitamin E
Sleep/recovery	May be disturbed and irregular at altitude, especially the first few nights	Afternoon naps may help until the nighttime sleep disturbances subside. Make sleeping environment as comfortable and similar to home as possible.
Body composition	Potential decrease in muscle mass at altitude, but not very common at elevations that athletes typically train at (1800 to 3050 m/6000 to 10,000 ft)	Adequate nutrition with possible increase in caloric intake. Regular monitoring of body composition.
Acute mountain sickness (AMS)	Potential for symptoms of headache and nausea, but not very common at elevations that athletes typically train at (1800 to 3050 m/6000 to 10,000 ft)	Prescription acetazolamide or aspirin in combination with adequate rest and recovery. Elimination of or significant modification to training until recovery.

workouts should be doubled initially. Because there is great individual variability among athletes' responses at altitude, some athletes may be able to replicate sea level training volume and/or intensity within a few weeks at high altitude without any negative effects. Other athletes, however, may never be able to replicate sea level workouts at altitude and may need more time to adjust than the recommended timetables shown in figures 8.9 and 8.10.

Away From Training

In addition to modifications related to training volume and intensity, athletes and coaches should follow nontraining guidelines to ensure a productive high altitude training experience. Most of these steps are either a continuation or modification of what the athlete would normally do at sea level. However, some of these recommendations are unique to the altitude situation. Table 8.4 summarizes the important nontraining issues that athletes and coaches should address prior to and during altitude training.

References

Adams, W.C., Bernauer, E.M., Dill, D.B., and Bomar, J.B. 1975. Effects of equivalent sealevel and altitude training on $\dot{V}O_2$max and running performance. *J Appl Physiol* 39:262-266.

Asano, K., Sub, S., Matsuzaka, A., Hirakoba, K., Nagai, J., and Kawaoka, T. 1986. The influences of simulated altitude training on work capacity and performance in middle and long distance runners. *Bulletin of Institute of Health and Sport Sciences* 9:195-202.

Ashenden, M.J., Gore, C.J., Dobson, G.P., Boston, T.T., Parisotto, R., Emslie, K.R., Trout, G.J., and Hahn, A.G. 2000. Simulated moderate altitude elevates serum erythropoietin but does not increase reticulocyte production in well-trained runners. *Eur J Appl Physiol* 81:428-435.

Ashenden, M.J., Gore, C.J., Dobson, G.P., and Hahn, A.G. 1999a. "Live high, train low" does not change the total haemoglobin mass of male endurance athletes sleeping at a simulated altitude of 3000 m for 23 nights. *Eur J Appl Physiol* 80:479-484.

Ashenden, M.J., Gore, C.J., Martin, D.T., Dobson, G.P., and Hahn, A.G. 1999b. Effects of a 12-day "live high, train low" camp on reticulocyte production and haemoglobin mass in elite female road cyclists. *Eur J Appl Physiol* 80:472-478.

Bailey, D.M., and Davies, B. 1997. Physiological implications of altitude training for endurance performance at sea level: A review. *Br J Sports Med* 31:183-190.

Bailey, D.M., Davies, B., Romer, L., Castell, L., Newsholme, E., and Gandy, G. 1998. Implications of moderate altitude training for sea-level endurance in elite distance runners. *Eur J Appl Physiol* 78:360-368.

Banchero, N., Sime, F., Penaloza, D., Cruz, J., Gamboa, R., and Marticorena, E. 1966. Pulmonary pressure, cardiac output, and arterial oxygen saturation during exercise at high altitude and at sea level. *Circulation* 33:249-262.

Bartsch, P. 1992. Treatment of high altitude diseases without drugs. *Int J Sports Med* 13(Suppl. 1):S71-S74.

Beidleman, B.A., Rock, P.B., Muza, S.R., Fulco, C.S., Gibson, L.L., Kamimori, G.H., and Cymerman, A. 2002. Substrate oxidation is altered in women during exercise upon acute altitude exposure. *Med Sci Sports Exerc* 34:430-437.

Bell, C. 1996. Morphology of the erythron. In *Hematology: Clinical and laboratory practice I*, edited by R.L. Bick. St. Louis: Mosby.

Berglund, B. 1992. High-altitude training: Aspects of hematological adaptation. *Sports Med* 14:289-303.

Berglund, B., and Ekblom, B. 1991. Effect of recombinant human erythropoietin treatment on blood pressure and some haematological parameters in healthy men. *J Intern Med* 229:125-130.

Birkeland, K.I., Stray-Gundersen, J., Hemmersbach, P., Hallen, J., Haug, E., and Bahr, R. 2000. Effect of fhEPO administration on serum levels of sTfR and cycling performance. *Med Sci Sports Exerc* 32:1238-1243.

Boning, D. 1997. Altitude and hypoxic training: A short review. *Int J Sports Med* 18:565-570.

Bouissou, P., Peronnet, F., Brisson, G., Helie, R., and Ledoux, M. 1986. Metabolic and endocrine responses to graded exercise under acute hypoxia. *Eur J Appl Physiol* 55:290-294.

Boyer, S.J., and Blume, F.D. 1984. Weight loss and changes in body composition at high altitude. *J Appl Physiol* 57:1580-1585.

Bradwell, A.R., Wright, A.D., Winterborn, M., and Imray, C. 1992. Acetazolamide and high altitude diseases. *Int J Sports Med* 13(Suppl. 1):S63-S64.

Braun, B., Mawson, J.T., Muza, S.R., Dominick, S.B., Brooks, G.A., Horning, M.A., Rock, P.B., Moore, L.G., Mazzeo, R.S., Ezeji-Okoye, S.C., and Butterfield, G.E. 2000. Women at altitude: Carbohydrate utilization during exercise at 4,300 m. *J Appl Physiol* 88:246-256.

Brooks, G.A., Butterfield, G.E., Wolfe, R.R., Groves, B.M., Mazzeo, R.S., Sutton, J.R., Wolfel, E.E., and Reeves, J.T. 1991. Increased dependence on blood glucose after acclimatization to 4,300 m. *J Appl Physiol* 70:919-927.

Brosnan, M.J., Martin, D.T., Hahn, A.G., Gore, C.T., and Hawley, J.A. 2000. Impaired interval exercise responses in elite female cyclists at moderate simulated altitude. *J Appl Physiol* 89:1819-1824.

Burtscher, M., Nachbauer, W., Baumgartl, P., and Philadelphy, M. 1996. Benefits of training at moderate altitude versus sea level training in amateur runners. *Eur J Appl Physiol* 74:558-563.

Buskirk, E.R., Kollias, J., Akers, R.F., Prokop, E.K., and Reategui, E.P. 1967. Maximal performance at altitude and on return from altitude in conditioned runners. *J Appl Physiol* 23:259-266.

Butterfield, G.E. 1996. Maintenance of body weight at altitude. In *Nutritional needs in cold and high-altitude environments*, edited by B.M. Marriott and S.J. Carlson. Washington, D.C.: Committee on Military Nutrition Research. pp. 357-378.

Butterfield, G.E., Gates, J., Flemming, S., Brooks, G.A., Sutton, J.R., and Reeves, J.T. 1992. Increased energy intake minimizes weight loss in men at high altitude. *J Appl Physiol* 72:1741-1748.

Capelli, C., and di Prampero, P.E. 1995. Effects of altitude on top speeds during 1 h unaccompanied cycling. *Eur J Appl Physiol* 71:469-471.

Chapman R.F., Emery, M., and Stager, J.M. 1999. Degree of arterial desaturation in normoxia influences $\dot{V}O_2$max decline in mild hypoxia. *Med Sci Sports Exerc* 31:658-663.

Chapman, R.F., Stray-Gundersen, J., and Levine, B.D. 1998. Individual variation in response to altitude training. *J Appl Physiol* 85:1448-1456.

Chung, D-S., Lee, J-G., Kim, E-H., Lee, C-H., and Lee, S-K. 1995. The effects of altitude training on blood cells, maximal oxygen uptake and swimming performance. *Korean Journal of Science* 7:35-46.

Daniels, J., and Oldridge, N. 1970. The effects of alternate exposure to altitude and sea level in world-class middle-distance runners. *Med Sci Sports* 2:107-112.

de Merode, A. 2000. International Olympic Committee list of classes of prohibited substances and methods of doping. Lausanne, Comite Internationale Olympique. Letter Feb. 15, 2000:2.

Dempsey, J.A. 1986. Is the lung built for exercise? *Med Sci Sports Exerc* 18:143-155.

Dempsey, J.A., and Forester, H.V. 1982. Mediation of ventilatory adaptations. *Physiol Rev* 62:262-346.

Dempsey, J.A., Hanson, P.E., and Henderson, K.S. 1984. Exercise induced arterial hypoxemia in healthy persons at sea level. *J Physiol* 355:161-175.

Desplanches, D., Hoppeler, H., Linoissier, M.T., Denis, C., Claasen, H., Dormois, D., Lacour, J.R., and Geyssant, A. 1993. Effects of training in normoxia and normobaric hypoxia on human muscle ultrastructure. *Pflugers Arch* 425:263-267.

Dill, D.B., and Adams, W.C. 1971. Maximal oxygen uptake at sea level and at 3,090-m altitude in high school champion runners. *J Appl Physiol* 30:854-859.

Eckardt, K-U., Boutellier, U., Kurtz, A., Schopen, M., Koller, E.A., and Bauer, C. 1989. Rate of erythropoietin formation in humans in response to acute hypobaric hypoxia. *J Appl Physiol* 66:1785-1788.

Ekblom, B., and Berglund, B. 1991. Effects of erythropoietin administration on maximal aerobic power. *Scand J Med Sci Sports* 1:88-93.

Fandrey, J., and Jelkmann, W.E. 1991. Interleukin-1 and tumor necrosis factor-alpha inhibit erythropoietin production in vitro. *Ann N Y Acad Sci* 628:250-255.

Faulkner, J.A., Daniels, J.T., and Balke, B. 1967. Effects of training at moderate altitude on physical performance capacity. *J Appl Physiol* 23:85-89.

Faulkner, J.A., Kollias, J., Favour, C.B., Buskirk, E.R., and Balke, B. 1968. Maximum aerobic capacity and running performance at altitude. *J Appl Physiol* 24:685-691.

Flaharty, K.K., Caro, J., Erslev, A., Whalen, J.J., Morris, E.M., Bjornsson, T.D., and Vlasses, P.H. 1990. Pharmacokinetics and erythropoietic response to human recombinant erythropoietin in healthy men. *Clin Pharmacol Ther* 47:557-564.

Frey W.O., Zenhausern, R., Colombani, P.C., and Fehr, J. 2000. Influence of intermittent exposure to normobaric hypoxia on hematological indexes and exercise performance. *Med Sci Sports Exerc* 32(Suppl. 5):S65.

Friedmann, B., Weller, E., Mairbaurl, H., and Bartsch, P. 2001. Effects of iron repletion on blood volume and performance capacity in young athletes. *Med Sci Sports Exerc* 33:741-746.

Fulco, C.S., Rock, P.D., and Cymerman, A. 2000. Improving athletic performance: is altitude residence or altitude training helpful? *Aviat Space Environ Med* 71:162-171.

Fulco, C.S., Rock, P.D., and Cymerman, A. 1998. Maximal and submaximal exercise performance at altitude. *Aviat Space Environ Med* 69:793-801.

Gale, G.E., Torre-Bueno, J.R., Moon, R.E., Saltzman, H.A., and Wagner, P.D. 1985. Ventilation-perfusion inequality in normal humans during exercise at sea level and simulated altitude. *J Appl Physiol* 58:978-988.

Goldenberg, F., Richalet, J.P., Onnen, I., and Antezana, A.M. 1992. Sleep apneas and high altitude newcomers. *Int J Sports Med* 13(Suppl. 1):S34-S36.

Gore, C.J., Craig, N.P., Hahn, A.G., Rice, A.J., Bourdon, P.C., Lawrence, S.R., Walsh, C.B.V., Barnes, P.G., Parisotto, R., Martin, D.T., and Pyne, D.B. 1998. Altitude training at 2690 m does not increase total haemoglobin mass or sea level $\dot{V}O_2$max in world champion track cyclists. *J Sci Med Sport* 1:156-170.

Gore, C.J., Hahn, A.G., Aughey, R.J., Martin, D.T., Ashenden, M.J., Clark, S.A., Garnham, A.P., Roberts, A.D., Slater, G.J., and McKenna, M.J. 2001. Live high:train low increases muscle buffer capacity and submaximal cycling efficiency. *Acta Physiol Scand* 173:275-286.

Gore, C.J., Hahn, A.G., Scroop, G.C., Watson, D.B., Norton, K.I., Wood, R.J., Campbell, D.P., and Emonson, D.L. 1996. Increased arterial desaturation in trained cyclists during maximal exercise at 580 m altitude. *J Appl Physiol* 80:2204-2210.

Gore, C.J., Little, S.C., Hahn, A.G., Scroop, G.C., Norton, K.I., Bourdon, P.C., Woolford, S.M., Buckley, J.D., Stanef, T., Campbell, D.P., Watson, D.B., and Emonson, D.L. 1997. Reduced performance of male and female athletes at 580 m altitude. *Eur J Appl Physiol* 75:136-143.

Green H., MacDougall, J., Tarnapolsky, M.A., and Melissa, N.L. 1999. Downregulation of Na+-K+-ATPase pumps in skeletal muscle with training in normobaric hypoxia. *J Appl Physiol* 86:1745-1748.

Grover, R.F., Reeves, J.T., Maher, J.T., McCullough, R.E., Cruz, J.C., Denniston, J.C., and Cymerman, A. 1976. Maintained stroke volume but impaired arterial oxygenation in man at high altitude with supplemental CO_2. *Circ Res* 38:391-396.

Grover, R.F., Weil, J.V., and Reeves, J.T. 1986. Cardiovascular adaptation to exercise at high altitude. In *Exercise and sport sciences reviews*, edited by K.B. Pandolf. New York: Macmillan.

Hahn, A.G. 1991. The effect of altitude training on athletic performance at sea level: A review. *Excel* 7:9-23.

Hahn, A.G., and Gore, C.J. 2001. The effect of altitude on cycling performance. *Sports Med* 31:533-557.

Hahn, A.G., Telford, R.D., Tumilty, D.M., McBride, M.E., Campbell, D.P., Kovacic, J.C., Batschi, R., and Thompson, P.A. 1992. Effect of supplementary hypoxic training on physiological characteristics and ergometer performance of elite rowers. *Excel* 8:127-138.

Hakkinen, K., Keskinen, K.L., Alen, M., Komi, P.V., and Kauhanen, H. 1989. Serum hormone concentrations during prolonged training in elite endurance-trained and strength-trained athletes. *Eur J Appl Physiol* 59:233-238.

Hansen, J.R., Stetler, G.P., and Vogel, J.A. 1967. Arterial pyruvate, lactate, pH and PCO_2 during work at sea level and high altitude. *J Appl Physiol* 24:523-530.

Hartley, L.H., Vogel, J.A., and Landowne, M. 1973. Central, femoral, and brachial circulation during exercise in hypoxia. *J Appl Physiol* 34:87-90.

Hinton, P.S., Giordano, C., Brownlie, T., and Haas, J.D. 2000. Iron supplementation improves endurance after training in iron-depleted, nonanemic women. *J Appl Physiol* 88:1103-1111.

Hogan, R.P., Kotchen, T.A., Boyd III, A.E., and Hartley, L.H. 1973. Effect of altitude on renin-aldosterone system and metabolism of water and electrolytes. *J Appl Physiol* 35:385-390.

Hoppeler, H., Kleinert, E., Schlegel, C., Claassen, E., Howald, H., Kayar, S.R., and Cerretelli, P. 1990. Morphologic adaptations of human skeletal muscle to chronic hypoxia. *Int J Sports Med* 11(Suppl. 1):S3-S9.

Huang, S.Y., Alexander, J.K., Grover, R.F., Maher, J.T., McCullough, R.E., McCullough, R.G., Moore, L.G., Sampson, J.B., Weil, J.V., and Reeves, J.T. 1984. Hypocapnia and sustained hypoxia blunt ventilation on arrival at high altitude. *J Appl Physiol* 56:602-606.

Ingham, E.A., Pfitzinger, P.D., Hellemans, J., Bailey, C., Fleming, J.S., and Hopkins, W.G. 2001. Running performance following intermittent altitude exposure simulated with nitrogen tents. *Med Sci Sports Exerc* 33(Suppl. 5):S2.

Ingjer, F., and Myhre, K. 1992. Physiological effects of altitude training on elite male cross-country skiers. *J Sports Sci* 10:37-47.

Jensen, K., Nielsen, T.S., Fiskestrand, A., Lund, J.O., Christensen, N.J., and Sechar, N.H. 1993. High-altitude training does not increase maximal oxygen uptake or work capacity at sea level in rowers. *Scand J Med Sci Sports* 3:256-262.

Kayser, B. 1992. Nutrition and high altitude exposure. *Int J Sports Med* 13(Suppl. 1):S129-S132.

Kayser, B. 1994. Nutrition and energetics of exercise at altitude. *Sports Med* 17:309-323.

Kayser, B. 1996. Lactate during exercise at high altitude. *Eur J Appl Physiol* 74:195-205.

Klausen, K. 1966. Cardiac output in man in rest and work during and after acclimatization to 3800 m. *J Appl Physiol* 21:609-616.

Knaupp, W., Khilnani, S., Sherwood, J., Scharf, S., and Steinberg, H. 1992. Erythropoietin response to acute normobaric hypoxia in humans. *J Appl Physiol* 73:837-840.

Koistinen, P., Takala, T., Martikkala, V., and Leppaluoto, J. 1995. Aerobic fitness influences the response of maximal oxygen uptake and lactate threshold in acute hypobaric hypoxia. *Int J Sports Med* 26:78-81.

Laciga, P., and Koller, E.A. 1976. Respiratory, circulatory, and ECG changes during acute
exposure to altitude. *J Appl Physiol* 41:159-167.

Laitinen, H., Alopaeus, K., Heikkinen, R., Hietanen, H., Mikkelsson, L., Tikkanen, H.,
and Rusko, H.K. 1995. Acclimatization to living in normobaric hypoxia and training at sea level in runners. *Med Sci Sports Exerc* 27(Suppl. 5):S109.

Lawler, J., Powers, S.K., and Thompson, D. 1988. Linear relationship between $\dot{V}O_2$max and
$\dot{V}O_2$max decrement during exposure to acute hypoxia. *J Appl Physiol* 64:1486-1492.

Levine, B. 2002. Intermittent hypoxic training: fact and fancy. *High Alt Med Biol* 3: 177-
1993.

Levine, B.D., and Stray-Gundersen, J. 1997. "Living high-training low": Effect of moderate-altitude acclimatization with low-altitude training on performance. *J Appl Physiol*
83:102-112.

Lundby, C., Saltin, B., and van Hall, G. 2000. The "lactate paradox," evidence for a transient change in the course of acclimatization to severe hypoxia in lowlanders. *Acta
Physiol Scand* 170:265-269.

MacDougall, J.D., Green, H.J., Sutton, J.R., Coates, G., Cymerman, A., Young, P., and
Houston, C.S. 1991. Operation Everest II: Structural adaptations in skeletal muscle
in response to extreme simulated altitude. *Acta Physiol Scand* 142:421-427.

Maher, J.T., Jones, L.G., Hartley, L.H., Williams, G.H., and Rose, L.I. 1975. Aldosterone dynamics during graded exercise at sea level and high altitude. *J Appl Physiol* 39:18-22.

Matilla, V., and Rusko, H. 1996. Effect of living high and training low on sea level performance in cyclists. *Med Sci Sports Exerc* 28(Suppl. 5):S157.

Mawson, J.T., Braun, B., Rock, P.B., Moore, L.G., Mazzeo, R., and Butterfield, G.E. 2000.
Women at altitude: Energy requirements at 4300 m. *J Appl Physiol* 88:272-281.

McComas, A.J. 1996. *Skeletal muscle form and function*. Champaign, Ill.: Human Kinetics.

Meeuwsen T., Hendriksen, I.J.M., and Holewijn, M. 2001. Training-induced increases in
sea-level performance is enhanced by acute intermittent hypobaric hypoxia. *Eur J
Appl Physiol* 84:283-290.

Melissa, L.M., MacDougall, J.D., Tarnapolsky, M.A., Cipriano, N., and Green, H.J. 1997.
Skeletal muscle adaptations to training under normobaric hypoxic versus normoxic
conditions. *Med Sci Sports Exerc* 29:238-243.

Mizuno, M., Juel, C., Bro-Rasmussen, T., Mygind, E., Schibye, B., Rasmussin, B., and
Saltin, B. 1990. Limb skeletal muscle adaptations in athletes after training at altitude. *J Appl Physiol* 68:496-502.

Moore, L.G., Cymerman, A., Huang, S.Y., McCullough, R.E., McCullough, R.G., Rock,
P.B., Young, A.J., Young, P.M., Bloedow, D., Weil, J.V., and Reeves, J.T. 1986. Propra-
nolol does not impair exercise oxygen uptake in normal man at high altitude. *J
Appl Physiol* 61:1935-1941.

Morris, D.M., Kearney, J.T., and Burke, E.R. 2000. The effects of breathing supplemental
oxygen during altitude training on cycling performance. *J Sci Med Sport* 3:165-175.

Nieman, D. 1997. Immune response to heavy exertion. *J Appl Physiol* 82:1385-1394.

Nieman, D.C., Ahle, J.C., Henson, D.A., Warren, B.J., Suttles, J., Davis, J.M., Buckley,
K.S., Simandle, S., Butterworth, D.E., Fagoaga, O.R., and Nehlsen-Cannarella, S.L.
1995a. Indomethacin does not alter the natural killer cell response to 2.5 hours of
running. *J Appl Physiol* 79:748-755.

Nieman, D.C., Miller, A.R., Henson, D.A., Warren, B.J., Gusewitch, G., Johnson, R.L.,
Davis, J.M., Butterworth, D.E., Herring, J.L., and Nehlsen-Cannarella, S.L. 1994.
Effects of high- versus moderate-intensity exercise on circulating lymphocyte sub-
populations and proliferative response. *Int J Sports Med* 15:199-206.

Nieman, D.C., Simandle, S., Henson, D.A., Warren, B.J., Suttles, J., Davis, J.M., Buckley, K.S., Ahle, J.C., Butterworth, D.E., Fagoaga, O.R., and Nehlsen-Cannarella, S.L. 1995b. Lymphocyte proliferation response to 2.5 hours of running. *Int J Sports Med* 16:406-410.

Nummela, A., and Rusko, H. 2000. Acclimatization to altitude and normoxic training improve 400-m running performance at sea level. *J Sports Sci* 18:411-419.

Olds, T. 2001. Modelling human locomotion: applications to cycling. *Sports Med* 31:497-509.

Olds, T. 1992. The optimal altitude for cycling performance: A mathematical model. *Excel* 8:155-159.

Ou, L.C., Salceda, S., Schuster, S.J., Dunnack, L.M., Brink-Johnsen, T., Chen, J., and Leiter, J.C. 1998. Polycythemic responses to hypoxia: Molecular and genetic mechanisms of chronic mountain sickness. *J Appl Physiol* 84:1242-1251.

Peronnet, F., Thibault, G., and Cousineau, D-L. 1991. A theoretical analysis of the effect of altitude on running performance. *J Appl Physiol* 70:399-404.

Piehl-Aulin, K., Svedenhag, J., Wide, L., Berglund, B., and Saltin, B. 1998. Short-term intermittent normobaric hypoxia: Haematological, physiological and mental effects. *Scand J Med Sci Sports* 8:132-137.

Porter, D.L., and Goldberg, M.A. 1994. Physiology of erythropoietin production. *Semin Hematol* 31:112-121.

Rahkila, P., and Rusko, H. 1982. Effect of high altitude training on muscle enzyme activities and physical performance characteristics of cross-country skiers. In *Exercise and sport biology*, edited by P.V. Komi. Champaign, Ill.: Human Kinetics.

Reeves, J.T., Wolfel, E.E., Green, H.J., Mazzeo, R.S., Young, A.J., Sutton, J.R., and Brooks, G.A. 1992. Oxygen transport during exercise at high altitude and the lactate paradox: Lessons from Operation Everest II and Pike's Peak. In *Exercise and sport sciences reviews*, edited by K.B. Pandolf. New York: Macmillan.

Richalet, J.P., Souberbielle, J.C., Antezana, A.M., Dechaux, M., Le Trong, J.L., Bienvenu, A., Daniel, F., Blanchot, C., and Zittoun, J. 1994. Control of erythropoiesis in humans during prolonged exposure to the altitude of 6,542 m. *Am J Physiol* 266:R756-R764.

Robergs, R.A., Quintana, R., Parker, D.L., and Frankel, C.C. 1998. Multiple variables explain the variability in the decrement in $\dot{V}O_2$max during acute hypobaric hypoxia. *Med Sci Sports Exerc* 30:869-879.

Roberts, A.C., Butterfield, G.E., Cymerman, A., Reeves, J.T., Wolfel, E.E., and Brooks, G.A. 1996a. Acclimatization to 4300-m altitude decreases reliance on fat as a substrate. *J Appl Physiol* 81:1762-1771.

Roberts, A.C., Reeves, J.T., Butterfield, G.E., Mazzeo, R.S., Sutton, J.R., Wolfel, E.E., and Brooks, G.A. 1996b. Altitude and β-blockade augment glucose utilization during submaximal exercise. *J Appl Physiol* 80:605-615.

Roberts, A.D., Daley, P.J., Martin, D.T., Hahn, A., Gore, C.J., and Spence, R. 1998. Sea level $\dot{V}O_2$max fails to predict $\dot{V}O_2$max and performance at 1800 m altitude. *Med Sci Sports Exerc* 30(Suppl. 5):111.

Rodriguez, F.A., Casas, H., Casas, M., Pages, T., Rama, R., Ricart, A., Ventura, J.L., Ibanez, J., and Viscor, G. 1999. Intermittent hypobaric hypoxia stimulates erythropoiesis and improves aerobic capacity. *Med Sci Sports Exerc* 31:264-268.

Rodriguez, F.A., Ventura, J.L., Casas, M., Casas, H., Pages, T., Rama, R., Ricart, A., Palacios, L., and Viscor, G. 2000. Erythropoietin acute reaction and hematological adaptations to short, intermittent hypobaric hypoxia. *Eur J Appl Physiol* 82:170-177.

Roi, G.S., Giacometti, M., and Von Duvillard, S.P. 1999. Marathons at altitude. *Med Sci Sports Exerc* 31:723-728.

Rose, M.S., Houston, C.S., Fulco, C.S., Coates, G., Sutton, J.R., and Cymerman, A. 1988. Operation Everest II: Nutrition and body composition. *J Appl Physiol* 65:2545-2551.

Rusko, H.K., Leppavuori, A., Makela, P., and Leppaluoto, J. 1995. Living high, training low: A new approach to altitude training at sea level in athletes. *Med Sci Sports Exerc* 27(Suppl. 5):S6.

Rusko, H.K., Tikkanen, H., Paavolainen, L., Hamalainen, I., Kalliokoski, K., and Puranen, A. 1999. Effect of living in hypoxia and training in normoxia on sea level $\dot{V}O_2$max and red cell mass. *Med Sci Sports Exerc* 31(Suppl. 5):S86.

Saltin, B., Kim, C.K., Terrados, N., Larsen, H., Svedenhag, J., and Rolf, C.J. 1995. Morphology, enzyme activities and buffer capacity in leg muscles of Kenyan and Scandinavian runners. *Scand J Med Sci Sports* 5:222-230.

Shannon, M.P., Wilber, R.L., and Kearney, J.T. 2001. Normobaric-hypoxia: Performance characteristics of simulated altitude tents. *Med Sci Sports Exerc* 33(Suppl. 5):S60.

Simon-Schnass, I. 1994. Risk of oxidative stress during exercise at high altitude. In *Exercise and oxygen toxicity*, edited by C.K. Sen, L. Packer, and O. Hanninen. Amsterdam: Elsevier.

Simon-Schnass, I., and Pabst, H. 1988. Influence of vitamin E on physical performance. *Int J Vitam Nutr Res* 58:49-54.

Squires, R.W., and Buskirk, E.R. 1982. Aerobic capacity during acute exposure to simulated altitude, 914 to 2286 meters. *Med Sci Sports Exerc* 14:36-40.

Stenberg, J., Ekblom, B., and Messin, R. 1966. Hemodynamic response to work at simulated altitude, 4000 m. *J ApplPhysiol* 21:1589-1594.

Stray-Gundersen, J., Alexander, C., Hochstein, A., deLemos, D., and Levine, B.D. 1992. Failure of red cell volume to increase to altitude exposure in iron deficient runners. *Med Sci Sports Exerc* 24(Suppl.):S90.

Stray-Gundersen, J., Chapman, R.F., and Levine, B.D. 2001. "Living high-training low" altitude training improves sea level performance in male and female elite runners. *J Appl Physiol* 91:1113-1120.

Svedenhag, J., Saltin, B., Johansson, C., and Kaijser, L. 1991. Aerobic and anaerobic exercise capacities of elite middle-distance runners after two weeks of training at moderate altitude. *Scand J Med Sci Sports* 1:205-214

Sylvester, J.T., Cymerman, A., Gurtner, G., Hottenstein, O., Cote, M., and Wolfe, D. 1981. Components of alveolar-arterial O_2gradient during rest and exercise at sea level and high altitude. *J Appl Physiol* 50:1129-1139.

Telford, R.D., Graham, K.S., Sutton, J.R., Hahn, A.G., Campbell, D.A., Creighton, S.W., Cunningham, R.B., Davis, P.G., Gore, C.J., Smith, J.A., and Tumilty, D.M. 1996. Medium altitude training and sea-level performance. *Med Sci Sports Exerc* 28(Suppl. 5):S124.

Terrados, N., Jansson, E., Sylven, C., and Kaijser, L. 1990. Is hypoxia a stimulus for synthesis of oxidative enzymes and myoglobin? *J Appl Physiol* 68:2369-2372.

Terrados, N., Melichna, J., Sylven, C., Jansson, E., and Kaijser, L. 1988. Effects of training at simulated altitude on performance and muscle metabolic capacity in competitive road cyclists. *Eur J Appl Physiol* 57:203-209.

Torre-Bueno, J.R., Wagner, P.D., Saltzman, H.A., Gale, G.E., and Moon, R.E. 1985. Diffusion limitation in normal humans during exercise at sea level and simulated altitude. *J Appl Physiol* 58:989-995.

Vallier, J.M., Chateau, P., and Guezennec, C.Y. 1996. Effects of physical training in a hypobaric chamber on the physical performance of competitive triathletes. *Eur J Appl Physiol* 73:471-478.

Vasankari, T.J., Kujala, U.M., Rusko, H., Sarna, S., and Ahotupa, M. 1997. The effect of endurance exercise at moderate altitude on serum lipid peroxidation and antioxidant functions in humans. *Eur J Appl Physiol* 75:396-399.

Vasankari, T.J., Rusko, H., Kujala, U.M., and Huhtaniemi, I.T. 1993. The effect of ski training at altitude and racing on pituitary, adrenal and testicular function in men. *Eur J Appl Physiol* 66:221-225.

Vogel, J.A., Hansen, J.E., and Harris, C.W. 1967. Cardiovascular responses in man during exhaustive work at sea level and high altitude. *J Appl Physiol* 25:531-539.

Vogel, J.A., Hartley, L.H., Cruz, J.C., and Hogan, R.P. 1974. Cardiac output during exercise in sea level residents at sea level and high altitude. *J Appl Physiol* 36:169-172.

Wagner, P.D., Gale, G.E., Moon, R.E., Torre-Bueno, J.R., Stolp, B.W., and Saltzman, H.A. 1986. Pulmonary gas exchange in humans exercising at sea level and simulated altitude. *J Appl Physiol* 61:260-270.

Welch, H.G. 1987. Effects of hypoxia and hyperoxia on human performance. *Exerc Sport Sci Rev* 15:191-220.

Wilber, R.L. 2001. Current trends in altitude training. *Sports Med* 31:249-265.

Wilber, R.L., Drake, S.D., Hesson, J.L., Nelson, J.A., Kearney, J.T., Dallam, G.M., and Williams, L.L. 2000. Effect of altitude training on serum creatine kinase activity and serum cortisol concentration in triathletes. *Eur J Appl Physiol* 81:140-147.

Wilber, R.L., Holm, P.L., Morris, D.M., Dallam, G.M., and Callan, S.D. 2002a. Effect of F_iO_2 on physiological responses and power output in trained cyclists at moderate altitude. *Med Sci Sports Exerc* 34(Suppl. 5):S269.

Wilber, R.L., Shannon, M.P., Kearney, J.T., Holm, P.L., and Hill, M.R. 2002b. Operational characteristics of a normobaric hypoxic system. *Med Sci Sports Exerc* 34(Suppl. 5): 92.

Witkowski, S., Karlsen, T., Resaland, G., Sivieri, M., Yates, R., Harber, M., Ge, R.L., Stray-Gundersen, J., and Levine, B.D. 2001. Optimal altitude for "living high-training low." *Med Sci Sports Exerc* 33(Suppl. 5):S292.

Wolfel, E.E., Selland, M.A., Mazzeo, R.S., and Reeves, J.T. 1994. Systemic hypertension at 4300 m is related to sympathoadrenal activity. *J Appl Physiol* 76:1643-1650.

Wolski, L.A., McKenzie, D.C., and Wenger, H.A. 1996. Altitude training for improvements in sea level performance. *Sports Med* 22:251-263.

Young, A.J., Evans, W.J., Cymerman, A., Pandolf, K.B., Knapik, J.J., and Maher, J.T. 1982. Sparing effect of chronic high-altitude exposure on muscle glycogen utilization. *J Appl Physiol* 52:857-862.

Young, P.M., Rock, P.B., Fulco, C.S., Trad, L.A., Forte, V.A., and Cymerman, A. 1987. Altitude acclimatization attenuates plasma ammonia accumulation during submaximal exercise. *J Appl Physiol* 63:758-764.

9

Nutrition for Competitive Cycling

Asker E. Jeukendrup

Cycling has seen enormous changes in nutritional practices in the last 30 years. In the 1960s and 1970s, cyclists were still fueling themselves with hot tea and chicken wings during stages. There are anecdotal reports of cyclists taking whiskey in their drink bottles to keep themselves warm during cold races, and there is photographic evidence of a whole peloton stopping at a milk car during a stage in the Tour de France to fill their bottles with fresh milk. In the 1960s, it was common practice to eat large amounts of red meat the day before and sometimes even the morning of an important race. Even during hot stages in the Tour de France, cyclists would carry only one water bottle on their bikes. Many cyclists trained without drinking, believing that this would make them stronger during the race.

Clearly, these practices have changed. Today pasta, rice, and bread are important components of the diet, and special sport drinks and energy bars have been developed for use during exercise. Enormous effort by various research groups has gone into the development of drinks that deliver both water and nutrients at high rates, preventing dehydration and depletion of energy stores.

This chapter will give an overview of the evidence-based nutritional recommendations and their scientific background. Although cycling has many disciplines, this chapter will apply mainly to events of 45 min or longer, particularly road cycling, time trialing, and off-road cycling.

Energy Cost of Cycling

It has been estimated that a cyclist with average efficiency and aerodynamics requires about 21 kcal/min (83 kJ/min) to ride at 40 kph (26 mph). The relatively small carbohydrate stores in the human body (2000 to 3000 kcal; 8 to 12 MJ) can fuel about 90 min of cycling at this speed. The amount of energy stored as fat for a 70-kg male and a 55-kg female cyclist of average body composition would provide 100,000 kcal (400,000 kJ) and 125,000 kcal (500,000 kJ), respectively.

In other words, if only fat or only carbohydrates could be used as fuel, the carbohydrate stores from exercising muscles would deliver energy for no more than 90 min of cycling at 40 kph, whereas energy derived from fat stores would theoretically be sufficient for 110 hours (4.5 days) of riding at this pace.

Since carbohydrate can deliver more energy per second than fat can, carbohydrate is often the preferred fuel. Especially during high-intensity exercise, carbohydrate can provide energy at very high rates. Well-trained

© Bruce Coleman, Inc.

The daily energy expenditure of an elite cyclist is very high. Therefore, serious cyclists should commit to a sound nutritional program to ensure that energy is available when needed.

cyclists can expend up to 30 kcal/min for longer periods of time, most of this derived from the breakdown of muscle glycogen.

Because of such high energy expenditures in combination with long training rides or races, the total daily energy expenditure of cyclists can be very high. In fact, cycling is among the sports with the highest energy expenditures ever reported.

During the Tour de France, energy expenditures may rise to 9000 kcal (36 MJ) per day. In such extreme conditions, it is a challenge to maintain energy balance (energy balance equals energy intake minus energy expenditure). In a study by Saris and colleagues (1989), energy expenditures and intakes were measured during the three weeks of the Tour de France (see figure 9.1). In this study, despite very high energy expenditures on some days, riders maintained energy balance fairly well. On some of the very hard days, when energy expenditure topped 6000 kcal (24 MJ), cyclists had difficulty matching the energy expenditure and often were in slightly negative energy balance (500 to 1500 kcal). On rest days, they seemed to compensate for this, and over the course of three weeks were able to maintain their body weights fairly well (Jeukendrup, Craig, and Hawley 2000).

Weight losses have often been reported during the Tour de France and similar stage races. This indicates the difficulties in maintaining energy balance. Hunger feelings often are suppressed for several hours after strenuous exercise, making it difficult for a cyclist to consume large amounts of solid food. During weeks 2 and 3 of the Tour de France, riders often suffer

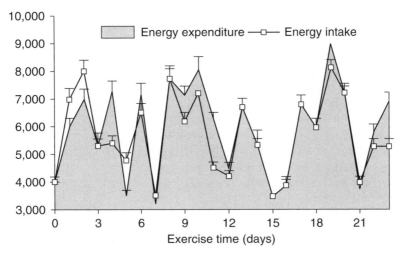

FIGURE 9.1   Energy intake versus energy expenditure during the Tour de France. Although energy intakes seems to match energy expenditure very well, cyclists have great difficulty maintaining energy balance on the days with extremely high energy expenditures (up to 9000 kcal).

Data adapted from Saris et al. 1989.

from gastrointestinal problems and may not be able to tolerate large amounts of food. The incidence of gastrointestinal problems is greater after hot stages, when dehydration may be considerable. At such times, riders must rehydrate before eating to reestablish normal gut function. In general, riders should be encouraged to eat and drink as much as possible during each stage. Aggressive riding tactics make it difficult to eat and drink a lot especially during the final two hours of a race. Anecdotal evidence shows that riders can be trained to eat and drink during races, which will increase their intake considerably.

Nutrition Before Exercise

The goal of carbohydrate ingestion in the days and hours before a one-day event is to maximize the body's carbohydrate stores (i.e., liver and muscle glycogen). The depletion of these energy stores has a detrimental effect on performance. Consuming carbohydrate can prevent depletion.

Cyclists must also ingest fluids in the days and hours before exercise to ensure proper hydration. Dehydration, like glycogen depletion, is a major cause of fatigue during sustained high-intensity exercise.

Carbo Loading

Scandinavian studies in the 1960s demonstrated that a cyclist can increase endurance capacity by eating a high-carbohydrate diet. A linear relationship seems to exist between muscle glycogen concentration and time to fatigue at a constant workload. Although the original glycogen-loading protocol included a so-called "depletion phase," more recent studies indicate that this is not necessary in trained athletes. Training likely induces adaptations in cyclists that enhance glycogen storage capacity.

Achieving high muscle glycogen stores is relatively easy and requires only a high dietary carbohydrate intake a few days prior to an event in combination with reduced training. For a 70-kg cyclist, total liver and muscle carbohydrate stores are in the order of 500 to 700 g. Intake of 7 to 10 g of carbohydrate per kg of body weight per day should be sufficient to replenish carbohydrate stores completely. In preparation for extreme situations, the recommendations are often slightly higher (8 to 11 g of carbohydrate per kg of body weight per day).

Carbohydrate Intake Three to Four Hours Before Exercise. Ingestion of a carbohydrate-rich meal of approximately 140 to 330 g of carbohydrate three to four hours before exercise has been shown to increase muscle glycogen levels (Coyle et al. 1985) and enhance exercise performance. An increase in preexercise muscle glycogen is one explanation for enhanced performance. In addition, the replenishment of liver glycogen stores may play an important role. After an overnight fast, liver glycogen levels can be substantially reduced, which may cause difficulty maintaining blood glu-

What About Fat Loading?

Carbohydrate loading has been recommended for athletes since the 1960s, but recently there has been some interest in fat loading. Fat-loading diets have a high fat content and relatively little carbohydrate. High-fat diets (in which more than 50% of the energy comes from fat) result in skeletal muscle adaptations similar to adaptations seen after endurance training. The ability to use fat as a fuel is increased even after only five days on a high-fat diet (Burke et al. 1999). The downside is that these diets reduce muscle glycogen content, especially when training is continued.

It has been suggested that the negative effects of a high-fat diet can be counteracted by one day on a high-carbohydrate diet. Researchers have investigated this idea (five days of a high-fat diet followed by one day of carbo loading) but found no effect on performance (Burke et al. 2002).

cose levels during the subsequent exercise bout. The ingestion of carbohydrate may replenish liver glycogen reserves and contribute, together with any ongoing absorption of the ingested carbohydrate, to the maintenance of blood glucose.

Carbohydrate intake in the hours before exercise has profound effects on metabolism. In general, carbohydrate use is stimulated, and less fatty acids are mobilized and used. Although these metabolic perturbations can persist for up to 6 hours after carbohydrate ingestion (Montain et al. 1991), they do not appear to be detrimental to exercise performance. The increased carbohydrate availability seems to compensate for the greater carbohydrate use.

Races such as the Tour de France usually start between 10 A.M. and noon. Between 7 and 9 A.M., riders have a large breakfast that contains mainly carbohydrate foods such as cereal, muesli, and bread. On days with very long stages, cyclists may eat a large plate of pasta or rice in addition to the normal breakfast. Such a breakfast is likely to contain more than 300 g of carbohydrate and will help riders maintain their 24-hour energy balance.

Carbohydrate Intake 60 Minutes Before Exercise. Ingesting carbohydrate results in a large increase in plasma glucose and insulin. However, when exercise is initiated 30 to 60 min after ingestion of carbohydrate, there is a rapid fall in blood glucose because of the combined stimulatory effects of high insulin levels and muscle contraction on muscle glucose uptake. Despite ongoing absorption of the ingested carbohydrate, plasma glucose levels may fall rapidly during the first 10 to 15 min of exercise.

Preexercise carbohydrate ingestion results in an enhanced uptake and use of blood glucose by skeletal muscle, which may account for the increased carbohydrate use often observed after ingestion. In addition, muscle glycogen breakdown may be accelerated, and the increase in plasma fatty acids with exercise is attenuated. Less fat is used as fuel because of lower plasma fatty acid availability (elevated plasma insulin concentrations inhibit the release of fatty acids from stores) and as a result of a reduction in the use of fat stored in the muscle.

Because these metabolic effects of preexercise carbohydrate ingestion are a consequence of high glucose and insulin levels, strategies to minimize the changes in plasma glucose and insulin before exercise are of high interest. Suggested strategies include ingesting fructose or carbohydrate types other than glucose, varying the carbohydrate load and ingestion schedule, adding fat, or including warm-up exercise in the preexercise period. In general, although these various interventions do modify the metabolic response to exercise, there appears to be no advantage to blunting preexercise glucose and insulin concentrations.

Some individuals may suffer more from the consequences of low blood glucose levels (hypoglycemia). Since hypoglycemia is associated with dizziness, lack of power, fatigue, nausea, and cold sweat, this could certainly affect performance. Many cyclists have experienced hypoglycemia; it is generally referred to as "hitting the wall."

When carbohydrate is ingested during prolonged exercise, the type of preexercise carbohydrate feeding has no effect on metabolism and performance (Burke et al. 1998).

Food items often are divided into different categories depending on their so-called glycemic index (GI). This index reflects the rate at which glucose becomes available after a meal. This is a measure of the rise in blood glucose after a certain food product is ingested compared to the rise in blood glucose after an equal amount of pure glucose is ingested. Thus, food products with a moderate to high glycemic index enter the circulation more rapidly and result in a higher rate of glycogen storage compared to low-glycemic index foods. The GI of a food product is influenced by many factors, including the type of carbohydrate and the content of dietary fat, protein, and fiber present in the food. Fat, protein, and fiber slow down the rate of gastric emptying; therefore, cyclists should avoid them in the postexercise diet when they want fast muscle glycogen repletion. Table 9.1 lists some food products with a high, moderate, and low GI. High- and moderate-GI foods should have priority in the postexercise period.

Glycemic response during exercise preceded by carbohydrate ingestion is determined by a number of factors, including the combined stimulatory effects of insulin and muscle contraction on muscle glucose uptake, the balance of inhibitory and stimulatory effects of insulin and catecholamines on liver glucose output, and the magnitude of ongoing intestinal absorption of glucose from the ingested carbohydrate (Kuipers, Fransen, and Keizer 1999). Furthermore, the inhibition of fatty acid release and use by the muscle occurs with just small increases in plasma insulin, for example, after fructose (low GI) ingestion.

TABLE 9.1 Foods With a High, Moderate, and Low Glycemic Index

The glycemic index is a measure of the change in blood glucose concentration and reflects the end result of digestion, absorption, and liver metabolism. The baseline is set at 100 and is based on the response to ingestion of pure glucose. In general, foods with a high glycemic index are recommended in the hours after exercise.

High glycemic index (> 85)	Medium glycemic index (60 to 85)	Low glycemic index (< 60)
Glucose	Bananas	Fructose
Sucrose	All-bran cereal	Apples
Corn syrup	Grapes	Applesauce
Maple syrup	Oatmeal	Cherries
Honey	Orange juice	Kidney beans
Bagels	Pasta	Lentils
Candy	Rice	Navy beans
Corn flakes	Whole grain rye bread	Chick peas
Carrots	Corn	Dates
Crackers	Baked beans	Figs
Potatoes	Potato chips	Peaches
Raisins		Plums
Bread (white)		Ice cream
Sport drinks		Milk
		Yogurt
		Tomato soup

Thus, it could be argued that if preexercise carbohydrate ingestion is the only mechanism by which a cyclist can increase carbohydrate availability during exercise, the cyclist would be well advised to ingest as much carbohydrate as possible while avoiding undue gastrointestinal distress. This would compensate for the reduced fat use and provide a pool of glucose that would become available for use during the later stages of exercise.

In summary, notwithstanding the well-documented metabolic effects of preexercise carbohydrate ingestion and the possibility of some negative consequences in susceptible individuals, evidence does not seem to support the practice of avoiding carbohydrate ingestion in the hour before exercise, provided sufficient carbohydrate is ingested. Individual practice must be determined on the basis of individual experience with various preexercise carbohydrate ingestion protocols.

Fluid Intake Before Exercise

In addition to carbohydrate depletion, dehydration is a major contributor to fatigue. Levels as low as 1 to 2% of body weight (600 to 1500 ml) are associated with impaired exercise performance (Walsh et al. 1994). Thus, cyclists preparing for one-day races should ingest sufficient quantities of fluid to ensure that they are well hydrated before exercise. This is best monitored by body weight.

Ingesting large amounts of water may result in hyperhydration before exercise, but it is also likely to increase diuresis (fluid excretion) and gastrointestinal distress. Some have suggested adding glycerol to hydration beverages to enhance fluid retention and maintain a relative hyperhydration before and during exercise. The studies in the literature (Hitchins et al. 1999; Latzka et al. 1998) have produced conflicting results, and there is the possibility that glycerol will promote intracellular dehydration with potential negative consequences such as headaches. It is perhaps premature to recommend glycerol hyperhydration at this stage.

Practical Recommendations for Carbohydrate and Fluid Ingestion Prior to Exercise

▶ For the two to four days leading up to a race, consume a high-carbohydrate diet containing 7 to 10 g of carbohydrate per kg of body weight per day. In preparation for extreme situations, increase to 8 to 11 g of carbohydrate per kg of body weight per day.

▶ Make sure you are fully hydrated. Drink relatively large volumes of fluid the days before and three to four hours before the race.

▶ Ingest 150 to 300 g of carbohydrate three to four hours before the race. Do not skip breakfast!

▶ Experiment with carbohydrate intake in the hour before the race. Most cyclists have no problem eating or drinking carbohydrate 30 to 60 min before exercise. Those who develop rebound hypoglycemia should wait until 5 min before the start before taking carbohydrate.

Nutrition During Exercise

During the race, cyclists need to replenish fluids and ingest energy to prevent depletion of carbohydrate stores. Several studies have shown that carbohydrate ingestion during exercise that lasts longer than 45 min can improve exercise performance. Early studies demonstrated that cyclists could ride 20 to 25% longer in rides to exhaustion at 65 to 70% $\dot{V}O_2$max. Jeukendrup and colleagues (1997) showed that simulated 40-km time trial performance improved by more than a minute with carbohydrate ingestion compared to a water placebo.

During exercise of longer than 90 min, performance improvement is likely to be the result of better maintenance of blood glucose concentrations and high carbohydrate utilization rates. During high-intensity exercise such as a 40-km time trial, the mechanisms are less clear.

Carbohydrate Intake During Exercise

The carbohydrate ingested during exercise reduces the breakdown of liver glycogen (Jeukendrup et al. 1999a, 199b). It is generally believed that a larger contribution of ingested carbohydrate to energy expenditure is beneficial, partly because it will reduce the breakdown of endogenous carbohydrate sources (i.e., liver glycogen). Jeukendrup and Jentjens (2000) demonstrated that certain types of carbohydrates are oxidized more readily than others. Glucose, maltodextrins, sucrose, maltose, and soluble starches are oxidized at relatively high rates, whereas fructose and galactose are oxidized at lower rates.

What's in the Bags?

During long stages, cyclists receive bags of food halfway through the race. Some races even have two feed zones. The rider quickly grabs a bag while passing the soigneurs at great speed, not an easy task considering that the bags often contain several bottles and are quite heavy. The bags usually include two 500-ml drink bottles, two energy bars, and a little cake. Often bags also contain a few gels (highly concentrated carbohydrate solution) or a small volume of an energy drink (20 to 30% carbohydrate solution). Riders know that these have to be taken with a relatively large volume of fluid to avoid gastrointestinal problems and reduce gastric emptying.

The more carbohydrate is ingested, the more it will be oxidized. However, when carbohydrate is ingested at a rate of about 1.0 to 1.2 g/min (60 to 70 g/hr), additional carbohydrate intake will not result in increased utilization (Jeukendrup and Jentjens 2000). Figure 9.2 summarizes the findings of many current studies. The use of ingested carbohydrate levels off at about 1 g/min. Even the ingestion of very large amounts of carbohydrate will not increase the use over about 1 g/min. Excess carbohydrate intake may cause reduced gastric emptying and gastrointestinal distress. The advice is simple: Try to ensure a carbohydrate intake of 60 to 70 g per hour of training or competition.

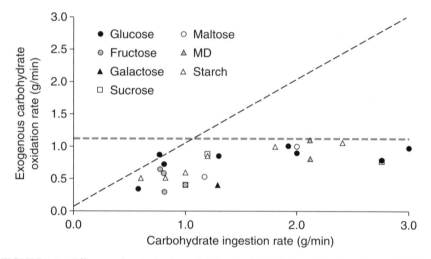

FIGURE 9.2   Efficacy of carbohydrate drinks. Carbohydrate utilization from a drink (exogenous carbohydrate oxidation) versus the rate of intake. Generally the more carbohydrate is ingested, the more carbohydrate is oxidized. However, there appears to be a maximum utilization of approximately 1 g/min. Ingestion of more than 1.0 to 1.2 g/min will not result in increased utilization rates. Clearly, some carbohydrates are oxidized at higher rates than others: glucose, glucose polymers, and maltose versus fructose and galactose.

Data adapted from Jeukendrup and Jentjens 2000.

Fluid Intake During Exercise

Increased muscular activity during exercise causes an increase in heat production in the body because of the inefficiency of the metabolic reactions involved in providing energy for muscle force development. For every liter of oxygen consumed during cycling, approximately 4 kcal (16 kJ) of heat are produced and only 1 kcal (4 kJ) is actually used to perform mechanical work. The human body is approximately 20% efficient when cycling (maximum is about 25%). This means that for all the energy used while cycling, only about 20% of it is used for propelling the bike forward. Most of the other 80% is "wasted" through heat production.

When climbing a mountain, a professional cyclist may produce more than 300 W of power for an hour or more. If that cyclist is 20% efficient, 1200 W of heat will be produced. This is the equivalent of approximately 900 kcal per hour.

Only a small proportion of the heat produced in active skeletal muscle is lost through the skin. Most of the heat is passed to the body core via the convective flow of venous blood returning to the heart. The rate of temperature increase in the belly of the quadriceps muscle group is close to 1°C per minute during the initial moments of high-intensity cycling. This rate of heat storage cannot persist, as damage to muscle proteins would occur within 10 min. Thus, most of the heat generated in the muscle is transferred to the body core.

Increases in body core temperature are sensed by receptors in the hypothalamus. This area of the brain also receives information from skin receptors and integrates this information to produce appropriate responses—such as increased blood flow to the skin and sweating—to increase heat loss and reduce or prevent further rises in body temperature.

Evaporation of sweat from the skin is an effective cooling mechanism. Complete evaporation of 1 L of water from the skin will remove 580 kcal (2.4 MJ) of body heat. Some people may lose 2 to 3 L of sweat per hour during strenuous activity in a warm environment. Even at low ambient temperatures (about 10°C), sweat loss can exceed 1 L per hour.

Exercise performance at moderate to high intensities is impaired when an individual is dehydrated by as little as 2% of body weight. Losses in excess of 5% of body weight can decrease the capacity for work by about 30%. The capacity to perform very high intensity exercise, resulting in exhaustion within only a few minutes, has also been shown to be reduced by as much as 45% by prior dehydration corresponding to a loss of only 2.5% of body weight.

Therefore, fluid intake during exercise is extremely important, even in cooler conditions. Many studies demonstrate the beneficial effects of fluid ingestion during exercise, yet most cyclists do not drink enough. Measurements during various professional cycling races (Tour de Andalusia, Mediterranean Tour, Tour of Switzerland, Tour de France) have shown that riders lose 2.1 to 4.5 kg of body weight per stage. Some of this weight loss (100 to 300 g) may be carbohydrate and fat used during exercise, but the majority is fluid loss. In some phases of the race, it is difficult to drink simply because the hands are needed on the handlebars or there is little time to drink. It is almost impossible to drink during steep uphills, steep downhills, or when other riders are attacking. Drinking may be even more difficult during off-road cycling.

Another problem is the fact that drink bottles are not always readily available, and a maximum of only about 1 L can be carried on the bike. Often bottles are provided by the team director from the team car. One or two riders will drop back to the team car to collect bottles for the whole team of five to eight riders.

Practical Recommendations for Carbohydrate and Fluid Ingestion During Exercise

▶ Try to compensate for fluid loss by drinking equal amounts of fluid.

▶ Ingest 60 to 70 g of carbohydrate per hour. If sweat loss is 1 L per hour, the preferred drink would be a 6% carbohydrate solution (60 g of carbohydrate in 1 L of water).

▶ Drink a large bolus at the start and top it with smaller volumes at regular intervals.

▶ Drinks should contain sodium (20 to 30 mmol/L).

▶ Drinks should be palatable to promote fluid intake.

▶ During long rides, solid food should be ingested to prevent an empty feeling in the stomach.

Nutrition After Exercise

After exercise, it is important to replenish fluid losses and restore muscle glycogen. It is especially important in stage races to recover quickly, and proper nutrition is one of the most powerful ways to speed up recovery. Depending on the situation, fluid replenishment may be more important than, less important than, or equally as important as the restoration of muscle glycogen. In most cases, riders should aim at achieving both of these goals at the same time.

Muscle Glycogen Recovery

The restoration of muscle glycogen depends on the amount of carbohydrate ingested, the timing of carbohydrate intake, and the type and form of carbohydrate intake after exercise. More recently it has been suggested that additional protein intake may help glycogen synthesis.

The amount of carbohydrate consumed after exercise is probably the most important factor that determines the rate of muscle glycogen synthesis. The rate of muscle glycogen storage is directly related to the quantity of carbohydrate consumed. When no carbohydrates are ingested after exercise, the rate of muscle glycogen synthesis is very low. A large carbohydrate intake can increase muscle glycogen rates up to about 25 g per hour.

More than 10 years ago, researchers claimed that a carbohydrate intake of 50 g every two hours after exercise resulted in maximal glycogen synthesis rates. More recent studies have manipulated the amount of carbohydrate given to athletes to determine the maximal rate of glycogen synthesis after exercise. A study by van Loon and colleagues (2000) showed that an increase in carbohydrate ingestion from 0.8 to 1.2 g per kg of body weight per hour provided at 30-min intervals resulted in faster muscle glycogen synthesis. It seems, therefore, that maximal muscle glycogen synthesis rates are not achieved at a carbohydrate intake of around 0.8 g per kg of body weight per hour as believed previously.

Figure 9.3 illustrates maximal muscle glycogen synthesis rates after the ingestion of different rates of carbohydrate in the early hours postexercise. The maximal rate of muscle glycogen resynthesis is reached at a carbohydrate intake of between 1.2 and 1.4 g/min (75 to 90 g of carbohydrate per hour). A carbohydrate intake of more than 90 g per hour provides no additional benefits in terms of muscle glycogen storage and may only increase the risk of gastrointestinal discomfort.

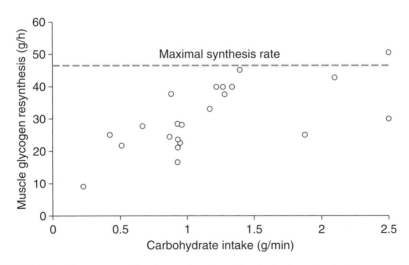

FIGURE 9.3   Glycogen synthesis as a function of carbohydrate intake. The more carbohydrate that is ingested, the more glycogen will be synthesized. However, above an intake of approximately 75 to 90 g per hour, no further improvement is observed.

From Jentjens and Jeukendrup, in press.

Timing of Carbohydrate Consumption.   The timing of carbohydrate intake is important when a fast recovery is required. Complete glycogen repletion can be accomplished within 24 hours providing the amount and timing is right. The most rapid replenishment of glycogen stores occurs in the first 60 to 90 min after exercise. One study found that the rate of glycogen storage is almost twice as fast if carbohydrate supplements are provided immediately after exercise compared to several hours later (Ivy et al. 1988).

The most important factor in the process of glycogen resynthesis seems to be the transport of glucose into the muscle cell. Several studies have demonstrated that endurance training results in an increased ability to accumulate muscle glycogen after exercise. This is related to the higher glucose transport capacity after training.

Besides an enhanced glucose transport, muscle contraction also increases the muscle's sensitivity to insulin. When carbohydrates are ingested after exercise, both glucose concentrations and insulin concentrations rise in the blood. The increase in circulating insulin not only increases muscle glucose uptake but also stimulates glycogen synthetase, the enzyme responsible for glycogen synthesis.

Therefore, it is recommended that athletes consume carbohydrate as soon as possible after exercise to enhance the restoration of muscle glycogen stores. The highest rates of muscle glycogen synthesis were reported in studies in which carbohydrates were provided at regular intervals every 15 to 30 min postexercise (Jentjens and Jeukendrup in press). This is most probably due to the maintenance of high blood glucose and insulin concentrations for a longer duration. Thus, eating frequent, small meals appears to have an extra benefit over eating a few large meals. Additionally, eating small meals is likely to reduce the risk of gastrointestinal discomfort.

Types of Carbohydrates.   Most carbohydrates will provide similar amounts of glucose for glycogen storage. When fructose is ingested, the rate of glycogen synthesis is relatively low because the liver has to convert fructose to glucose before it can be used for glycogen synthesis in the muscle. Most types of carbohydrate, however, result in similar muscle glycogen resynthesis rates (glucose, sucrose, glucose polymers). When mixed meals are consumed, the availability of glucose may differ depending on the composition of the meal. Preferably, athletes should consume meals with a high glycemic index (see table 9.1).

Does it matter if the carbohydrate consumed after exercise is in liquid or solid form? Probably not. Liquid and solid forms of carbohydrates consumed in the first few hours after exercise do not appear to differ in their capacity to elicit muscle glycogen synthesis. However, experts often recommend liquid forms of carbohydrate or carbohydrate foods with a high fluid content because they are easy to digest and less filling and do not tend to adversely affect normal appetite. Liquid carbohydrate supplements also provide a source of fluid that may be beneficial for rapid rehydration.

Effect of Added Protein

Insulin promotes muscle glycogen synthesis after exercise. Any means by which insulin concentrations can be elevated could help the resynthesis of glycogen after exercise. Some amino acids and proteins cause the pancreas to release insulin. Several studies have shown that coingestion of protein and/or amino acids with carbohydrate almost doubled insulin response. Muscle glycogen synthesis also was increased by 40 to 100% (van Loon et al. 2000; Zawadzki, Yaspelkis, and Ivy 1992).

However, a more recent study (Jentjens et al. 2001) showed that when total carbohydrate intake is very high (1.2 g per kg of body weight per hour), the presence of a protein–amino acid mixture does not further increase the rate of muscle glycogen synthesis despite a much higher insulin response. Therefore, there is no need to ingest proteins or amino acids with carbohydrate to maximize glycogen synthesis when total carbohydrate intake is sufficient.

Although protein intake may not always have an effect on muscle glycogen synthesis, evidence suggests that intake of essential amino acids in the hours after exercise may increase protein synthesis (Rasmussen et al. 2000). Increased protein synthesis after exercise could help in repairing muscle damage and in synthesizing various enzymes and mitochondria.

Fluid Intake After Exercise

Dehydration is associated with impaired thermoregulation and increased cardiovascular strain. With progressive dehydration, losses of intracellular as well as extracellular fluid volume will occur. The loss of intracellular volume may have important implications for recovery from exercise in view of the emerging evidence of a role for cell volume in the regulation of cell metabolism. A reduced intracellular volume can reduce rates of glycogen and protein synthesis, whereas a high cell volume (cell swelling) can stimulate these processes.

The effectiveness of postexercise dehydration is determined mainly by the volume and composition of the fluid consumed. Contrary to common belief, plain water is not the ideal postexercise rehydration beverage when rapid and complete restoration of body fluid balance is necessary. Ingestion of water alone results in a rapid fall in the plasma sodium concentration and a drop in the plasma osmolality. These changes have the effect of reducing the stimulation to drink (thirst) and increasing urine output, both of which impair the rehydration process.

Complete rehydration after exercise can only be achieved if the sodium lost in sweat is replaced as well as the water. In order to achieve euhydration after exercise, sodium intake must be greater than sodium loss. Plasma volume is more rapidly and completely restored in the postexercise period if some sodium chloride (77 mmol/L or 0.45 g/L) is added to the water consumed (Nose et al. 1988). This sodium concentration is similar to the upper limit of the sodium concentration found in sweat, but is considerably higher than the sodium concentration of many commercially available sport drinks, which usually contain 10 to 25 mmol/L (0.06 to 0.15 g/L).

Ingesting a beverage containing sodium not only promotes rapid fluid absorption in the small intestine, but also allows the plasma sodium concentration to remain elevated during the rehydration period and helps to maintain thirst while delaying the stimulation of urine production.

The inclusion of potassium in the beverage consumed after exercise would be expected to enhance the replacement of intracellular water and thus promote rehydration, but currently there is little experimental evidence to support this. The rehydration drink should contain carbohydrate (glucose or glucose polymers) because the presence of glucose will stimulate fluid absorption in the gut and improve beverage taste. Following exercise, the uptake of glucose into the muscle for glycogen resynthesis should also promote intracellular rehydration.

Until recently, experts generally recommended that athletes consume a volume of fluid equivalent to their sweat loss incurred during exercise in order to adequately rehydrate in the postexercise recovery period. In other words, it was recommended that they consume about 1 L of fluid for every kg lost during exercise. It is now clear that this amount is insufficient because it does not take into account the obligatory urine losses incurred following beverage consumption over a period of hours. Existing data indicate that ingestion of 150% or more of weight loss (i.e., 1.5 L of fluid consumed during recovery for every kg of weight lost during exercise) may be required to achieve normal hydration within six hours following exercise (Shirreffs et al. 1996).

In most circumstances, athletes should be encouraged to consume solid food as well as drink between exercise bouts, unless food intake is likely to result in gastrointestinal disturbances. In one study, the same fluid volume consumed as a meal plus water combination compared with a sport drink resulted in a smaller volume of urine being produced and hence greater fluid retention (Maughan, Leiper, and Shirreffs 1996). The greater efficacy of the meal plus water treatment in restoring whole body fluid balance was probably a consequence of its greater total sodium and potassium content.

In exercise situations in which sweat losses are large, the total amount of sodium and chloride lost will be high. For example, the loss of 10 L of sweat, with a sodium concentration of 50 mmol/L, amounts to a loss of about 29 g of sodium chloride. Obviously, food intake can be important in restoring these salt losses since most commercially available sport drinks contain only about 10 to 25 mmol/L (0.06 to 0.15 g/L) of salt.

It is now clear that rehydration after exercise can be achieved only if electrolyte losses through sweat as well as water are replaced. One of the problems is that drinks with high sodium content (i.e., 40 to 80 mmol/L) are unpalatable to some people, resulting in reduced drink consumption. However, drinks with low sodium content, such as most soft drinks, are ineffective for rehydration and also reduce the stimulus to drink.

Practical Recommendations for Carbohydrate and Fluid Ingestion After Exercise

▶ Ingest 1.2 g of carbohydrate per kg of body weight as soon as possible after exercise. Aim for a carbohydrate intake of 1.2 g per kg of body weight per hour during the first four hours postexercise.

▶ Consume carbohydrate every 15 to 30 min.

▶ Aim for a total carbohydrate intake of 8 to 10 g per kg of body weight within 24 hours.

▶ The addition of protein to enhance insulin response does not seem to be more beneficial in terms of glycogen synthesis when the total amount of carbohydrate intake is adequate.

▶ Drink 150% of the weight loss in the form of a sodium-containing carbohydrate drink in the hours after exercise to achieve normal hydration within six hours following exercise.

▶ Although liquid and solid forms of carbohydrate seem to result in similar rates of muscle glycogen synthesis, a liquid supplement is highly recommended after exercise since this also provides a source of fluid for rehydration.

Nutritional Supplements

Are nutritional supplements necessary? The answer is, it depends. Over 600 different supplements are currently on the market. Studies have claimed that 40 to 100% of all top athletes use nutritional supplements, ranging from sport drinks and vitamin and mineral supplements to exotic herbal products that contain over a thousand different substances. Surely they cannot all work. In fact, most supplements have no effect other than maybe a placebo effect.

Prior to discussing specific supplements, it is important to have some knowledge of supplement regulation and the difference between medicinal and nutritional supplements. Medicines must undergo rigorous clinical trials prior to being approved and becoming available on the market; nutritional supplements do not. In addition, the purity of medicines must be established and guaranteed, which is not the case for nutritional supplements. As a result, when you purchase vitamins, minerals, herbs, or other nutritional or nonnutritional supplements, the purity of that product cannot be guaranteed, and the actual amounts listed on the label and the quality of substances within supplements may not be accurate. A study of 16 dehydroepiandrosterone (DHEA) supplements showed that three brands did not contain any DHEA, five contained less than 75% of what was stated on the label, and one contained 150% of what was stated on the label.

Recently a number of athletes who tested positive for nandrolone claimed that this was due to the use of contaminated nutritional supplements. In fact, evidence suggests that certain supplements can result in a positive doping test for nandrolone.

Creatine

Creatine became a popular supplement after the 1992 Olympics in Barcelona. Linford Christie, the gold medal winner in the men's 100-m dash, reportedly used creatine supplements. By the 1996 Olympic games in Atlanta, approximately 80% of all athletes used creatine. Creatine consumption by athletes all over the world is now estimated to be over 3 million kg per year.

Creatine is a naturally occurring compound mostly present in meat and fish. Creatine can be synthesized within the human body and is therefore not an essential supplement. In normal, healthy individuals, diet and oral ingestion together provide approximately 2 g of creatine per day. At the same time and at approximately the same rate (2 g per day), creatine is broken down to creatinine and excreted in the urine.

The primary dietary sources of creatine are fish and red meat. Strict vegetarians and vegans will have negligible creatine intake because plants contain only trace amounts of creatine. Therefore, they are dependent on endogenous synthesis of creatine.

Oral ingestion of creatine suppresses the biosynthesis of compound. When a diet is deficient in creatine, urinary excretion of creatine and creatinine is reduced. Creatine is synthesized in the human body from the amino acids arginine, glycine, and methionine. The majority of creatine synthesis occurs in the liver and kidneys. In a 70-kg man, the total body creatine content is approximately 120 g, 95% of which is found in muscle.

A person can increase total creatine stores (creatine and phosphocreatine) in the muscle by simply ingesting creatine monohydrate. Intake of 5 g of creatine four times per day for five days (the equivalent of 8 kg of raw meat) seems to be the optimal regimen; no further improvements occur with increased ingestion. This protocol can increase total creatine concentration by an average of 25 mmol/kg dry weight with 30% of the increase in total creatine content being in the form of phosphocreatine. The majority of studies have now confirmed such increases in muscle creatine and have demonstrated positive effects on repeated sprint performance.

However, there is considerable variation among subjects in initial total creatine concentration in the muscle. If you have naturally high levels of creatine, you are less likely to benefit from supplementation. The largest increase in muscle creatine concentration is observed in individuals with the lowest initial concentration. A concentration of 160 mmol/kg dry weight appears to be the natural ceiling. However only about 20% of subjects reached this high level after creatine supplementation. About 30% of all individuals will not display such large increases in muscle creatine and will therefore not benefit from supplementation. These are often referred to as nonresponders.

During most cycling events (except for sprints), most adenosine triphosphate (ATP) is resynthesized by oxidative phosphorylation in the mitochondria. Net phosphocreatine breakdown and the net contribution of phosphocreatine to energy production are minimal. However, creatine and phosphocreatine in that case have been shown to provide a shuttle system for the transfer of high-energy phosphate groups from the ATP production site (the mitochondria) to the ATP consumption site (the contracting myofibrils). Theoretically, creatine could facilitate aerobic energy production and enhance performance in prolonged exercise.

In contrast to the very large number of studies investigating high-intensity exercise, few studies address the potential effects of creatine on endurance exercise. These studies, however, indicate that creatine supplementation has no effect on maximal oxygen uptake or endurance capacity. However, in one study creatine loading improved intermittent sprint capacity at the end of endurance exercise to fatigue. Interestingly, this effect was not observed when creatine was also ingested during exercise. Endurance capacity was not affected by creatine supplementation in this study.

In conclusion, at this stage few studies have investigated the effects of creatine supplementation on endurance performance. These studies generally do not report ergogenic effects.

Carnitine

Carnitine is normally found in meat. It has been suggested that carnitine supplementation could increase maximal oxygen consumption ($\dot{V}O_2max$) and reduce lactate production during maximal and supramaximal exercise. The most important claim relates to the role of carnitine in fat metabolism. It is often claimed that carnitine improves fat metabolism, reduces fat mass, and increases muscle mass. Generally advertised as a "fat burner," carnitine is often used to lose weight, lose body fat, and improve "sharpness." Cyclists often use carnitine in the hope that it will increase fat use, spare muscle glycogen, and help reduce body fat.

We derive carnitine from diet, but it is also synthesized in the body. Total carnitine stores in the body are about 27 g, 98% of which can be found in muscle. Carnitine plays a very important role in transporting fatty acids into the mitochondria where they can be oxidized. Those with a carnitine deficiency cannot oxidize fatty acids, as carnitine is very important in this process. Studies do not support the claim of carnitine as a "fat burner." More recently it was demonstrated that this is because carnitine is not taken up by the muscle. Ingesting large amounts of carnitine may increase the concentration of carnitine in plasma, but muscle carnitine concentration will be unaffected. Even long-term supplementation of two to three weeks does not have the desired effect.

In conclusion, oral carnitine supplementation in humans for periods of two to three weeks does not increase carnitine concentration in muscle and therefore cannot have an effect on muscle metabolism at rest and during exercise. Carnitine supplementation does not help individuals lose weight or reduce body fat mass and does not increase fat utilization or reduce glycogen breakdown during prolonged exercise. In addition carnitine supplementation does not increase $\dot{V}O_2$max or reduce lactate accumulation during maximal and supramaximal exercise.

Coenzyme Q10

Coenzyme Q10 (CoQ10), or ubiquinone, is an integral part of the electron transport chain of the mitochondria. CoQ10 therefore plays an important role in oxidative phosphorylation. CoQ10 is present in heart muscle and has been used therapeutically to treat cardiovascular disease and help patients recover from cardiac surgery. It has been demonstrated that CoQ10 supplementation in those conditions improves oxidative metabolism—the use of fat and carbohydrate in the presence of oxygen—and exercise capacity in these patients, and it also functions as an antioxidant promoting the scavenging of free radicals. These findings were soon extrapolated to trained athletes: CoQ10 is claimed to increase $\dot{V}O_2$max and increase stamina and energy.

A few studies investigated the effects of CoQ10 supplementation in athletes. Although most of these studies reported elevated plasma CoQ10 levels, no changes were observed in $\dot{V}O_2$max, performance, or lactate at submaximal workloads.

Svensson and colleagues (1999) reported that ingestion of 120 mg of CoQ10 per day for 20 days resulted in marked increases in plasma CoQ10 concentrations, but the muscle CoQ10 concentration was unaltered. Of course if CoQ10 supplementation does not alter muscle CoQ10 concentration, it is expected to have no effect on any performance-related variables.

CoQ10 may even have some negative effects. It has been reported that during high exercise intensity, when there is an abundance of hydrogen ions in the cells, CoQ10 can augment free radical production (Malm et al. 1997). Paradoxically, this is the opposite effect of what CoQ10 is claimed to do.

Vitamin and Mineral Supplements

Vitamins and minerals are probably the most popular nutritional supplements used by athletes. Vitamins and minerals are essential for a variety of body processes such as energy production (B vitamins), hemoglobin synthesis (iron), immune system health (vitamin A, zinc), prevention of oxidative damage and repair of tissue (antioxidants), healthy bone maintenance (calcium, vitamin D), and the synthesis and maintenance of muscle tissue during exercise.

It is generally believed that cyclists can obtain the daily requirements of vitamins and minerals by consuming a well-balanced diet. Poor diets are probably the main reason for any micronutrient deficiencies found in cyclists, although in certain cases regular strenuous exercise may contribute to the deficiency. An inadequate knowledge of proper dietary practices, lack of time for food preparation, misleading advertisements for micronutrient supplements, and a lack of qualified dietary advice can all add to suboptimal micronutrient intakes in athletes. When energy intake is very high (more than 5000 kcal per day; 20,000 kJ per day), athletes tend to consume a large number of snacks and high-energy sport drinks, often composed mainly of refined carbohydrate but low in protein and micronutrients. As a consequence, the nutrient density for vitamins drops. So, do cyclists need supplements? The answer again is, it depends.

In some situations, supplementation can be very important. For example, amenorrheic female cyclists should certainly take calcium supplements, and other female athletes should consider taking calcium supplements to ensure adequate calcium status and maintain healthy bones. Athletes who train and compete in hot environments should also consider increasing their intake of minerals—particularly iron, zinc, and magnesium—because mineral losses in sweat can be considerable. Even so, daily supplements of these minerals should not exceed two times the recommended daily intake. As with vitamins, excessive intakes of minerals can be toxic and can impair the absorption of other essential trace elements.

Vegetarian athletes will have problems obtaining sufficient intakes of some vitamins, particularly vitamin B_{12} (cobalamin) since its only natural dietary source is meat.

Clear evidence exists to show that antioxidants provide an important defense mechanism against the damaging effects of free radicals. Many athletes consume large doses of antioxidant vitamins (vitamins C, E, and betacarotene). However, excessive antioxidant ingestion may not be uniformly helpful. The controversy continues as to whether physically active individuals should consume antioxidant compounds in amounts that are well in excess of RDI values. Certainly, at present, the data are insufficient to strongly recommend antioxidant supplements for athletes. Further research is needed to fully document the efficacy and safety of long-term antioxidant supplement use.

The bottom line is that in most conditions vitamin and mineral supplementation is not necessary and will not improve performance. If you want to take a multivitamin and mineral supplement as an insurance policy, take a supplement that contains one time the RDI. The intake of excessive amounts of vitamins and/or minerals should be strongly discouraged.

Common Nutritional Practices of Cyclists

In this chapter so far we have described the theory, what cyclists *should* do. But what do cyclists *really* do?

Several studies have investigated the nutritional habits of cyclists. Most of these studies have used dietary records, which often tend to underestimate food intake. Nevertheless, studies of high-level male road cyclists provide important information about nutrient intake and food practices during training and major stage races. Typically, male cyclists engaged in intensive training programs report energy intakes of 3000 to 8000 kcal (12 to 32 MJ) per day and carbohydrate intakes of 8 to 11 g per kg of body weight per day. Intake of protein and micronutrients usually meet recommended intake levels simply because of the large amounts of food consumed. Less information is available on female cyclists.

Current dietary practices during stage races appear to favor greater reliance on prestage intake and poststage recovery meals to achieve nutritional goals. Recent reports suggest that current riding tactics interfere with recommended practices of consuming substantial amounts of fluid and carbohydrate while cycling. Fluid intake is often marginal, and training to drink and eat during the race would be beneficial. Garcia-Roves and colleagues (1997) reported that during the three major stage races cyclists ingested, on average, 13% of their daily energy intake during the race, mostly in the form of sport drinks (carbohydrate solutions). However, in this particular study, fluid intake during the race was extremely low, and it is likely that fluid and carbohydrate intake was underestimated. Carbohydrate intake during the race averaged 25 g per hour, substantially lower than the recommended 60 to 70 g per hour (see the section on nutrition during exercise).

To increase daily energy intake in the form of carbohydrate, maltodextrins can be added to various foods and meals. These carbohydrates have the advantage of not having a strong flavor and as such can be added as invisible calories.

In conclusion, the nutritional practices of cyclists are not optimal; even at the highest levels of cycling there is still room for improvement. Performance in road and off-road cycling is highly dependent on nutrition, much more so than in most other sports. Inadequate nutritional practices can have immediate and dramatic effects on performance. The advice given in this chapter should help to optimize nutritional practices and enhance performance.

References

Burke, L.M., Angus, D.J., Cox, G.R., Gawthorn, K.M., Hawley, J.A., Febbraio, M.A., and Hargreaves, M. 1999. Fat adaptation with carbohydrate recovery promotes metabolic adaptation during prolonged cycling. *Med Sci Sports Exerc* 31:297.

Burke, L.M., Claassen, A., Hawley, J.A., and Noakes, T.D. 1998. Carbohydrate intake during prolonged cycling minimizes effect of glycemic index of preexercise meal. *J Appl Physiol* 85:2220-2226.

Burke, L.M., Hawley, J.A., Angus, D.J., Cox, G.R., Clark, S.A., Cummings, N.K., Desbrow, B., and Hargreaves, M. 2002. Adaptations to short-term high-fat diet persist during exercise despite high carbohydrate availability. *Med Sci Sports Exerc* 34:83-91.

Coyle, E.F., Coggan, A.R., Hemmert, M.K., Lowe, R.C., and Walters, T.J. 1985. Substrate usage during prolonged exercise following a preexercise meal. *J Appl Physiol* 59:429-433.

Garcia-Roves, P., Terrados, N., Fernandez, S., and Patterson, A. 1997. Macronutrients intake of top level cyclists during continuous competition: Change in the feeding pattern. *Int J Sports Med* 19:61-67.

Hitchins, S., Martin, D.T., Burke, L., Yates, K., Fallon, K., Hahn, A., and Dobson, G.P. 1999. Glycerol hyperhydration improves cycle time trial performance in hot humid conditions. *Eur J Appl Physiol* 80:494-501.

Ivy, J.L., Katz, A.L., Cutler, C.L., Sherman, W.M., and Coyle, E.F. 1988. Muscle glycogen synthesis after exercise: Effect of time of carbohydrate ingestion. *J Appl Physiol* 64:1480-1485.

Jentjens, R.L, and Jeukendrup, E. In press. Carbohydrate intake to optimize glycogen resynthesis. *Sports Med.*

Jentjens, R.L, van Loon, L.J., Mann, C.H., Wagenmakers, A.J., and Jeukendrup, A.E. 2001. Addition of protein and amino acids to carbohydrates does not enhance postexercise muscle glycogen synthesis. *J Appl Physiol* 91:839-846.

Jeukendrup, A., Brouns, F., Wagenmakers, A.J., and Saris, W.H. 1997. Carbohydrate-electrolyte feedings improve 1 h time trial cycling performance. *Int J Sports Med* 18:125-129.

Jeukendrup, A.E., Craig, N., and Hawley, J.A.H. 2000. The bioengergetics of world class cycling. *J Sci Med Sport* 3(4): 414-433.

Jeukendrup, A.E., and Jentjens, R. 2000. Oxidation of carbohydrate feedings during prolonged exercise: Current thoughts, guidelines, and directions for future research. *Sports Med* 29(6): 407-424.

Jeukendrup, A.E., Raben, A., Gijsen, A., Stegen, J.H., Brouns, F., Saris, W.H., and Wagenmakers, A.J. 1999a. Glucose kinetics during prolonged exercise in highly trained human subjects: Effect of glucose ingestion. *J Physiol (Lond)* 515:579-589.

Jeukendrup, A.E., Wagenmakers, A.J., Stegen, J.H., Gijsen, A.P., Brouns, F., and Saris, W.H. 1999b. Carbohydrate ingestion can completely suppress endogenous glucose production during exercise. *Am J Physiol* 276:E672-683.

Kuipers, H., Fransen, E.J., and Keizer, H.A. 1999. Pre-exercise ingestion of carbohydrate and transient hypoglycemia during exercise. *Int J Sports Med* 20:227-231.

Latzka, W.A., Sawka, M.N., Montain, S.J., Skrinar, G.S., Fielding, R.A., Matott, R.P, and Pandolf, K.B. 1998. Hyperhydration: Tolerance and cardiovascular effects during uncompensable exercise-heat stress. *J Appl Physiol* 84:1858-1864.

Malm, C., Svensson, M., Ekblom, B., and Sjodin, B. 1997. Effects of ubiquinon-10 supplementation and high intensity training on physical performance in humans. *Acta Physiol Scand* 161:379-384.

Maughan, R.J., Leiper, J.B., and Shirreffs, S.M. 1996. Restoration of fluid balance after exercise-induced dehydration: Effects of food and fluid intake. *Eur J Appl Physiol Occup Physiol* 73:317-325.

Montain, S.J., Hopper, M.K., Coggan, A.R., and Coyle, E.F. 1991. Exercise metabolism at different time intervals after a meal. *J Appl Physiol* 70:882-888.

Nose, H., Mack, G.W., Shi, X., and Nadel, E.R. 1988. Role of osmolality and plasma volume during rehydration in humans. *J Appl Physiol* 65:325-331.

Rasmussen, B.B., Tipton, K.D., Miller, S.L., Wolf, S.E., and Wolfe, R.R. 2000. An oral essential amino acid-carbohydrate supplement enhances muscle protein anabolism after resistance exercise. *J Appl Physiol* 88:386-392.

Saris, W.H.M., van Erp-Baart, M.A., Brouns, F., Westerterp, K.R., and ten Hoor, F. 1989. Study on food intake and energy expenditure during extreme sustained exercise: The Tour de France. *Int J Sports Med* 10:S26-S31.

Shirreffs, S.M., Taylor, A.J., Leiper, J.B., and Maughan, R.J. 1996. Post-exercise rehydration in man: Effects of volume consumed and drink sodium content. *Med Sci Sports Exerc* 28:1260-1271.

Svensson, M., Malm, C., Tonkonogi, M., Ekblom, B., Sjodin, B., and Sahlin, K. 1999. Effect of Q10 supplementation on tissue Q10 levels and adenine nucleotide catabolism during high-intensity exercise. *Int J Sport Nutr* 9:166-180.

van Loon, L.J., Saris, W.H., Kruijshoop, M., and Wagenmakers, A.J. 2000. Maximizing postexercise muscle glycogen synthesis: Carbohydrate supplementation and the application of amino acid or protein hydrolysate mixtures. *Am J Clin Nutr* 72:106-111.

Walsh, R.M., Noakes, T.D., Hawley, J.A., and Dennis, S.C. 1994. Impaired high-intensity cycling performance time at low levels of dehydration. *Int J Sports Med* 15:392-398.

Zawadzki, K.M., Yaspelkis III, B.B., and Ivy, J.L. 1992. Carbohydrate-protein complex increases the rate of muscle glycogen storage after exercise. *J Appl Physiol* 72:1854-1859.

10

Physiology of Professional Road Cycling

Alejandro Lucía • Jesús Hoyos • José L. Chicharro

A road cycling race, especially a three-week race, is one of the best models for studying the physiological adaptations of the human body to extreme endurance exercise. In this chapter, we place special emphasis on the evaluation of performance from a practical point of view—which physiological characteristics (the ones that can be routinely evaluated in a laboratory setting) are somewhat more typical of pro cyclists compared to other endurance athletes, including elite road cyclists of a lower fitness level? When can we say that a cyclist has the potential to compete professionally? We also outline the results of several field studies conducted during three-week races such as the Tour de France.

Main Characteristics of Road Cycling: Racing Calendar and Training Over the Season

Road cycling, especially professional cycling, is an extreme endurance sport. Today's pro cyclist covers approximately 35,000 to 45,000 km each year in training and competition. The training program of a professional road cyclist generally includes three periods, which vary in both training volume and intensity: the precompetition phase, the competition phase (which usually includes an active rest period), and the postcompetition, or active rest, phase (see figure 10.1). During the two to three weeks of the rest phase, most riders adopt an almost sedentary lifestyle.

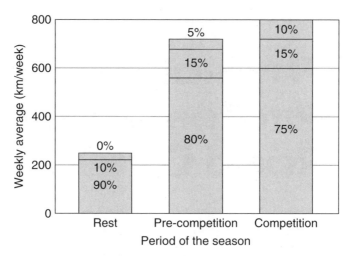

FIGURE 10.1 Training periods of professional road cyclists. Usually the season is divided into three training periods: rest (November to December), precompetition (December to mid-February), and competition (mid-February to October, usually with an active rest period). The percentage of training performed in intensity zones 1 (light), 2 (moderate), and 3 (intense) is specified from bottom to top. (See the text for more explanation on the limits of the three zones.) Average data collected from cyclists of the Banesto professional team during the 1998 season.

The typical racing season of a road cyclist starts in mid-February and finishes at the end of summer/beginning of fall. Usually the cyclist has 90 to 100 competition days, including several one-day races (classics of 200 to 300 km), several one-week tour races (four to five consecutive daily stages of 150 to 200 km and an individual time trial), and 1 or 2 three-week tour races (Giro d'Italia, Tour de France, or Vuelta a España). The three-week tour race includes 21 to 22 daily stages of about 200 km each, or four to five hours per stage with only one to two days of rest. In other words, a pro cyclist on a tour faces 90 to 100 hours of competition covering 3500 to 4000 km. Most professional races take place in western Europe (France, Italy, Spain, Belgium, the Netherlands, and Germany). Figure 10.2 shows the 1996 competition calendar of a professional cyclist, including 2 three-week races (Giro and Vuelta).

A particular characteristic of road cycling compared to other endurance sports is the high number of competition days. During the season, nearly

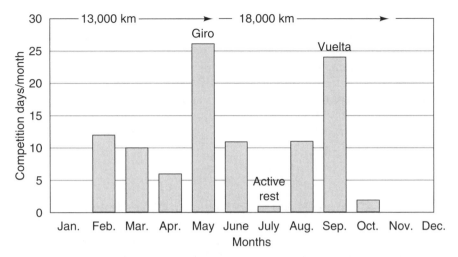

FIGURE 10.2   Example of the distribution of competition days over a professional racing season. A total of 90 competition days including 9 one-week stage races, 2 three-week races (Vuelta a España and Giro d'Italia), and 5 one-day races (classics). An active rest period is included in the middle of the competition season during the month of July.

one out of every three days is a competition day. This implies that, during the competition period, a good number of competition days can be used as hard training sessions. Team leaders such as Lance Armstrong or Jan Ullrich are allowed to use several races during the late winter and early spring as part of their training programs so they peak later in the season, usually for the Tour de France during the month of July.

It is commonly thought that a cyclist needs at least 30 competition days to start the Tour de France in good condition. For instance, the 2001 Giro d'Italia served as an excellent training macrocycle for Jan Ullrich. During this race, he was free to adjust exercise intensity in each daily stage, regardless of the race outcome.

Further, it is not uncommon to see some cyclists continue their daily training after crossing the finish line of a particular race in order to build up their endurance capacity. For instance, a 21-year-old Lance Armstrong surprised many team directors during the 1993 Vuelta a Galicia (a one-week tour race in Spain) by putting in some 70 km of extra training after each daily stage. Some weeks later, he won the world championship. Some riders adopt a similar approach when they prepare for the spring classics (Milano-San Remo, Liège-Bastogne-Liège, etc.).

Training prescription in professional cycling is not usually as precise as in other endurance sports, partly because competitions are used spontaneously as training and the distribution of exercise intensity during races is often random and difficult to predict. Indeed, road cycling is a complex sport in which many uncontrollable variables (weather conditions, altitude, wind direction, team tactics, etc.) can influence exercise intensity. The current tendency of many professional riders is to focus their efforts on long-duration, low-intensity training, especially during the winter months. This type of approach allows them to build up an excellent aerobic background so that a few weeks of high-intensity training (including competitions) later on in the season is sufficient for them to reach their peak for the most important stage in the season.

Calendar for Road Cycling

Professional road racing is a unique sport in that a rider's normal season includes close to 100 competition days. The road cyclist's training program typically involves long-duration, moderate-intensity workouts. Intense workouts are usually left to the races themselves.

Three-Week Tour Races

The three-week races are the most remarkable cycling events. The most renowned, the Tour de France, is nearly 100 years old.

The first Tours (1903 to 1909) were marvelous, mad adventures dreamed up by Henri Desgranges. These were heroic times. Cyclists obtained food in bars along the way and drank from fountains. They did their own bicycle repairs on bikes weighing almost 20 kg (modern bikes weigh less than 9 kg). In those days, the average length of the Tour was 136 hours for the winner (but much longer for those crossing the line last) and included only 11 stages. In other words, each stage lasted some 12 hours. Cyclists would reach each day's finish line in the dark. Participants had little time to recover before the next grueling day of competition. Little was known about nutrition; there was scarce awareness of the need to consume carbohydrates (pasta, rice, bread) to help competitors withstand the demands of the race. The Tour at the turn of the century was not such an agonizing or intense race, but more of a tough trial of elimination. Fats, rather than carbohydrates, were the main energy source.

From 1910 to 1926, the average length of the Tour was some chilling 211 hours for the winner, spread across 15 stages of around 14 hours each. Competitors set off with spare inner tubes and tires looped around their necks. A novel feature was added—the Tour crossed the Pyrenees and the Alps. New roads were specifically laid for the race through some mountain passes, although other roads were still unpaved. In these wild days, some cyclists were even scared to ride alone in the colossal Alps for fear of bumping into bears. The Tour started to take on a more intense character. It was therefore no surprise that the cyclists began to be known as "les forçats de la route" (meaning "the strongmen of the road"). The Tour of 1926 was 5745 km, the longest in history. For many competitors it was also the hardest, and it became known as "le Tour de la Souffrance" (the Tour of Suffering).

From 1927 to 1939, the Tour began to take on a more familiar look. It lasted 22 days (160 hours total), and the average stage was seven hours. Amphetamines made their debut, and with their arrival came the capacity to increase agonizing efforts. Marcel Bidot, one of the professionals of the era, stated that flat stages (of some 200 km) from beginning to end were an against-the-clock dash.

After World War II, the Tour entered the era of the legendary Coppi and Bobet. From 1947 to 1960, the Tour became more like today's race—135 hours shared over 22 stages, approximately six hours per stage.

The Tour gained in popularity from 1961 to 1979. Millions watched the Tour on TV. These were the times of Anquetil and Merckx, who like today's competitors were capable of sustaining a power output of over 400 W. The Tour covered 22 five-and-a-half-hour stages in 123 hours, almost the same as today's race. Since sport nutrition and training science were still embryonic, racers could not give their all for too long.

The era of 1980 to the end of the 20th century was the age of the modern champions (Hinault, LeMond, Indurain), of brightly colored racing suits and sprinting bicycles. Automatic pedals hit the scene, their use spreading toward the end of the 1980s. It was also the era of sport physiology and scientific publications on cycling that described the Tour's intensity in figures (Fernández-García et al. 2000; Lucia, Hoyos et al. 1999; Padilla et al. 2000; Padilla et al. 2001). In round numbers, the general picture of the Tour of the last 20 years is as follows: 100 hours of effort for the cyclist who classifies first, shared over 21 stages of nearly five hours each.

In the 1990s, most riders in the peloton wore heart rate monitors during daily stages. This allowed researchers and team physiologists to determine the exercise intensity of tour races, based on the overall linear relationship between heart rate and exercise intensity during dynamic exercise involving large muscle groups, such as running, cycling, and swimming (Gilman 1996).

Exercise intensity can be divided into three zones according to reference heart rate values. In zone 1 (less than 70% of the predicted maximal heart rate or HRmax), exercise intensity is low and aerobic metabolism accounts for the great majority of energy production (Skinner and McLellan 1980). In zone 2 (from 70 to 90% of HRmax), blood lactate production increases since some fast muscle fibers (type II) are recruited to sustain the required force production. Finally, at the intensity corresponding to zone 3 (more than 90% of HRmax), blood lactate accumulates in the blood and several body adjustments (such as a marked increase in ventilation) occur in an attempt to compensate for the rising lactic acidosis.

Roughly speaking, exercise intensity during the five hours of an average stage in a three-week race (combining flat stages, time trials, and mountain stages) could be divided into 3 hours and 30 min in zone 1 (70%), 1 hour in zone 2 (20%), and 30 min in zone 3 (10%) (Lucia, Hoyos et al. 1999). Because of advances in sport nutrition and training, one of the main characteristics of current three-week races is the ability of competitors to maintain near-maximal intensity (zone 3) during periods of more than 30 min (Fernández-García et al. 2000; Lucia, Hoyos et al. 1999; Padilla et al. 2000; Padilla et al. 2001). The modern champion can be distinguished by the capacity to withstand the many minutes of a time trial or the climb to the top of a mountain pass at almost 100% maximum capacity (zone 3). The present-day Tour is perhaps the most intense.

The current trend is toward shorter, more intense races. For instance, in 2002 the total distance covered in each Vuelta, Giro, and Tour was under 3500 km. Interestingly, this new era might provide a good option for elite mountain riders to succeed in road races, given their well-known ability to tolerate extremely high workloads (zone 3). Indeed, some world-class MTB riders were hired by pro road teams for the 2002 season.

Figure 10.3 shows the total time spent racing by the winner of the Tour de France throughout its history. The graph illustrates the tendency toward a decrease in exercise duration, which implies an increase in exercise intensity.

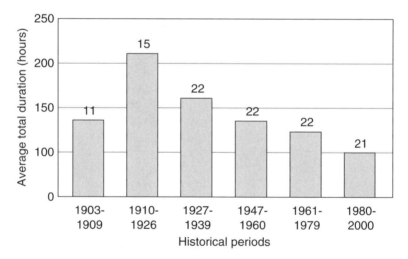

FIGURE 10.3   Total duration (in hours) of the Tour de France throughout its history. The average times of the winners in each historical period are shown. The average numbers of stages are displayed on top of the bars.

Trends in Tour Races

Since the beginning of the 20th century, three-week tour races have been extremely demanding. Compared to the old days, the current trend is toward shorter, more intense daily stages. In the years to come, it is expected that the average amount of time a cyclist spends in zone 3 per stage will be more than 30 min.

Physiological Demands of the Different Phases of Tour Races

In general, three-week tour races have three main competition requirements (see table 10.1): flat and long parcours (usually ridden at high speeds inside a large group of riders), individual time trials (40 to 60 km over level terrain), and uphill cycling (high mountain passes).

Every tour race includes seven or more flat stages of about 200 km, lasting four to five hours. Most of the time, cyclists ride in large groups of 150 to 200 cyclists. This considerably reduces the major force—air resistance—to be overcome in this type of terrain. As a result, the energy requirement of cycling can be decreased by as much as 40% (McCole et al. 1990), making the overall exercise intensity low to moderate. The proportion of the total stage time spent in zone 3 barely reaches 5% (Lucia, Hoyos et al. 1999).

A great mastery of technical skills (such as drafting or the ability to avoid crashes) would seem most important in this type of stage, in which most riders are able to finish within the same time. In fact, these stages usually do not determine the final outcome of a tour race.

The high average speeds (approximately 45 kph) at which riders are able to cover these stages require that they push high gears (53×12 to 11) during long periods. This inevitably results in some muscle damage. Previous research has reported increased levels of muscle damage markers during cycling tour races (Mena, Maynar, and Campillo 1996). This phenomenon may have a negative impact on performance during the second part of a three-week race, during which accumulated muscle fatigue may considerably limit performance in the phases of competition that determine the winner—the time trials and high mountain passes.

Tour races typically include three time trials (TT) performed over overall flat terrains: a short, opening TT of 5 to 10 km and two long TT of 40 to 60 km. This phase of the competition usually influences the final outcome of the race.

Air resistance is the main force that the cyclist encounters during TT. Thus, aerodynamic factors (the cyclist's riding posture, the size of the frontal wheels, etc.) play a major role (Lucia, Hoyos, and Chicharro 2000a).

Those who seek top performance (average velocity of 50 kph) must tolerate high constant workloads, mostly in zone 3, during the entire 60 min of the TT (Lucia, Hoyos et al. 1999). Some authors have estimated that the mean absolute power output sustained during long TT averages 350 W,

TABLE 10.1 Main Characteristics of Flat Stages, High Mountain Stages, and Individual Time Trials

	Flat stage	Individual time trial	High mountain stage
Distance (km)	~ 200 (overall flat)	40 to 60	~ 200
Exercise time (hours)	4 to 5	~ 1	5 to 6
Mean exercise intensity	Low to moderate	High	Moderate to high (high during ascents)
Prevailing metabolism	Aerobic (fat)	Aerobic (CHO) and anaerobic	Aerobic (fat and CHO) and aerobic/ anaerobic (CHO) during ascents
Mean velocity (km/hour)	~ 45	~ 50 (time trial specialists)	~ 20 during ascents
Cycling position	Traditional (sitting)	Aerodynamic (triathlon bars)	Alternating sitting and standing
Main requirements	Technical	Physiological and aerodynamics	Physiological
Specific concerns	Crashes, muscle damage	Aerodynamics	Moderate hypoxia in some ascents (altitude > 1500 m)
Estimated average power output	200 to 250 W	350 W (≥400 W in time trial specialists)	6 or more W/kg during ascents

Both the flat and high mountain stages are mass starts.

Adapted, by permission, from A. Lucia, J. Hoyos, and J.L. Chicharro, 2001,"Physiology of professional road racing,"*Med Sci Sports Exerc* 31:325-337.

although TT specialists probably generate much higher power outputs (greater than 400 W) (Padilla et al. 2000).

Some mass-start stages of approximately 200 km (the so-called high mountain stages) include three to five mountain passes of 5 to 10% mean gradient, and thus require cycling uphill during several 30- to 60-min periods over a total time of five to six hours.

High-mountain stages in road races require climbing specialists to cycle in intensity zones 2 and 3.

When climbing at low speeds (about 20 kph), the cyclist must mainly overcome the force of gravity (Swain 1994). Because of its effects on gravity-induced resistance, body mass has a major influence on climbing performance. A high power-output-to-body-mass ratio at maximal or near-maximal intensities (6 or more W/kg) is necessary for professional road riders (Lucia, Hoyos, and Chicharro 2000a; Padilla et al. 1999).

In addition, rolling resistance resulting from the interaction between the bicycle tires and the road surface increases considerably at lower riding speeds and on the rough road surfaces of most mountain routes (Lucia, Hoyos, and Chicharro 2000a). To overcome these forces, cyclists frequently switch from the conventional sitting position to a less economic standing posture to exert more force on the pedals. Climbing specialists perform high mountain ascents at intensities in zones 2 and 3 (Fernández-García et al. 2000; Lucia, Hoyos et al. 1999). Because of team requirements, however, some riders are not required to perform maximally during high mountain stages.

Figure 10.4 shows an example of the exercise intensity distribution shown by one of the best world riders during the 1997 Tour de France.

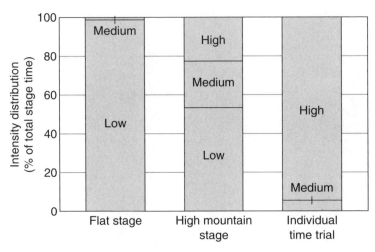

FIGURE 10.4 Example of exercise intensity distribution in a world-class cyclist during the 1997 Tour de France. Exercise intensities of low, medium, and high correspond to zones 1 (less than 70% HRmax), 2 (70 to 90% HRmax), and 3 (greater than 90% HRmax).

Data from Lucía, Hoyos et al. 1999.

Race Smart

Those who seek top performance in the two competition phases that determine the final outcome of tour races—individual time trials and uphill cycling—must continue in zone 3 for more than 30 min.

Effects on Body Systems: Signs of Overtraining and Hormonal Disturbances

Three-week tour races are so hard on a cyclist's body that a certain state of hormonal exhaustion was noted in riders completing the 1999 Vuelta a España (Lucia et al. 2001). Basal levels of the following hormones were measured before the corresponding stages throughout the Vuelta:

▶ Cortisol, a stress hormone secreted by the adrenal gland during exercise. Cortisol has a catabolic effect—that is, it stimulates the mobilization of substrates.

▶ Testosterone, an anabolic hormone secreted by the testes. Testosterone, among other effects, contributes to repairing damaged muscle after exercise.

▶ Melatonin, a hormone secreted by the pineal gland during nighttime hours only. Melatonin regulates the internal body clock.

Levels for each of these hormones decreased by the third week of the race, probably because the secretion rate during the four to five racing hours per day is so high that the glands (adrenal, testes, and pineal) do not have sufficient time to recover overnight.

We could draw an analogy with the decrease in catecholamines (adrenaline) reported in overtrained distance runners, attributed to adrenal exhaustion or the so-called parasympathetic form of overtraining (Mackinnon and Hooper 2000). Like cortisol, catecholamines are also secreted by the adrenal glands but have a quicker action. They stimulate the cardiac pump by increasing the strength of each beat and the number of beats per minute.

Because of the effects of adrenaline on the heart, adrenal exhaustion is mainly reflected by a somewhat paradoxical decrease in HRmax during maximal intensity exercise. For instance, the heart rate of an overtrained cyclist barely surpassed 90% HRmax during the mountain stages of the 1997 Tour de France, in spite of maximum perception of effort. This tendency to decline in HRmax is actually fairly common at the end of a long tour race.

In contrast, when cyclists are at their peak, their heart rate rises quickly to reach its highest level, which can be maintained for long periods. Further investigation may serve to determine the physiological mid- or long-term consequences of this state of hormonal exhaustion on other body systems (e.g., the immune system).

Signs of Overtraining

A certain degree of overtraining is common by the end of a three-week race. This state is reflected by reduced basal levels of several stress hormones and an inability to reach HRmax during maximal effort.

Anthropometric Variables of Professional Cyclists

As we already know, road cycling requires performing over a great variety of terrains and in many competitive situations. In turn, cycling performance over each competition terrain is to some extent determined by the morphological characteristics of body mass, height, body surface and frontal areas, and body mass index (BMI).

Anthropometric variables might differ greatly depending on the cyclist's speciality. Time trial or flat terrain specialists are usually taller and heavier (180 to 185 cm, 70 to 75 kg, BMI around 22) than those who excel in uphill climbing (175 to 180 cm, 60 to 66 kg, BMI of 19 to 20) (Lucia, Hoyos, and Chicharro 2000a; Padilla et al. 1999). The BMI of some sprint specialists might even surpass 22.

The morphometric characteristics of modern champions who are able to excel in both types of terrains are close to those of time trialists (about 180 cm, 70 kg). This could be the profile for years to come. Increased muscle mass and glycogen stores are advantages associated with heavier weights, which appear to be needed in modern intense races. Indeed, higher intensity means a higher reliance on glycogen stores. A good amount of muscle mass is also crucial to generate the forceful muscle contractions now required to push very hard gears over flat terrain.

Body fat percentage, on the other hand, does not significantly differ among the different types of cyclists, including the heavier ones. Body fat percentages begin close to 10% (using skinfold techniques) during the winter months, then gradually decrease during the season to values around 9% during the spring and close to 8% during three-week tour races at the end of the spring and summer months (Lucia, Hoyos, and Chicharro 2001).

Body Effect on Racing

Although those who excel in time trials and flat terrain are traditionally taller and heavier than climbers, the morphometric characteristics of modern champions are close to those of time trialists.

Physiological Variables of Professional Road Cyclists

In contrast to other endurance athletes such as runners or cross-country skiers, the physiological variables of professional cyclists was not available in the scientific literature until the late 1990s. Up until then, much of what was assumed was based on studies conducted on well-trained but amateur cyclists. Today, it is possible to get a broad picture of the physiological profile of professional riders. Several variables have been measured during routine physiological evaluated (gradual tests until exhaustion) and include both maximal variables (e.g., maximal oxygen uptake) and submaximal variables (e.g., the anaerobic threshold).

Maximal Power Output and Maximal Oxygen Uptake

Average values of maximal power output attained during an incremental test vary depending on the protocol used. Lower values of 400 to 450 W (6.0 to 6.5 W/kg) are recorded during tests involving 4-min increments of 35 W, staring at 110 W (Padilla et al. 1999). Power outputs of 450 to 500 W (6.5 to 7.5 W/kg) can be obtained during shorter, ramp protocols involving 1-min increments of 25 W, starting at 20 W (Lucia, Hoyos, and Chicharro 2001). Maximal power outputs clearly above 500 W are not unusual in top-level time trialists such as Abraham Olano and Alex Zulle using the latter type of ramp protocols.

Mean values of maximal oxygen uptake ($\dot{V}O_2max$) reported in pro riders range between 5.0 and 5.5 L/min or between 70 and 80 ml/kg/min when expressed in absolute or relative units, respectively (Lucia, Hoyos, and Chicharro 2001). Uphill climbing specialists exhibit the highest relative values (around 80 ml/kg/min), comparable to elite distance runners. Lowest values (around 70 ml/kg/min) usually correspond to TT specialists or rouleurs (Lucia, Hoyos, and Chicharro 2000a).

While high $\dot{V}O_2max$ values (usually greater than 70 ml/kg/min) are required for cycling performance at a professional level, other physiological variables that relate to the ability to perform at high but submaximal intensities are far more important. For instance, similar values of $\dot{V}O_2max$ are recorded in elite amateur cyclists of a lower competitive level (Lucia et al. 1998; Lucia, Hoyos, Santalla, Perez, and Chicharro 2002). It could be generalized that a high $\dot{V}O_2max$ is a prerequisite for succeeding as a road cyclist, but this characteristic alone is clearly insufficient.

$\dot{V}O_2max$ and Performance

Although the $\dot{V}O_2max$ of pro riders is usually high (between 70 and 80 ml/kg/min), it is often comparable to that of cyclists at lower competition levels. Other physiological variables are more important in determining performance.

Submaximal Variables

During gradual exercise tests that use either ramplike or longer protocols, the anaerobic threshold (AT) is the exercise intensity at which type II fibers, formerly known as fast-twitch fibers, are inevitably recruited to sustain the required power output (Wasserman, Beaver, and Whipp 1990). This results in lactic acidosis and increased pulmonary ventilation to buffer this acidosis. Thus, a shift of the AT toward higher intensities in a given cyclist can be interpreted as a favorable training adaptation.

However, much controversy exists over the different methods used to determine AT in elite athletes. Some authors prefer long protocols of 4-min increments to measure blood lactate concentration and thus determine exercise intensity, eliciting a blood concentration of 4 mM, the so-called onset of blood lactate accumulation (OBLA) (Padilla et al. 1999) or the individual anaerobic threshold (IAT) (Fernández-García et al. 2000).

In contrast, several studies performed in our laboratory describe the use of ventilatory parameters during shorter, ramplike protocols to establish the workload at which the second ventilatory threshold, also termed respiratory compensation point (RCP), occurs (Lucia, Hoyos, and Chicharro 2001). Keeping the different methodologies used for AT evaluation in mind, most authors agree that the AT of pro riders (OBLA, IAT, or RCP) corresponds to about 90% of both their $\dot{V}O_2$max and maximal power output.

Although the literature is full of conflicting results, in about two thirds of professional riders the increase in heart rate that occurs during gradual ramplike protocols is attenuated at high intensities (Lucia, Carvajal et al. 1999). This phenomenon was originally observed more than 50 years ago and is now known as the heart rate deflection point (HR_d).

The HR_d usually occurs at the workload that also elicits AT, as first reported by Conconi and colleagues (1996). Given that both HR_d and AT occur at similar workloads and HR_d is easy to determine in the field (only a heart rate telemeter is needed), the so-called Conconi test that detects HR_d is the most popular test in pro cycling for performance evaluation and prescription of training intensity.

However, HR_d does not occur in all cyclists (see figure 10.5), and the physiological meaning of this phenomenon is not yet clearly understood. For this reason, we recommend the use of constant-load tests at high, submaximal intensities (80 to 90% $\dot{V}O_2$max) for the evaluation of elite road cyclists.

Constant-Load Tests

Although it may seem paradoxical, oxygen uptake ($\dot{V}O_2$) and exercise intensity slowly rise during any prolonged exercise bout of more than 6 min at a constant power output involving sustained lactic acidosis (zone 2 and mostly zone 3) (see figure 10.6). This phenomenon is the slow component of $\dot{V}O_2$ and mainly is attributable to a progressive recruitment of type II fibers with exercise duration, caused by gradual fatigue of previously recruited type I fibers (Gaesser and Poole 1996). For a given power output, type II fibers are indeed less efficient—they consume more O_2—than type I fibers (Coyle et al. 1992).

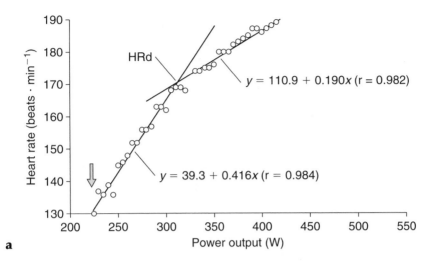

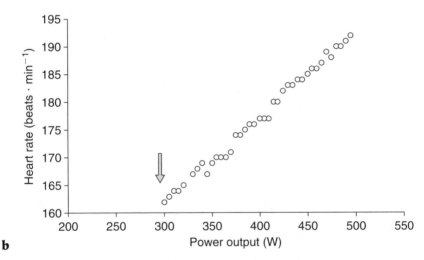

FIGURE 10.5   Example of *(a)* heart rate deflection (HR$_d$) occurrence and *(b)* linear response of heart rate (HR) during a ramp protocol until exhaustion in two world-class cyclists (Lucia, Hoyos, Santalla, Perez, Carvajal, and Chicharro 2002). According to experts in the field (Hofmann et al. 1997), the HR-to-power output relationship must be analyzed once the so-called lactate threshold is reached (vertical arrows). For most professional cyclists, this corresponds to 70 to 80% of HRmax.

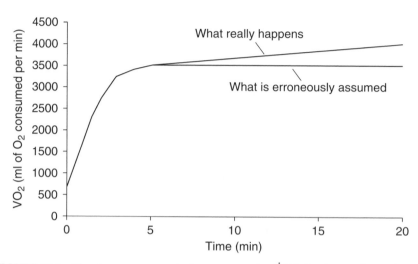

FIGURE 10.6   The slow component of oxygen uptake ($\dot{V}O_2$). During prolonged exercise lasting more than 6 min at a given constant power output involving sustained lactic acidosis (greater than 70 to 80% HRmax), $\dot{V}O_2$, and thus exercise intensity, inevitably shows a gradual increase and theoretically could reach $\dot{V}O_2$max if the exercise is prolonged for a long period.

One adaptation pro cyclists make through training and competition is a decrease in the magnitude of the $\dot{V}O_2$ slow component. Therefore, although sport professionals rarely keep in mind the $\dot{V}O_2$ slow component, a part of training regimes for elite cyclists should be aimed at decreasing its magnitude. For instance, during a 20-min bout at a mean power output as high as 400 W (or approximately 80% $\dot{V}O_2$max), the average $\dot{V}O_2$ of world-class cyclists increases only by 130 ml from the start to the end of exercise (Lucia, Hoyos, and Chicharro 2000b). In noncyclists working at similar relative intensities (80% $\dot{V}O_2$max) and much lower power outputs (below 200 W), the magnitude of the slow component can be three to four times higher (Gaesser and Poole 1996). This low value of the slow component in pro riders suggests their great efficiency, which might be linked to their probable high proportion of type I fibers in their knees.

Economy and Efficiency.   Gross mechanical efficiency (GE) is the ratio of work accomplished to energy expended. GE should be ideally determined during a constant-load test, for example, a 20-min test at 80% $\dot{V}O_2$max. For any given power output, GE can be easily estimated using the following equation:

$$GE = 60 \times W/20{,}934 \times \dot{V}O_2$$

where W is power output in watts, 20,934 is the caloric equivalent (in joules) of 1 L of oxygen, and $\dot{V}O_2$ is oxygen uptake in L/min (Jeukendrup, Craig, and Hawley 2000). GE is an estimate of whole body efficiency and thus might be relevant from a practical point of view (Coast 1996).

The mechanical efficiency of pedaling, which relies mainly on concentric work of the knee extensors, is much lower than that of running, in which eccentric contractions and efficient stretch–shortening movements play an important role (Billat et al. 1998). Bearing this efficiency limitation of the pedaling cycle in mind, it is obvious that an exceptionally high GE is one of the best possible training adaptations for endurance cycling. Such an adaptation is required at the highest competition level to sustain extremely high power outputs greater than 400 W during prolonged periods at the lowest metabolic cost (Lucia, Hoyos, and Chicharro 2001).

In fact, at the workloads most important competition phases are tackled (zones 1 and 2 or from about 300 to 500 W), the GE of pro riders averages some 25% (Lucia, Hoyos, Santalla, Perez, and Chicharro 2002), clearly above values normally shown by noncyclists at similar relative intensities, on average around 20% (Moseley and Jeukendrup 2001). Although the physiological and metabolic determinants of this variable are not yet fully understood, in pro riders GE could be determined largely by the percentage distribution of efficient type I fibers in the main muscles involved in cycling, the knee extensor muscles, particularly the vastus lateralis. That is, the greater the number of type I fibers, the higher the GE.

Few reports in the literature provide data derived from muscle biopsies taken in pro riders of the highest competition level, but it is widely known that human work efficiency is positively related to the percentage distribution of type I fibers in exercising muscles. Previous research on endurance-trained cyclists has shown that a higher percentage of type I fibers in the vastus lateralis is associated with a greater efficiency during prolonged exercise (one hour) at moderate to high intensity (Coyle et al. 1992).

A variable with a similar meaning to GE is cycling economy (CE). Measured in $W/\dot{V}O_2$ (the latter in L/min), this variable refers to the power output generated at a cost of 1 L of oxygen per minute of exercise (Coyle et al. 1991). The CE of pro cyclists generating a power output of approximately 400 W during 20 min averages around 85 W/L/min. This mean value is clearly above those previously reported for highly trained amateur riders during a simulated time trial of one hour at power outputs of 256 to 376 W in which the mean was around 75 W/L/min (Coyle et al. 1991). Like GE, CE is positively related to the percentage distribution of type I fibers in knee extensor muscles (Coyle et al. 1991).

We recently showed an inverse relationship between GE/CE and $\dot{V}O_2$max in world-class pro riders (unpublished data). Riders with the lowest $\dot{V}O_2$max values showed the highest economy and efficiency and vice versa. One could speculate that in the natural selection process for success in world-class cycling, a relatively low $\dot{V}O_2$max—a parameter mainly limited by the maximal capacity of the cardiac pump—could be compensated for, at least partly, by an especially high percentage of efficient type I fibers in knee extensors. Moreover, once a certain fitness level is reached, submaximal variables such as CE and GE performed at intensities corresponding to zones 2 and 3 become more important determinants of cycling performance than $\dot{V}O_2max$ (Lucia et al. 1998).

Interestingly, one of the best riders ever tested in our laboratory, a two-time world champion, has a relatively low $\dot{V}O_2max$ value (less than 70 ml/ kg/min), yet his CE and GE during a 20-min test at 400 W are very high, clearly above 90 W/L/min and 25%, respectively. We could draw an analogy with elite endurance running. It has been shown that the best athletes, particularly marathon racers, are usually the most economizing. Moreover, the relatively low $\dot{V}O_2max$ values of some world-class marathoners, including Olympic champions, are compensated for by an exceptionally high running economy (Morgan and Daniels 1994). Saltin and colleagues (1995) also reported that the remarkable dominance of Kenyan distance runners compared to Caucasians is partly attributable to their greater running economy.

For all of these reasons, we propose that the type of constant-load exercise used in our laboratory (20 min at 80% $\dot{V}O_2max$), which is well tolerated by elite cyclists, be included in the routine evaluation of these athletes. There is an obvious need for future research in this area. It would be interesting to analyze which aspects of training—for example, volume versus intensity—have the greatest impact on GE/CE. This type of study would be of practical applicability, given the efficiency limitations of the pedaling cycle per se, which relies mostly on concentric work.

World-Class Cyclists

During prolonged exercise at power outputs as high as 400 W, the economy and gross mechanical efficiency of world-class cyclists averages around 85 W/L/min and around 25%. Both variables are crucial determinants of sport performance.

Figure 10.7 summarizes the main physiological characteristics of top-level (pro) road cyclists.

Climbers Versus Time Trialists. The final outcome of a tour race is determined mainly by the cyclist's ability to perform successfully in uphill cycling and time trials over overall flat terrain. The large difference between these two feats implies that most cyclists will show a greater skill in one or the other, such that a clear division often may be made between hill climbers and time trialists or rouleurs.

In Europe, many cycling professionals think that the differences between these types of cyclists are determined mainly by genetics. It is true that the

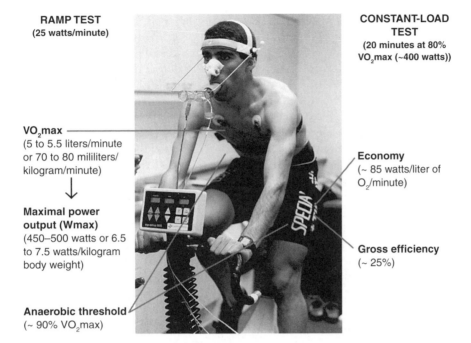

RAMP TEST
(25 watts/minute)

CONSTANT-LOAD TEST
(20 minutes at 80% VO₂max (~400 watts))

$\dot{V}O_2$max
(5 to 5.5 liters/minute or 70 to 80 mililiters/ kilogram/minute)
↓

Maximal power output (Wmax)
(450–500 watts or 6.5 to 7.5 watts/kilogram body weight)

Anaerobic threshold
(~ 90% VO₂max)

Economy
(~ 85 watts/liter of O₂/minute)

Gross efficiency
(~ 25%)

FIGURE 10.7   The professional road rider in the physiology laboratory illustrating the most important physiological variables that can be routinely obtained during a ramp or submaximal constant-load test. $\dot{V}O_2$max, which in turn determines Wmax, is mainly limited by the maximal capacity of the cardiac pump, whereas anaerobic threshold is an overall integrative parameter, determined by both cardiorespiratory and muscle factors. The most important characteristic variables—economy and gross efficiency—probably can be obtained during a constant-load test. Both economy and gross efficiency are related largely to the percentage of type I fibers in the knee extensor muscles, mainly the vastus lateralis.

Photo courtesy of Alejandro Lucía.

previously mentioned differences in anthropometric characteristics between climbers and time trialists (the latter tend to be taller and heavier) are determined at least partly by the genetic heritage of each cyclist. This is reflected also in $\dot{V}O_2$max values expressed in relative units (around 80 ml/kg/min in climbers and around 70 ml/kg/min in time trialists).

A closer observation, however, reveals that other differences might be conditioned, and thus suppressed, by training. Constant-load tests are necessary to identify such differences. During constant bouts of exercise conducted at 80% $\dot{V}O_2$max, we measured $\dot{V}O_2$ and blood pH (to estimate each cyclist's buffering capacity and ability to cope with lactic acidosis) and used surface electrodes placed over the vastus lateralis muscle to evaluate the electromyographic activity of the knee extensor muscles (Lucia, Hoyos, and Chicharro 2000a). The results showed that climbing specialists have a

greater ability to recruit fibers and to buffer acidosis, whereas TT specialists show a more efficient pedaling pattern, lower fiber recruitment to generate comparable power output. These differences may explain the ability
of climbers to switch rapidly from an already demanding pace of around
respiratory compensation point (RCP) or about 90% $\dot{V}O_2$max to higher
speeds up to 100% $\dot{V}O_2$max during mountain ascents. Moreover, a select
few (Marco Pantani, José María Jiménez) are able to perform repeated short
bouts of maximum intensity exercise during long ascents. This type of exercise probably demands great adaptation on behalf of both anaerobic (recruitment of type II fibers) and buffer systems. In contrast, during TT
(especially those exceeding 40 km), the exercise intensity is still near maximum (at or above RCP) but is more stable. Thus, efficiency is an important
concern.

Figure 10.8 summarizes the main differences between climbing and time
trial specialists. The characteristics that usually distinguish climbers from
time-trialists are not only those derived from genetic or morphometric factors. Specific training also plays a significant role.

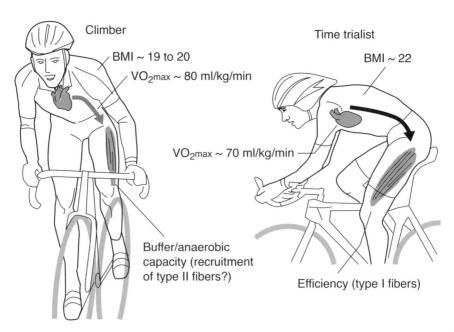

FIGURE 10.8   Climbers versus time trialists. Differences are not just due to morphometric factors such as BMI. Climbers probably have a higher anaerobic capacity,
whereas time trialists exhibit a more efficient pedaling pattern. The maximum
amount of oxygen available to working muscles ($\dot{V}O_2$max) is usually higher in
climbers because of to their lower body weight. When expressed in absolute terms
(L/min), $\dot{V}O_2$max is similar in both types of cyclists.

Physiological Applications to Cycling

An important issue in cycling is to adequately quantify exercise intensity during both training and competition based on data obtained in previous laboratory incremental tests. Heart rate data can be used to divide exercise intensity into zones: zone 1 is less than 70% HRmax, zone 2 is between 70 and 90% HRmax, and zone 3 is greater than 90% HRmax. In fact, this was the first approach used to report exercise intensity during the Tour de France (Lucia, Hoyos et al. 1999).

In addition to the fact that heart rate is really easy to monitor using telemeters such as the famous Polar devices without disturbing the cyclist during workouts or competitions, heart rate is the best possible indicator of exercise intensity during endurance exercise, since it is overall linearly related to $\dot{V}O_2$, independent of the HR_d phenomenon (Gilman 1996). For these reasons, heart rate has been the variable most frequently used to evaluate the level of intensity attained during training and competition in professional cycling since the 1990s.

When based on heart rate data, training orientation does not necessarily require periodic readjustment of target heart rate (for example, at the RCP) by repeated testing during the season. We recently showed that target heart rate values corresponding to performance markers such as RCP remained stable (around 175 beats per minute) during the course of a complete season in professional cyclists, despite a significant improvement in performance throughout the training season as shown by increases in the power output eliciting the RCP (Lucia, Hoyos, Perez, and Chicharro 2000).

Comparable findings have also been reported in cyclists (Hoogeveen 2000) and speedskaters (Foster, Fitzgerald, and Spatz 1999). There were no seasonal changes in target heart rate values corresponding to AT.

Interestingly, maximal heart rate does not change significantly during the season, whereas recovery values (recorded at 3 and 5 min postexercise) show a consistent decrease (Lucia, Hoyos, Perez, and Chicharro 2000). Accordingly, it is a common mistake to stop collecting physiological data at the point of exhaustion since the most interesting information might emerge during recovery.

Recent technological developments have made it possible to measure power output (W) on a bicycle with a power-measuring device such as the SRM Training System and thus prescribe training loads based on power output eliciting AT. In fact, Lance Armstrong and other cyclists use the SRM system during training.

Power output is obviously the best indicator of cycling performance. However, from a strictly physiological point of view, heart rate is a better indicator of exercise intensity than power output. Because of the $\dot{V}O_2$ slow component phenomenon, the fact that power output remains stable does not necessarily mean that exercise intensity also remains constant. Far from it. $\dot{V}O_2$ inevitably increases despite a constant power output. This physiological misconception could increase the risk of overtraining. For instance, a 20-min workout originally aimed at training at AT intensity could turn out to be an exhaustive $\dot{V}O_2$max type of workout. Both heart rate and power output are necessary tools for a scientific prescription of training.

Heart Rate

Heart rate is probably the most scientific indicator of exercise intensity in endurance road cycling, whereas power output is the best indicator of performance. Ideally, both variables should be monitored in training and competition.

Directions for Future Research

Exercise physiology did not become an important tool for performance improvement in professional road cycling until late in the 1980s. Thus, at least from a scientific perspective, road cycling is probably lagging behind other endurance sports such as marathon running. Over the last few decades, some of the most prestigious physiologists have studied Olympic-class marathoners and Kenyan runners; physiological data on professional cyclists was not available in the scientific literature until late in the 1990s.

Scientific advances in nutrition, ergogenic aids (banned or not), aerodynamics, and equipment are responsible for the major improvements in road cycling performance over the last century. Precise training prescription based on scientific variables and laboratory tests has played a minor role. Thus, the major challenge of the future is to adequately analyze the sport from a scientific point of view to help cyclists develop the best possible training programs. For example, $\dot{V}O_2$max—a variable we know is determined mainly by the maximal capacity of the heart to pump oxygenated blood to working muscles—does not increase during the season in pro cyclists (Lucia, Hoyos, Pardo, and Chicharro 2000). Future studies should be conducted to determine which type of training intervention can increase $\dot{V}O_2$max in a pro cyclist.

Finally, another important issue is to adequately mimic actual cycling in the laboratory, a difficult task especially when considering the long duration of most races. In contrast to other sports, cyclists are rarely required to perform maximally under ideal conditions. Instead, they must tolerate maximal efforts when they are close to chronic fatigue (e.g., during the final week of the Tour de France). This should be kept in mind when testing cyclists and prescribing training programs.

References

Billat, V., Richard, V.L., Binsse, V.M., Koralsztein, J.P., and Haouzi, P. 1998. The $\dot{V}O_2$ slow component for severe exercise depends on type of exercise and is not correlated with time to fatigue. *J Appl Physiol* 85:2118-2184.

Coast, J.R. 1996. Optimal pedaling cadence. In *High-tech cycling*, edited by E.R. Burke. Champaign, Ill.: Human Kinetics. pp. 101-117.

Conconi, F., Grazzi, G., Casoni, C., Guglielmini, C., Borsetto, C., Ballarin, E., Mazzoni, G., Patracchini, M., and Manfredini, F. 1996. The Conconi test: Methodology after 12 years of application. *Int J Sports Med* 17:509-519.

Coyle, E.F., Feltner, M.E., Kautz, S.A., Hamilton, M.T., Montain, S.J., Baylor A.M., Abraham, L.D., and Petrek, G.W. 1991. Physiological and biomechanical factors associated with elite endurance cycling performance. *Med Sci Sports Exerc* 23:93-107.

Coyle, E.F., Sidossis, L.S., Horowitz, J.F., and Beltz, J.D. 1992. Cycling efficiency is related to the percentage of type I muscle fibers. *Med Sci Sports Exerc* 24:782-788.

Fernández-García, B., Pérez-Landaluce, J., Rodríguez-Alonso, M., and Terrados, N. 2000. Intensity of exercise during road race pro-cycling competition. *Med Sci Sports Exerc* 32:1002-1006.

Foster, C., Fitzgerald, D.J., and Spatz, P. 1999. Stability of the blood lactate-heart rate relationship in competitive athletes. *Med Sci Sports Exerc* 31:578-582.

Gaesser, G.A., and Poole, D.C. 1996. The slow component of oxygen uptake kinetics in humans. *Exerc Sport Sci Rev* 24:35-71.

Gilman, M.B. 1996. The use of heart rate to monitor the intensity of endurance training. *Sports Med* 21:73-79.

Hofmann, P., Pokan, R., Seibert, F.J., Zweiker, R., and Schmid, P. 1997. The heart rate performance curve during incremental cycle ergometer exercise in healthy young male subjects. *Med Sci Sports Exerc* 29:762-768.

Hoogeveen, A.R. 2000. The effect of endurance training on the ventilatory response to exercise in elite cyclists. *Eur J Appl Physiol* 82:45-51.

Jeukendrup, A.E., Craig, N.P., and Hawley, J.A. 2000. The bioenergetics of World Class Cycling. *J Sci Med Sport* 3:414-433.

Lucía, A., Carvajal, A., Boraita, A., Serratosa, L., Hoyos, J., and Chicharro, J.L. 1999. Heart dimensions may influence the occurrence of the heart rate deflection point in highly trained cyclists. *Br J Sports Med* 33:387-392.

Lucía, A., Díaz, B., Hoyos, J., Fernández, C., Villa, G., Bandrés, F., and Chicharro, J.L. 2001. Hormone levels of world class cyclists during the Tour of Spain stage race. *Br J Sports Med* 35:424-430.

Lucía, A., Hoyos, J., Carvajal, A., and Chicharro, J.L. 1999. Heart rate response to professional road cycling: The Tour de France. *Int J Sports Med* 20:167-172.

Lucía, A., Hoyos, J., and Chicharro, J.L. 2000a. Physiological response to professional road cycling: Climbers vs. time trialists. *Int J Sports Med* 21:505-512.

Lucía, A., Hoyos, J., and Chicharro, J.L. 2000b. The slow component of $\dot{V}O_2$ in professional cyclists. *Br J Sports Med* 34:367-374.

Lucía, A., Hoyos, J., and Chicharro, J.L. 2001. Physiology of professional road racing. *Sports Med* 31:325-337.

Lucía, A., Hoyos, J., Pardo, J., and Chicharro, J.L. 2000. Metabolic and neuromuscular adaptations to endurance training in professional cyclists: A longitudinal study. *Jpn J Physiol* 50:381-388.

Lucía, A., Hoyos, J., Perez, M., and Chicharro, J.L. 2000. Heart rate and performance parameters in elite cyclists: A longitudinal study. *Med Sci Sports Exerc* 32:1777-1782.

Lucía, A., Hoyos, J., Santalla, A., Perez, M., Carvajal, A., and Chicharro, J.L. 2002. Lactic acidosis, potassium and the heart rate deflection point in professional road cyclists. *Br J Sports Med* 36(2):113-117.

Lucía, A., Hoyos, J., Santalla, A., Perez, M., and Chicharro, J.L. 2002. Kinetics of $\dot{V}O_2$ in professional cyclists. *Med Sci Sports Exerc* 34:320-325.

Lucía, A., Pardo, J., Durantez, A., Hoyos, J., and Chicharro, J.L. 1998. Physiological differences between professional and elite road cyclists. *Int J Sports Med* 19:342-348.

MacKinnon, L.T., and Hooper, S.L. 2000. Overtraining and overreaching: Causes, effects, and prevention. In *Exercise and sport science*, edited by W.E. Garrett Jr. and D.T. Kinkerdall. Philadelphia: Lippincott Williams & Wilkins. pp 487-498.

McCole, S.D., Claney, K., Conte J-C., Anderson, R., and Hagberg, J.M. 1990. Energy expenditure during bicycling. *J Appl Physiol* 68:748-753.

Mena, P., Maynar, M., and Campillo, J.E. 1996. Changes in plasma enzyme activities in professional racing cyclists. *Br J Sports Med* 30:122-124.

Morgan, D.W., and Daniels, J.T. 1994. Relationship between $\dot{V}O_2$max and the aerobic demand of running in elite distance runners. *Int J Sports Med* 15:426-429.

Moseley, L., and Jeukendrup, A.E. 2001. The reliability of cycling efficiency. *Med Sci Sports Exerc* 33:621-627.

Padilla, A., Mujika, I., Cuesta, G., and Goiriena, J.J. 1999. Level ground and uphill cycling ability in professional road cycling. *Med Sci Sports Exerc* 31:878-885.

Padilla, S., Mujika, I., Orbañanos, J., and Angulo, F. 2000. Exercise intensity during competition time trials in professional road cycling. *Med Sci Sports Exerc* 32:850-856.

Padilla, S., Mujika, I., Orbananos, J., Santisteban, J., Angulo, F., Jose Goiriena, J. 2001. Exercise intensity and load during mass-start stage races in professional road cycling. *Med Sci Sports Exerc* 33:796-802.

Saltin, B., Kim, C.K., Terrados, H., Larsen, J., Svedenhag, J., and Rolf, C. 1995. Morphology, enzyme activities and buffer capacity in leg muscles of Kenyan and Scandinavian runners. *Scand J Med Sci Sports* 5:222-230.

Skinner, J.S., and McLellan, T.H. 1980. The transition from aerobic to anaerobic metabolism. *Res Q Exerc Sport* 51:234-238.

Swain, D.P. 1994. The influence of body mass in endurance bicycling. *Med Sci Sports Exerc* 26:58-63.

Wasserman, K., Beaver, W.L., and Whipp, B.J. 1990. Gas exchange theory and the lactic acidosis (anaerobic) threshold. *Circulation* 81(Suppl. II):14-30.

11

Physiology of Mountain Biking

Holden S-H. MacRae

To be a successful mountain cyclist requires optimally conditioned physiological systems, a level of technical skill not required of road cyclists, and the ability to integrate these traits during training and competition to produce optimal performance. The cross-country event in particular requires unique technical skills; appropriate pacing and race tactics; and the ability to maintain a high work rate, tolerate adverse environmental conditions, and resist the effects of mental and physical fatigue due to energy depletion and dehydration.

Cross-country (XC) riding is the most popular of the three mountain bike disciplines. Typical XC races last approximately 2 to 3 hours for elite men and 1.75 to 2.5 hours for elite women. Typical downhill (DH) competitions last 4 to 7 min, and dual slalom (DS) competitions last approximately 30 to 60 s. All three disciplines of mountain biking require the cyclist to generate high power outputs for short durations, with this requirement being more important for DH and DS. Aerobic or endurance power, the dominant energy system used in XC riding, is less important for DH and DS riding. This chapter addresses the physiology of XC cycling, primarily since research data on the physiology of DH and DS are not available.

A large number of scientific investigations of distance runners, cyclists, rowers, XC skiers, swimmers, and triathletes have determined the minimum physiological requirements for any individual wishing to compete at a high level in continuous, moderate- to high-intensity endurance events lasting longer than 30 min such as XC mountain biking. They are as follows (Hawley and Burke 1998):

▶ High maximal aerobic power ($\dot{V}O_2$max)—greater than 60 ml/kg/min for women and 65 ml/kg/min for men

▶ High power-to-weight ratio

▶ Low level of body fat

▶ Ability to train and race at a high percentage of $\dot{V}O_2$max (or high percentage of heart rate maximum) for sustained periods

▶ High power output or speed at the so-called anaerobic or lactate threshold

▶ Ability to maintain high absolute power outputs or speeds and to resist the onset of muscular fatigue

▶ Efficient and economical technique

▶ Ability to use fat as a fuel during sustained exercise at high work rates and thus spare the body's own carbohydrate reserves

The physiological demands of mountain biking include most of these requirements and encompass four broad areas: cardiovascular power, muscle power, energetic power (energy system), and resistance to fatigue.

Cardiovascular power describes the ability of the cyclist to consume, transport, and use oxygen. Cardiovascular performance is assessed by determining the cyclist's maximum oxygen uptake ($\dot{V}O_2$max)—consumption, transport, and use—either directly in a laboratory setting using gas exchange measurement or indirectly through estimation based on heart rate data or time trial performance. This is currently one of the best assessments of an athlete's capacity to perform endurance activities.

Muscle power refers to the ability of the cyclist to generate high leg power outputs measured in watts (W) and is usually assessed by short-duration, high-intensity cycling (e.g., the Wingate bicycle sprint test) or from longer tests (12 to 14 min) that determine the peak power output (Kuipers et al. 1985). This latter type of assessment is usually performed in conjunction with a $\dot{V}O_2$max test.

Energetic power refers to the capacity of an individual to produce adenosine triphosphate (ATP) to sustain cellular processes including muscular contraction. In cycling, this means the capacity to produce mechanical power (Hawley and Hopkins 1995). Four metabolic pathways—the phosphagen, anaerobic glycolytic, aerobic glycolytic, and aerobic lipolytic metabolic pathways—are involved in the resynthesis of ATP, the body's universal energy carrier, in muscle cells (Hawley and Hopkins 1995). The contributions of these power systems to the total energy requirements of exercise can be assessed by having individuals perform a maximal amount of work in a set amount of time or a given amount of work in the shortest possible time.

Resistance to fatigue describes the ability of the individual to maintain a given power output or speed by matching the rate of ATP delivery to the rate of ATP use; establishing an adequate buffering of acid metabolites, mainly hydrogen ions (H^+) and inorganic phosphate (Pi) (Westerblad, Allen, and Lannergren 2002); and minimizing the depletion of the muscle's energy stores.

Cardiovascular Power Demands

The physiology of elite XC mountain bikers is comparable to that of elite road cyclists (Lucia et al. 1998; Padilla et al. 2000). National-level male and female mountain bikers have high mean peak power outputs of around 420 W and 313 W, respectively; power-to-body-weight ratios of 5.9 W/kg and 5.3 W/kg, respectively; and maximal aerobic capacities of 70.0 ml/ kg/min and 58 ml/kg/min, respectively (Baron 2001; Wilber et al. 1997). Thus, to perform at a high level, XC mountain bikers appear to require a physiological makeup similar to that of elite road cyclists. See table 11.1 for a comparative summary of physiological laboratory data for mountain bikers.

The primary requirement for high performance cycling is the ability to generate a high maximal aerobic power ($\dot{V}O_2$max). This capacity is usually expressed relative to the body mass of the individual (ml/kg/min), but it has been suggested that the absolute aerobic capacity (in L/min) may better reflect the cycling potential of the individual.

Why is a high $\dot{V}O_2$max so important? Competitive XC mountain bike racing requires average power outputs that can exceed 300 W over a 120-min race when a cyclist is competing at around 90% of heart rate maximum (HRmax). The oxygen cost of generating a power output of 300 W is approximately 4.0 L/min. Thus, if the $\dot{V}O_2$max of the cyclist is 4.0 L/min or less, then the likelihood that he or she will be able to generate and/or sustain that level of power output for more than a few minutes is extremely low. High aerobic capacities are thus necessary to generate the sustained high power outputs required for competitive XC racing. The relationship between power output and aerobic capacity is shown in figure 11.1.

What do we know about the cardiovascular demands during mountain biking? Both elite and competitive cyclists maintain high heart rates during

TABLE 11.1 Comparative Maximal Exercise Characteristics of Competitive (Subelite) and Elite Mountain Bikers

	MacRae, Hise, and Allen 2000 (subelite) n = 6	Wilber et al. 1997 (elite) n = 10	Baron 2001 (elite) n = 25	Gregory 2001 (elite) n = 5	Wilber et al. 1997 (elite women) n = 10
Height (cm)	180 ± 7	176.7 ± 7	179 ± 5	179 ± 7	162 ± 5
Body mass (kg)	76.9 ± 3.6	71.5 ± 7.8	69.4 ± 6.5	68.8 ± 6.2	57.5 ± 4.7
Body fat (%)	8.5 ± 0.9	5.8 ± 1.1	NA	7.8 ± 1.2	13.2 ± 2.0
$\dot{V}O_2max$ (L/min) (ml/kg/min)	4.5 ± 0.5 58.4 ± 2.3	4.99 ± 0.4 70.0 ± 2.3	4.75 ± 0.3* 68.4 ± 3.8	5.2 ± 0.4 75.4 ± 2.3	3.33 ± 0.3 57.9 ± 2.8
Heart rate (bpm)	182 ± 3	192 ± 12	NA	188 ± 8	178 ± 7
Power (W)	389 ± 41	420 ± 42	382 ± 26*	415 ± 25	313 ± 24
Power (W/kg)	5.1 ± 0.3	5.9 ± 0.3	5.5 ± 0.4	6.0 ± 0.2	5.4 ± 0.4

Values are mean ± SD.

* = estimated from data presented.

NA = not available.

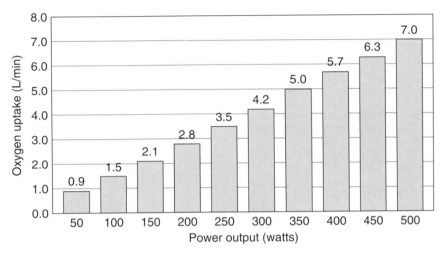

FIGURE 11.1   Relationship between power output and oxygen uptake.

off-road racing. Seifert and colleagues (1997) reported that trained XC cyclists performing a 10.4-km off-road time trial averaged 93% of their peak heart rates. When those cyclists rode a course with manufactured bumps, their $\dot{V}O_2$ averaged 2.68 L/min. Unfortunately, no maximum HR or $\dot{V}O_2$ data were reported in that study, so the relative exercise intensities of the cyclists are unknown.

MacRae, Hise, and Allen (2000) studied competitive subelite mountain bikers during sustained climbing time trials. The on-road trials lasted 8 min and covered 1.62 km at a 183-m elevation gain. The off-road trials lasted 10 min, covering 1.38 km at a 123-m elevation gain. We measured heart rate and $\dot{V}O_2$ with a portable metabolic unit and measured power output with an SRM training system. During the uphill cycling, $\dot{V}O_2$ averaged 3.8 L/min (about 84% of $\dot{V}O_2$peak), and heart rate averaged 168 beats/min (about 92% of HRmax).

Do elite mountain bikers perform at higher relative intensities under field conditions, that is, when exercising outside of a laboratory setting? In an unpublished master's thesis, Gregory (2001) studied three Australian National Team members preparing for competition on the Sydney 2000 Olympic XC course. These cyclists completed two laps for 13.8 km at a 646-m elevation gain. The cyclists' heart rates averaged 176 beats/min or about 91% of peak heart rate. No $\dot{V}O_2$ data are available from that study, so the oxygen cost of performing XC racing where the course includes flat riding, ascending, and descending has yet to be determined.

Table 11.2 summarizes the cardiovascular performance data from the three mentioned studies. No data are available describing the cardiovascular demands of off-road cycling in women.

TABLE 11.2 Cardiovascular Performance During Off-Road Cycling

	Seifert et al. 1997 (subelite, elite) n = 12	MacRae, Hise, and Allen 2000 (subelite) n = 6	Gregory 2001 (elite) n = 3
Average heart rate (bpm)	168 ± 5.1	168 ± 6.1	176 ± 7.0
Average % HRmax	93	92	91
Average $\dot{V}O_2$ (L/min) (ml/kg/min)	2.60 ± 0.4 39.6 ± 3.7	3.85 ± 0.8 49.8 ± 8.3	NA NA
Average % $\dot{V}O_2$max	NA	85 ± 2	NA
Average power (W)	NA	266 ± 46	307 ± 14
% max power (W)	NA	68	72
Mean cadence (rev/min)	NA	72 ± 5.0	68 ± 4.3

Values are mean ± SD.
NA = not available.

Training Implications

These studies seem to indicate that during climbing and XC riding and racing, heart rates are maintained at high levels (greater than 90% HRmax). Therefore, preparation requires training at intensities that replicate the expected intensity during competition. Furthermore, if $\dot{V}O_2$ during XC racing is close to our measured $\dot{V}O_2$ during uphill riding—around 4.0 L/min (and it could be higher)—then it is to be expected that the $\dot{V}O_2$max of a competitive male cyclist will need to be at least 4.5 L/min, given that he likely will be riding at a relative $\dot{V}O_2$ of around 85 to 90%. The data from laboratory testing shown in table 11.1 confirm this requirement.

Therefore, training should be directed at improving maximal capacity for oxygen consumption ($\dot{V}O_2$max) and, perhaps more important, should replicate as often as possible the expected intensity that will be required of the cyclist during riding or competition. The amount by which $\dot{V}O_2$max improves will depend primarily on the fitness level of the cyclist (high levels of cardiovascular fitness will limit the amount by which $\dot{V}O_2$max can be increased) and on training volume and intensity.

Most aerobic training studies, studies with an average duration of approximately three months, show improvements in $\dot{V}O_2$max of around 16%. Whether cyclists training for several years can elicit further improvements in $\dot{V}O_2$max has yet to be shown. Long-term training studies lasting several years have elicited $\dot{V}O_2$max increases of around 42% (Ekblom et al. 1968; Saltin and Rowell 1980).

Although a high $\dot{V}O_2$max is necessary for success at the highest levels of competition, the cyclist who is able to ride for several hours at a high intensity will likely be the best competitor. Therefore, training that does not include a sufficiently high volume conducted at a high intensity will probably result in a subpar performance during competition.

Muscle Power Demands

Little is known about the power output demands of mountain biking. Gregory (2001) measured power output on a XC course in elite and competitive mountain bikers. Average power output in the elite cyclists represented only 72% of laboratory-measured peak power output (PPO), but all the climbing sections on the course used for that study required power outputs in excess of the laboratory-measured PPO. Table 11.3 shows a summary of that data collected with an SRM training system during uphill and XC off-road riding.

TABLE 11.3 Off-Road Cycling Performance During Uphill Riding and Cross-Country Trial Laps Using an SRM System

	MacRae, Hise, and Allen 2000 (uphill, subelite) n = 6	Gregory 2001 (cross-country, elite) n = 3
Average heart rate (bpm)	166 ± 6	176 ± 7
Average % HRmax	91 ± 1	91 ± 1
Average $\dot{V}O_2$ (L/min) (ml/kg/min)	3.85 ± 0.8 49.8 ± 8	NA NA
Average % $\dot{V}O_2$max	85 ± 2	NA
Average power (W)	266 ± 46	307 ± 14
% peak power (W)	68 ± 12	72 ± 8
Average cadence (rev/min)	72 ± 5	68 ± 4
Average speed (km/h)	9.0 ± 0.5	20.3 ± 1.2

We have also used SRM cranks to measure power output during uphill mountain biking (MacRae, Hise, and Allen 2000; table 11.3). That data demonstrated large fluctuations in average power output on a minute-by-minute basis even though $\dot{V}O_2$ was maintained at a steady rate (see figure 11.2).

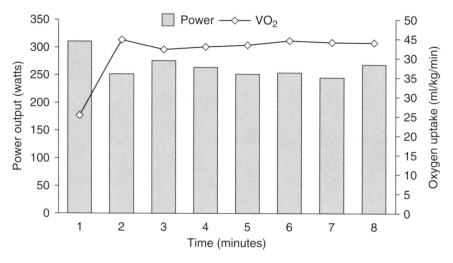

FIGURE 11.2   Power output and oxygen uptake during uphill off-road cycling.

Power output fluctuations were even more pronounced when the time scale was reduced to fractions of a minute (data not shown). Thus, the demands placed on the contracting muscles, particularly during the uphill portions, are quite different from those placed on the cardiovascular system. Therefore, the average power outputs recorded during laboratory time trials (a common test used by physiologists for predicting race performance) or during on-road time trials likely will not be very accurate indicators of the power demands expected of mountain bikers under real-world circumstances.

High power outputs are important, but so is the ability to sustain these outputs over extended periods. Using an SRM system, road cyclist Chris Boardman's coach, Peter Keen, estimated that Boardman's average power output during his record-breaking hour ride was 442 W.

Larger individuals are able to produce more power than smaller individuals, mainly because larger individuals have greater muscle mass. When cycling on the flat, larger cyclists are able to outperform smaller cyclists because of their greater power-to-body-weight ratio. However, during uphill cycling, which accounts for a significant portion of mountain bike training and competition, the heavier cyclist has to do more work compared to the lighter cyclist.

In uphill cycling, the cyclist with the higher or best power-to-weight ratio will likely be the most successful. Perhaps more important, the rider's physiology and the type of terrain primarily will determine the cyclist's power output at any time on a XC course.

No data at this time address the issue of power-to-weight ratio in XC cycling and to what extent, if any, it determines performance in mountain biking. We evaluated several physiological and performance parameters to try to predict which parameter(s)—$\dot{V}O_2$max, Wingate test peak power output, $\dot{V}O_2$max test peak power output, body composition, or lean thigh volume—would best predict uphill cycling performance (unpublished data from MacRae et al. 2000).

Multivariate regression analysis revealed that the best predictor of uphill cycling performance was the maximal power W/kg (5.1 ± 0.3) achieved during a progressive incremental laboratory cycling test to exhaustion. This observation confirms the findings on road cyclists in which the peak power output generated on a progressive incremental exercise test was highly related to time trial performance ranging from 16 to 40 km (Balmer, Davison, and Bird 2000; Hawley and Noakes 1992; Weston et al. 1997).

One standard laboratory measurement frequently used to assess training status and predict exercise performance, in addition to $\dot{V}O_2$max, is anaerobic threshold (AT) or lactate threshold (LT). Since the early 1970s, the ability to sustain a high power output at AT or LT has been used to predict cycling performance from laboratory measurements. When venous or capillary blood samples are taken at frequent intervals during progressive exercise testing in the laboratory—for example, during a test in which the cyclist exercises from relatively light power outputs to maximum power output—researchers commonly observe that blood lactate concentrations (BLa-) increase. Conceptually, the increase in blood lactate accumulation is ascribed to an increase in the rate of glycolysis (glucose conversion to pyruvic acid or lactic acid) and is erroneously believed to be a threshold response consequent to inadequate oxygen delivery. It is commonly believed that this threshold increase in BLa- is indicative of the optimal race pace or power output, and that sustained exercise above this threshold will result in premature fatigue.

The premise that provision of a substrate (oxygen) to muscle could limit exercise performance by inducing fatigue originated in the 1920s (Hill, Long, and Lupton 1924a, 1924b), was expanded in the 1930s (Bock and Dill 1931; Owles 1930), and was perpetuated in the 1960s following research conducted on cardiac disease patients (Wasserman and McIlroy 1964). These researchers assumed that breathing changes (pulmonary ventilation) during exercise of increasing work rate was a response to oxygen-deprived (hypoxic) muscle that caused increased lactic acid production. These observations led to the subsequent development of the anaerobic threshold hypothesis in the 1960s (Wasserman and McIlroy 1964) and the lactate threshold hypothesis in the 1980s (Buono and Roby 1982; Young and Maughan 1982).

The underlying theory behind these hypotheses is that, at some point during exercise, high rates of anaerobic glycolytic ATP production occur, resulting in interference with energy production and skeletal muscle cross-bridge cycling (force production in muscle), primarily caused by acid production and accumulation. This causes fatigue and a failure of muscle contraction, or in practical terms, a reduction in exercise performance.

However, all of these studies are based on the assumption that increased rates of carbohydrate breakdown (glycolysis) produce lactic acid, and that the dissociation of this acid produces hydrogen ions (H^+) that interfere with energy production and muscle force production. That H^+ can interfere with muscle force production (cross-bridge cycling) is well known from measures taken on in vitro (in an artificial environment) isolated muscle fibers (Fitts 1994). What is not appreciated from those studies is the fact that at physiological temperatures, H^+ accumulation (reflected in a reduced pH) does not inhibit muscle cross-bridge activity (Bruton, Lannergren, and Westerblad 1998; Pate et al. 1995; Westerblad, Bruton, and Lannergren 1997; Wiseman, Beck, and Chase 1996).

Also not appreciated in these early studies is the fact that the formation of lactate from lactic acid does not result in a net accumulation of H^+, but rather that high rates of ATP breakdown are the likely sources of H^+ accumulation (Dennis, Gevers, and Opie 1991; Gevers 1977; Hochachka 1994; MacRae and Dennis 1995), and that fatigue is more likely associated with inorganic phosphate (Pi) accumulation than lactate and H^+ accumulation (Westerblad, Allen, and Lannergren, 2002).

More to the point, in vivo studies (within the living body) show a wide range of muscle pH concentrations reached at exhaustion during intense exercise. If an accumulation of H^+ limits high-intensity exercise in vivo, then considerable interindividual differences must exist in the pH sensitivities of the various processes involved (Mannion, Jakeman, and Willan 1995).

Given the evidence, what is the practicality of measuring changes in blood lactate concentration for estimating cycling performance? First, given the biochemical evidence indicating that accumulation of lactate is unlikely to be implicated in the fatigue process, the usefulness of this measurement appears to be limited in that respect.

Second, we have demonstrated using radio-labeled lactate tracers that even at low work rates (around 30% $\dot{V}O_2$max), there is an appreciable appearance of lactate in the blood, but the BLa- is not altered since its disappearance rate matched the appearance rate (MacRae et al. 1992). Furthermore, both lactate appearance and disappearance rose as curvilinear functions of increasing work rate (with no threshold effect), and at the higher work rates the appearance of lactate exceeded its disappearance, so that blood lactate concentrations began to rise.

These techniques clearly demonstrate that blood lactate concentration is a function of its rate of production and rate of removal from the blood. Given that lactate is also transported by a sarcolemmal membrane–specific transporter (Roth and Brooks 1990a, 1990b), it is extremely difficult to assess whether changes in blood lactate concentration during exercise reflect changes in its production rate, transport rate, or removal rate. As such, measuring blood lactate concentration (or more specifically, attempting to determine a blood lactate threshold) likely has little if any usefulness for estimating cycling performance, particularly since blood lactate concentrations of 5 to 9 mM/L^{-1} can be maintained by highly trained endurance cyclists exercising at 85 to 90% $\dot{V}O_2$peak for around an hour or longer (Coyle et al. 1988; Myburgh, Viljoen, and Tereblanche 2001; Romijn et al. 1995; Stepto et al. 2001).

What is important to remember is that lactate is merely a three-carbon fragment of a glucose molecule (glucose is a six-carbon molecule), and as such it should be viewed as a usable fuel (Brooks 1986). More to the point, we have shown that the rate of lactate oxidation (lactate conversion to CO_2 and H_2O for production of ATP) increases with increasing exercise intensity, that exercise training improves an individual's capacity to oxidize lactate, and that the major fate of lactate formed during exercise is oxidation (MacRae, Noakes, and Dennis 1995). As such, lactate oxidation may contribute a substantial amount to fuel use during very prolonged exercise (Rauch et al. 1998), and may also contribute substantially to fuel use during high-intensity events lasting one to three hours.

While these latter contentions have yet to be demonstrated, XC cyclists may benefit from generating and sustaining high levels of lactate, which may serve as an important fuel source when glycogen and blood glucose levels drop. Indirect evidence for this can be seen in our study of uphill cycling in which cyclists generated BLa- of around 8 mM/L^{-1} (MacRae, Hise, and Allen 2000), and from the work of Gregory (2001) with elite mountain bikers who maintained BLa- of around 9.6 mM/L^{-1} in a 30-min time trial (93% HRmax). It is feasible that these cyclists' BLa- would likely have been similar during the XC race simulation on the Sydney Olympic mountain bike course where they rode at 91% HRmax. No data are available describing the muscle power demands of off-road cycling in women.

Given the current understanding of lactate metabolism, effective training should not be based on a particular blood lactate concentration or on some arbitrary threshold. There is no physiological or biochemical support for an anaerobic or lactate threshold, and there is no evidence to support the use of a definitive blood lactate concentration to optimize training. Replicating in training the expected intensities and durations of a competition together with replicating in training those intensities as frequently as possible will more effectively prepare the cyclist for competition than using a hypothetical threshold.

Training Implications

Since the sustainable power outputs during XC racing need to be around 300 W or higher for men, cyclists should be exposed to workloads of this intensity and greater during significant portions of their training. A work rate of around 300 W should require an oxygen consumption rate of around 4 L/min, or for a 70-kg cyclist, a $\dot{V}O_2$ of around 57 ml/kg/min. This intensity would be equivalent to around 84% $\dot{V}O_2$max, or 92% HRmax and 73% of peak power output (assuming a $\dot{V}O_2$max of around 66 ml/kg/min).

Obviously, access to a sport science laboratory will allow the cyclist to determine $\dot{V}O_2$max, HRmax, and peak power output. However, since this possibility is not always feasible and is typically a time-intensive and expensive proposition, there are other means for quantifying the appropriate training loads. SRM cranks or similar devices can quantify instantaneous power, and portable or wireless monitors can accurately measure heart rate.

In addition, a close relationship exists between a cyclist's field-measured heart rate and power output and laboratory-measured oxygen consumption data as shown in figure 11.3. Therefore, a cyclist who knows his or her maximal heart rate can use the information in figure 11.3 to develop a training program that will not require laboratory testing.

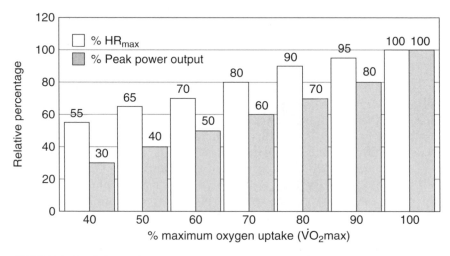

FIGURE 11.3   Relationship among oxygen consumption, heart rate, and power output.

Efficiency and Economy of Pedaling

Mechanical efficiency is a measure of work that assesses the ratio of energy input to energy output, or the percentage of total energy expended that produces external work. Movement economy refers to the energy required (usually measured as $\dot{V}O_2$) to maintain a constant velocity of movement (power output).

There is little conclusive information about the factors that determine or influence efficiency (Mosely and Jeukendrup 2001), but the importance of this measure can be demonstrated through modeling software, which predicts that for a trained rider averaging 300 W over 40 km, a 1% improvement in efficiency will give a 63-s improvement in a 40-km time trial. The time gain in less skilled riders would be even greater (Jeukendrup, Craig, and Hawley 2000). Mechanical efficiency in most cycling studies is generally around 20%, implying that around 80% of all the energy obtained from ATP breakdown is wasted as heat.

Neither cycling efficiency nor cycling economy for mountain bikers has been reported in the scientific literature, but the latter value may be important to competitive performance (the amount of oxygen consumed in liters of energy transferred to the bicycle, or W/L).

The ratio of type I (slow-twitch) to type II (fast-twitch) skeletal muscle fibers has also been used as an index of cycling economy. In vitro studies have suggested that type I fibers are more resistant to acidosis, which can cause fatigue, than are type II fibers. Having a larger proportion of type I fibers would likely make a cyclist more resistant to fatigue. Furthermore, Coyle and colleagues (1992) demonstrated that muscular efficiency varied greatly in a group of competitive road cyclists, and that most of the variability was related to differences in their percentage of type I muscle fibers. That study expanded on previous findings with elite cyclists (Coyle et al. 1991) and led the researchers to suggest that cyclists with a greater proportion of type I fibers are more efficient than cyclists with a greater proportion of types II fibers.

However, Mannion, Jakeman, and Willan (1995) found that in contrast to in vitro studies and to the correlational data published by Coyle and colleagues (1991, 1992), subjects with the highest proportion of type II muscle fibers were able to perform high-intensity exercise at the lowest muscle pH concentrations, with the greatest accumulation of acid. They also found that subjects with the highest skeletal muscle buffering capacity (capacity to resist acid accumulation) did not accumulate more lactate during exercise and also were not able to exercise longer than did those with lesser muscle buffering capacity.

Taken together, these data would suggest that muscle fiber type does not play an important role in cycling performance conducted at race intensities. More to the point, the majority of studies conducted on cycling efficiency have required the cyclists to cycle at intensities less than 75% $\dot{V}O_2$max, well below the intensities commonly observed in mountain bike racing. Again, as for the cardiovascular and muscle power components described, no data are available describing cycling efficiency or economy in women.

Training Implications

Performance improvements following high-intensity training (HIT) that approximates competition intensity may be due to improved cycling economy. HIT has been shown to improve skeletal muscle buffering capacity (Weston et al. 1997) and allow cyclists to maintain higher relative work rates and carbohydrate breakdown rates (Stepto et al. 2001; Westgarth-Taylor et al. 1997). Thus, incorporating HIT on a regular basis into XC race preparation might improve cycling efficiency and economy and also will likely improve the capacity of the cyclist for high rates of carbohydrate utilization.

Energetic Power Demands

The importance of maintaining a balance between energy demand and energy supply is well known. A mismatch between the two typically results in reduced performance or cessation of exercise. Unfortunately, most studies of metabolic regulation (e.g., matching energy supply to energy demand) have focused on ATP-yielding pathways and have overlooked or ignored the regulation of ATP utilization (Arthur et al. 1992; Rumsey et al. 1990).

However, the biologically relevant pathways for exercising muscle necessarily include ATP utilization. The most meaningful end products of the pathway in exercising muscle are work, force development, or power output, not carbon dioxide (CO_2), water (H_2O), lactate, H^+, or creatine. Similarly, the most crucial metabolic rate is the ATP turnover rate (the ability to break down and resynthesize ATP), not O_2, CO_2, or carbon fuel fluxes (Hochachka 1994). Tight energy coupling between ATP synthesis and ATP flux (breakdown) indicates a high level of metabolic efficiency. This should be reflected in the cyclist's ability to generate high power outputs.

Four major energy power systems provide the energy necessary to cycle off road. These systems are responsible for maintaining an adequate availability of ATP, the energy currency of the body.

The first system is the ATP-PCr phosphagen system, where the body's limited stores of ATP can be replenished rapidly by using stored phospho-creatine (PCr). The breakdown of PCr provides a mechanism for resynthe-sizing ATP, but generates a highly reactive metabolite (Pi) involved in many enzyme reactions in metabolism. Therefore, the quantity of PCr stored in skeletal muscle is probably limited or not largely altered by training to mini-mize the accumulation of Pi during high-intensity exercise. There is sub-stantial recent support for increased Pi having a role in skeletal muscle fatigue, whereas the role of acidosis via generation of lactic acid in depress-ing muscle contraction is limited (Westerblad, Allen, and Lannergren 2002).

The O_2-independent (anaerobic) glycolytic (carbohydrate) system is the main mechanism for ATP replenishment once phosphagen supplies are depleted. This system is activated to support high-intensity muscular work and is capable of supplying ATP at high rates using primarily stored muscle glycogen. During anaerobic work, PCr utilization approaches completion before glycolysis is fully activated. This phase in behavior arises because, as an ATP-synthesizing process, glycolysis is competing with creatine ki-nase (CK), the enzyme involved in the breakdown of PCr, for limiting amounts of ADP, which is necessary for ATP resynthesis.

The O_2-dependent (aerobic) glycolytic system involves the complete breakdown of carbohydrates, thereby amplifying ATP formation immensely above that which is generated by the ATP-PCr system and the anaerobic/glycolytic system.

The O_2-dependent (aerobic) lipolytic (fat) system involves the complete breakdown of fats. This system also is capable of yielding immense quan-tities of ATP, quantities several times greater than those formed by the aerobic/glycolytic system.

What do we know about the energy requirements of XC cycling? It is well known that during prolonged, continuous, moderate-intensity cycling (greater than 90 min at 70 to 80% $\dot{V}O_2$max), the onset of fatigue is associated with very low muscle glycogen concentrations and hypoglycemia (Bergstrom et al. 1962; Bosch, Dennis, and Noakes 1993; Coyle et al. 1986). Consequently, years of research investigated ways to delay the onset of fatigue by increas-ing muscle glycogen stores prior to exercise. This was accomplished by ma-nipulating training intensity and volume, by modifying diet, or by feeding individuals carbohydrate during exercise to maintain blood glucose levels. See Hawley and colleagues (1997) for a review of those studies.

Those studies concluded that cycling performance could be enhanced and the onset of fatigue delayed by carbohydrate loading prior to exercise or carbohydrate feeding during exercise. Unfortunately, those studies all involved constant-load exercise and were not placebo controlled. Also, many researchers considered fatigue to be based on how long a person could exercise rather than the more practical expectation of how fast a given distance could be covered.

To date, only two placebo-controlled studies have examined carbohydrate loading and its effect on cycling performance (Hawley, Palmer, and Noakes 1997), including one that involved exercise lasting longer than one hour, a 100-km time trial that also included stochastic exercise (periods of higher intensity exercise to simulate race conditions) (Burke et al. 2000). Neither of those placebo-controlled studies documented an improvement in cycling performance when the subjects were carbohydrate loaded prior to exercise or fed carbohydrate during exercise.

Limited information is available regarding the energy requirements of XC cycling. At the intensity likely to be experienced during hard training or competition—$\geq 80\%$ $\dot{V}O_2$max or $\geq 90\%$ HRmax—it is expected that the major fuel used to resynthesize ATP will be muscle glycogen. Glucose and glycogen utilization are known to increase exponentially with increasing exercise intensity, and the rate glycogen utilization increases with increasing intensity is greater than that of glucose utilization (Brooks 1997). Trained cyclists exercising for up to one hour at > 300 W will be able to sustain oxygen uptakes greater than 4.0 L/min and will generate 90 to 94% of their energy requirements from carbohydrate breakdown, with glycogen contributing about 90% to the overall rate of carbohydrate usage (Stepto et al. 2001). Again, no information is available on the energy demands of mountain biking in women.

Training Implications

What does this information mean in practical terms, when cyclists are exercising hard during training or competition? Using the $\dot{V}O_2$ data of Seifert and colleagues (1997) on mountain bikers, it can be estimated that the cyclists in that study were expending energy at a rate of around 13 kCal/min. During uphill cycling trials, MacRae, Hise, and Allen (2000) measured an average energy expenditure of around 19 kCal/min. In laboratory trials that included high-intensity interval training, Stepto and colleagues (2001) measured average energy expenditures of around 21.5 kCal/min on road cyclists during the time periods when exercise occurred at the high intensities (around 85% $\dot{V}O_2$max, 340 W).

Based on the limited information available, the majority of energy for high-intensity training and competition will likely be derived from muscle glycogen breakdown. The energy requirements for cycling at high intensity will be around 20 kCal/min or higher. Thus, training needs to focus on improving the cyclist's capacity for carbohydrate usage. Perhaps more important, the cyclist needs to pay particular attention to the appropriate replenishment of glycogen in training or competition so that the subsequent training session or race performance will not be compromised by suboptimal fuel reserves.

Resistance to Fatigue

The ability to maintain a high absolute power output or speed and resist the onset of muscular fatigue is critical to successful mountain bike race performance. Fatigue is generally defined as a reduced capacity to maintain a given power output or speed. Physiological fatigue during cycling is multifaceted and includes central nervous system, cardiovascular, muscular, and energetic (which incorporates nutritional) fatigue. By examining the requirements of the event—duration of the activity, intensity of effort required, environmental conditions expected, course profile—and reflecting on past experience in similar circumstances, the cyclist should be able to identify likely sources of fatigue and then assume strategies to diminish or delay the onset of fatigue.

A review article by Noakes (2000) provides a well-rounded summary of the current concepts that describe the fatigue process during exercise of moderate to high intensity. It also provides four additional models that need to be considered when evaluating factors limiting either short-duration, maximal, or prolonged submaximal exercise.

1. The energy supply/energy depletion model of fatigue suggests that provision of substrate to muscle limits exercise performance, thereby producing fatigue. Fatigue during high-intensity exercise may result from an inability to provide ATP at rates rapid enough to sustain the exercise. The information in the muscle power section related to AT and LT, the efficiency of cycling section, as well as the energetic power section address issues related to this model.

2. The muscle power/muscle recruitment model of fatigue suggests that the processes involved in skeletal muscle recruitment (central or nervous system fatigue), excitation, and contraction during exercise limit exercise performance. St. Clair Gibson, Schabort, and Noakes (2001) studied neuromuscular activity in endurance-trained cyclists during a 100-km time trial that included five 1-km and four 4-km high-intensity bouts of exercise (around 90% $\dot{V}O_2peak$) during the 100-km time trial. This study established that peripheral skeletal muscle neuromuscular activity declined with the reduction in power output during bouts of high-intensity exercise. The reduction in power output occurred when more than 20% of the available muscle was recruited during the time trial. This finding suggests that a central neural governor controls muscle recruitment during prolonged exercise.

3. The biomechanical model describes the role of muscles as elastic energy return systems, suggesting that the greater the muscle's capacity to act as a spring, the less torque it must produce, hence the more efficient it is.

4. The psychological/motivational model suggests that exercise performance is influenced by conscious effort.

No available data specifically address the role fatigue plays in mountain biking performance, particularly since vibration-induced fatigue may contribute to performance changes. Most of the studies of the fatigue process during endurance cycling examined energetic factors associated with fatigue, primarily by determining the role of substrate (carbohydrate and fat) availability in attenuating fatigue during laboratory studies (Bergstrom et al. 1962; Coyle et al. 1986). Those studies either examined if cyclists could accomplish more work before fatigue (increased time to exhaustion) or whether they could complete a set distance or work task in a shorter time (Bosch, Dennis, and Noakes 1993; Hawley et al. 1997; Kang et al. 1995; Widrick et al. 1993). The results from those studies show that exercise performance improves when altering substrate availability (e.g., through consumption of carbohydrate), but the mechanisms involved for the improved performance are unknown.

Performance improvements are generally assumed to be due to alterations in skeletal muscle metabolism (McConnell et al. 1999), which delays the onset of muscle glycogen depletion, or by preventing or reversing hypoglycemia (Coggan and Coyle 1989).

Most laboratory studies of the fatigue process are problematic in that they require the subject to exercise at a constant load for the duration of the activity. However, constant work rates are not typical of cycling competition. Most cycling, whether in training or competition, involves exercise in which power output varies in a random and stochastic fashion. Burke and colleagues (2000) showed that during prolonged exercise, including bouts of high-intensity exercise designed to simulate stochastic exercise, a progressive reduction in power output occurred during the bouts of high-intensity exercise. Thus, since XC mountain biking involves periods of high-intensity exercise and also includes periods of supramaximal exercise, it is to be expected that the ability to maintain high power outputs will be diminished as a competition progresses.

The other area of fatigue research in cycling has focused on performance related to the anaerobic threshold and lactate threshold. As indicated in the muscle power section, measurements of lactate accumulation are often made to assess the exercise intensity beyond which the development of fatigue is increased.

Training Implications

Cyclists will likely improve their resistance to physiological fatigue by optimizing training for the cardiovascular, muscular, and energetic systems. Whether training can prevent the decline in muscle power output that results from high-intensity exercise (St. Clair Gibson, Schabort, and Noakes 2001), thus by implication favorably altering central nervous system governing of muscle recruitment, is yet to be determined.

Effects of Suspension Type on Mountain Biking Performance

The majority of mountain bikes produced at present are equipped with either a front suspension (FS) or a front and rear dual suspension (DS) system. The use of a DS bicycle may increase rider comfort, could promote better control on harsh trails, and may result in improved cycling performance by reducing physical trauma due to excessive vibration. The reluctance of XC racers to use DS bicycles is conceptually attributed to the idea that riding a DS bicycle is less economical (requires a greater energy output) than riding an FS bicycle. The loss of pedaling energy caused by compression of the suspension system followed by spring dampening on a DS bicycle may result in greater energy expenditure compared to an FS bicycle.

Since a large amount of time is spent riding uphill in XC riding, we assessed whether uphill cycling performance was adversely affected by riding a DS (four-bar linkage) compared with an FS bicycle on the road and on an off-road course (MacRae, Hise, and Allen 2000). The major finding of that study was that cardiovascular performance was similar in both road conditions irrespective of bicycle type, but that the power output necessary to pedal the DS bicycle uphill was significantly higher. The average power output at each time interval during the uphill ride was approximately 80 W/min higher on the DS compared with the FS bicycle.

This power output should have resulted in approximately a 1 L/min or around 13 ml/kg/min higher metabolic rate for the DS bicycle, but this was not the case. Bicycle type did not affect the time to complete each uphill trial, the oxygen cost of riding ($\dot{V}O_2$), or the heart rate responses of the cyclists during the trials. This latter finding was surprising since we expected that not only the larger mass of the DS bicycle but also the energy cost of compressing the rear suspension during pedaling would result in a higher $\dot{V}O_2$.

In an earlier study, Seifert and colleagues (1997) also found no differences in oxygen cost between riding an FS and DS bicycle on a flat, looped course with manufactured bumps. Unfortunately, that study, which also included an uphill time trial, provided no data as to the oxygen cost or power output of riding the different suspension system bicycles uphill.

Our cyclists performed the uphill trials at about 84% of $\dot{V}O_2$peak and about 92% of HRmax, irrespective of road condition or bicycle type, and around 69% and 88% of $\dot{V}O_2$peak power output on the FS and DS bicycles, respectively.

Even though oxygen consumption, cardiovascular performance, average cycling velocities, and time to complete the time trials were similar on both bicycles, it is probable that the higher power outputs required to pedal the DS bicycle uphill were generated to overcome the compression of the rear suspension. The rear suspension spring may have absorbed some of the torque energy being applied to the pedals, resulting in higher torques having to be applied to the drivetrain to maintain uphill speed.

Can a DS bicycle be used effectively in XC racing in which a large portion of the race involves uphill riding, particularly since the power output data (see figure 11.4) suggest that the energy cost of generating around 80 W/min more power on a DS bicycle may negatively impact performance? Since neither of the metabolic/cardiovascular or cycling performance variables (other than power output) were affected by bicycle type, we hypothesized that the generation of a higher power output to cycle uphill on the DS bicycle was likely conserved by the rear suspension spring and, during rebound of the spring following compression, contributed to the forward momentum of the bicycle. Thus, on that particular type of DS bicycle, cycling performance did not appear to be negatively impacted, and the rider may have benefited from riding a DS bicycle because of reduced vibration, more control on rough trails, and the potential to descend downhill at greater velocities.

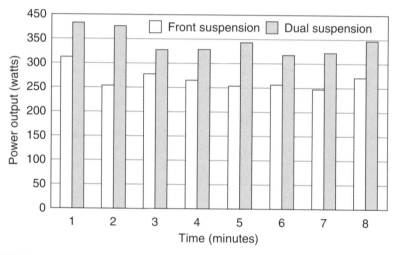

FIGURE 11.4   Power output during uphill cycling on front suspension (FS) and dual suspension (DS) bicycles.

Directions for Future Research

The paucity of data on the physiological responses of women in cycling in general, and mountain biking in particular, is at best disappointing, particularly since there is no reason studies on women cannot be conducted within the same framework and design as those conducted on men. Although it is feasible that the research findings from physiological studies on men can be applied to women, no definitive research supports this contention. Thus, a concerted effort to study the physiological demands of cycling on women, both in laboratory and field conditions, is urgently needed.

Clearly, research physiologists who study cycling performance need to move from the laboratory to the field. Laboratory research is valuable up to a point, but advances in technology have now made it possible to measure physiological performance in real-world circumstances. As such, more studies of cyclists exercising in the field need to be conducted.

The most practical illustration of a laboratory finding not being replicated in the field was seen in our own work. The typical increase in oxygen consumption was observed as power output increased in the lab, but an almost complete dissociation between oxygen consumption and power output occurred when the cyclists exercised in the field (MacRae, Hise, and Allen 2000).

There is also limited information on the effects of different bicycle suspension designs on mountain biking performance, or whether DS bicycles can be effectively raced in competition. Physiological data from the two published studies on bicycle suspension systems (MacRae, Hise, and Allen 2000; Seifert et al. 1997) and how they impact cycling exercise performance suggest that DS bicycles can be raced as competitively as FS bicycles. This observation needs confirmation on a typical XC course under race simulation conditions.

No data are available on the physiological requirements of downhill (DH) and dual slalom (DS) mountain biking. Research into the specific requirements of these mountain bike disciplines is needed. Relevant to this topic, as well as to XC cycling, is the lack of information available regarding appropriate training to prepare for effective competition in the three mountain bike disciplines—DH, DS, and XC.

Appropriate pacing and race tactics; the maintenance of a high work rate; the ability to tolerate and resist mental and physical fatigue caused by energy depletion and dehydration; and the tolerance of adverse environmental conditions such as altitude, dust, and hyperthermia are factors that a mountain biker has to be aware of in training and competition. Purely from a physiological standpoint, no training studies have attempted to determine the appropriate volume and intensity of training necessary to optimally prepare for mountain bike competition. More to the point, it has yet to be shown which variables—percent of HRmax or $\dot{V}O_2$max, percent of peak power output, sustainable power output, and so on—need to be monitored during training to maximize the training response and whether one or more of these variables is more effective than the others.

We must also consider that training for competition by recreational, intermediate, subelite, and elite cyclists will be quite different. The physiological information we have on mountain bikers is very limited and based on a small number of cyclists. More laboratory and field studies need to be conducted on mountain bikers of different levels of experience to determine the unique responses likely to be observed in each category of experience.

References

Arthur, P.G., Hogan, M.C., Bebout, D.E., Wagner, P.D., and Hochachka, P.W. 1992. Modeling the effects of hypoxia on ATP turnover in exercising muscle. *J Appl Physiol* 73:737-742.

Balmer, J., Davison, R.C., and Bird, S.R. 2000. Peak power predicts performance power during an outdoor 16.1-km cycling time trial. *Med Sci Sports Exerc* 32:1485-1490.

Baron, R. 2001. Aerobic and anaerobic power characteristics of off-road cyclists. *Med Sci Sports Exerc* 33(8): 1387-1393.

Bergstrom, J., Hermansen, L., Hultman, L., and Saltin, B. 1962. Diet, muscle glycogen and physical performance. *Acta Physiol Scand* 71:140-150.

Bock, A.V., and Dill, D.B. 1931. *The physiology of muscular exercise.* 3rd ed. London: Longmans, Green and Company.

Bosch, A.N., Dennis, S.C., and Noakes, T.D. 1993. Influence of carbohydrate loading on fuel substrate turnover and oxidation during prolonged exercise. *J Appl Physiol* 74:1921-1927.

Brooks, G.A. 1986. Lactate production under fully aerobic conditions: The lactate shuttle during rest and exercise. *Fed Proc* 45:2924-2929.

Brooks, G.A. 1997. Importance of the "crossover" concept in exercise metabolism. *Clin Exp Pharmacol Physiol* 24:889-894.

Bruton, J.D., Lannergren, J., and Westerblad, H. 1998. Effects of CO -induced acidification on the fatigue resistance of single mouse fibres at 28∞C. *J Appl Physiol* 85:478-483.

Buono, M.J., and Roby, F.B. 1982. Acid-base, metabolic, and ventilatory responses to repeated bouts of exercise. *J Appl Physiol* 53:436-439.

Burke, L.M., Hawley, J.A., Schabort, E.K., St. Clair Gibson, A., Mujika, I., and Noakes, T.D. 2000. Carbohydrate loading failed to improve 100-km cycling performance in a placebo-controlled trial. *J Appl Physiol* 88:1284-1290.

Coggan, A.R., and Coyle, E.F. 1989. Metabolism and performance following carbohydrate ingestion late in exercise. *Med Sci Sports Exerc* 21(1): 59-65.

Coyle, E.F., Coggan, A.R., Hemmert, M.K., and Ivy, J.L. 1986. Muscle glycogen utilization during prolonged strenuous exercise when fed carbohydrate. *J Appl Physiol* 61:165-172.

Coyle, E.F., Coggan, A.R., Hopper, M.K., and Walters, T.J. 1988. Determinants of endurance in well-trained cyclists. *J Appl Physiol* 64:2622-2630.

Coyle, E.F., Feltner, M.E., Kautz, S.A., Hamilton, M.T., Montain, S.J., Baylor, A.M., Abraham, L.D., and Petrek, G.W. 1991. Physiological and biomechanical factors associated with elite endurance cycling performance. *Med Sci Sports Exerc* 23(1): 93-107.

Coyle, E.F., Sidossis, L.S., Horowitz, J.F., and Beltz, J.L. 1992. Cycling efficiency is related to the percentage of Type I muscle fibers. *Med Sci Sports Exerc* 24(7): 782-788.

Dennis, S.C., Gevers, W., and Opie, L.H. 1991. Protons in ischemia: Where do they come from; where do they go to? *J Mol Cell Cardiol* 23:1077-1086.

Ekblom, B., Astrand, P.O., Saltin, B., Stenberg, J., and Wallstrom, B. 1968. Effect of training on circulatory response to exercise. *J Appl Physiol* 24:518-528.

Fitts, R.H. 1994. Cellular mechanisms of muscle fatigue. *Physiol Rev* 74:49-94.

Gevers, W.A. 1977. Generation of protons by metabolic processes in heart cells. *J Mol Cell Cardiol* 9:867-874.

Gregory, J. 2001. The physiological and physical determinants of mountain bike cross country cycling. Master's thesis, University of Tasmania.

Hawley, J.A., and Burke, L. 1998. *Peak performance: Training and nutritional strategies for sport.* St. Leonards, Australia: Allen and Unwin.

Hawley, J.A., and Hopkins, W.G. 1995. Aerobic glycolytic and aerobic lipolytic power systems. *Sports Med* 19(4): 240-250.

Hawley, J.A., and Noakes, T.D. 1992. Peak power output predicts maximal oxygen uptake and performance time in trained cyclists. *Eur J Appl Physiol* 65:79-83.

Hawley, J.A., Palmer, G.S., and Noakes, T.D. 1997. Effects of 3 days of carbohydrate supplementation on muscle glycogen content and subsequent utilization during a 1 h cycle time trial. *Eur J Appl Physiol* 75:407-412.

Hawley, J.A., Schabort, E.J., Noakes, T.D., and Dennis, S.C. 1997. Carbohydrate loading and exercise performance: An update. *Sports Med* 24:73-81.

Hill, A.V., Long, C.N.H., and Lupton, H. 1924a. Muscular exercise, lactic acid, and the supply and utilization of oxygen: Parts I-III. *Proceedings of the Royal Society of Britain* 97:155-176.

Hill, A.V., Long, C.N.H., and Lupton, H. 1924b. Muscular exercise, lactic acid, and the supply and utilization of oxygen: Parts VII-VIII. *Proceedings of the Royal Society of Britain* 97:438-475.

Hochachka, P.W. 1994. *Muscles as molecular and metabolic machines.* Boca Raton, Fla.: CRC Press.

Jeukendrup, A.E., Craig, N.P., and Hawley, J.A. 2000. The bioenergetics of world class cycling. *J Sci Med Sport* 3(4): 414-433.

Kang, J., Robertson, R.J., Denys, B.G., DaSilva, S.G., Visich, P., Suminski, R.R., Utter, A.C., Goss, F.L., and Metz, K.F. 1995. Effect of carbohydrate ingestion subsequent to carbohydrate supercompensation on endurance performance. *Int J Sport Nutr* 5:329-343.

Kuipers, H.F., Verstappen, F.T., Keizer, H.A., Guerten, P., and van Kranenburg, G. 1985. Variability of aerobic performance in the laboratory and its physiological correlates. *International Journal of Sports Med* 6:197-201.

Lucia, A., Pardo, J., Durantez, A., Hoyos, J., and Chicharro, J.L. 1998. Physiological differences between professional and elite road cyclists. *Int J Sports Med* 19(5): 342-348.

MacRae, H.S., and Dennis, S.C. 1995. Lactic acidosis as a facilitator of oxyhemoglobin dissociation during exercise (letter). *J Appl Physiol* 78:758-759.

MacRae, H.S., Dennis, S.C., Bosch, A.N., and Noakes, T.D. 1992. Effects of training on lactate production and removal during progressive exercise in humans. *J Appl Physiol* 72:1649-1656.

MacRae, H.S., Hise, K.J., and Allen, P.J. 2000. Effects of front and dual suspension mountain bike systems on uphill cycling performance. *Med Sci Sports Exerc* 32(7): 1276-1280.

MacRae, H.H., Noakes, T.D., and Dennis, S.C. 1995. Effects of endurance training on lactate removal by oxidation and gluconeogenesis during exercise. *Pflugers Arch* 430:964-970.

Mannion, A.F., Jakeman, P.M., and Willan, P.L. 1995. Skeletal muscle buffer value, fibre type distribution and high intensity exercise performance in man. *Exp Physiol* 80:89-101.

McConell, G., Snow, R.J., Proietto, J., and Hargreaves, M. 1999. Muscle metabolism during prolonged exercise in humans: Influence of carbohydrate availability. *J Appl Physiol* 87(3): 1083-1086.

Mosely, L., and Jeukendrup, A.E. 2001. The reliability of cycling efficiency. *Med Sci Sports Exerc* 33(4): 621-627.

Myburgh, K.H., Viljoen, A., and Tereblanche, S. 2001. Plasma lactate concentrations for self-selected maximal effort lasting 1 h. *Med Sci Sports Exerc* 33(1): 152-156.

Noakes, T.D. 2000. Physiological models to understand exercise fatigue and the adaptations that predict or enhance athletic performance. *Scand J Med Sci Sports* 10:123-145.

Owles, W.H. 1930. Alterations in the lactic acid content of the blood as a result of light exercise, and associated changes in the CO_2 combining power of the blood and alveolar CO_2 pressure. *J Physiol* 69:214-237.

Padilla, S., Mujiką, I., Orbananos, J., and Angulo, F. 2000. Exercise intensity during competition time trials in professional road cycling. *Med Sci Sports Exerc* 32(4): 850-856.

Pate, E., Bhimani, M., Franks-Skiba, K., and Cooke, R. 1995. Reduced effect of pH on skinned rabbit psoas muscle mechanics at high temperatures: Implications for fatigue. *J Physiol* 486:689-694.

Rauch, H.G., Hawley, J.A., Noakes, T.D., and Dennis, S.C. 1998. Fuel metabolism during ultra-endurance exercise. *Pflugers Arch* 436:211-219.

Romijn, J.A., Coyle, E.F., Sidossis, L.S., Zhang, X.J., and Wolfe, R.R. 1995. Relationship between fatty acid delivery and fatty acid oxidation during strenuous exercise. *J Appl Physiol* 79(6): 1939-1945.

Roth, D.A., and Brooks, G.A. 1990a. Lactate transport is mediated by a membrane-bound carrier in rat skeletal muscle sarcolemmal vesicles. *Arch Biochem Biophys* 279(2): 377-385.

Roth, D.A., and Brooks, G.A. 1990b. Lactate and pyruvate transport is dominated by a pH gradient-sensitive carrier in rat skeletal muscle sarcolemmal vesicles. *Arch Biochem Biophys* 279(2): 386-394.

Rumsey, W.L., Schlosser, C., Nuutinen, E.M., Robiollo, M., and Wilson, D.F. 1990. Cellular energetics and the oxygen dependence of respiration in cardiac myocytes isolated from adult rat. *J Biol Chem* 265:15,392-15,402.

Saltin, B., and Rowell, L.B. 1980. Functional adaptations to physical activity and inactivity. *Fed Proc* 39:1506-1516.

Seifert, J.G., Luetkemeier, M.J., Spencer, M.K., Miller, D., and Burke, E.R. 1997. The effects of mountain bike suspension systems on energy expenditure, physical exertion, and time trial performance during mountain bicycling. *Int J Sports Med* 18(3): 197-200.

St. Clair Gibson, A., Schabort, E.J., and Noakes, T.D. 2001. Reduced neuromuscular activity and force generation during prolonged cycling. *Am J Physiol Regul Integr Comp Physiol* 281:R187-R196.

Stepto, N.K., Martin, D.T., Fallon, K.E., and Hawley, J.A. 2001. Metabolic demands of intense aerobic interval training in competitive cyclists. *Med Sci Sports Exerc* 33(2): 303-310.

Wasserman, K., and McIlroy, M.B. 1964. Detecting the threshold of anaerobic metabolism in cardiac patients during exercise. *Am J Cardiol* 14:844-852.

Westerblad, H., Allen, D.G., and Lannergren, J. 2002. Muscle fatigue: Lactic acid or inorganic phosphate the major cause? *News Physiol Sci* 17:17-21.

Westerblad, H., Bruton, J.D., and Lannergren, J. 1997. The effect of intracellular pH on contractile function of intact, single fibres of mouse muscle declines with increasing temperature. *J Physiol* 500:193-204.

Westgarth-Taylor, C., Hawley, J.A., Rickard, S., Myburgh, K.H., Noakes, T.D., and Dennis, S.C. 1997. Metabolic and performance adaptations to interval training in endurance-trained cyclists. *Eur J Appl Physiol* 75:298-304.

Weston, A.R., Myburgh, K.H, Lindsay, F.H., Dennis, S.C., Noakes, T.D., and Hawley, J.A. 1997. Skeletal muscle buffering capacity and endurance performance after high-intensity interval training by well-trained cyclists. *Eur J Appl Physiol* 75:7-13.

Widrick, J.J., Costill, D.L., Fink, W.J., Hickey, M.S., McConell, G.K., and Tanaka, H. 1993. Carbohydrate feedings and exercise performance: Effect of initial muscle glycogen concentration. *J Appl Physiol* 74(6): 2,998-3,005.

Wilber, R.L., Zawadzki, K.M., Kearney, J.T., Shannon, M.P., and Disalvo, D. 1997. Physiological profiles of elite off-road and road cyclists. *Med Sci Sports Exerc* 29(8): 1,090-1,094.

Wiseman, R.W., Beck, T.W., and Chase, P.B. 1996. Effect of intracellular pH on force development depends on temperature in intact skeletal muscle from mouse. *Am J Physiol* 271:C878-C886.

Young, K., and Maughan, R.J. 1982. Physical training in humans: A central or peripheral effect. In *Biochemistry of exercise (Vol. 13)* edited by H. Knuttgen, J. Vogel, and J. Poortmans. Champaign, Ill.: Human Kinetics. pp. 433-438.

Index

Note: The italicized *f* and *t* following page numbers refer to figures and tables, respectively.

Contributors

David R. Bassett, Jr., Exercise Science Unit, University of Tennessee at Knoxville

Jeffrey P. Broker, PhD, Department of Biology, University of Colorado, Colorado Springs

José L. Chicharro, MD, PhD, Departamento de Enfermería y Unidad de Investigación en Fisiología del Deporte Universidad Complutense de Madrid, Spain

Conrad Earnest, PhD, FACSM, The Cooper Institute, Division of Clinical Applications, Dallas, Texas

Jesús Hoyos, MD, Asociación Deportiva Banesto, Madrid, Spain

Asker E. Jeukendrup, School of Sport and Exercise Sciences, University of Birmingham at Edgbaston, Birmingham, United Kingdom

Chester R. Kyle, PhD, Department of Mechanical Engineering, California State University at Long Beach

Alejandro Lucía, MD, PhD, Facultad de Ciencias de la Actividad Física y el Deporte, Universidad Europea de Madrid, Spain

Holden S-H. MacRae, PhD, Department of Sports Medicine, Pepperdine University, Malibu, California

John Olsen, MSME

Andrew L. Pruitt, EdD

Randall L. Wilber, PhD, United States Olympic Committee, Colorado Springs

About the Editor

Before his untimely death in late Fall 2002, **Edmund R. Burke, PhD,** was the pre-eminent author of books and articles on cycling. He wrote or edited more than 16 books on health, fitness, and cycling, including *Serious Cycling* and *Fitness Cycling.* He completed this second edition of *High-Tech Cycling* just prior to his death.

Renowned for translating the latest scientific research into practical application, Dr. Burke served as a columnist for *Adventure Cycling, Cycle Sport Magazine,* and *Performance Conditioning for Cycling.* He has also wrote extensively on cycling physiology, training, nutrition, health, and fitness for *VeloNews, Bicycling,* and *Inside Triathlon.* He served as executive editor of *Cycling Science* and managing editor of *Performance Conditioning for Cycling.*

Dr. Burke was the physiologist for USA Cycling for seven years. He worked with the 1980, 1984, and 1996 Olympic cycling teams, which won nine medals, as well as many world championship teams. He was a consultant with several companies in the areas of cycling, fitness equipment design, nutritional products, and fitness programs. His professional memberships included a role as fellow of the American College of Sports Medicine and also as vice president of research for the National Strength and Conditioning Association from 1993 to 1995.

Dr. Burke earned a doctorate in exercise physiology from The Ohio State University. He was a professor and director of the exercise science program at the University of Colorado at Colorado Springs, where he lived with his wife, Kathleen.